EIGHT WAYS OF LOVING GOD

JEANETTE FLOOD

Eight Ways of Loving God

Revealed by Love Himself

IGNATIUS PRESS   SAN FRANCISCO

Cover art:
The Three Crosses under the Stars
© iStockphoto/NCHANT

Cover design by Enrique J. Aguilar

© 2019 by Ignatius Press, San Francisco
All rights reserved
ISBN 978-1-62164-045-5
Library of Congress Catalogue number 2018949811
Printed in the United States of America ∞

With all my love, to Love Himself

CONTENTS

ABBREVIATIONS

(Abbreviations of books and translations of the Bible cited herein)

Old Testament Books

Gen	Genesis
Ex	Exodus
Lev	Leviticus
Num	Numbers
Deut	Deuteronomy
2 Kings	Second Book of Kings
Job	Book of Job
Ps	Psalms
Prov	Proverbs
Song	Song of Songs
Wis	Books of Wisdom
Sir	Sirach (*aka* Ecclesiasticus)
Is	Book of the Prophet Isaiah
Jer	Book of the Prophet Jeremiah
Joel	Book of the Prophet Joel
Zech	Book of Zechariah
2 Mac	Second Book of Maccabees

New Testament Books

Mt	Matthew
Mk	Mark
Lk	Luke
Jn	John
Acts	Acts of the Apostles
Rom	Letter to the Romans
1 Cor	First Letter to the Corinthians
2 Cor	Second Letter to the Corinthians
Eph	Letter to the Ephesians
Phil	Letter to the Philippians
Col	Letter to the Colossians
1 Thess	First Letter to Thessalonians
2 Thess	Second Letter to Thessalonians
1 Tim	First Letter to Timothy
2 Tim	Second Letter to Timothy
Heb	Letter to the Hebrews
Jas	First Letter of James
1 Pet	First Letter of Peter
2 Pet	Second Letter of Peter
1 Jn	First Letter of John
Rev	Revelation

Bible Translations

DRA	Douay-Rheims 1899 American Edition
KJV	King James Version
NAB	New American Bible
NABRE	New American Bible (Revised Edition)
NIV	New International Version
NRSV	New Revised Standard Version
RSVCE	Revised Standard Version, Catholic Edition
RSV2CE	Revised Standard Version, Second Catholic Edition

PREFACE

This book is filled with analogies in the hope that they might help explain the Catholic faith. Some of them are a little quirky, no doubt because the author is a little quirky.

If any analogy, quirky or otherwise, doesn't help you, then just ignore it. As apologist Jimmy Akin often states on Catholic Answers Live, an analogy differs more from the reality it depicts than it has in common with it. We might liken a shy person to a mouse, but that person has very little in common with a mouse—for example, size, intelligence, fur, and a tail, for starters. So please keep that in mind if the limitations of an analogy loom larger to you than the intended illumination. In that case, just drop it; it hasn't fulfilled its purpose. Focus more on what the Church has to say. She's been thinking and writing about these things far longer than I.

Note also that many topics herein overlap, so you will see something discussed in one section while another aspect of it will appear in another. I've included cross-references here and there, but for a more thorough exploration of any topic, use the index.

Church Documents

If you're interested in perusing any of the Church documents referenced in this book, they can be found online. Many Vatican II and papal documents can be found on the Vatican website (http://w2.vatican.va /content/vatican/en.html) and in the EWTN online document library (http://www.ewtn.com/v/library/search.asp). The entire *Catechism of the Catholic Church* is available online at http://ccc.usccb.org/flipbooks /catechism/index.html.

A Note to Non-Catholic Readers

This book is written primarily for a Catholic audience.

I state this not to ward off all others (quite the contrary!—rather, to everyone I extend a warm welcome) but to explain that there are some things in this book that a Catholic audience will take for granted but with which others may not be as comfortable or familiar. Unfortunately, explaining those specifically Catholic ways of thinking or practices in *full* is beyond the scope of this book. There will be *some* explanation, as even many Catholics these days do not always understand why we believe what we believe or do what we do. But to, say, an Evangelical or an agnostic, those explanations will probably seem incomplete.

It's not that these topics are inexplicable. It's just that if I tried to tackle them all, this book would be ten times longer. Many topics could use a book-length explanation. Moreover, explaining something to an Evangelical would require a diametrically different set of arguments than what would meet an agnostic's objections; the former would want to know where this idea was in the Bible, and the agnostic couldn't care less about that. Add in the mainline Protestants, Muslims, Jews, atheists, etc., and I would have to add that many more angles.

On the other hand, the curious *can* find scores of books on these subjects. Ignatius Press, the Coming Home Network, Emmaus Road Publishing, Sophia Institute Press, Catholic Answers, and other publishers have numerous works on apologetics (explaining the Catholic faith).

I do hope that readers of different faith backgrounds will read this book. I couldn't help but think of you when addressing some of these points and did try to offer a little insight on them with you in mind. I've also added more detail to some issues in the footnotes and suggested reading for a more in-depth view. And of course, the book isn't limited to these controversial areas. There are many points of agreement and, I imagine, mutual interest. I hope that, despite the Catholic perspective, most of the book will still inspire anyone striving to follow Jesus, or anyone considering doing so, to take up the challenge of learning to love Him better or, as St. Paul put it, to "try to learn what is pleasing to the Lord."[1]

---

[1] Eph 5:10.

PART ONE

"LOVE THE LORD YOUR GOD"

I

WHY SHOULD I LOVE GOD?

You may see this as a perfectly legitimate question, or you may be rather shocked by it. Wherever you may be on that spectrum, I think it's a good idea to begin with the *why* of loving God before addressing the *how*. Some aren't sure God is even real or that they want a relationship with Him. But looking at *why* can also benefit those to whom this question has never occurred, because there's no guarantee that it never will. We all have to face such thoughts at times; many saints, such as Teresa of Calcutta and Thérèse of Lisieux, had to face profound doubts that disturbed them. We're also prone to forgetfulness and need reminders. Furthermore, friends and relatives may ask us this question, so it is helpful to consider possible answers.

Not Sure about Loving God

Of course, not everyone believes that God exists or Jesus is the Son of God. This book isn't designed to tackle such questions, but there are plenty of great books on those topics.[1] Rather, the present work builds on a faith in, or at least an openness to, the Christian God and His goodness.

I understand the questions people have; I've had to deal with many of them myself in my own journey. (Asking questions isn't a problem—as long as we persist in seeking Truth.) You may believe God exists, but you have other impediments. Maybe you don't know Him. If so, you can ask His help in getting to know Him. Faith isn't something we can muster up; it's a gift. In fact, faith (along with hope and love) is one of the three theological virtues, and they can be obtained only as a gift from God.[2] It's not that He's holding out on us: He gives these gifts to

---

[1] Please see the Recommended Works, at the end of this book.

[2] See *Catechism of the Catholic Church*, 2nd ed. (Washington, D.C.: United States Catholic Conference, 1997), (hereinafter abbreviated *CCC*), nos. 1812–29, 1840–44, and the glossary: "virtues, theological" (p. 903).

those who want to follow Him. He's dying to give you those virtues. Indeed, He already died in order to give them—and more—to you. All you need to do is ask.

Maybe you can't comprehend how a good God could allow evil in this world. Or maybe you believe and had a relationship with Him in the past or have one now but aren't too happy with Him. (I was one of the latter myself at one time.) This book will discuss trusting God and grapple with the problem of suffering. For right now, I'll pass on the sound advice my spiritual director gave me when I was too angry with God to pray: Pray anyway. Talk to God about it; tell Him what's bothering you. "He's a big guy", Fr. Blair used to say to me. "He can take it." But He can't give you any answers if you're not speaking (or listening) to Him.

Obstacles We All Face

Those who believe and follow God also face impediments in loving Him. Some obstructions are part of the human condition; others belong to our particular age.

First among the timeless difficulties in loving God is the fact that when Adam and Eve disobeyed God, they lost something—divine grace—and thus they could not pass it on to us. Once its flame has been snuffed out, one candle can no longer light another. So we're missing something essential. We can be "relit" through Baptism, but we still struggle with the consequences, like an inclination to sin ("concupiscence").

Instead of divine grace, we have inherited from our first parents a fallen nature, with a robust streak of self-centeredness. Pride plagues us all. It can take a lot of forms, but essentially it is the hearty preference we have for our own way over anyone else's, including God's.

The *modern* challenges to loving God come from the world in which we live. Philosophical trends have fostered a cheekiness toward God, while skepticism has become ubiquitous. Moreover, the prosperity many free countries enjoy has a downside: a sense of entitlement, for one thing. We take our myriad comforts, pleasures, and freedoms for granted and are miffed if they are interfered with in any way. All the while we live and move and breathe in a culture polluted by a smog of materialism, where the desire for instant gratification and the inclination to look out for Number One are heartily nurtured by incessant advertising. All these combine to swell our self-centeredness.

What is more, we are inundated by graphic media, affecting not only our minds, but potentially our souls as well. Back in the 1980s, in his book *Amusing Ourselves to Death*, Neil Postman showed how the pacing of television—then, an average of 3.5 seconds per image—was shrinking viewers' span of attention.[3] In the forty-plus years since his book first came out, the pace has only increased, and the images themselves have become more graphic. Postman also decried the effects of the media on our ability to think and discuss. In an interview, he said the shift from reading to television "tends to make people less aware, less intelligent, less reflective, less analytical" and less capable of comprehending long and intricate discourse. Unlike those at the heady Lincoln–Douglas debates in the nineteenth century, "Today, it's inconceivable that any group of Americans could endure seven hours of such discourse."[4]

With surfing on the Internet, our ability to think deeply is even more challenged. In *The Shallows: What the Internet Is Doing to Our Brains*, Nicholas Carr points out, "The Net's cacophony of stimuli short-circuits both conscious and unconscious thought, preventing our minds from thinking either deeply or creatively."[5] He also warns that the Internet "is altering the depth of our emotions as well as our thoughts".[6] (Even as I'm writing this, I have to fight the temptation to check my email.) There's always a new distraction. Now that we can carry the Internet in our pockets and get multiple notifications throughout the day on our phones, the distractions never seem to end. None of this helps us contemplate the things that matter most.

In addition, millions are caught up in the race of consuming ever more—more stuff and more entertainment. Education and work are degenerating into means merely to pay for what we consume. When we're not at work or amusing ourselves, we're running around shopping or fixing/maintaining what we have. Those raising children schlepp them around to various activities—many of which may be quite worthwhile individually but together add up to frenetic mayhem. But parents deem it necessary for their kids to get into college someday: they've got to get into a good school so they can get a good job to pay for all this.

[3] Neil Postman, *Amusing Ourselves to Death: Public Discourse in the Age of Show Business* (New York: Penguin Books, 1985), p. 86.

[4] Neil Postman interview, "Literacy Lost", PBS Currents, www.youtube.com/watch?v=VWNHLKW7n5c.

[5] Nicholas Carr, *The Shallows* (New York: Norton, 2010), p. 119.

[6] Ibid., p. 221.

Entertainment and consumption have practically become the point of life in our modern culture. Without time for serious thought processes, we are losing the ability to think deeply. We don't even have time to wonder, *What is the meaning of it all?* Do we possess our possessions, or do they possess us? Do we consume pleasures and entertainment, or do they consume us?

Living mostly in man-made environments also has an effect on us. We can start having the false impression that everything is under our control, forgetting our smallness and how limited we are. This delusion is harder to maintain out in nature. On the peak of a great mountain, at the edge of a seemingly endless sea, at the foot of soaring sequoias, or beneath the canopy of countless stars, we are more likely to experience a sense of awe and wonder and, if we let ourselves, perhaps even a notion that the Creator of all this must be even more majestic and awe-inspiring. An earthquake, hurricane, or tsunami occasionally reminds us how puny we really are, how far less powerful than we would like to believe. All these things that make us feel so small and helpless remind us that we need Someone big enough to handle them all. Most of the time, however, we are in or surrounded by buildings or vehicles and using the latest new gadgets, all of which feed our swollen sense of control. But it is an illusion. Control over hundreds of channels ceases instantly when the electricity goes out. Sculpting the ultimate physique and maintaining it with Botox and surgery will not keep us from dying someday.

So we walk around in a myopic bubble, blind to reality. This is truly ironic for an age priding itself on its dedication to realism, even "gritty" realism. It is almost laughable, given how much of our lives are spent watching fiction, fantasy, or virtuality on various screens. What *does* absorb our attention, even when it's real, is so fleeting, while what matters most—the ultimate, lasting, *real* reality, the point of our existence—scarcely enters our consciousness. Most of us are so caught up in the here-and-now we're too busy to bother much about the hereafter.

All these difficulties—our fallen nature, self-centeredness, spiritual blindness, the cultural attitudes around us, and the temptations and distractions beckoning to us constantly—make the aim to love God challenging. They could all be summed up as, "What's in it for me?"

Love doesn't ask that question. But God has placed earthly desires in our hearts, so it's not an invalid question. Before we can get to love, let's look at it head-on.

What's in It for Me?

Whatever you think of the Rolling Stones, you have to admit they're right in pointing out that lasting satisfaction cannot be had, even when we try and we try and we try and we try.[7] Everyone can relate to this experience; it's the story of our lives.

Sure, we experience satisfactions here and there, but they don't last. "Snickers really satisfies", the ads used to repeat *ad nauseam*. Hah! Snicker at the thought. Any Snickers addict—as I once was—knows how false that is. A yummy candy bar or even a chocolate truffle might be intensely enjoyable, but it only lasts a few moments, and then it's over. The satisfaction of a delicious meal will last longer, but you will still get hungry again. Likewise, you can take satisfaction in a job well done, but you can't sit on your laurels for the rest of your life.

At least at some point in our lives, we all try to find lasting happiness in the things of this world, but the effort inevitably fails, even as we produce more and more comfort-giving and fun commodities. "Technological society has succeeded in multiplying the opportunities for pleasure, yet it has great difficulty in generating joy."[8] Instead, says Pope Francis, such pursuits lead to a "covetous heart", "blunted conscience", "desolation and anguish".[9] Even actor Jim Carrey observed: "I think everybody should get rich and famous and do everything they ever dreamed of so they can see that it's not the answer."[10]

C. S. Lewis was very astute on why we can never be perfectly satisfied in this life:

> The settled happiness and security which we all desire, God withholds from us by the very nature of the world: but joy, pleasure, and merriment He has scattered broadcast. We are never safe, but we have plenty of fun, and some ecstasy. It is not hard to see why. The security we crave

---

[7] See Mick Jagger and Keith Richards, "(I Can't Get No) Satisfaction" (1965).

[8] Pope St. Paul VI, Apostolic Exhortation *Gaudete in Domino* on Christian Joy (May 9, 1975), 1. (Quotations from this and all papal and conciliar documents have whenever possible been taken from the Vatican website.)

[9] Pope Francis, Apostolic Exhortation *Evangelii Gaudium* on the Proclamation of the Gospel in Today's World, *The Joy of the Gospel* (November 24, 2013), no. 2. His predecessor similarly noted, "When we try to spare ourselves the effort and pain of pursuing truth, love, and goodness,... we drift into a life of emptiness" and a growing sense of meaninglessness. Pope Benedict XVI, Encyclical Letter *Spe Salvi* on Christian Hope, *Saved in Hope* (November 30, 2007), no. 37.

[10] Widely quoted; original source is reportedly *Reader's Digest*, March 2006.

would teach us to rest our hearts in this world and oppose an obstacle to our return to God: ... Our Father refreshes us on the journey with some pleasant inns, but will not encourage us to mistake them for home.[11]

It's as though God has placed a homing device within each of us. He has planted an indefinable—quiet but persistent—yearning in our hearts. When viewing a beautiful landscape, a sunrise or sunset at the beach, or someplace with a great vista, have you ever felt a mysterious longing? A longing for ... you know not what? It seems a desire to *be* in that place. Seeing some distant hills, Laura Ingalls remarked, "They are so beautiful that they make me want to go to them." But her friend Ida replied, "Oh, I don't know.... When you got there, they would just be hills, covered with ordinary buffalo grass like this", kicking a tuft of it.[12]

This longing must be more than a curiosity to see faraway places or what lies beyond, because Ida is right: when we reach those places, the longing is never satisfied. There might be a certain satisfaction in seeing new places, but the imagined magic they had from afar fades away upon arrival. I think the longing is for something unreachable here. The beauty of creation reminds us of the Creator and makes us homesick for Beauty Himself. That is why that ache is not merely to stand in another *place*; the ache is for union, a desire to be *one* with that beauty ... a desire that can only be fulfilled in heaven, in the Beatific Vision.[13]

It is only natural that we keep failing to find satisfaction in created things, because we were created for something more. Something better than all the pleasures, exciting experiences, the most wonderful accomplishments, and even the best relationships of this world put together. St. Augustine famously put it: "Our hearts are restless until they rest in You, O Lord."

So, to those not sure about loving God and wondering, *What's in it for me?*, know that there really is something for us. Any description will fall short, but God alone truly quenches our deepest thirst; we've got a God-shaped ache in our hearts, and only He can fill it. And if we live accordingly, then seeing Him face to face will not merely be thrilling

---

[11] C. S. Lewis, *The Problem of Pain* (New York: Simon & Schuster, 1996), p. 103.

[12] Laura Ingalls Wilder, *These Happy Golden Years* (New York: HarperCollins, 1971), pp. 204–5.

[13] In doing research for this book, I was pleasantly surprised to discover a similar sentiment in C. S. Lewis, *Weight of Glory* (New York: HarperOne, 2001), pp. 30–31.

and fantastic and inexpressibly wonderful, it will be the total and unending fulfillment of our very being.

Unbelievably Lovable

Why love God? Why do we love anyone? Because we see something in that person: something beautiful, good, admirable— intellect, wit, virtue, strength—something lovable.

> The joy of the gospel fills the hearts and lives of all who encounter Jesus. Those who accept his offer of salvation are set free from sin, sorrow, inner emptiness and loneliness. With Christ, joy is constantly born anew.
>
> —POPE FRANCIS Box 1

Ever been infatuated? Ever admired someone from afar or idolized a celebrity? A gorgeous singer? An incredible athlete? Just to be noticed by this star would be thrilling. There's a reason we call such a person a "teen idol" or speak of "idolizing" someone. It's because we're mixed up. When we outgrow such infatuation, we look on it as silly and on those still in the grips of it as immature or blind. But the truth is, the experience, while misguided, is actually natural to humans. We are meant to worship, to adore—just not to adore other people. Idolatry is putting someone or something in the place of God. But adoration itself is wrong or silly only when we're adoring the wrong one. Transfer those adoring looks, those longing sighs, that willingness to do anything just to be near the adored one, *to God*, and you're on the right track.

When we see God someday, we will see the Source of all goodness, of all beauty; we will see Truth Himself, who is also All-Mighty. Our hearts will be drawn to Him; He will be infinitely attractive to us because He is the fulfillment of all our desires; indeed, the fulfillment of our very being. The more one comes to know God, the more one realizes how lovable He is. He is infinitely good, infinitely more powerful, infinitely more wise, infinitely more appealing than anyone we know or could ever imagine.

He Loves Us!

While many take God's love for granted, on a deeper level, we find it hard to believe in His love. My sister told me of a speaker who said, "It's like I'm this piece of —— that the world revolves around." We're self-centered and at the same time can't stand ourselves. When we really think about His greatness and pristine holiness, we feel small and unworthy. How could He love *me*? And *why* would He love me?

But the surprising, delightful thing is that somehow He loves each of us. He loves us just the way we are, where we are. He desires us to be united with Him forever in heaven—He wants it so much that He's gone to stupendous lengths to achieve it.

First, He fashioned material creation to reflect His attributes to us.[14] The intricate and varied beauties of a rose, a thoroughbred, a spectacular sunset, a sparkling waterfall all exhibit the incredible creativity and beauty of the Divine Artist. The size of the universe with its multiple galaxies testifies to the inexpressible greatness and might of the One who created it all. The wondrous ways in which all these created things work together and interact and the order of the universe display His wisdom. Joy, laughter, harmony, love, cooperation, generosity, self-sacrifice all echo His goodness. Creation reveals to us these admirable attributes of God.

> Has not God in fact won for himself a claim on all our love? From all eternity he has loved us.... It was for [us] that he created heaven and earth and such an abundance of things. He made all these things out of love for man, so that all creation might serve man, and man in turn might love God out of gratitude for so many gifts.
>
> —St. Alphonsus Liguori [Box 2]

But He didn't stop there; He wanted us to know Him better. So He set aside a people and revealed Himself and His ways to them. That wasn't enough either.

Some people view God as the Great Clockmaker who created everything, set it on auto-pilot, and sat back to watch or wandered away. Jesus, however, unveils an astoundingly different God, who is anything but indifferent and aloof, far from absent. He was so present that He came down from heaven and became one of us. You can't get much more involved than that.

He didn't have to do it that way. He has myriad angels who could have been sent. Instead, the Son of God came to teach His people face to face. Even so, He could have just temporarily taken on a human *appearance*. He could have just appeared in all His glory, delivered His message, *voila!* handing over a Bible pre-printed by Heavenly Press, and infused the disciples with the knowledge they would need. But no: He "did not count equality with God a thing to be grasped, but emptied himself, taking the form of a servant".[15] His condescension

[14] See *CCC* 32.
[15] Phil 2:6.

(which means "come down to be with") is literal and incredible.[16] He was willing to give up all the infinite richness of His divine privileges, stoop to our level, and become one of us. That would be like one of us becoming an ant and going to live in an ant farm.

It's amazing enough that God would come to earth at all, but even more incredible is the way He came. Why come as a baby? In weakness, obscurity, and poverty? Why did He live an ordinary life as a craftsman in a poor village for nearly *thirty* years? Why spend three years teaching, preaching, and healing? In our fast-paced, bottom-line society, all this seems so inefficient, such a waste of valuable time. Nor did He need to suffer on the Cross to attain our salvation. Some theologians say, given the infinite value of His Blood, a single drop could save the universe. He could have saved us by undergoing a minor cut.

Why did He do it the way He did? Because He loves us. He wanted to spend time with us. And because He came not merely to *tell* us how to live but to *show* us.

Children often want to grow up quickly, to gain skills in a day. We know they can't become a virtuoso in a week or a month; we laugh at their impatience. But we're the same: we want to lose weight or gain a virtue right away, without any work. But that's not the way God set things up. Anything worthwhile takes time and effort. And instead of merely telling us, "This is the way it is; deal with it", He came down here—as one of us—and lived it too.

He knew that human language is limited, so words wouldn't be enough. To walk with us, to heal us, to live with us would be so much more effective in showing us His love. In the life of Jesus, we learn that God is down-to-earth, generous, selfless, thoughtful, caring, funny, wise beyond compare, wondrous and mighty in His marvelous cures and miracles.[17]

All that was still not enough.

He expressed His love by dying for love. As the man-God, He healed the breach between mankind and God, which we caused but couldn't fix. Not with a wave of His hand, but by laying His hands and feet

---

[16] Lucifer evidently found it incredibly distasteful—rumor has it he foresaw the Incarnation and that was what led to his rebellion: he couldn't stand the thought of bowing to a God who had become human.

[17] Take a look at the stories about Him recorded by Matthew, Mark, Luke, and John; also check out modern perspectives, such as Frank Sheed's *To Know Christ Jesus* or Dorothy Sayers' incomparable *The Man Born to Be King*.

down on a cross and letting them be nailed there. He suffered and died, as we do, so that He could transform pain and death into a pathway to heaven. He lived a full human life and died a horrible death to show us the depth of His love. In the death of Jesus, we learn that He is determined, courageous beyond words, honorable, self-sacrificing, merciful, heroic. To the conundrum of suffering, He answered not in words but with Himself: He suffered with us, He suffered for us; He suffered more than anyone. He is the definition of selflessness. In Him, we learn what love looks like, what love means.

Having been murdered by His own creatures, God the Son didn't take this wholesale rejection and head straight back to heaven, chalking up His earthly life as a failed attempt to connect with us. No, He resurrected His body to prove His divine identity and manifest His victory over death, making sure we knew about it. In His Resurrection, we learn that He has boundless mercy, can't be beaten, doesn't hold grudges, and not only can defeat evil but can transform the worst evil into the best good.

Then He ascended into heaven. His mission accomplished, He didn't need a human body anymore, yet He will keep His humanity forever. Wow. It's amazing enough that, to save us, He took on our human condition for thirty-three years. How mind-boggling that He will retain it for ever and ever, long after our salvation has been accomplished.

This is only a glimpse of what He's done for us, and yet it amounts to another, very powerful reason to love God. We love those who love us, who have been there for us. And no one has been there for us like God has.

Will We Reciprocate?

Amazingly, He actually longs for our love.[18] God *wants* a relationship with us. We tend not to think about His perspective, about what He thinks if we notice Him or not.

It's true that the Church teaches that if what motivates a soul to obey God is a fear of hell, that's good enough. God is merciful. But He would *far* rather that we followed Him out of love.

---

[18] The Bible is chock-full of evidence of this. Beyond the famous John 3:15, consider, e.g., the Book of Hosea, Song of Songs, the parables of the lost sheep, lost coin, prodigal son (all in Luke 15), Mt 23:37, and Rev 2:4.

Parents get this. Most parents would be at least relieved if not satisfied if their kids obeyed them, even if it was only to avoid the consequences. But the same parents would be absolutely thrilled if their kids actually "got it"—if they did their chores and duties, and even tried to appreciate their parents, because they loved them and wanted to please them and believed that if their parents said certain things were good for them or bad for them, then that must be true, even if the kids weren't mature enough to see it themselves yet. Wow, that would be tremendous! So too would our Lord prefer that we trust Him and what He says and follow Him out of *love*.[19]

Thus it is best if we can get beyond fear, guilt, and duty. Those of course are far better than indifference, irresponsibility, and rebellion. For your sake, He'll accept your efforts for those former reasons, but He would rather you were motivated by love.

Nor does He like being used any more than anyone else. No one appreciates hearing from someone claiming to be a friend only when they need a favor. What if someone blew off one invitation you sent them after another, or when they *did* come, they acted as if they were doing you a big favor by accepting? What if they came late, looked bored, didn't pay attention, and then left early? Would you feel loved? God wants His love reciprocated too.

ᴣ◐ ᴣ◐ ᴣ◐

Why should we love Him? Aside from His being our Creator and thus our owing Him love as well as worship, obedience, and gratitude, the main reason is that He is infinitely lovable. He is more admirable, awe-inspiring, captivating than any superstar. And because He loves us. His infinite mercy, generous Providence, and His unfathomable love for us have been demonstrated by His becoming one of us and dying for us. Here is a loving God, and a very lovable one as well.

What we're made for, deep down what we're really longing for, is God. Nothing else will satisfy us in the long run. Nothing. And while we can get a foretaste here of what that ultimate union with Him will be like, this yearning in our hearts can never be fully satisfied in this life.

---

[19] The parable of the prodigal son illustrates God's acceptance of "imperfect contrition"; Peter hints at the merit of perfect contrition: "[L]ove covers a multitude of sins" (1 Pet 4:8). *CCC* 1452–53 explains these terms.

But we can begin here. In fact, that is what our life story is supposed to be all about.

The challenge is to keep that fact in the forefront of our minds. Some people have never learned this; many others forget. Even those who know it and strive to practice it struggle to live by it every day. Loving God is not always easy to do.

Moreover, we are influenced by certain attitudes in the air. When we hear the phrase "loving God" or "the love of God", we usually think of *His* love for *us*. In a culture like ours, I might easily question if He loves me, how much He loves me, whether His love is good enough for me, or if I'm good enough for His love. No matter what form that type of question takes, it's all about me. I forget the real question of my life is: How well am I loving God? Does He "feel the love"?

What Does It Mean to Love God?

Once you've decided you do want to love God better, how do you go about it? What does loving God mean, anyway?

What Do You Give a God Who Has Everything?

Everything we have is a gift from God: intellect, personality, body, faculties, strengths (and weaknesses), faith, situation in life, the grace we need to do any good thing—all were given to us by our Creator. Anything we try to give to Him we find, really, was His to begin with. The only thing that is truly ours, in a sense, is our free will. Of course, He gave that to us too—so the only thing we can give back to Him is the use of that will.

So what can you give God, then, who has it all? Your love.

And along with your heart, your will. Your life. Yourself. Your all. To give Him these things is to give Him your love.

What Is Love?

Love desires the good of the loved one. Love puts the good of the beloved before self.

> To love is to will the good of another.
> —St. Thomas Aquinas Box 3

Love is more than a feeling; it is an act of the will. So, what we can give back to God with our free will is our love, ourselves. This is why He gave us free will, so we could love Him freely, by our own choice.

Love is more than lip service. St. Teresa of Avila said: "Love is proved by deeds." Our daily choices and what we do when no one is looking are what prove our love for God is real.

Indeed, true love desires to prove itself. Jesus illustrates how entirely without self-interest love is when He speaks of going two miles when forced to go one; of also giving a coat when someone demands your cloak.[20] Do more, go farther, above and beyond, expecting nothing in return, and you will be imitating the love of God, "for he is kind to the ungrateful and the selfish".[21]

Remember what we said earlier about teen idols and celebrities? How thrilling it would be just being noticed by your favorite superstar? What if your hero did more than notice you and asked you a favor? What would you be willing to do for that person? Just about anything, right? It would feel like an honor and a privilege to be singled out. The more difficult the task, the greater the honor you would feel in being entrusted with it. That willingness to do anything is what our love for God should look like. Love welcomes sacrifice.

Fortunately, opportunities are all around us. "Love is a fruit in season at all times and within the reach of every hand", St. Teresa of Calcutta said.[22]

God's Love Language

Gary Chapman has described five "love languages" by which people express and understand love. For some people, what really says "I love you" is a gift; for others, it is an act of service; for still others, it is quality time, touch, or words of affirmation. Chapman has books applying these love languages to marriages, parenting, school, single life, the workplace, and more.

What about God? What's *His* love language? What can we do that really speaks love to *Him*? I believe this is one reason Jesus came: to reveal the love language of God.

When studying literature, we look at more than just what the narrator says. While the heart of a story could be stated explicitly or implied in what the narrator says, it is also revealed in the plot, the characters, what they say, and what they do. We glean the message by looking at all

---

[20] See Mt 5:41; Lk 6:27–37.

[21] Lk 6:35.

[22] Mother Teresa, *Love: A Fruit Always in Season; Daily Meditations from the Words of Mother Teresa of Calcutta*, ed. Dorothy S. Hunt (San Francisco: Ignatius Press, 1987), back cover.

these things. In the same way, we can learn the love language of God by studying the story of Jesus: His life, His words, and His actions.

Nothing compares with the love of God. In both senses of the phrase: nothing is better than being loved by God, and there is nothing better than loving Him in return. If we love Him, we'll *want* to know how the Lord wants to be loved. This book helps to unpack what Jesus revealed, offering you the chance to learn how to love God better.

SECTION ONE

LOVING GOD MEANS
TRUSTING HIM

"I tell you, do not be anxious . . .
If you . . . know how to give good gifts to your children,
how much more will your Father who is in heaven
give good things to those who ask him!"

(Mt 6:25, 7:11)

Perfect love casts out fear.

(1 Jn 4:18)

2

HURDLES TO TRUST

Trust is needed for every step in following Christ because to be a Christian is not just to go out on a limb, but to live out there.

Trust Is Crucial

Trust is foundational to a loving relationship. Even those who already trust in God need to trust Him more. We're never done learning to trust God. Each new rung He asks us to climb in the spiritual life requires trust in Him. And everyone has trust issues: starting with Eve (who trusted the serpent more than God), down through the ages, to every one of her children.

How many sins do we commit because we don't trust enough in God's grace or His plan?

Often when tempted, we don't believe God's promise, "My grace is sufficient for you."[1] We may put up a little fight, but we tend to crumble before putting that verse to the test. And frequently we don't trust the Holy Spirit's promptings, turning a deaf ear because we don't want to leave our comfort zone or do something too "extreme". We don't trust that His idea is worth it.

Not trusting in His plan is another common pitfall. When our plans are ruined, we cling to them instead of discerning His plan. Either we forget He *has* a plan or we don't care what it is.

Hardest of all, of course, is trusting Him in the face of suffering: when things go from bad to worse, when dreams are crushed, when pain takes over, when tragedy strikes. That's when it's really hard to trust in God's love, in His wisdom, and sometimes in His very existence.

Without trust, then, it's very hard to grow in virtue. We can't overcome our habitual sins without trust in God, and smaller sins can lead to mortal sin. Without trust, it's almost impossible to make it through a

[1] 2 Cor 12:9.

31

period of real suffering with one's faith intact. Whatever our issues with trust might be, we have to get past them. Trust is absolutely necessary in a vibrant spiritual life.

Worrywart-ism

Probably the most common form of distrust is worry. At the rate we do it, worrying could be a national pastime.

When Jesus told His followers to leave off worrying, in his famous "Consider the lilies" discourse,[2] His audience had a lot more reason to worry than I do. Most of them were poor, and they were living in an occupied country, under Pontius Pilate, who had shown little respect for their lives. Yet Jesus said to them, "[D]o not be anxious about your life, what you shall eat or what you shall drink, nor ... what you shall put on."[3] Many of us worry about things far less basic to survival. We worry about being liked, paying for all we want, success, what people think of us, etc. We also worry about more important things, but things we have little or no control over: job security, the economy, the safety of our loved ones, our country, and so on.

But worrying over *anything* in this world, even the most justifiable— one's own life, for instance—Jesus says is a waste of time: "[W]hich of you by being anxious can add one cubit to his span of life?"[4] Rather, He asserts that being a child of God means trusting that our heavenly Father will care for us. Worrying is even something of an insult to God; it shows a lack of confidence in His love for us.[5] Rather, I should entrust the things that worry me to God. I should build my trust by recalling what He has done in the past when I gave my concerns to Him. "The moment you realize you are worrying, make very quickly an act of confidence: 'No, Jesus, You are there.... I have no right to worry.' "[6]

---

[2] See Mt 6:25–34.

[3] Mt 6:25.

[4] Mt 6:27.

[5] Anxiety as a mental condition, on the other hand, is different. For a variety of reasons—from chemical imbalance to trauma—one can experience anxiety beyond one's ability to control. This should not be a cause to feel guilty on top of that, but a reason to seek professional help. The Sacraments of Confession and Anointing (both healing sacraments) are also very helpful.

[6] Fr. Jean C.J. d'Elbée, *I Believe in Love: A Personal Retreat Based on the Teaching of St. Thérèse of Lisieux* (Manchester, N.H.: Sophia Institute Press, 2001), p. 92. He also notes: "Nature always worries.... The main thing is not to consent consciously to anxiety or a troubled mind" (pp. 91–92).

Instead of worrying, Christ urges us to seek "first the kingdom of God, and his righteousness".[7] Doing that naturally kicks me out of center stage and puts God there, where He belongs. It also gives me His perspective and helps me get my priorities straight. And seeking God's Kingdom and righteousness before all else yields the opposite of anxiety: peace and joy. It is only when we stop fooling ourselves in thinking we can serve God and our own interest that we can have peace. Otherwise, we become anxious to get our way and greedy to keep it, whether it is a small pleasure or achieving a five-year plan. When we let go of all these things—when we become like St. Paul, who was content to feast or do without—only then will we have peace in God's will, only then can we "rejoice at all times".

Beware of Useless Fear

Among the possible motives for sin, pleasure comes to mind, selfishness seems to cover all the bases, and the "love of money" has St. Paul's vote as "the root of all evils".[8] With those obvious contenders, fear may not even make a blip on the radar screen. But fear is a big sin–stimulator.

It's not usually obvious. If we lived under a dictatorship, it would be unmistakable: out of fear, people (including you and me) might sin in ways we wouldn't otherwise. But if you live in a free country, fear might not seem to play much of a role in your day-to-day life. And since we don't like to admit we have any fears, we certainly don't go hunting our psyche for them.

It's when you start going deeper in your spiritual life that you discover fear. When you try to root out sin, you must ask yourself, *Why do I do that?* Sometimes you ask it again for each new answer before you stumble on the real reason, and not infrequently that reason is fear.

Let's say you keep blowing up at your family members when they make you late. Why does that make you explode? You might say it's because you *really* hate to be late. But why is that? If it's not an important event, could it be that you're afraid of what people might think? Maybe it's the fear that the person waiting for you will be annoyed and

---

[7] Mt 6:33, KJV.
[8] 1 Tim 6:10.

like you less. Or that the person will lose respect for you. Maybe you're afraid that an instance of tardiness will tarnish your image as having it all together, either in the eyes of someone else or in your own.

Or let's say you keep putting work before family. That could spring from a lot of reasons—maybe your self-image is too caught up in being successful. But fear could play a role too: the fear of being a failure or of being average. You've got to be Somebody, or you're nothing. Maybe it's more serious: a fear of being passed over for a promotion or of losing your job.

It takes courage to admit fears, let alone overcome them. Usually it's only during a retreat or a time of ongoing prayer and reflection that we can open ourselves to admitting these things. We build up walls to keep from seeing these deeper areas of ourselves; if we do get a glimpse, we find the sight rather alarming and look away.

But we need to recognize fear, because it can cause us to sin. We might hurt others or be rude, indifferent, or blind to them in trying to avoid what we fear. What is needed is trust.

The Challenge of Trusting in God

When I first became a mother, I soon found myself anxious about my child's well-being. There was nothing wrong with her—just with me. I realized there were many dangers beyond my power to prevent that could befall my helpless darling.

At that time, I was losing hold of my trust in God to take care of what I could not. My father-in-law had passed away prematurely the year before, and one of my dearest friends died shortly after. I had begun to experience disturbing flashbacks of a repressed childhood trauma. My husband's nerve injury was worsening, and it was dawning on us that our dreams of a concert career for him might be not merely delayed but snuffed out.

I mention all this only to show that when I advocate trusting in God, I'm not doing so airily, with no personal experience of how hard it can be.

Overcoming Fear

I'm not belittling fear. It is a powerful force, and sometimes we are wise to pay heed to it.

Yet the Bible says, "Fear not!" over and over. The idea is said to appear in the Bible 365 times—one for each day of the year.[9] Pope St. John Paul II echoed this. Though he had lived under Nazi occupation and Communist totalitarianism, "Be not afraid" was his refrain. How could one who had faced truly fearful circumstances say that? He could because he found God to be faithful.

The best way to overcome a fear is to face it. When you run from a fear, its shadow looms over you. But when you stop, turn around, and examine it, it shrinks considerably. What if X did happen? When you think about it, you realize it wouldn't be the end of the world.

But even if it were something truly terrible, Christ has promised that with His grace we could endure it. If we give it over to Him, He could and would bring good out of it. With His help, we could bring good out of it too if, by nothing else, by offering it up.[10] Even if the worst scenarios we can imagine were to happen, ultimately it wouldn't matter, so long as we were seeking first God's Kingdom and His righteousness. The only tragedy in this life, Leon Bloy wrote, is not to become a saint.[11] Any suffering we undergo can help us fulfill our purpose: to get to heaven and bring as many souls with us as we can.

Everything Is a Gift

You gasp. Surely I can't mean that—*every*thing is a gift? Hah!

But I do mean it. Every*thing* and every circumstance is or holds, on some level, a gift.

Yeah, right. Tell that to those in the hospital or who are unemployed or . . .

Yes, it is possible to share that view with *some* who are in the hospital or unemployed—but not at a time of tragedy (more on that later). It helped me when I was hospitalized and when I was laid off. A priest once told my dad, when he was going through hard times, that God had given him "the gift of catastrophe". The reminder can actually bring some level of comfort.

---

[9] No, I have not counted them personally, but I've seen that number quoted often. Matthew Kelly, however, puts it even higher: 1,000 times! *Rediscover Catholicism* (Cincinnati, Ohio: Beacon, 2010), p. 304.

[10] More on this in section 5 below, on carrying the cross.

[11] Leon Bloy, *The Woman Who Was Poor* (New York: Sheed & Ward, 1947), p. 356.

Granted, not every gift appears to be a gift. Not every gift from God brings joy to the recipient upon its arrival.

Some gifts are obvious. Beauty, wealth, health, friendship, love, success, admiration, intelligence, talent, house, car, food. These are the kinds of gifts we desire, easily recognize as gifts, and (one hopes) are thankful to have. However, we don't always remember that the word *gift* implies a Giver; nor do we ponder *why* we received this or that particular gift, what a gift is for.

Beauty, for instance, draws people's attention and admiration. It can give a certain weight to the beautiful person's words and actions. Many beautiful people, however, use their gift simply to soak up attention and admiration for themselves. But beauty has its disadvantages too. Sometimes it draws unsavory people and unwelcome conversations and situations. And people don't always take a beautiful person seriously: they're too enthralled with the person's looks to listen, or they assume beauty and brains don't go together. So plainness can be a gift as well.

Some gifts we would rather not have. But we need to learn to see them as God does.

The Hiding Place recounts the true story of two sisters sent to a concentration camp. If that weren't bad enough, all the beds are infested with fleas. Betsy thanks God even for the fleas; Corrie can't go that far. The sisters, having smuggled in a Bible, share God's Word with the other female prisoners, drawing many of them to their bunk for Bible studies every night. Later, they discover they got away with this flagrant rule-breaking precisely due to the fleas: it was because of the fleas that guards didn't come into the barracks.[12] In that sense, the fleas were a gift.

In some languages, the word for *crisis* is the same as the one for *opportunity*. We usually don't recognize poverty or illness as the gift of opportunity. But it is. The lack of a certain desired gift holds many opportunities: the opportunity to trust in God more, to exercise patience, to offer it up[13] as a prayer for someone else, to grow in charity, to ponder the superiority of the next life to this one, to wake up, recognize one's sin, and repent.

---

[12] Corrie Ten Boom, with John and Elizabeth Sherrill, *The Hiding Place* (New York: Bantam Books, 1971), pp. 197, 198, 209.

[13] *Offering up* is Catholic-ese for "giving to God as a prayer" or "giving up for the love of God".

The lack of a good can also be the opportunity to be served. Each Christian is called to be Christ to others, and sometimes that means being Christ-in-need, to be a "least one". It's very humbling, but how can people serve Christ in their brethren if none are in need? Sometimes I must accept being the needy one. My need is a gift of opportunity for someone else.

Thus difficulties and trials are or hold tremendous gifts of spiritual opportunity.

Accepting His Answers to Prayers of Petition

Asking God for something always requires trust; the *Catechism of the Catholic Church* calls it "the principal difficulty" in trusting in God.[14] Turning to Him, though, gives us the proper attitude: a recognition that He is God and we are not. "*Humility* is the foundation of prayer", the *Catechism* adds. "Man is a beggar before God."[15] Realizing we need Him is a great start.

We don't turn to Him as much as we could or should. Sometimes we forget; sometimes we live in habitual self-sufficiency; sometimes we're too proud. Meanwhile God is a gentleman; He doesn't intrude in our lives. "Our Father knows what we need before we ask him, but he awaits our petition because the dignity of his children lies in their freedom."[16]

Still, He longs for us to turn to Him with our needs and desires. In fact, the *Catechism* states that our prayer is a *response* to God seeking us.[17] He loves us. He wants to give us good things, to heal and help us. He doesn't get annoyed or tired of helping. He is an *infinitely* patient, loving Father, who delights in helping, even more than a devoted mother caring for her baby.

Whenever we put a situation, need, or desire in His hands, we have immediately bettered it. Even with requests He deems better not to grant, He can always make the situation better. Fr. Martin Connor, L.C., an excellent retreat master, says God has three answers to our

---

[14] *CCC* 2734.
[15] *CCC* 2559, quoting St. Augustine, *Sermo* 56, 6, 9: PL 38, 381.
[16] *CCC* 2736; cf. Mt 6:8.
[17] See *CCC* 2560, 2561.

prayers of petition: (1) "Yes"; (2) "Not yet"; and (3) "I have a better idea." Accepting Answer Two or Three requires faith, grace, love, and spiritual maturity. Every answer comes from His love for us and is the best for us. Waiting or accepting a different answer is an opportunity for us to grow in faith and hope, as well as to express our love for God and grow in it. Still, such answers can be hard to accept and, in our day and age, hard to understand.

Acknowledging the Yeses

Yeses do come. We must acknowledge that; we must rejoice and remember them. Too often we forget. We're more likely to remember what we perceive to be Nos.

In fact, however, it's very possible that God wants to give us even more Yeses than we now receive, but we're not asking. Jesus tell us five times in the Gospel of John that He will give us whatever we ask in His name.[18] Maybe, like Huckleberry Finn, we tried that as kids, asking for some prized item, didn't get it, and gave up on that idea. But why did Jesus say it if He didn't mean it?

What does that verse mean? Was it only for apostolic times? Well, miracles in the lives of the saints disprove that idea. If you look at those saints who performed miracles, you notice a few things: the miracles were never things that they asked for themselves (aside from help in serving others); they were totally dedicated to the will of God; and they were full of loving trust not only in God's power but in His will.

Maybe if we were like that and if we asked for more, we would receive more Yeses too.

Handling the Suspense

Answer Number Two—a situation where you don't know what is going to happen or how long this will go on—is a type of affliction that deserves to be recognized; it deserves a name. Let's call it "the cross of suspense". But if we don't get a Yes right away, we must not give up. Take the timeless advice of a fourth-century hermit: "Do not be troubled if you do not immediately receive from God what you ask him; for he desires to do something even greater for you, while you cling to him in prayer."[19]

---

[18] See Jn 14:13; 14:14; 15:16; 16:23; 16:24.
[19] Evagrius Ponticus, *De oratione* 34: PG 79, 1173. Quoted in *CCC* 2737.

Some years ago, the Lord enlightened me on His perspective on the "Not yet" answer. Our daughter as a toddler would ask for a hot dog, and I would say, "Okay", and start making it. Seconds later, she would come back and repeat the request. Another minute, and she was back again, complaining and whining as though I were refusing her. I would explain, "Honey, I *am* making you a hot dog; it just takes some time to cook it. It's coming!" Then it struck me how like her I am. I ask God for something, but I have no idea what's involved. I get impatient and don't understand why it's taking so long. But why don't I trust Him? God is cooking up something good for me, and all I do is complain.

Looking at creation, I notice that God likes to take time with things. Aside from lightning, not much happens in a flash. Most things take time to develop, to grow, to ripen. Even lightning comes only after the storm clouds have gradually gathered. Why should I expect His answers to my prayers to be any different?

I suspect He has His reasons. Maybe He enjoys the process as much as the result. Maybe He's trying to teach me something. Good chance it has to do with coordinating His answer with what's good for other people too. But His timing is always perfect. I need to remember that and not demand what isn't ready yet. If it's still unripe, it won't be as good for me anyway.

God's delay can also teach us patience. That time of suspense tests our trust. The temptation to doubt Him or to give up is a chance to pray again, to renew and deepen our hope in Him. Continuing to pray during a delay gives us the grace to wait, and if we persevere, we'll gain a more profound trust. Delay, then, can result in greater virtue in us.

Jesus urges us to persist in prayer like a man knocking and knocking at his neighbor's door in the middle of the night.[20] Perseverance in prayer shows confidence in God because by it one continues the conversation; he trusts that God does hear him, does care. Our perseverance also shows God (and ourselves) how serious we are about our petition. Having to wait can motivate us to pray more, and more fervently. It can also motivate us to fast and make sacrifices.

In fact, though we're thinking about the petition, God is thinking about us; the *Catechism* states His first answer to our request is a "transformation of the praying heart".[21] If it causes us to look at ourselves and our lives to see if something needs to be changed, this is a very good

---

[20] See Lk 11:5–8.
[21] *CCC* 2739.

possible reason for the delay. Perhaps there is some sin we need to give up. "We know that God does not listen to sinners," pointed out the young man blind from birth, "but if any one is a worshiper of God and does his will, God listens to him."[22]

Moreover, waiting gives us time to reflect, which can help purify our prayer. Reflection may lead us to amend our petition or let go of *how* He answers it. Saint Augustine says prayer enables us "to receive what he is prepared to give".[23] This leads, naturally, to the possibility that He will respond to our petition in another way.

> If God seems slow in responding, it is because He is preparing a better gift. He will not deny us. God withholds what you are not yet ready for. He wants you to have a lively desire for His greatest gifts. All of which is to say, pray always and do not lose heart.
>
> —St. Augustine [Box 4]

Who's Got the Best Ideas?

Answer Three is the hardest to accept. It requires learning to think as He does in order to recognize that what might feel like a No (or worse) is actually a better idea. When He doesn't do things *our* way, we doubt. That's why He said, "Blessed are the meek", blessed are those who trust anyway.[24] Often we won't understand His answer until we reach heaven, so trust is indispensable.

Trusting God means trusting that He knows what He's doing and has our best interests at heart. However, we need to humble ourselves and admit that we don't know everything; we don't know better than He does. Maybe, just maybe, being all-knowing—caring about everyone, and seeing the big picture—actually puts Him in a better position to decide what's best in any given situation than my limited, self-interested outlook puts me.

> Trust in the LORD with all your heart, and do not rely on your own insight.
>
> —Proverbs 3:5 [Box 5]

I've seen this many times. When I was applying to graduate school, for instance, everything kept going awry. I wasn't accepted at my first choice; I missed an entrance test at my second; and a recommendation

---

[22] Jn 9:31. See also Is 58:6–11.
[23] St. Augustine, *Ep.* 130, 8, 17: PL 33, 500, as quoted in *CCC* 2737.
[24] Mt 5:5.

for my third was missing, so I wasn't considered for a scholarship. Not a catastrophe, but I was disheartened and confused, since I was pretty sure God was calling me to graduate school. But it all turned out for the best. I later learned that my first choice was very biased; I would have hated it there. The second choice was in a different field and would not have worked as well for God's plan for me. My third choice later had another round of scholarships, and I ended up getting a free ride. He actually did know what He was doing!

C. S. Lewis gives a striking depiction of trust in God in *Perelandra*. In this novel, the first woman and the first man on the planet Venus have *not* fallen, but they are about to be tested. Ransom, a man from Earth, is sent to help them. One day Ransom discusses with the woman the concept of disappointment——something she's never experienced. When she understands, she says:

> I never saw it before.... One goes into the forest to pick food and already the thought of one fruit rather than another has grown up in one's mind. Then, it may be, one finds a different fruit.... One joy was expected and another was given.... You could send your soul after the good you had expected, instead of turning it to the good you had got. You could refuse the real good; you could make the real fruit taste insipid by thinking of the other.[25]

Sadly, clinging to the desired good is much more familiar to us. But we can adopt her attitude and see everything as coming from the hand of God and, therefore, ultimately for our good.

Jesus said that to enter the Kingdom of heaven we must become like little children. They trust their parents so much more than we trust our heavenly Father. We're like a baby in a carrier on her daddy's chest: happy when he takes us where we want to go, but when he goes elsewhere or won't let us grab what we want, we get angry. While we can do more than a baby, we're even more dependent, for she can exist without her earthly father, but we can't exist without our heavenly Father. We could prefer our own way so much as to try to escape from the carrier—with tragic results. Or we can appreciate where He takes us and try to learn what He's showing us.

Mary presents us with a beautiful example of steadfast dedication to God's way. At the wedding in Cana, when she noticed the couple's

---

[25] C. S. Lewis, *Perelandra* (New York: Macmillan, 1978), pp. 68–69.

embarrassing dilemma, she came to ask Jesus for help. Notice, though, that she didn't tell Him *how* to help; she didn't dictate the solution. She simply stated the problem: they have no more wine. She knew He could come up with a great solution on His own. We can imitate her trust in God, bringing our troubles to Him with faith that He cares and will help us, but without telling Him what to do, trusting instead that His solution will be the best possible. Fr. Jean d'Elbée says God finds such "humble confidence" irresistible.[26] It shows, on the one hand, a childlike dependence on Him—a confidence not only in His power but also in His love—as well as a charming humility. It is the picture of trust.

We need to keep in mind that when God's idea differs from our own, we're not always disappointed, even in this life. Sometimes we're absolutely delighted. Think of Mary Magdalen on Easter morning. She was so distressed that Jesus' body was missing that she could think of nothing else. She was so beside herself that she didn't recognize the living Jesus when He came up to her. Here was something she had not even dreamed of asking for.

Each of us will experience that joy and thrill someday, if not in this life, then in the next, where all our ills will be healed and we'll see that all our prayers have been answered in the best way possible, far beyond what we could even imagine.

[26] Fr. Jean C.J. d'Elbée, *I Believe in Love* (Manchester, N.H.: Sophia Institute Press, 2001), p. 38.

3

SCALING TRUST MOUNTAINS

Trusting God in Suffering

In the previous chapter, I stated one could (delicately) share with those who are ill or struggling financially that their situation could be seen as a gift or holds a gift. Of course, one would have to be careful with the wording, timing, and tone.

But one shouldn't say it to someone who had just undergone a tragedy. You couldn't walk up to someone who had just lost a child or been given a diagnosis of terminal cancer and declare that to be a gift. That would be even worse than saying it was God's will.

This is not to say the notion that everything is a gift is false, any more than the idea that whatever happens is God's will is false. Both statements just need explanation. And when you're reeling from a tragedy, you can't be bothered with conundrums that need long explanations.

The statement that whatever happens is God's will definitely needs a few paragraphs following it; otherwise it makes God sound arbitrary, indifferent, or downright evil. The key point is that there is a difference between God's perfect will and His permissive will. God's perfect will is that we all do what is right and are holy and happy. However, He also wants us to have free will, and, unfortunately, that means when we choose to do what is wrong, we and/or others will be hurt. But without free will, we could no more return His love than a robot could. Also, in order for us to be eternally happy, we must be one with Jesus, and that means going through the Cross to get to heaven. So sometimes God *permits* bad things to happen to us in order to achieve some greater good— especially salvation or a growth in holiness for us or someone else.

For instance, Jesus didn't *want* Judas to betray Him. He didn't cause him or inspire him to do so. Nor did He want the Sanhedrin to arrest and condemn Him; they did all that on their own. But He didn't stop them either. He permitted it because He saw in their actions the opportunity to prove His love for His Father and for us. His enemies had been unable to kill Him earlier, though they had wanted to, because He didn't permit it then. *Their* will was the same—to kill him—but they could do Him no harm until His permissive will allowed it.

Similarly, if I were running joyously through a meadow and someone suddenly tackled me, I wouldn't be all that pleased. But if I found out that three feet ahead of me was the edge of a cliff and my life had just been saved, my attitude would naturally change. Sometimes God needs to allow the drastic to occur so that something worse does not.

Thus the idea that something tragic is a "gift" can't be stated in isolation. Indeed, it is so startling as to be offensive. Of course, the tragedy itself is not a gift. Christianity doesn't hold that suffering itself is good, only that God is so great that He can bring good out of anything, including suffering. After all, He turned the worst thing that ever happened in human history—the murder of God—into the best thing that ever happened. God is present in every tragic situation, and He has gifts for us even there, though we may not recognize them as such for years, or perhaps not until the next life. He must offer a gift even in the worst situation, or how else could St. Paul say, "Give thanks in all circumstances"?

Every moment, good or bad, provides a platform upon which to meet God. The good, the bad, and the tragic moments will all pass, but the relationship with God that is strengthened and deepened by turning to Him in all of those will never pass away. Such ideas can be shared successfully with someone who has undergone a tragedy only when some time has passed and when the person is searching and open to hearing complex answers requiring explanation.

Trusting God after He Let You Down

It's hard to trust someone who has hurt you or with whom you're angry. We can even feel that way about God. I never understood that ... until it happened to me.

I didn't have much trouble trusting God when I was younger. As time went on and tragedies came into my life and petitions dear to my heart were not answered and the vicissitudes of adult life accumulated, my trust began ebbing away. Still, it was a surprise to find myself fuming at God in my late twenties.

It never occurred to me that going to the theater to see a movie—about Beethoven, of all things—could change my life ... for the worse. But it did. There's a scene in *Immortal Beloved* in which a minor character is raped. The stupid grin on the assaulting soldier's face filled me with such rage I had to leave. I paced and paced in the restroom, adrenalin coursing to my fingertips, my whole body ready to attack. A fairly extreme pacifist in high school, I now found myself wanting to mangle every rapist there ever was. It infuriated me that a man could force himself upon a woman, inflicting long-term trauma, anger, fear, and humiliation—wounds for a lifetime—for his own momentary self-satisfaction. And get away with it. Time and again, it has happened, across cultures, across continents, across millennia. I was filled with fury and further frustrated that there was no such one upon whom I could unleash it.

A strangely strong reaction, perhaps. But it did have a personal connection. A close relative of mine had been raped decades before. I had never really experienced any emotion about it before; perhaps it was denial. But there was more. As a little girl, I had been left alone with that same rapist a day or two before he attacked my relative. He took me on an errand; after a while, my mother became worried because we were gone so much longer than expected. Years later, symptoms of molestation, including faceless flashbacks, arose. Now this rape-scene-inspired rage seemed to confirm it.

I couldn't shake it. I stepped out of that theater and fell into a deep depression.

I started seeing a priest with a master's degree in counseling, who explained what was going on psychologically. Such aggressors treat their victims as shameful objects who deserve abuse. Victims subconsciously take on this identity and view themselves as shameful objects too.

The hardest part for me was feeling abandoned by God. Why had He let it happen? I couldn't fathom it. I understood that suffering is part of life, and as a Catholic, I believed that suffering linked to Christ's could be redemptive. I was in the habit of offering things up. But this was different. I had read plenty of lives of the saints. Quite a few female saints over the ages faced would-be rapists and were miraculously rescued. Why hadn't God protected me?

Moreover, in my mind, sexual assault was different from other kinds of suffering. If He had sent physical pain or loss or other kinds of "clean" suffering, I could have handled that (I thought), with His grace.

It wouldn't have been easy, of course. But rape and molestation were something else altogether. Dirty, shameful, unbearable. So I was pretty angry at God too.

I had already been experiencing some dryness in prayer. I thought, surely *now*, He'll let me feel His presence, let me feel His love, when I need Him so badly. Nope. Nothing. So I said, "Fine. If you're not going to show up—even when I need you most—then I'm not either." And I stopped even trying to have a prayer time anymore.

Still believing in Him and in everything the Church taught, I didn't abandon my spiritual life though. I did talk to God at times during the day. I went to Mass every Sunday. I even went to Confession once in a while—and eventually started seeing my priest-counselor. He advised me to "pray my anger", but I was too angry at first even to try that.

I had been dealing with this for over a year when another priest offered to give me the Sacrament of Anointing of the Sick. There aren't sparkling lights and mystical music when we receive a sacrament, yet I knew something had happened. I knew I was on the road to healing.

So, not long afterward, I decided to try meditation again. I decided to meditate on a Scripture passage I knew God had been stirring up in my memory but that I had until then been unwilling, out of anger, to contemplate: *Whatever is done to the least of His brothers is done to Him.*[1]

Okay, I admitted, if that's true, then it somehow applies to my situation as well. Maybe God hadn't watched me get molested with a detached shrug, chalking it up as another unfortunate consequence of free will. Maybe He hadn't abandoned me. Could He ... could it be possible, that somehow He was there, *identifying* with me, as one of His least ones?

Impossible! What a revolting thought! *Jesus* could not be an object of shame.

Then it occurred to me that if that was true for Him, then it could be true for me. Maybe I hadn't been rendered a shameful object after all.

Before that day, I had begged the Lord to heal me of this horror on many occasions and been frustrated that He hadn't. *How long, O Lord?* I would cry with the Psalmist. When the time came at last, it took only about ten minutes. Once I realized that He had not abandoned me but had been there with me and suffered with me that changed everything. My anger at Him vanished. Once I went on to forgive my assailant (see

[1] See Mt 25:40.

p. 251 below), my wound was miraculously healed. My ability to trust God and move forward in our relationship was restored.

I share this very personal story only in the hope that it might help others suffering heartaches to give God a chance too.

Why Should We Trust God?

We live in a culture saturated with the illusion of control. We *do* have an extraordinary amount of control over our lives compared to times past, but it's still an illusion. Occasionally, something enormous will break through and wake us up: earthquakes, hurricanes, terrorism. But if the incident has not touched us personally, we quickly fall back into a doze. The recession some years ago had a temporary impact, showing that hard work and worldly prudence are not fail-proof protection from financial ruin. All of us will eventually encounter illness or accident ourselves or in our families. Indeed, any of us could die at any moment. When this truth does get through to us, it usually terrifies us. Or it makes us angry, usually at God.

There is a certain attitude prevalent today, originating from atheistic writers and philosophers, that God cannot be all-good, all-loving, all-powerful, *and* allow suffering in the world. As C. S. Lewis put it, they've put "God in the dock":[2] *If* He exists, He must answer to us.

The problem is in how we view God. If we see Him as a Big Prayer-Answering Machine in the Sky or an Almighty but Easy-Going Gramps, we'll think He should just give us what we want and protect us from everything unpleasant, let alone painful or catastrophic. But that's not who God is. He is the Father. Every good parent knows that loving your children does not mean giving them whatever they want, for they frequently want what isn't good for them. Love even means letting them suffer something they don't understand (say, a toddler getting stitches) in order to prevent greater suffering.

God knows it's a struggle for us to trust Him in everything; Jesus said, "What father among you, if his son asks for a fish, will ... give him a

---

[2] "The ancient man approached God (or even the gods) as ... his judge. For the modern man the roles are reversed.... Man is on the Bench and God in the Dock." C. S. Lewis, *God in the Dock: Essays on Theology and Ethics*, ed. Walter Hooper (Grand Rapids, Mich.: William B. Eerdmans, 1970), p. 244.

serpent; or if he asks for an egg, will give him a scorpion?"[3] The only problem is that sometimes it sure *looks* like a serpent or scorpion.

Even the *Catechism* acknowledges evil and suffering "can shake our faith and become a temptation against it".[4] So how does the *Catechism* account for the scandal of evil?

> No quick answer will suffice. Only Christian faith as a whole constitutes the answer to this question: the goodness of creation, the drama of sin, and the patient love of God who comes to meet man by his covenants, the redemptive Incarnation of his Son, his gift of the Spirit, his gathering of the Church, the power of the sacraments, and his call to a blessed life.... *There is not a single aspect of the Christian message that is not in part an answer to the question of evil.*[5]

The Meaning of Suffering

Christians must take a different attitude to suffering from that of the world. Christ said plainly that to be His disciple one must deny himself, pick up his cross, and follow after Him.[6] If we love Him, then we must trust Him. If we want to partake in the Resurrection, in the glory, we have to follow the Way—which includes a stop at Calvary. We get to heaven by being members of His Body, and He took His whole body with Him to the Cross. There is no avoiding the cross.

While awaiting execution by the Nazis, Lutheran pastor Dietrich Bonhoeffer reflected: "Discipleship means allegiance to the suffering Christ, and it is therefore not at all surprising that Christians should be called upon to suffer.... To endure the cross is not a tragedy.... The cross is laid on every Christian.... Suffering, then, is the badge of true discipleship."[7]

Sometimes we eventually come to see at least some reasons why God allowed us to suffer, why God's plans were actually better for us, or how our going through a hardship helped someone else. One

[3] Lk 11:11–12.
[4] *CCC* 164.
[5] *CCC* 309; italics in original.
[6] See Mt 16:24; Mk 8:34.
[7] Dietrich Bonhoeffer, *The Cost of Discipleship* (New York: Macmillan Publishing, 1963), pp. 101, 98, 99, 100.

instance of this I'll always remember because I would not otherwise have survived my teens. One day, when I was young and stupid, I was running late for work. I was stuck behind a slowpoke on a winding, hilly road. At last, I couldn't stand it anymore and passed him on a brief straightaway, getting back into my lane shortly before the brow of a hill. As I came over the crest, I saw a stalled car in the opposite lane, with another car coming up behind it. I realized that if the first car had not broken down and brought the second car to a halt, I would very likely have gotten into a head-on collision with that second car. I also realized that nobody else knew this. Those in the first car were probably pretty peeved that their car broke down. Even the people in the second car might have been momentarily annoyed by the obstacle in their path. They didn't know that God allowed it to happen so that lives would be saved.

Many times God's reasons for a suffering remain a mystery, and we'll never understand it perfectly during our lifetime. However, we don't really need to know all of His reasons for a specific suffering in order to find meaning in it. What is essential is to believe it has meaning.

> When we fail to find meaning in our suffering, we can easily fall into despair. But once we find meaning in our suffering, it is astounding what we can endure. The key is not the suffering itself, but the meaning found within it.
> ... Who among us would refuse to endure even years of pain for the sake of a daughter or son? We would be willing and even eager to suffer, because our love for our children would give meaning to such suffering.[8]

Pope St. John Paul II describes suffering as a call, a vocation. And it is in answering that call, in following Christ and carrying our crosses, that we discover the meaning of suffering.

> Christ does not explain in the abstract the reasons for suffering, but before all else he says: "Follow me!" Come! Take part through your suffering in this work of saving the world, a salvation achieved through my suffering! Through my Cross. Gradually, as *the individual takes up his cross*, spiritually uniting himself to the Cross of Christ, the salvific meaning of suffering is

---

[8] Jeff Cavins, "Power Made Perfect in Weakness", in *Amazing Grace for Those Who Suffer*, ed. Jeff Cavins and Matthew Pinto (West Chester, Penn.: Ascension Press, 2002), pp. 261–62.

revealed before him. . . . It is then that man finds in his suffering interior peace and even spiritual joy.[9]

Crazy as that sounds, it's what Jesus promised: those who take His yoke find it sweet.[10]

The acts of the early Christian martyrs are full of evidence which shows how Christ transfigures for his own the hour of their mortal agony by granting them the unspeakable assurance of his presence. In the hour of the cruellest torture they bear for his sake, they are made partakers in the perfect joy and bliss of fellowship with him. To bear the cross proves to be the only way of triumphing over suffering.[11]

To unite our sufferings to Christ's makes them an honor to bear; it changes everything. "Once we discover meaning in our suffering, we gain a key to spiritual treasures, both in our earthly life and in the life to come. We obtain a wisdom that enables us not only to survive but to *thrive*, even while adversity continues."[12]

The Benefits of Suffering

The idea that suffering has value is foreign to many people and sounds ridiculous to them.[13] The nature of suffering's value is as mysterious to us mortals as fluctuating stock-market values are to a six-year-old. But all who love Christ recognize that *His* suffering was very valuable— indeed, of infinite value; we must trust that, linked to His, our suffering has value too. While we'll never know in this life all the reasons for certain sufferings, there are still benefits we can comprehend.

First, suffering reminds us of the big picture and that we need God. It also wakes us up. We become aware of and gain deeper sympathy for others who are suffering, especially those with worse trials than our own, and the sufferings resulting as a natural consequence of our sins

---

[9] Pope St. John Paul II, Apostolic Letter *Salvifici Doloris* on the Christian Meaning of Human Suffering, *On Human Suffering* (February 11, 1984), no. 26.

[10] See Mt 11:30, DRA.

[11] Bonhoeffer, *Cost of Discipleship*, p. 101.

[12] Cavins and Pinto, introduction in *Amazing Grace for Those Who Suffer*, p. 12.

[13] As it has since Christ's day; see 1 Cor 1:23.

invite us to reconsider and repent. Suffering also sparks big questions, such as: What is life really all about? What happens when we die?

Suffering also offers the chance to do good for others and ourselves.

Restitution and Intercession

We tend to think more of how we've *been* wronged than how we've wronged others. But listening to Fr. Spitzer explaining on the radio[14] that to forgive is to leave one's vindication in God's hands, even when the offender never apologizes, made me wonder if there were people to whom I owed apologies, whom I had unknowingly hurt along the way. What vindication will those I've injured receive for my sins? Suddenly I *felt* the need to make reparation.[15] Such a realization transforms how we perceive the crosses God allows in our lives, making us actually grateful for them.

Suffering can have incredible spiritual power. If we humbly accept a cross, link it to Christ's, and offer it with His as a prayer, our suffering can have great value. It can then make reparation to those harmed by our past sins and/or help those for whom we are interceding.

Moreover, linking our sufferings to Christ's brings His into our present day. A cartoon figure could not comprehend the third dimension, yet that doesn't mean it doesn't exist. Similarly, we cannot perceive the spiritual dimension, but it is just as real. When we unite with Christ in suffering, His Passion and sacrifice are extended into our time and place. This can only be of benefit to all involved.

Building Virtue through Discipline

Suffering, if we let it, can also help us; it can strengthen and purify us. Scripture drops hints on these potential benefits by describing suffering as "discipline" or "trial".

The word *discipline* has three meanings that apply here. First is "punishment", as when a parent "disciplines" a disobedient child. The purpose is the good of the child. Swatting a toddler who runs into the road, for instance: the small pain is meant to imprint a lesson and prevent catastrophically greater pain.[16] Of course, children are no fans of

---

[14] Fr. Robert Spitzer, *Fr. Spitzer's Universe*, on EWTN Radio (September 23, 2017).

[15] Reparation is discussed at greater length in chaps. 15, 16, and 26 below.

[16] This idea is sprinkled throughout the Bible; see e.g., Prov 5:23: "He dies for lack of discipline."

discipline, but as we mature we realize its necessity in order for us to survive and thrive. Similarly, "the Lord disciplines him whom he loves, and chastises every son whom he receives."[17] The natural consequences of sin are designed precisely to make us stop and think, to realize that wrongdoing is not such a hot idea after all. The Second Book of Maccabees makes a similar point: "[T]hese punishments were designed not to destroy but to discipline our people. In fact, not to let the impious alone for long, but to punish them immediately, is a sign of great kindness ... in order that [the Lord] may not take vengeance on us afterward when our sins have reached their height."[18]

The second meaning of *discipline* is "training", and the goal here is virtue. Though God's part is indispensable, no virtue can develop in us without our cooperation.[19] We can gain no virtue without His help, but we will develop no virtue without hard work. *Virtue* means "strength", and we have to work for it because He wants us to own it. There would be no glory in being virtuous if we had nothing to do with it, and God wants us to have a share in heavenly glory.[20]

Like a good coach or parent, God continually calls us onward and upward. A coach doesn't say, "Okay, you're good enough; no more practice for you." No, he calls us to keep working, to get stronger and hone our skills further. Nor does the Lord say, "You're holy enough; now you can just cruise to heaven." No, He says, "You are good enough for my love. My love can always reach you, no matter how far you have fallen. But let's see how high you can go." God is a father who lovingly urges us to stretch ourselves more and more, and a little more, delighting in our reaching new heights. "[H]e disciplines us for our good, that we may share his holiness."[21] Enduring a cross with love

---

[17] Heb 12:6; this in turn is an echo of Deut 8:5.

[18] 2 Macc 6:12b–13, 15.

[19] The Lord creates us with certain strengths and talents (natural virtues); He infuses the baptized with supernatural virtues, especially the theological virtues of faith, hope, and charity, without which we cannot reach heaven. We can gain and increase natural virtues through repeated acts (*virtue* is also defined as "habit"), but only God can increase the theological virtues in us. He does so, though, when we act on them: e.g., acts of faith predispose us to receiving more faith, which God then gives. All supernatural virtues except faith and hope are lost when a mortal sin is committed, but can be restored through repentance and Confession. See Martin A. Waldron, "Virtue", in *The Catholic Encyclopedia* (New York: Robert Appleton Co., 1912). Accessed September 28, 2017, from New Advent: http://www.newadvent.org/cathen/15472a.htm, and *CCC* 162 and 1810; cf. also *CCC* 1803–45 and 2010.

[20] See e.g., Rom 2:9–10; Col 3:4; and 1 Pet 5:4; see also *CCC* 2025–26.

[21] Heb 12:10. See also Job 23:10: "[W]hen he has tried me, I shall come forth as gold."

requires us to die to ourselves and rely on His grace, and it results in greater virtue in us.

Suffering offers a training ground in which we can develop virtues (such as patience, compassion, fortitude) as well as self-mastery—a third pertinent meaning of *discipline*. We call one who rises early to exercise or practices music for hours "disciplined". Those who embrace their training gain self-mastery and are not held back by vices or the consequences of vices. Being disciplined enables us to do our best and stretch that best. This applies to the spiritual life as well. "For the moment all discipline seems painful rather than pleasant; later it yields the peaceful fruit of righteousness to those who have been trained by it."[22]

A cross can also be like a brace. Leg braces correct a bone growing askew or support a weak limb that might otherwise go astray. Dental braces fix teeth that are out of place. Like braces, crosses are rigid, unyielding, painful, and/or annoying, *but* over time, they will straighten out what is crooked in us—if we let them.

Trial by Fire

Another recurring image for suffering in Scripture is being put in fire. "For you, O God, have tested us; you have tried us as silver is tried."[23] Sirach and Zechariah speak of testing gold in fire, a "surefire" way to see if it is genuine.[24] Similarly, "trials and tribulations" put *us* to the test, to see how authentic our love and fidelity to God are.

> [F]or a little while you may have to suffer various trials, so that the genuineness of your faith, more precious than gold which ... is tested by fire, may redound to praise and glory and honor.
>
> 1 PETER 1:6–7 Box 6

When we come before the Judgment Seat of God, Satan (which means "Accuser") will be there too, pointing out all our sins. If our lives were carefree and God did everything for us, Satan could accuse us of not loving God, but loving merely His benefits, as he did with Job.[25] But if we suffer for God, if we're faithful to Him when it's difficult, we demonstrate our love.

---

[22] Heb 12:11.

[23] Ps 66:10. See also Sir 31:26; 1 Cor 3:13.

[24] See Sir 2:5 and Zech 13:9.

[25] See Job 1:9–12; Rev 12:10.

Love is proved by what we do when things get tough. Are we like the one who "when tribulation or persecution arises on account of the word, immediately ... falls away"?[26] It's easy to love when things are going well, to be a fair-weather friend. All our crosses are chances to prove that our love for the Lord is real and deep. Suffering with Christ then speaks volumes of love to Him (which He rewards even in this life, for suffering draws us "interiorly close to Christ").[27]

Fire also purifies. It is the best way to separate any alloys or impurities from a precious metal. "I will put [them] into the fire, and refine them as one refines silver."[28] Suffering can have the same effect on our souls, if we let it. It can burn away our pride, self-sufficiency, worldliness, indifference, and self-interest, and a myriad of sinful tendencies.

ॐ ॐ ॐ

The overarching purpose of our sufferings is to help us and others reach heaven. "Blessed is the man who endures trial, for when he has stood the test he will receive the crown of life which God has

> Oh, great is the soul that, [a]midst suffering, stands faithfully by God and does His will.... For God's pure love sweetens her fate.
>
> —St. Faustina [Box 7]

promised to those who love him."[29] So great are God's promises to those who carry their crosses that St. Peter even says to *rejoice* when we share in Christ's sufferings.[30] In the end, we'll find all trials and tribulations, all pangs and pains, all sorrows and woes, have been more than worth it. "Only ... when we see God 'face to face,' will we ... know the ultimate meaning of the whole work of creation and ... salvation and understand the marvellous ways by which his Providence led everything towards its final end. The Last Judgment will reveal that God's justice triumphs over all the injustices committed by his creatures and that God's love is stronger than death."[31]

---

[26] Mt 13:21.

[27] John Paul II, *Salvifici Doloris, Human Suffering*, no. 26.

[28] Zech 13:9.

[29] Jas 1:12. Cf. also Wis 3:5–6.

[30] See 1 Pet 4:13. See also 2 Tim 2:11–12: "If we have died with him, we shall also live with him; if we endure, we shall also reign with him."

[31] *CCC* 314, 1040.

4

SOARING TRUST

What Trust Looks Like

Does anyone actually trust as depicted in the last chapter? Oh yes. Examine the life of a saint—any saint. They had to trust. Besides the canonized saints, we can find examples in our own day.

One example is someone I knew personally. Anne Dull was a delightful young woman, a model of femininity. A professional chef with a natural gift for bringing beauty into any environment, she was pretty, humble, and quick to laugh, and she seemed to swing-dance through life. She was one of my dearest friends.

At a time when Anne didn't have health insurance, a mole on the back of her leg began to hurt. A few months later, she heard we were praying for one of my co-workers who had just had a cancerous mole removed. Learning about devotion to one's guardian angel, Anne turned in prayer to hers for advice and felt her angel was screaming at her to get to a doctor.

The news wasn't good. She was diagnosed with level-three malignant melanoma. Each step of her journey would be one of renunciation.

The doctors first decided to remove all the lymph nodes in the affected leg. Anne was not vain, but she wasn't exactly thrilled to hear that without those lymph nodes her leg would get puffy. She went through with it and made jokes about it.

The next treatment was agonizing. Her greatest desire was to be a wife and mother, and this next step would probably render her infertile. She was heartbroken.

Later, she had another surgery, expecting recovery to last about a week. It was six weeks. She spent them in her brother's apartment, alone for hours, far from friends and the rest of her family. She had to give up her job, her friends, and her life in San Francisco.

Meanwhile, my husband and I had moved across the country to Maryland. It was awful to be so far away and unable to help. But being at a distance highlighted for me the ways Anne was changing. Early on, she didn't want to talk about her condition. If I said I was praying for her, she would lightly respond, "I'm praying for you too!" Then there was a period of struggling with her faith, feeling disgruntled with God and confused.

Yet somehow Anne's faith survived. It even began to thrive in astonishing ways. She had wanted so much to get married. So when she told me, some sixteen months after her diagnosis, that if she recovered she would become a nun, I found it hard to believe. She seemed designed to be an ideal wife and mother. But through her suffering and loss, she had grown so close to the Lord, she wanted to give her life to Him. Over time, she not only became resigned to God's will, she became dedicated to it. Then she offered Him her life as a prayer for her family.

The Lord accepted her gift. She developed four brain tumors. But she developed something else too: practically palpable holiness. Through this ordeal, she had to let go of her dreams of motherhood; she went on voluntarily to renounce married love and even life itself.

During Anne's battle with cancer, a dear mutual friend and her roommate, Patty, was going through her own turmoil, losing both her brother and a beloved aunt to cancer in close succession. I composed this poem in 1991, when Patty told me her mother was diagnosed with cancer too, and Anne was getting worse. (Revised 2015.)

O my God, oh, please ...
I can't think what to say,
but hear me, please hear me.
Hear a desperate prayer.
Spare us, Lord, please spare us;
leave us life a while.
Let not pain take one,
nor grief the other.
Let us *be* a while.

Wandering glazed eyes
searching the holy apse,
blind to beauty, dull to meaning,
find themselves upon a glass,
a wondrous, colored glass.

Who am I, Lord; who am I?
An ignoramus
watching an artist
work in the dark.
Yes, and screaming out,
"Too much blue too much red!
What are You doing?
What are You thinking!"

Yes, but when the sun shines through ...
who am I, God, who am I?

Now I see the beauty of Your pattern,
wondering at a pattern
as much as in the beauty.
Blue and red and glorious gold
dancing in majesty
round a solid stone cross.

(continued)

> *Yes, who are you to say*
> *too much red too much blue,*
> *too much blood too much grief?*
> *Would you lessen a beloved's glory?*
>
> Thank You, Lord, for hearing me
> and flashing a glimpse of understanding.
> However You answer a desperate prayer,
> turn our thoughts from mysterious panes
> to the glory of the day
> Your Son will shine through.
>
> Box 8

She was in a lot of pain at the end, but she had so much peace, more peace than anyone I've ever known. The last time I talked to her, it was almost uncomfortable for a sinner like me: she was so shining, so pure, so loving, so holy. I was convinced I was talking to a saint.

Her life did not go as she had initially hoped and planned. But it was a beautiful life, a life that was an amazing testimony of love for God. His plans for her were far more glorious.

There are many such stories. Some are found in *Amazing Grace for Those Who Suffer*, a book strangely brimming with hope. It tells the stories of "ten ordinary people who have endured extraordinary pain who ... discover[ed] in their ordeals that God was there to meet them and bring meaning to what the world would consider senseless circumstances" and "the treasures they gained in the midst of their pain".[1]

Solidarity of God

There are much worse sufferings. I can't explain how certain horrible tragedies could be good for us; all I can do is point to the Cross. Jesus is the best possible example.

Though suffering is a mystery, we know God cares. He made it very evident in His Passion and death on the Cross. We may not always understand His plan or His permissive will, but we know that He hasn't asked us to do anything He hasn't done. His solidarity with us in suffering is clear. How many of us have suffered or will ever suffer like He did? He lives up to the name *Emmanuel*—God with us. He is with us, in all things.

[1] Jeff Cavins and Matthew Pinto, eds., introduction in *Amazing Grace for Those Who Suffer* (West Chester, Penn.: Ascension Press, 2002), p. 12.

We already saw in chapter 1 above the absolute solidarity of His Incarnation. But He didn't stop there. He went on to give the ultimate answer to the question of why we must endure evil and suffering. That answer was not in words but in example. Not a mild illustration, but the Cross—the origin of the word *excruciating*. Furthermore, His agony included a whole host of unseen spiritual sufferings, of which we know nothing. Foreseeing all the rejection, ridicule, and indifference His Passion would meet through the ages could only have added to His sufferings.

He endured sorrow, dread, betrayal, rejection, false accusations, hatred, mockery, humiliation, blows, spitting in the face, flesh-ripping sadistic whipping all over His body (which alone could have killed Him), a crown of thorns, a heavy Cross on His lacerated shoulders in His weakened state (no sleep or food, beaten and bleeding profusely), falling repeatedly on wounded knees, being stripped naked and nailed to a Cross, and three hours of unimaginable agony, where every breath required pushing up against the nails in His pierced feet to draw air into His lungs. All this was endured by One who could have effortlessly defeated His enemies. Instead, He embraced suffering to show us His love.

Imagine the Lord, sagging on the Cross in exhausted torment, lifting His bloody, thorn-crowned head to look at you tenderly, deep into your eyes. See the streams of blood caked on His cheeks. See the suffering in His tortured eyes and haggard face. He struggles to speak; you hear Him say gently to you, to you alone, "*Now* do you believe that I love you?"

No one in all the universe since its creation has expressed such solidarity as God did in taking on human life and then willingly laying it down like that. Solidarity defined.

Perfect Trust

In all of this, Jesus simultaneously provides the prime model of trust in the midst of suffering. We might think He never had to struggle with trusting God: How could He? He *was* God.

We have to remember though that He was also human—fully human.[2] Suffering wasn't any less painful for Him than for us. He clearly

[2] He also had two wills: a human will and a divine will (*CCC* 475).

more than shared our dread of it; I've never experienced so intense a dread that capillaries in my skin burst and I began sweating blood. His response is our example: He turned to His Father in prayer—distressed prayer, but also loving, obedient, trusting prayer. He turned to Him again and again, pleading, but always concluded with, "Not my will, but yours be done." The Father's will was made evident in the arrival of the armed crowd.[3] Once His Father's will was clear, Jesus welcomed each facet of His Passion.

Some think Jesus lost that trust at the end, when He cried out, "My God, my God, why have you forsaken me?" While such a cry may mean He *felt* forsaken, it doesn't imply a lack of trust. He was still calling on His Father. Moreover, He said those words for our sake. That God Himself could emit such a cry shows He had descended into the depths of human suffering, revealing the totality of His solidarity with us. Further, those words were also a quotation: the opening words of Psalm 22. Many who heard Him would recognize them and would recall the rest of the psalm. It might occur to them then that maybe Jesus was the Messiah after all, for the prophecy of the Suffering Servant in Psalm 22 was being fulfilled before their eyes.[4] Overall, Psalm 22 is one of hope and ends with trust in God.[5] Finally, Jesus' continued trust in the Father is also evident in His dying words, "Father, into your hands I commit my spirit!"[6] This is another direct quote from the Psalms—Psalm 31, another messianic psalm proclaiming trust in God.

> I trust in you, O LORD,
>   I say, "You are my God."...
>
> ... you heard my supplications,
>   when I cried to you for help.
> Love the LORD, all you his saints!
> The LORD preserves the faithful....
> Be strong, and let your heart take courage,
>   all you who wait for the LORD!
>
> —PSALM 31:14, 22–24   Box 9

All this speaks of Jesus' vast trust in His Father. Even when His prayers were not answered as He had hoped, even in the worst of suffering, even feeling abandoned, He never stopped trusting His Father. Jesus demonstrated how to trust God no matter what.

---

[3] See Jn 18:11 and Mt 26:53.
[4] See in particular Ps 22:7–8, 16, 18.
[5] See especially Ps 22:4–5, 24.
[6] Lk 23:46.

The Heart of Holiness

The essence of trust in God is expressed in "The Universal Prayer" of Pope Clement XI:

> I want whatever You want
> because You want it,
> the way You want it,
> for as long as You want it.[7]

Such a prayer requires a gargantuan amount of trust—limitless, really. It means turning everything over to God and accepting His will unconditionally.

This is not the same as rolling over and doing nothing. That would be Quietism, a heresy that equates accepting God's will with total passivity. When a problem enters our lives, embracing His will often means accepting the challenge of struggling to overcome it. What we learn in the process and how we grow are often the fruits He had in mind when He permitted that difficulty in our lives. Matthew Kelly even asserts, "We're not here to solve problems. Problems are here to solve us."[8] Sometimes we may not be able to solve them, but either way, we can offer the attempt to God as a prayer. The (original) "Serenity Prayer" sums it up nicely: "God, give us grace to accept with serenity [and offer up] the things that cannot be changed, courage to change the things that should be changed, and the wisdom to distinguish the one from the other."[9]

Pope Clement's prayer might be too hard to pray at first; I started with, "Lord, I *want* to want whatever you want ..." If you can't pray even that, ask for the grace, love, and trust to pray it. The eternal view is critical. Jesus said there was really only one thing we needed to be worried about. The "one thing needful"[10] is to love God, to please God, to choose God. Choosing God and loving Him in daily life means

---

[7] *Prayer Book* (Circle Press, 2003), pp. 22–25. For an online version of the prayer, see http://www.catholicity.com/prayer/universal-prayer.html.

[8] Matthew Kelly, *Rediscover Catholicism* (Cincinnati, Ohio: Beacon Publishing, 2010), p. 55.

[9] This is the original form—with a little Catholic addition—of the popular prayer, per the author: Reinhold Niebuhr, *The Essential Reinhold Niebuhr*, ed. Robert McAfee Brown (New Haven: Yale University Press, 1986), p. 251.

[10] See Lk 10:41–42.

choosing His way, His will. He assures us that His plans are "plans for welfare and not for evil, to give you a future and a hope".[11] We can come to want what He wants when we know that *what* He wants is our good.

St. Faustina says the Lord asked her to write: "From today on, my own will does not exist.... I do the will of God everywhere, always, and in everything." He assured her: "Be afraid of nothing; love will give you strength and make the realization of this easy."[12] Saints and doctors of the Church have said the essence of holiness is conforming one's will to the will of God. Only a great love can do so. "The highest and most complete proof of love is to surrender ourselves completely, giving all our confidence to Him whom we love. Be with Jesus as a friend with his friend, very loving and very beloved."[13] A life lived with that attitude is one of peace and joy.

Continual Call to Trust More

Sometimes when we think we've learned to trust in God, it feels like He says, *Oh yeah, how 'bout now?* and takes it up another notch.

I love St. Teresa of Avila's comeback on this. Once when she was traveling on a difficult journey, she slipped and fell into a river. She was peeved and said, "Lord, when will You stop putting obstacles in our path?" A mystic, she heard the reply, "I treat all my friends this way." And she retorted: "No wonder You have so few then."[14]

But Fr. Jean d'Elbée has some ideas as to *why* He treats His friends this way:

> I have often noticed that to reward an act of confidence, Jesus gives us the occasion to make an even greater act of confidence....
>
> This is what Jesus is like with those who love Him. He does not grant the first prayer; He permits a greater trial.... Because God loves you, He

[11] Jer 29:11.

[12] St. Faustina, *Divine Mercy in My Soul: Diary of Saint Maria Faustina Kowalska* (Stockbridge, Mass.: Marian Press, 2015), p. 167.

[13] Fr. Jean C.J. d'Elbée, *I Believe in Love* (Manchester, N.H.: Sophia Institute Press, 2001), p. 51.

[14] Based on the account in Adelaide Marie du Sacré Coeur, O.C.D., *The Life of Saint Teresa: Taken from the French of "A Carmelite Nun" by Alice Lady Lovat* (London: Simpkin, Marshall, Hamilton, Kent, 1920), p. 548.

wants to see how far you will push your confidence. He wants to be able to say to you, as He did to the Canaanite woman, "How great is your faith!"

... [Be] like Martha and Mary before the tomb of Lazarus, with confidence unto death. Believe, believe in the divine omnipotence! Believe in Love![15]

Trials are opportunities to become more like Him: stronger, holier, more trusting, more loving, more worthy of the praise and rewards He wants to heap on us in eternity.[16]

Each of us is called to have a soaring trust too.

---

[15] Ibid., pp. 48, 50.
[16] See also more on this in sec. 5 below (chaps. 15 and 16), on carrying the cross.

5

HOW DO WE GROW IN TRUST?

You may be thinking, *That all sounds good, but how do I do it?* Fortunately, there are practical steps we can take to grow in trust.

Gaining the Right Mind-Set

The first step is to learn to think straight (i.e., as He does) and to realize how trustworthy He is.

Grow in Gratitude

All around us are the works of His hands, and our lives are dappled with acts of God, but we don't remember or reflect on them. We are surrounded by what His love has wrought: the beauty and bounty of nature, people to love and who love us, temporal blessings, myriad forms of goodness. Scripture and the lives of the saints abound with demonstrations of His faithfulness, His wisdom, His love. Everything we have ultimately comes from His hand. We can deepen our trust by noticing His abundant, loving Providence in our own lives; appreciating all this leads to gratitude and welcoming opportunities to show Him love in return.

Expect and Accept Crosses

"When we survey human history, it becomes evident that suffering is simply a given for human beings. It is not a matter of *whether* we will suffer during our lives, but *when*. And more specifically, *how* will we suffer: poorly or well?"[1] Peter, who initially ran from the Cross, later

---

[1] Jeff Cavins, afterword: "Power Made Perfect in Weakness", in *Amazing Grace for Those Who Suffer*, ed. Jeff Cavins and Matthew Pinto (West Chester, Penn.: Ascension Press, 2002), p. 261.

wrote: "Beloved, do not be surprised at the fiery ordeal which comes upon you to prove you, as though something strange were happening to you."[2] Realizing and accepting this is a huge step in trust.

Expecting crosses can actually add to our gratitude if it causes us to consider the suffering God does *not* permit to befall us. How often do we thank Him for all the terrible things that *could* have happened to us and our loved ones, but didn't? God filters sufferings through His loving fingers, holding back most and allowing through only those that will somehow bring us a greater good. Believe that, and you can rest in His will. If we trust that what He wants for us is good, we can want that good too, even if it comes in an unpleasant package. He's a good judge of value; we can trust that He knows which goods are greater.

Recognize Divine Compassion

Another important element in trusting God is to recognize His compassion for us. It's easy to think He doesn't care, as if He watches us suffer with a divine shrug, saying, "Yeah, well, you've got to suffer. This is good for you. What, you want a different cross?"

As a parent, I sometimes have to let my children suffer, but that doesn't mean I don't care. Just because I let the nurse give my sweet little baby a shot (and even hold her down to help!) doesn't mean I don't care that the shots hurt. I care tremendously, and it hurts me to see it. It breaks my heart that she doesn't understand I'm permitting *this* suffering because it's less than the suffering it prevents. Surely the Father, model of perfect parenthood, has infinite sympathy and love for us in our sufferings. So the next step is to believe in God's loving compassion.

Acts of Trust

Ask for the Grace to Trust

Trust in God, like much in the spiritual life, is a gift, and we need to ask for it. Telling Him how you feel may be the best type of prayer in such times, something like these:

----

[2] I Pet 4:12.

Okay, Lord, You said to come to You and You would lighten my burden. Here I am; I've come. Things are really tough right now. Please help me, please strengthen me. Jesus, I trust in You; help me trust Your loving Heart even more.

Lord, You said Your grace would be enough for me. I'm feeling really tempted right now. Help me not to give in. You promised to provide a way out of every temptation; show it to me. Shower me with Your grace, and help me to believe in it. Remind my heart that what I want most is to please You. All things are possible with You.

Rely on His Grace

"With God, all things are possible."[3] We must remember this when things get hard. We feel like we can't manage it, we can't get through this crisis—because we can't. At least not by ourselves. With Him, though, we can do anything He calls us to do, for He Himself will strengthen us.[4]

My husband and I experienced this when he developed a serious nerve condition. Gradually he lost more and more function in his arms: from interfering with his ability to play guitar (right after he had completed his master's in classical guitar, with a string of concerts lined up) to interfering with everyday tasks like washing his hair. It wasn't diagnosed correctly, and a more serious nerve condition developed, which threatened permanent disability. Through all this, God's grace was tremendous. Though very distressing, it was simultaneously a peace-filled time. We went to Mass every day, and God's grace was very evident. James' acceptance of God's will was truly remarkable (and far more complete than mine). Even when we heard his arms might become paralyzed, we were able to trust—*obviously* a great miracle of God's grace.

It was when James thought it was starting to affect his legs too that I broke down. I told God that that was just too much. The Lord reminded me that His grace was already enabling us to endure more than our own natural capabilities; why should I assume it wouldn't be enough for any other tribulation? I was trying to traverse a bridge before I got to it. I couldn't imagine carrying this possible cross because I did not yet have the grace to carry it. If it came, the grace would come too. If ever we

[3] Mt 19:26.
[4] See Phil 4:13.

got to that bridge, the grace would be there waiting for us. "God provides us with as much strength to resist in every calamity as we need. But he does not give it in advance, so that we trust Him alone. In such a trust, all anxiety about the future must be overcome."[5]

Focus on the Triumph

Another vital step in trusting God is to realize that all difficulties, all problems, all suffering will pass. When we're undergoing a trial, we feel like it will go on and on and on. But it won't: "All things pass." Though our ordeals seem long at the time, none are—in the light of eternity. And just as Christ's death was not the end of the story, neither is our suffering. If we join it to His Cross, then He will bring about a victory. Every dark night ends with a sunrise. Everyone who dies to himself in Christ will rise with Him.

The Lord emphasizes this repeatedly in Scripture. Isaiah, for instance, prophesied: "For behold, I create new heavens and a new earth; and the former things shall not be remembered or come into mind."[6] And Jesus pointed out: "When a woman is in labor, she has pain, because her hour has come; but when she is delivered of the child, she no longer remembers the anguish, for joy that a child is born into the world. So you have sorrow now, but I will see you again and your hearts will rejoice, and no one will take your joy from you."[7] It's a matter of not putting all our eggs in the basket of this world, but remembering that it is fleeting and not our home. It is for another world—an everlasting paradise with God—that we were created.

In light of that, all suffering dims. "I consider that the sufferings of this present time are not worth comparing with the glory that is to be revealed to us", St. Paul wrote.[8] He knew what he was talking about. He had suffered much for the sake of the gospel: he had often gone "without food, in cold and exposure", been shipwrecked, imprisoned, beaten numerous times, and stoned, and he faced many dangers and much

---

[5] Cf. Dietrich Bonhoeffer, *Letters and Papers from Prison* (New York: Collier Books, 1972), p. 11. This translation found in Michael F. Möller, "The Child, the Fool, the Sufferer: Dietrich Bonhoeffer: A Reflection on His Life and Ministry", *Trinity Seminary Review* 26, no. 2 (Summer/Fall 2005): 109.

[6] Is 65:17.

[7] Jn 16:21–22.

[8] Rom 8:18.

rejection.[9] But he had also had a vision, an experience, of heaven.[10] He did not even try to describe what he experienced, saying only, "No eye has seen, nor ear heard, nor the heart of man conceived, what God has prepared for those who love him."[11] Having seen heaven, he regarded suffering as a "slight momentary affliction", thoroughly worth enduring, given what it prepares us for: "an eternal weight of glory beyond all comparison".[12]

When we're undergoing trials and suffering, we must remember this: God will triumph. Indeed, His victory has already begun. "In the world you have tribulation", Jesus said at the Last Supper; "but be of good cheer, I have overcome the world."[13] When we're at the end of our rope, we must recall that "he will wipe away every tear from [our] eyes, and death shall be no more, neither shall there be mourning nor crying nor pain any more, for the former things [will] have passed away."[14] And in the meantime, if the fruits of suffering include growing closer to God, becoming more like Him, showing Him our love, purifying us, and helping others and ourselves reach heaven, then it's more than worthwhile.

Conclusion

If what we're really seeking from God is *His* compliance, we have good grounds not to trust Him. We can't trust Him to do *our* will.

We *can* trust that His will is superior to ours and that what He wants is better—for everyone. Love means desiring the best for the beloved, and no one loves us more or knows better than He what is best for us. If we believe all that, then we can trust Him.

The Lord promised, "in everything God works for good with those who love him."[15] Our job then is to love Him, for "perfect love casts out fear."[16] We can also grow in trust by trying to trust. Trust is like a muscle: it grows stronger the more you use it. Try it, see what happens.

[9] 2 Cor 11:23–27.
[10] See 2 Cor 12:3–4. Many Scripture scholars hold that Paul was speaking of himself here.
[11] 1 Cor 2:9.
[12] 2 Cor 4:17.
[13] Jn 16:33.
[14] Rev 21:4.
[15] Rom 8:28.
[16] 1 Jn 4:18.

SECTION TWO

LOVING GOD MEANS
SPENDING TIME WITH HIM

And in the morning, a great while before day,
[Jesus] rose and went out to a lonely place,
and there he prayed.

(Mk 1:35)

[Jesus] went out to the hills to pray;
and all night he continued in prayer to God.

(Lk 6:12)

"For where your treasure is, there will your heart be also."

(Mt 6:21)

6

GOD'S #1 LOVE LANGUAGE: PRAYER

"Please don't get me anything for my birthday or Christmas", someone dear to me once said. She explained that after her parents' divorce, she didn't see her dad often, even on her birthday or holidays. Instead, he would send her an expensive gift. It felt like he didn't care about her and was just trying to placate her. She didn't want the things nearly as much as she wanted *him*. Similarly, the Lord spells the word *love* with the letters T-I-M-E. This is His first love language.[1]

The best way to express our love for God is by spending time with Him, talking to Him. In other words, praying. So in the quest to love God, prayer necessarily comes first.

It comes first whether one is just starting and not sure one even has a relationship with God or one has already been committed to Him for years. You can't love someone you don't know; reading about God or those who know and love Him will only take you so far. It's just not the same as knowing Him yourself. Spending time is the best way to get to know Him. Yet no matter how long we've known Him, we never outgrow prayer. We never become so spiritually advanced that we don't need prayer anymore. For one thing, we can always grow in how well we know God; we can never know Him thoroughly. We're always learning new things about our loved ones on earth; how much more so with God.

So prayer is the primary way to love God, in both senses of the word *primary*, both "first" and "the most important". First and foremost.

Adapted from "Prayer—Nourishing the Soul" by the author, in *Voices* (Michaelmas 2013): 24–27.

[1] We began with trust, as it's a big issue today; if you don't trust Him, you're not likely to spend time with Him.

We *Need* Prayer

Prayer happens to be good for us too. Well . . . much more than "good", actually; it's essential.

Expecting to get by spiritually without prayer is like planting a sapling in your cellar and expecting it to survive without light or water. Prayer provides the sun and rain our souls need to live and grow. While artificial light and a watering-can might work with a plant, for the soul, there are no real substitutes for prayer. Of course, we try all kinds of substitutes—entertainment, food, romance, vacations, etc.—all good things, but merely gifts and no replacement for the Giver. The soul can't thrive in the basement of our being: it needs to be exposed to the Son.

Though He was God, even Jesus, in His humanity, needed to pray. Not only did He *want* to pray, because He was all-holy and loved the Father, but He *needed* to pray. We see Him getting up early, staying up late, and slipping away by Himself whenever He could in order to pray. And if *He* needed to pray, who am I ever to think that I don't?

You see, apart from God, man is like a severed finger. It can't do much on its own. Sure, maybe it could wiggle a little, but what

> Apart from me, you can do nothing.
> —JOHN 15:5 BOX 10

good is that? So connecting with God is essential; otherwise, we will die, period. If we're baptized, that's a great start, but there's more to it: Baptism is like the surgery attaching us to the Body of Christ,[2] but the stitches keeping us in place are only temporary. If we close ourselves off to Him, we become a desiccated, lifeless appendage, and on the Day when the Divine Physician snips the stitches, we will fall off . . . dead.[3] Instead, *we* must actively fuse with Christ. We must open ourselves wide to Christ and grow into Him. Just as blood delivers life-giving oxygen and nutrition to every cell of the body, so Jesus is the Lifeblood of our souls. We must open ourselves more and more to Him, welcoming Him within us.

---

[2] Baptism is the ordinary means of becoming a member of Christ; however, it is not the only means. Nor is it an automatic guarantee of salvation. See *CCC* 837, 1257, 1267, 1281; cf. also 1253–54.

[3] Baptism leaves a permanent mark on the soul, even for those who lose their salvation (in this analogy, similar to the shorn stitches remaining in the dead finger). Baptism bestows a real, tremendous transformation, but to benefit from it, we must, before death, actualize and maintain the union with Christ it offers. See *CCC* 1272.

Prayer is the process by which the nerves in that finger fuse to the central nervous system. Only through prayer can we begin to know and unite with the mind and will of God. A person who tries to do it all on his own, without connecting to God, is like a finger attached only externally. It has no feeling; it is useless, not responding to the bidding of the Mind.

Connecting with God in prayer is also a major channel of grace. We cannot follow Him merely by our own power, but with His grace we can do amazing things: "I can

> Not to pray is to bring death upon a soul, it being impossible to lead a virtuous life without the aid of prayer.
>
> —ST. JOHN CHRYSOSTOM Box 11

do all things in him who strengthens me", says St. Paul.[4] St. Teresa of Calcutta recognized this: "I don't think there is anyone else who needs God's help and grace more than I do.... I cannot claim any credit for what gets done. On the contrary, I need His help twenty-four hours a day. And if days were longer, I would need even more of it."[5]

Every good thing we do is preceded by and dependent upon God's help. Even if that severed finger could wiggle a little, it would only be a temporary, leftover ability gained from the Body from which it came. But when we are joined to Him, then the power can really flow. The more deeply we are attached and the more often we seek and embrace His ways, the more we can do with Him, through Him, and for Him. Grace is that help, and prayer and the sacraments are the chief means by which we receive grace.[6]

Challenges to Prayer

Let's Be Honest: Prayer Is Not Always Easy or Fun

Prayer is an out-and-out fight. The *Catechism* grants this in the phrase "The Battle of Prayer". While one might expect the *Catechism* to be a dry rule book, it's loaded with great material, including a long and marvelous section on prayer. Its frankness is refreshing, observing that

---

[4] Phil 4:13.

[5] Mother Teresa, *Love: A Fruit Always in Season* (San Francisco: Ignatius Press, 1987), p. 244.

[6] See *A Catechism of Christian Doctrine, No. 3* (Paterson, N.J.: St. Anthony Guild Press, 1949), p. 86, no. 117.

prayer "always presupposes effort" and how common are "discouragement during periods of dryness", "disappointment over not being heard according to our own will", and feeling like a "failure in prayer" (that last one resonates with me). The *Catechism* recognizes how easy it is to conclude, "What good does it do to pray?" But the guidebook also provides the answer: confront temptations with humility, trust, and perseverance.[7]

The good news is that difficulty in prayer can actually be an ally in the quest to love God, for love is compellingly demonstrated by fidelity in adversity. Sometimes the best we can

> Love is the source of prayer; whoever draws from it reaches the summit of prayer.
> — *CCC* 2658 Box 12

do is show up for prayer and try and try to pray. Remember, love is sacrifice; love thinks of the Beloved before self. We won't know until heaven just how touched He was by our efforts.

God is not expecting us to become prayer champions overnight. Rather, He's like a mother who delights in watching her child begin to toddle about. If she constantly carried him or picked him up after every little tumble, he would never learn to walk. Instead, she helps him and comforts him as needed, but she also lets him struggle so he can gain the power and joy of walking and, later, running. In the same way, God allows us to struggle with prayer.

St. Teresa of Calcutta experienced forty years of dry prayer— emotionless prayer times, without any sense of God's presence. Yet she persevered, rising early each morning to begin her day with an hour of prayer before Christ in the Eucharist. And how richly God blessed her for it! She may not have *felt* anything during those prayer times, but He was definitely working in her; her life reveals the abundant graces[8] with which He enabled her to do what she did and the heavenly insights she needed to lead her order. Mother Teresa's example shows that love is the key to persevering in prayer. If we keep focusing on love as the goal, then nothing else will matter.

It also helps to remember how much God desires us to seek Him in prayer. "It is [God] who first seeks us"; Jesus "thirsts that we may thirst

---

[7] *CCC* 2728, 2753.

[8] Theologically speaking, *actual grace* is the power from God to do anything good; *salvific grace* is what we receive at Baptism and need to live in heaven: divine life within our souls. See *CCC* 1999–2000.

for him".[9] Realizing that God longs for you can enkindle a longing for Him in return. And when we persevere, He makes prayer a joy.

Making Time for God

At the outset, the biggest hurdle to prayer is finding the time.

In fact, you can't *find* the time to pray. The world, the flesh, and the devil will do everything possible to keep this time from you or help you fritter it away. You can't "find" the time; you have to *make* the time. And to do that, you have to be convinced that you need prayer.

Somebody once said that the busier your day, the greater your need to pray. That is so counterintuitive for people living in a busy culture like ours. On a busy day, my inclination is to hit the floor running—not kneeling. But, in reality, that is as foolish as dashing out the door to an important meeting across town, shouting over my shoulder, "I don't have time to get in the car, strap myself in, turn it on, and all that. I've got to go *now!*" Sure, I could run down my driveway and even get to the corner before my husband could reach it by car. But he would very soon pass me by and leave me miles behind. Making prayer your top priority is like getting into God's car and asking Him to take you where you need to go and get done what needs to be done ... which, come to think of it, He knows better than we do.

An ancient tale tells of a man searching the whole world trying to find God. It turns out He was with him all the time: hiding within the man's soul. The presence of God is like that, and so is His Providence. Spiritually, we are like a newborn who has so much to learn. While little babies are attracted to faces, recognize their parents' voices, and are comforted by being held and touched, they don't put it together at first that this face, this voice, and these loving arms all belong to one person. Nor do we always see these blessings here, that coincidence there, and this opportunity now as all coming from God's hand at work in our lives.

We're also like a baby who's a little older and whose father puts her, facing out, in an infant carrier secured to his chest. She can become so interested in the world around her from this new perspective and so eager to touch things that she forgets he is even there. We too can be unaware of how close our Father is, forget our need of Him, and focus on getting our way and trying to get where we want to go. Prayerful

---

[9] *CCC* 2560.

reflection is the chance to stop and remember Who is carrying us and caring for us. Though we can't see Him, we can appreciate that He's "got our back". And we can try to tune in to His presence, nestling in close and letting our love grow.

Praying through the Day

Work as Prayer

Some speak of making work a prayer. That could be a great idea or a defective one, depending on what is meant by it. Offering up your work as a prayer is commendable and beneficial, but *limiting* your prayer to work—i.e., offering your work as your *only* or main form of prayer—is not such a hot idea. Think of the Gospel story of Martha and Mary. Jesus didn't say to Mary: "Go help your sister, and that will be as good as listening to me."

On the other hand, neither did He say to Martha: "What you're doing is wrong. Stop it, and get in here." He said that Mary had chosen the *better* part, not the only worthwhile part. We all need to do some work. We have to attend to our physical lives and take care of others too. Remember, Jesus Himself probably spent eight times more of His life working for his family than He did in His public ministry (three years). So yes, we should work, and, as members of Christ's Body, we can join our work to His and consecrate it, making it a prayer. Absolutely, that is a beautiful and worthwhile thing to do. *But* we must give God some undivided attention too. Similarly, praying as we go about our business throughout the day is great ... but it's not enough.

This is true even if our work is directly *for* Him. St. John of the Cross says that those

> eaten up with activity ... and who imagine they are able to shake the world with their preaching and other outward works ... would be *much more useful* to the Church and more pleasing to the Lord ... if they devoted more time to prayer.... Without prayer, all they do amounts to nothing more than noise and uproar. No good work can be done without the power of God.[10]

---

[10] St. John of the Cross, quoted in Dom Jean-Baptiste Chautard, O.C.S.O., *The Soul of the Apostolate* (Charlotte, N.C.: TAN Books, 2012), pp. 113–14. Chautard views the attempt to do God's work without His help as insane, like saying, "My God,... just keep out of my way, and I guarantee to produce the best results!" *Soul of the Apostolate*, p. 12.

Think of a healthy marriage. A husband and wife need to talk about logistics and problems like the plumbing. But they need couple time too. They need to look at one another and discuss deeper things, reaffirm their love for one another, share what's burdening them, share their joys. Be there for each other. So also with God. Each of us needs to spend one-on-one time with Him. He doesn't need to hear our burdens and our joys, but He wants to. And He knows *we* need to share them with Him. We also need to hear what He has to say. We have so much to learn. And it's always nice to hear again His message of love and mercy.

This timeworn little paradox actually sums it up rather well:

Jack asked a monk, "Can I smoke a pipe while I'm praying?"
"No."
"Can I pray while I'm smoking a pipe?"
"Absolutely."

Yes, you can pray anytime: involve God in every moment of your day, whether you're working or playing. But don't multitask every time you pray; set aside some time just for Him.

He deserves it. And we need it.

Living a Prayer

There is another way to make one's work a prayer, springing from a different spirit: one makes one's whole life a prayer and offering to God. This is very different from tossing Him a token prayer while relying on oneself and in reality worshipping one's own activities. It *includes* work as a prayer but doesn't *limit* prayer to work. Instead, it seeks to "pray constantly".[11]

Brother Lawrence, in *Practicing the Presence of God*, advocated connecting with the ever-present God throughout the day by seeing His hand in everything, moment by moment. The seventeenth-century French monk maintained that each moment holds an opportunity to show God our love in a duty to be done or a suffering to be endured. That might sound negative, but many duties are pleasant—appreciating creation, praising God, reaching out to others, reasonably taking care of oneself with sleep, meals, exercise, recreation. Making such duties and

[11] 1 Thess 5:17.

blessings a prayer helps us to see God's Providence in everything and inspires gratitude.[12]

Ways to Pray

All this talk of prayer leads to the practical question, *How do I pray?* People often think of prayer as "saying prayers" or asking for something. But there's a lot more to it than that.

While we have as much need for spiritual nourishment as we do physical, we don't seem to be aware of it; we have poor spiritual appetites. We're so busy glutting our bodies that we're starving our souls. Or sometimes we give ourselves spiritual junk food—which leaves us worse off than before. Meanwhile, the Church offers an abundance of delicious, wholesome fare.

There are prayers for just about every personality, every need, every situation. The Church lays out a sumptuous banquet from which to choose, whether you're hungry for beauty, eloquence, awe, forgiveness, strength, guidance, hope, comfort, fellowship, inspiration, or just help meeting the Lord. There are litanies, novenas, the Rosary, chaplets, devotions; Vesper services, festivals of praise, holy hours, Benediction, Taizé, the Angelus, the Liturgy of the Hours; pilgrimages, and processions, just to name a few.

With so many options, how does one choose? We can try different kinds of prayer and see which work well for us. At the same time, we can keep a few principles in mind. First of all, one should try to cover the basics, such as beginning and ending the day with prayer. A morning offering is a great way to put God first in your life by putting Him first in your day. And at the end of the day, looking back over it with an examination of conscience gives one a chance to see what went well and what didn't, a chance to thank

> Never forget that it is at the beginning of each day that God has the necessary grace for the day ready for us. He knows exactly what opportunities we shall have to sin ... and will give us everything we need if we ask him then. That is why the devil does all he can to prevent us from saying our Morning Prayers or to make us say them badly.
>
> —St. John Vianney (Curé of Ars) [Box 13]

---

[12] See also n. 13 on p. 204 below.

and a chance to repent. Morning and night prayers make the One who is Alpha and Omega of the universe the beginning and end of your day too.

Next, our souls need a balanced diet—a variety of types and forms of prayer, not limited merely to petitions. Four general *types* of prayer are often summed up in the acronym "ACTS": adoration, contrition, thanksgiving, and supplication. Broadly speaking, all prayer can be classified as one or more of these types. For instance, a novena to St. Jude is a prayer of supplication; the Magnificat is a prayer of praise or adoration; the Mass incorporates all four types. Supplication is probably the most common type of prayer, but there's a reason it's last in the list. The first three are at least as necessary as the last: reminding us who God is, who we are, and what we owe Him. Loving prayer does not treat God as the Ultimate Vending Machine in the Sky, but seeks a living, loving, growing relationship with Him. It is helpful then to incorporate these three other types into our prayer times as well.

There are also various forms of prayer. A particularly valuable form is *liturgical* prayer, the public worship of the Church. Liturgical prayer is rich and enables us to worship the Lord in ways we could not achieve on our own, as it is based on the words of Scripture, the saints, and Church Fathers. Liturgical prayer is also corporate, and the Body of Christ should pray at times as a body. Doing so helps us remember that we are not alone in our relationship with God, but a family, His family.

The Little-Known Liturgy of the Hours

Aside from Mass, the most prevalent liturgical prayer is the Liturgy of the Hours (*aka* the Divine Office).* For centuries, clergy, monks, and nuns have committed to praying these prayers daily.

Much of the Divine Office consists in reciting or chanting the Psalter. Praying the Psalms expands one's spiritual vocabulary as they express every emotion and cover any situation. Also included is excellent material for meditation.

Vatican II encouraged the laity to pray at least some of the hours, especially in public celebrations such as Vespers. But even when one is physically alone, the Divine Office is considered a liturgical prayer because one is spiritually connected with all the other members of the Church praying the same prayers that day.

* The four-volume set is pricy, but one can use the single-volume *Christian Prayer* instead. Or one can view the Daytime and Night Prayers at ebreviary.com; subscribers have access to more content.

Box 14

We must also give God a chance to talk too. A relationship is stilted if one party does all the talking. No, He usually won't speak audibly, but He's given us His Word. Scripture is not always easy to understand, however, so it's a good idea to begin with the easier books, such as the Gospels and Epistles of the New Testament and the Psalms and wisdom literature in the Old Testament. A faithful translation with sound commentary serves like a ranger in a beautiful forest where one could otherwise get lost. The Ignatius Study Bible and the Navarre Bible are two great options.

Times of silence are also critical—giving the Lord a chance to speak to our hearts. Hearing Him usually doesn't happen all at once. We need to quiet our minds, which are spinning with the concerns and the ups-and-downs of relationships and daily life and all the images and words we've taken in from the media. Finding a place apart from distractions is indispensable. We also need to learn to recognize His voice—often a whisper—and that takes practice.

Finally, of all the different ways to pray, there are three golden paths to encounter God that stand out and deserve chapters of their own: meditation, Mass, and adoration.

7

MEDITATION: THE DIVINE MIND-MELD

The Art of Pondering

Wonderful as the Internet is, it can muddle our minds. Heavy use of our new technologies "can literally reroute our neural pathways.... We are becoming ever more adept at scanning and skimming, but what we are losing is our capacity for concentration, contemplation, and reflection."[1]

Of course, the Internet is not the only challenge to deep thinking; one's daily planner provides sufficient distraction. Decades before the web, Fr. Philip Dion wrote of the problem with surface-level thinking: "We judge of things chiefly by their effects on our material welfare and our physical well-being. In other words, it is possible to live practically without thinking; ... to live a most superficial kind of animal existence ... without ever becoming familiar with the whole thrilling world of spirit within us."[2]

Because there are so many other things competing for our attention, we can easily forget what we know or believe. What we know in our minds has not made its way down to our hearts. This is why we can say we love God but still neglect Him. Or why when we go to church, we can sit there as though we're waiting for a bus rather than marveling that we're mystically present with Christ at the greatest salvific events of history, while surrounded by the heavenly host. Or why we can say we believe in the Real Presence of Jesus in the Eucharist, yet file up to receive Him with as much excitement as when getting in line at the grocery store. "Use it or lose it" applies not only to the body but also to the mind and, even more frighteningly, to the spirit too.

Adapted from "Pondering—Path to Holiness: The Benefits of Meditation", by the author, in *Voices* (Christmastide 2013–2014): 19–21.

[1] Nicholas Carr, *The Shallows: What the Internet Is Doing to Our Brains* (New York: Norton, 2010), dust jacket.

[2] Fr. Philip Dion, *A Handbook of Spiritual Perfection* (Manchester, N.H.: Sophia Institute Press, 2001), p. 18.

So how can we realize—that is, *make real* to ourselves—what we know and believe? It is when we reflect on these things that they sink into our hearts, when we ponder these truths in prayer with the Holy Spirit, as Mary did, that they take root in our hearts, grow, and bear fruit.

Meditation Commendation

While there's a vast array of good ways to pray, many saints stress how crucial meditation is to the spiritual life. St. Teresa of Avila thought it could make the difference between heaven and hell. St. Alphonsus Liguori explains why: "It is impossible for him who perseveres in mental prayer to continue in sin: he will either give up meditation or renounce sin."[3]

Another strength of meditation is it's much less prone to deteriorating into phariseeism, something merely external, than other types of prayer. One could say a dozen devotions and attend Mass each day without having one's mind engaged or heart involved. If that's due to complacency or pride, then the graces are likely to roll right off. We could fool not only others with our apparent piety but even ourselves. I suppose it's theoretically possible to do that with meditation, but it would be much harder. Meditation is a one-on-one conversation with God requiring me to speak my own words and—far more difficult—to listen. That's pretty hard to fake.

This form of prayer is the most vital to a soul's growth and perseverance, engaging one's heart, one's mind, one's true self. All prayer is conversation with God, but meditation in some ways is the most intimate, because here we speak from the heart, we ourselves speak; and we strive to hear what He wants to say to us.

If a teenage son meets all his father's minimum rules, coming to Sunday dinner and staying out of serious trouble, but never talks to his father—aside from asking for a raise in his allowance or for the latest gizmo—what kind of relationship is that? How well will they know each other? And how long will the son's minimal obedience last? Our heavenly Father wants a real, personal relationship with each of us. We can't build that through *only* rote or group prayer.

---

[3] St. Alphonsus de Liguori, *The Great Means of Salvation* (London: Aeterna Press, 2015), p. 139. Meditation falls under mental prayer, one of three basic forms of prayer (along with vocal and liturgical prayer).

Don't get me wrong. I'm not disparaging vocal prayer or the Mass, both of which are very important and effective. *Vocal* prayers (those composed by someone else) are fundamental—they are the first we learn and the last we forget. They are helpful too when we don't know what to say or our own words seem inadequate. Similarly, group prayer is also important, and Mass is the most powerful prayer. (More on that in the next chapter.)

Nor am I saying that if our minds wander during any of these forms of prayer that our prayers are therefore worthless. If that were so, then I, Maj. Space Cadet, would be in big trouble. No, what matters is our intention and our efforts. If we want to pray from the heart, and keep trying, the Lord will care more for that than for our success (which is a gift from Him anyway).

Rather, I am merely echoing ...

... St. Teresa of Avila, who wrote: "It is then of the utmost importance to bear this truth in mind, that our Lord is within us, and that we ought to strive to be there with him."[4]

... And St. Alphonsus Liguori: "All the saints have become saints by mental prayer. Mental prayer is the blessed furnace in which souls are inflamed with the divine love."[5]

... And Venerable Archbishop Fulton Sheen, who explained that daily meditation on the love of God leads to "a gradual seepage of love down to the level of what is called the subconscious, and finally these good thoughts emerge, of themselves, in the form of effortless good actions."[6]

... And St. Teresa of Calcutta: "Holiness is impossible without it."[7]

Don't Freak Out

Now before I go on, I should reassure those whose state in life makes it seemingly impossible to do this, at least right now. There could be various situations that would make this very hard to do. You could be very sick, for instance, and either too fatigued, woozy, or distracted by pain to be able to meditate. In that case, just do the best you can,

---

[4] St. Teresa of Avila, *St. Teresa's Own Words: Or, Instructions on the Prayer of Recollection*, ed. James, Bishop of Hexham and Newcastle (London: Burns and Oates, 1910), p. 7.

[5] St. Alphonsus de Liguori, *The Great Means of Salvation and Perfection* (Brooklyn: Redemptorist Fathers, 1927), p. 258.

[6] Fulton J. Sheen, *Go to Heaven* (San Francisco: Ignatius Press, 2017), p. 173.

[7] Mother Teresa, *No Greater Love* (Novato, Calif.: New World Library, 2002), p. 5.

when you can. You can also just commune with God without words. Imitate the old peasant who came to church to pray every day; when asked by his pastor, St. John Vianney, what he did during those times, he replied, "I look at Him, and He looks at me." You can also join your sufferings to Christ's on the Cross and think about His Passion. You might be surprised to discover how close He is to you.

Another common state of life that makes prayer challenging is when you're at home full-time with young children. The idea of finding fifteen minutes for quiet prayer sounds insurmountable when you can rarely get even a minute alone in the bathroom. But if you ask the Lord to show you and you think outside the box, you can find a way.

For the time-challenged: if you're a morning person, you can get up a little earlier and pray first thing. It's a very peace-inducing practice to spend this time with God in the stillness before anyone else is up and requiring your attention. If you're a night owl, you can set aside some time before going to bed for meditation. This allows one to go to bed thinking of the things of God. Keep in mind too that you can begin with just five minutes and gradually work up to more. However you can manage it, spending time with God is the best deal in the universe.

Dividends of Divine Time Investment

If time is like a river, then prayer is an island upon which we can land to take a breather from the turbulence of life. While we are there, the river keeps flowing—time still passes—but in some mysterious, miraculous way, when we set out again, we find that, even if we couldn't afford the time, somehow it all works out. God either smooths out the rapids or directs our boat more efficiently or multiplies our time. What had seemed impossible to do in the time we had becomes possible after we take some of that limited time and invest it with God. St. Isidore, patron saint of farmers, for instance, used to attend daily morning Mass. When his employer learned of Isidore's resulting tardiness, he was annoyed ... until he saw the angel plowing in Isidore's place.

This is not to say, however, that we can use prayer as an escape from our duties. Longfellow recalls the story of a monk to whom Jesus appeared. When a bell tolled, calling the monk to feed the poor at the gate, he hesitated to leave the Lord, but went and did his duty. Returning, he saw a glow emanating from his cell and, entering, found the Lord still there. Jesus explained, "Hadst thou stayed, I must have fled!"[8]

I'm not saying that prayer guarantees you will accomplish every task on your to-do list. There is no "accomplishment gospel" any more than a "prosperity gospel". Our hearts always have to be in the right place. But our to-do list itself might be transformed. Perhaps a friend might surprise you by dropping off the bread and milk you need, or your boss might decide to go in a different direction on that project, giving you more time, or you realize an easier way to do X or that it would be better to wait on Y or drop Z altogether.

If you ask the Lord's help, He will open up a pocket of time for you.

What Is Meditation?

Simply put, meditation is a conversation with God, a mulling things over with Him—especially the things He cares about most. Unlike other types of meditation, Christian meditation is focused on Him and what He has revealed. The *Catechism* describes meditation as a "prayerful quest" to consider His revelation in faith and how it applies in our own lives.[9] It "silences the ego with its clamorous demands, in order that it may hear the wishes of the divine heart ... stir[s] up the will to conform more perfectly with His ... and strengthens our desire that all the good things we do shall be done for His Honor and Glory."[10]

While the word *contemplation* is sometimes used interchangeably with meditation, nowadays it is more often used for a special experience of union with God that can spring from meditation. True contemplation—a supernatural union with God—is not something we can cause; it is wholly a gift from God. While we cannot *make* it happen, we shouldn't lose hope of it ever happening. Carmelite mystics Ss. Teresa of Avila and John of the Cross both say that God desires everyone to enter into contemplation. We can open ourselves to it by being faithful in seeking Him in meditation, for it is often there that God gives the gift of contemplation.

[8] Henry Wadsworth Longfellow, "The Theologian's Tale; The Legend Beautiful", *Henry Wadsworth Longfellow: A Maine Historical Website*, www.hwlongfellow.org/poems_poem.php?pid=2064.

[9] CCC 2723.

[10] Archbishop Fulton Sheen, *Go to Heaven* (New York: McGraw-Hill, 1960), p. 158.

All in all, meditation is a sure and simple (though challenging) means to growing in holiness, available to everyone. Sometimes we can be like Naaman the Syrian,[11] seeking for the extraordinary and disdaining the plain, unimpressive method that God offers.

When the Praying Gets Tough, Who Keeps Praying?

Beyond making the time for meditation, the primary obstacle is how hard it is.

Learning Curve

Meditation is an art. It takes time to learn to do it well.

One thing that makes it hard is how harried and hurried we are; it takes a while to enter into prayer. We get discouraged because we want things to happen in our scheduled time frame, but we can't get God to fit there. We look up and find the time gone with evidently nothing to show for it. But how can we expect to go whizzing about all day long, multi-tasking, and then be able to sit down and—bam!—slide straight into mediation mode?

Our minds need time to settle down. Imagine scooping up water from a swollen creek after a storm: it will be murky. But if we set the jar down and leave it alone for a while, all the junk will sink to the bottom

---

HOW TO MEDITATE

For many who don't know how to meditate, here's one method. (A good time *goal*, by the way, is fifteen minutes. You can work up to it.)

1. Begin by making yourself present to God, who is always with you.
   A. The ideal place is in His physical presence, in a church or chapel with the Blessed Sacrament (Eucharistic Jesus in the tabernacle). This isn't practical for many of us, however; so try to create a sacred space at home or at least find a quiet corner for prayer. This helps minimize distractions.

(continued)

---

[11] See 2 Kings 5:1–14, esp. 10–12, where Naaman is offended that Elisha didn't heal him personally, but simply sent a message that he should wash in the river Jordan. But Naaman's servant wisely points out, "If the prophet had commanded you to do some great thing, would you not have done it?" (v. 13).

B. Acknowledge His presence by confirming your faith, hope, and love for Him; worship Him, thank Him for all He has done for you, and ask His forgiveness. It's tempting to gloss over this step, but if done well, it can lead to real closeness to Him. It also helps you transition from your workaday mind-set into a prayerful interior state.

2. Invoke the Holy Spirit in your own words or through a traditional prayer such as "Come, Holy Spirit". Open your heart and mind to Him. You don't want to have a conversation with yourself or mistake the voice of the world, the flesh, or the devil for His.

3. Read a text, preferably from Scripture. The Word of God, with its timeless wealth, is our primary source. You can also use the writings of saints or trustworthy spiritual writers on a virtue you're trying to develop or related to the liturgical season. Occasionally, the best "text" will be an occurrence in your own life on which the Lord is calling you to reflect.

4. Reflect on the text—especially something that strikes you—and what it means to you. Ask the Lord what He is trying to tell you through this. Ask Him to help you to be silent and open to Him and truly listen. (This is hard, but don't give up. Keep trying.)

   If you choose a Scripture passage, you can try the Ignatian method: Put yourself in the scene, either as someone explicitly in the story or as a bystander. Imagine what it looked like, what it smelled and sounded like. If it's from the Gospel, try to imagine what it would have been like to hear and see Jesus saying and doing these things.

   Other personalities might find it easier to concentrate if they write their reflections in the form of a letter to God.

   Another method that works for many people of various personalities is *lectio divina*: read the text slowly several times, and see what phrases strike you.

   A fruitful practice is to write down any insights gained. This can help you remember what you learned and see patterns in your life and in God's work, and it provides material on which to reflect again in the future.

5. Make a resolution. To be effective, prayer must spill over and change other areas of our lives. Think of something you can do *that day* to put into practice what the Lord is teaching you. (Examples: refrain from complaining but offer up difficulties instead; pay a visit to the Blessed Sacrament; do something thoughtful for someone else.)

Box 15

and the water will become clear. Our minds can do that too, but it takes patience and practice. The first part of prayer is entering into silence, disengaging from the world for a time.

Distractions, then, are to be expected. Usually, the best thing to do is just say, "Oops—sorry about that" and get back to prayer. (You may have to do this ten times in ten minutes.) If the same distraction keeps tugging at your attention, then you need to figure out why. If it's something you need to do later and you're worried you'll forget, write it down. Nothing to write on? Ask your guardian angel to remind you. If it's something you're anxious about, entrust it to the Lord. Still bothering you? Then make it the topic of discussion between you and the Lord. Tell Him why it's concerning you, and ask Him for His input and the help you need.

Ups and Downs

Difficulties are a standard feature of meditation. Sometimes, especially when people first discover God, He blesses their prayer times in ways they can feel, with fervor, joy, or a sense of His presence. But we don't always experience that, and it can be discouraging. It's imperative to know what's happening. It's not that God isn't real, that He doesn't care about us, or that we've failed. Granted, sometimes prayer falters because we've put something ahead of God, but even prayer done well and faithfully will become difficult.

This is normal. We have sunny prayer times and rainy ones. The former are traditionally characterized by "consolations", which refresh the soul and strengthen resolve. A *consolation* is any interior joy that attracts us to heavenly things. Sometimes we have them; sometimes we experience "desolation" instead. To the modern mind, *desolation* suggests a condition near despair, but here it denotes rather "deprivation", the opposite of consolation. The characteristic signs are dryness, feeling sad, tepid, slothful, or far from God, or doubting one's past faith experiences.[12]

Just as many prefer a sunny day to a rainy one, so also we naturally much prefer consolation to desolation. However, just as a plant needs both, so do our souls. A plant that received constant sunshine and no rain would wither up and die. Likewise, a soul receiving only consolations

---

[12] St. Ignatius of Loyola speaks at length of consolations and desolations and how to handle them in his rules for the discernment of spirits (*Spiritual Exercises*, nos. 313–36).

would get "burnt": it would likely become complacent and fail to grow, and might even die through falling into spiritual pride. Knowing what we need, the Lord sends us both sun and rain.

Growing Pains

We can see why He sends us the sunny times. During them, we feel encouraged and eager to do His will and help our neighbor. We're excited by new insights and are on fire with love for Him. But why do we need those rainy times? Because they too are critical to our growth: they remind us how much we need God and how little we can do on our own. Thus we have the chance to deepen our humility and dependence on God. And it is while we are enduring desolation that we can really grow in virtue. Like biceps, spiritual muscles grow when they are put to work, when they are challenged, even resisted.

Someone once said that when we feel close to God in prayer and ready to do anything for Him, that is His gift to us. When we persevere in prayer that is dry and dull and seems pointless, that is our gift to Him. In a similar vein, then-Bishop Fulton Sheen observes: "At the beginning one loves God for only His gifts or for the emotions He sends us.... The moment the Lover is loved for Himself, then the nature of the gifts ceases to matter. If God withdraws all sensible gifts it is only because He wants the union between the soul and Himself to be more personal and less dependent on His generosity."[13]

Mother Angelica echoes this in a book on the *gift* of dryness in prayer:

Only through the pain of dryness—where we decrease and He increases—can we begin to love God in the way He wishes us to love....

Faith tells us that God is present when we pray and Hope tells us He listens, but only Love makes us continue to pray when darkness, boredom and even disgust fill our souls to overflowing. Only a true love will persevere in praying despite darkness and confusion.[14]

To get through cold, rainy times, we need to gather and treasure the fruits of sunny prayer times. Recording them in a prayer journal prevents

---

[13] Bishop Fulton J. Sheen, ed., *That Tremendous Love* (New York: Harper and Row, 1967), p. 2.

[14] Mother Angelica, *Mother Angelica on Suffering and Burnout* (Irondale, Ala.: EWTN Publishing, 2017), p. 106; originally found in mini-book *Dawn on the Mountain: The Gift of Dryness in Prayer* (1973); https://www.ewtn.com/library/mother/madawn.htm.

forgetting, misremembering, or slighting them when the feelings have gone. One of the most inspiring books I've read has this advice:

> Profit, profit from these dark hours when your nature grieves, when your heart is cold, when you believe, wrongly, that Jesus is very far from you and even, perhaps, that He is turning His eyes away from you, because you see yourself to be so imperfect and wretched; profit from them to make heroic acts of faith and confidence out of pure will. These are the most precious acts—they have immense merit because in those times they are acts of pure faith, without consolation and without sensible aid.[15]

We don't know all the ways God is working in us in such trials. Just as the rain sinks into the earth to reach the plant's roots, however, He is feeding our souls in unseen ways.

Whether struggling with distractions or desolations, we can take steps to support our prayer times. Go to a place that elevates your spirit; light candles; put on music or bring out pictures that touch and inspire you. You can also rekindle and foster a love for God in your heart by looking for signs of His love throughout the day and recalling frequently what He's done for you. Also try meditating on the tremendous gift of His love. Think of the vast universe and its amazing detail, down to the cells and atoms. The Creator of all this knows *you*. He cares about you. He loves you; He loves *each one* of us. Incredible! Lastly, remember that just as the rain won't last forever, neither will the desolations. Sunny times will come again.

Goal: Unitive Prayer

These are normal stages in spiritual development. Saints and doctors of the Church who have gone through them have left us accounts. Whether you call these stages the "Three Ways" with two "dark nights" or you go by St. Teresa of Avila's "interior mansions", there is a pattern. Just as each of us passes through the stages of physical and intellectual development in our own unique way, so it is in the spiritual life. A relative few whiz through early stages; others, like Mother Teresa, might find themselves trudging through dark years rather than dark "nights".

---

[15] Fr. Jean C.J. d'Elbée, *I Believe in Love* (Manchester, N.H.: Sophia Institute Press, 2001), pp. 77–78.

God gives us these guides to encourage us to persevere. It's comforting to discover that a long period of dryness in prayer is quite normal and an indication of growth. Wherever we are on the road, we can rejoice that we're on it and making progress. Those who have reached the heights are calling down: telling us what it's like up there and what to expect along the way. Through them, the Lord reveals what we can attain with His help if we persevere: peace, joy, absolute love, heroic virtue, and (best of all), union with Him.

Communing with God through meditation is one of most effective ways to pray and to express love to Him. Once one experiences how vital meditation is, one can respond with Archbishop Fulton Sheen to the question "Why do you pray?" with "Why do you breathe?"

8

MASS: HITTING THE JACKPOT

Imagine it's your first day working at a lottery redemption office. In comes a scruffy guy in a shabby sportscoat and holey sneakers. He ambles up to the desk, eyes glued to an old Gameboy. Your co-workers greet him loudly, but he just plays on. They come around and start stuffing bills into his coat pockets.

"What are you doing?!" you exclaim.

"Oh, Joe won $500 million a few years ago and comes in to get his $250K every week."

"Yes, but ...", you sputter, "why don't you just send him a check?"

"This is the only way he'll get any of it. He kept losing the checks, or forgetting about them", says one. "He never cashed them."

"He knows to come in here every week," adds another, "but he doesn't seem to remember why. We resorted to putting cash in his pockets in the hope he'll retain at least some of it."

When they try to stuff his inside coat-pocket, he resists. They finally get some in; then Joe turns and goes out. You watch him walk down the street, bills fluttering, some floating off in the breeze. Little urchins creep up and pluck out handfuls. Joe doesn't notice.

"Will he have any left by the time he gets home?" you wonder aloud.

"Well, we always try to put a big wad in his inside pocket. He must be using some of it: he has a place to live, and he's obviously eating."

"He's better off than Jane", they add, pointing out the window. You see a scrawny, homeless woman in rags passing by. "She won an even bigger pot, but she's never even turned in her ticket. We've tried and tried to get her in here, but she won't hear of it. She can't stand us."

"What a crying shame", you think.

I wonder ... how often do our guardian angels think the same?

God has given us an unfathomable gift, and what we do? We ignore it, forget about it, or lose it. How many times have we acted like Joe Catholic, showing up for Mass with our minds a million miles away and shedding graces all the way home? Or maybe like Jane Catholic—we don't even bother going to Mass anymore. We're clueless about the incomparable value of what is offered us and how little of it we actually end up receiving.

Grumbling Obligation or Golden Opportunity?

Most of us don't realize all that's going on at Mass or how vital it is. If we're even aware that the Mass is so stupendously beneficial and crucial that the Church still teaches that we need to attend every Sunday or risk serious consequences to our souls, most don't know why. Such an idea may not only be surprising, but, to some, ridiculous or even objectionable. What's the big deal?

Think of it this way: skipping Sunday Mass is like a husband blowing off date night with his wife. Receiving Communion at Mass the following Sunday, without first going to Confession, is like that husband showing up two weeks later and hopping into bed with his wife—without apologizing for standing her up or even communicating with her for weeks—and expecting her to be perfectly fine with that arrangement. While most people wouldn't dare try that with a spouse, many unwittingly do just that to Jesus. Holy Communion is a union more intimate than the marital bed, and yet we sometimes treat it like a mundane duty or a dull surplus.

Most of us are aware of the Third Commandment: *Remember to keep holy the Sabbath day.* But some wonder why we can't keep it holy our own way. Well, the Church says, you can—and should—but you also need to come celebrate with the rest of us. The *minimum* of what God asks here is Mass.[1] If you want to go pray in a grove of trees, meditate on the beach, or sing songs with friends, you can do those things too. Your heavenly Father absolutely wants one-on-one time with you. But He has stipulated that on Sunday He wants us all gathered around the table as a family (the *whole* family, not just the ones we like). We may not know all the reasons; we just know He wants it, and ideally that should be enough for us.

Many of us began going to Mass when we were infants, and though we learned all the responses and when to stand, sit, and kneel, we may

---

[1] See *CCC* 2168–88, especially 2181–82; cf. 1166–67.

have never learned what it's really all about, missing its deep richness.
Here are some reflections that may help.

Crazy Love

And when the hour came, he sat at table, and the apostles with him. And
he said to them, "I have *earnestly desired* to eat this Passover with you
before I suffer...." And he took bread, and when he had given thanks
he broke it and gave it to them, saying, "This is my body which is given
for you. Do this in remembrance of me." And likewise the chalice after
supper, saying, "This chalice which is poured out for you is the new
covenant in my blood."[2]

Jesus says He has "earnestly desired"—or, in another translation,
"longed"—for this Last Supper with His disciples. Why? He gives Himself as food and drink to them; what does He get out of it? All the benefits are theirs.

It can only be love. And this is not just any love. This is crazy love.

At this Passover meal, He will establish a new covenant. In the Old
Testament, a covenant usually required a blood sacrifice. In this new
covenant, Christ offers Himself as the sacrifice—a living sacrifice—a
total gift of self. This gift, moreover, is a pledge to enact this sacrifice on
the Cross. It's astounding that He would "long" for this Supper.

He has longed for it only because He loves them. He's been with
them these three years and longed to give them His abundant graces. He
longs to see them become the saints they were created to be. He loves
them and wants to be united with them in this sacrament.

This longing began at the Fall and extends to all people of all time.
Communion between God and man had been broken since Adam and
Eve. The Lord longed for this Passover because, in His crazy love for
mankind, He longed to restore grace in and communion with us. He
longed to make this sacrifice for us, not because He longed for suffering
itself; rather, He longed for the *effects* of His sacrifice: our salvation and
sanctification. He established the disciples as priests and bishops so as
to extend this gift throughout the ages. Even to today ... even to you
and me.

"*Me?*" you may be thinking. "Seriously?"

---

[2] Lk 22:14–15, 19–20; emphasis added.

We may know, at least in theory, how infinite the Lord's love is for us. And yet how often we forget and seek something or someone else to fill the aching void in our hearts. This Scripture passage can help us grasp better the reality of this truth. How incredible must His love be that He would long to give Himself, to be united with each one of us no matter how unworthy. That He would actually *long* to sacrifice Himself for you and me.

The Last Supper was all about love: the washing of feet; the rich, sublime discourse; and most of all, the gift of Himself in the Eucharist. It was all about expressing His love and teaching His followers how to love. What He began at the Last Supper and consummated on the Cross is pure love: completely selfless and total, nothing held back.

The Mass we attend today is an extension of that same Supper. It is God's greatest gift of love to us. It's our chance to encounter the crazy love of God up close and personally.

Party-Poopers

If we really understood the Mass, we would never want to miss it. We're like the deluded people in the parable who came up with lame excuses to avoid going to a *king's* banquet.[3]

The Mass is even better than a party at a palace. In the first half, *God* is speaking to us in the readings. (Think about that: the Almighty has a message for *you*.) Scripture is His love letter to us. It's amazing sometimes how perfectly the readings can address a personal need, give you a solution to a problem or hope in a tough situation. Other times, the Lord's message is a hidden nugget. We need to stay alert so we don't miss it. We should go to Mass *"expecting God to communicate with us"*, says author and speaker Matthew Kelly. So we need to perk up our ears. "Listen to what God is saying to you in the music, through the readings, in the homily. Listen to the prayers of the Mass, and listen to the quiet of your heart."[4]

---

[3] See Lk 14:16–24.

[4] Matthew Kelly, *Rediscover Catholicism* (Cincinnati, Ohio: Beacon, 2010), pp. 197, 198; emphasis added. He also recommends bringing a journal and writing down one thing you hear God saying to you at each Mass. It focuses the mind and makes it more likely that we will heed and carry out His message.

In the second half of the Mass, we are participating in Christ's sacrifice of Himself on the Cross to the Father.[5] We are spiritually transported to Bethlehem and the Last Supper, Calvary and the Upper Room on Easter, all at once. We *are* there, only our physical eyes are blind to this spiritual reality. Plus we have the chance to be a part of Christ's gift: to offer ourselves *with* Christ as He offers Himself to the Father. Talk about riding on someone's coattails: it's like a toddler adding a penny to her dad's billion-dollar donation and getting listed as a benefactor.

As if that weren't enough, Christ then offers Himself to us as *food*. Think what people would do if somehow, somewhere, a mere berry plucked from heaven were possible to obtain—they would travel thousands of miles and pay top dollar. Yet people sometimes deem it too much trouble to go to their local parish, where they can receive God Himself.

People would flock to eat fruit plucked from heaven because they would assume it had healing properties and it increased goodness. Well, that's even truer for the precious food from heaven the Lord does offer us in the Eucharist. After all, the Eucharist is GOD. What could possibly be more helpful or healing than having God Himself within you?

Remember the old health motto "You are what you eat"? Well, it's an even older idea than you may realize, being evidently the motive for cannibalism. St. Jean de Brébeuf, a seventeenth-century Jesuit missionary, for instance, underwent horrific tortures with such courage that his Iroquois persecutors ate his heart in order to gain his courage. It may be that there were certain hormones or chemicals in Fr. Brébeuf's system accompanying his acts of courage, but I'm sure cannibals couldn't gain his virtues that way.

When we partake of the Body and Blood of our Lord in the Eucharist, on the other hand, it is not cannibalism because Christ is alive and giving Himself to us entirely. But it is a gift that, if we're open, *will* impart to us the virtues and characteristics of Him whom we consume. In *The Sacrament of Charity*, Pope Benedict pointed out that this is no ordinary consumption: "It is not the eucharistic food that is changed into us, but rather we who are mysteriously transformed by it."[6] This echoes St. Augustine's reflection: "You shall feed upon me; nor shall

---

[5] See *CCC* 1362–70.

[6] Pope Benedict XVI, Post-Synodal Apostolic Exhortation on the Eucharist as the Source and Summit of the Church's Life and Mission, *Sacramentum Caritatis, Sacrament of Charity* (February 22, 2007), no. 70.

you change me, like the food of your flesh, into yourself, but you shall be changed into me."[7] Perhaps this is why a consecrated Host does not change in appearance: just as the Host is truly Christ, though it still looks and tastes like bread, so too, if we receive Him with our souls wide open, we can become other Christs, and He will live and act and love in us though we still look the same externally.

Real Presence—For Real?

Of course, not all Catholics know or believe this. They missed the memo somehow and haven't grasped that chapter 6 of John's Gospel, where Jesus teaches about the Eucharist, is to be taken literally, that in the Eucharist Jesus is really, truly, physically present.

Biblical and Historical Grounds

There are both biblical and historical grounds for this Church teaching, primarily the words of Jesus Himself. His words are particularly powerful, for He repeats "eat my flesh and drink my blood" multiple times. Not only that, but the word used in this passage, *trōgō*, is better translated as "chew" or "gnaw" than "eat". Scripture scholars Scott Hahn and Curtis Mitch note: "The graphic and almost crude connotation of this verb thus adds greater force to the repetition of his words."[8]

His audience clearly thought Jesus was speaking literally, not metaphorically, for they said, "How can this man give us his flesh to eat?" Even His disciples found it difficult: "'This is a hard saying; who can listen to it?'... After this many of his disciples drew back and no longer walked with him." If Jesus simply meant this symbolically, He would have called them back and clarified. He explained on other occasions when they misunderstood Him. Instead, He let them go and simply turned to the Twelve, asking, "Will you also go away?"[9]

The early Church Fathers (great Christian writers living in the early centuries after the apostolic era) all understood Jesus to be speaking

---

[7] St. Augustine, *Confessions*, VII, 10, 16: PL 32:742, quoted in ibid.

[8] *Ignatius Catholic Study Bible: The New Testament*, with introduction, commentary, and notes by Scott Hahn and Curtis Mitch (San Francisco, Ignatius Press, 2010), p. 175, word study on "Eats" (Jn 6:54).

[9] Jn 6:52, 60, 66, 67.

literally here. St. Justin Martyr, writing around A.D. 155, says of the Eucharist: "Not as common bread nor common drink do we receive these; but since Jesus Christ our Savior was made incarnate by the word of God and had both flesh and blood for our salvation, so too, as we have been taught, the food which has been made into the Eucharist by the Eucharistic prayer set down by Him ... *is both the flesh and the blood of that incarnated Jesus.*"[10] Likewise St. Irenaeus, about twenty-five years later, writes something similar, speaking of the Eucharist as indeed Jesus' "own Blood" and "His own Body".[11]

St. Ignatius of Antioch (born ca. A.D. 50), one of the earliest Church Fathers and a disciple of St. John the Apostle, writes: "I desire the bread of God, the heavenly bread, the bread of life, which is the flesh of Jesus Christ, the Son of God...; and I desire the drink of God, namely, His blood, which is incorruptible love and eternal life."[12] He also lists as an error of heretics that they "do not confess that the Eucharist is the Flesh of our Savior Jesus Christ".[13]

Throughout her two-thousand-year-long history, the Catholic Church has continued to teach that although the gifts continue to *look* like bread and wine, they actually and physically *become* the Body and Blood of Jesus Christ. Believing this is not easy. It never has been. And so, periodically, the Lord will give the Church a Eucharistic miracle.

Miraculous Evidence

One of the most famous—because it has been ongoing for twelve hundred years—is that of Lanciano, Italy. In the eighth century, there was a priest who, while saying Mass, was struggling with disbelief in the Real Presence. Then, at the moment of Consecration, the Host in his hands visibly transformed into flesh and the wine into blood. The congregation marveled at the miracle and then spread the word throughout the town. The Host and Blood were preserved in reliquaries and can still be seen in the Church of St. Francis in Lanciano today.

---

[10] St. Justin Martyr, *The First Apology of Justin*, no. 66, in *The Faith of the Early Fathers*, ed. William A. Jurgens, vol. 1 (Collegeville, Minn.: Liturgical Press, 1970), p. 55, emphasis added.

[11] See St. Irenaeus, *Against Heresies*, 5, 2, 2, in *Faith of the Early Fathers*, 1:99.

[12] St. Ignatius of Antioch, *Epistle to the Romans*, in *The Ante-Nicene Fathers: The Writings of the Fathers down to 325 A.D.*, ed. Alexander Roberts, James Donaldson, and A. Cleveland Coxe, vol. 1, *The Apostolic Fathers—Justin Martyr—Irenaeus* (New York: Charles Scribner's Sons, 1903), p. 77.

[13] St. Ignatius of Antioch, *Epistle to the Smyrnaeans*, 6, 2, in *Faith of the Early Fathers*, 1:25.

Over the centuries, the Catholic Church has investigated this phenomenon six times. In 1970–1971, Dr. Odoardo Linoli, a professor in anatomy, pathological histology, and chemistry, and Dr. Ruggero Bertelli, professor emeritus of human anatomy, conducted a series of examinations. Their studies established the following: The flesh is real flesh and the blood real blood; both are human and have the same blood type, AB (the same found on the Shroud of Turin). Neither blood nor flesh contains any preservatives or chemical agents, such as those used in mummifying. Furthermore, the protein tests indicate the blood to be fresh.[14]

The flesh is heart tissue, taken from the heart wall, and includes part of the left ventricle. "Arterial and venous vessels and two thin branches of the vagal nerve" also appear in this cross-section of a human heart.[15] The slice could not have been taken from a dead body, for it would have required a hand trained in anatomical dissection, a practice that did not begin until after the fourteenth century—six centuries after the miracle occurred.[16]

This preservation of the flesh and blood can only be called miraculous:

Dr. Linoli further noted that the blood, had it been taken from a cadaver, would have altered rapidly through spoilage and decay. His findings conclusively exclude the possibility of a fraud perpetrated centuries ago.... The doctor ended his report by stating that while the flesh and blood were conserved in receptacles not hermetically sealed, they were not damaged, although they had been exposed to the influences of physical, atmospheric and biological agents.[17]

In our own time, an eerily similar miracle has occurred. In the 1990s, in Buenos Aires, a discarded Host was found on the floor after Mass. Following the usual procedure, it was placed in a container with water and put in the tabernacle. After a few days, instead of being dissolved,

---

[14] In 1981, Dr. Linoli ran new tests, using new technology, which confirmed his 1971 results. Both studies were published in *Quaderni Sclavo di Diagnostica Clinica e di Laboratori*.

[15] Fr. Nicola Nasuti, O.F.M. Conv., *The Eucharistic Miracle of Lanciano: Historical, Theological, Scientific and Photographic Documentation* (Lanciano, Italy: Santuario del Miracolo Eucaristico, 1988), p. 70.

[16] Ibid., p. 76.

[17] Joan Carroll Cruz, *Eucharistic Miracles and Eucharistic Phenomena in the Lives of the Saints* (Rockford, Ill.: TAN Books, 1987), pp. 6–7.

it had become an enlarged bloody tissue. The priest contacted Cardinal Bergoglio (now Pope Francis), who decided to investigate.

> On October 5, 1999, in the presence of the Cardinal's representatives, Dr. Castañón-Gomez took a sample of the bloody fragment and sent it to New York for analysis. Since he did not wish to prejudice the study, he purposely did not inform the team of scientists of its provenance. One of these scientists was Dr. Frederic Zugibe, the well-known cardiologist and forensic pathologist. He determined that the analyzed substance was real flesh and blood containing human DNA. Zugibe testified that, "the analyzed material is a fragment of the heart muscle found in the wall of the left ventricle close to the valves.... The heart muscle is in an inflammatory condition and contains a large number of white blood cells. This indicates that the heart was alive at the time the sample was taken ... since white blood cells die outside a living organism.... What is more, these white blood cells had penetrated the tissue, which further indicates that the heart had been under severe stress, as if the owner had been beaten severely about the chest."[18]

The blood type here, by the way, is once again AB, one of the rarest of blood types, though more common in the Middle East. Ron Tesoriero, an attorney involved in the scientific investigation, adds these details:

> The flesh was heart muscle. The heart had suffered traumatic injury about 3 days before. The heart could only have come from a living person.
> The sample had been kept in water for three years prior to the testing. The cardiac tissue and white blood cells, contrary to scientific principles, had remained vital and without degeneration.
> Also contrary to expectation, DNA testing failed to give a genetic profile of the "person" whose heart it was.[19]

God knows us; He provides solid data for our skeptical, evidence-demanding time.

Gift Beyond Belief: Blood Brother

Blood is thicker than water, they say. So when a childhood friend and I wanted to prove our loyalty to each other, to deepen our bond of

[18] Fr. M. Piotrowski, S.Chr., "Eucharistic Miracle in Buenos Aires", *Love One Another!* (online magazine); see https://aleteia.org/2016/04/22/eucharistic-miracle-beheld-by-pope-francis/.

[19] *Unseen*; http://unseen.net.au/. See also Ron Tesoriero and Lee Han, *Unseen: New Evidence* (Kincumber, New South Wales, 2013), especially pp. 43–60.

friendship, I said, "Let's each prick a thumb, and we put our thumbs together and mix the blood—that makes us 'blood-sisters'."

We thought it was a great idea. (My mom thought otherwise. She was, well, horrified when she heard about it and started talking about blood diseases and other sundry pleasantries.)

The idea of blood brotherhood is cross-cultural, with legends and rituals among such diverse peoples as Norsemen, Native Americans, and Chinese. Why such widespread appeal?

For the same reason it appealed to two nine-year-old suburban girls. Everyone knows you're supposed to be loyal to your own family. So how do you express a deep friendship or the immovability of your loyalty to a friend—a bond that is lifelong and unbreakable? Family members are said to be related "by blood", so from that I suppose arose the idea of mixing your blood with that of a friend who is like a sibling, so you would share the same blood.

The Lord recognizes the longings of the human heart—after all, He made our hearts. So not only did the Son come to earth to save us, not only did He become *one* of us, but in doing so, He even made His Father *our* Father.[20] We are the adopted children of *God*. He also knows that, as fallen creatures in a fallen world, we're a little insecure and long to be "blood brothers". So He undertook a much greater ritual: not the mere prick of a needle to His thumb, but nails right through His hands and feet. Shedding, not a mere drop, but pints and pints of Blood.

But how do we receive His Blood? Prick our thumbs? Be crucified too? He does call us to carry our cross and follow Him, but most of us won't have to shed our blood literally for Him. Instead, He instituted a more deeply unifying way to share His Blood than by rubbing pricked thumbs together: He gives us His own Blood and Body to consume in the Eucharist.[21]

It is a gift that unifies us with Him and truly makes us His blood brothers. In fact, there is no greater union possible on this earth.

Power of the Mass

We're always looking for the most bang for our buck, but every day most of us pass by the most stupendous deal of all time. Numerous

---

[20] See Jn 20:17.

[21] Both the Body and Blood are present in the Host and in the cup, for it is the living, entire Christ under both "species" in the Eucharist. (See *CCC* 1377.)

saints and doctors of the Church have stressed the infinite power and value of the Mass. St. John Vianney once said, "All good works taken together cannot have the value of one Holy Mass, because they are the works of men, whereas the Holy Mass is the work of God."[22] Vatican II echoed this in its document on the liturgy, calling the Mass the "font from which all [the Church's] power flows".[23] In other words, Mass is the greatest source of grace.

But it's not only what the Mass does for us that makes it priceless; as "a sacred action surpassing all others",[24] it's also the best means we have to do something for God. There's no higher prayer; there's nothing we can do more pleasing to God than praying the Mass.

If we really understood the Mass, our only problem with going every Sunday would be that it wouldn't be often enough. We would want to go more often than once a week.

How to Pray the Mass Better

It's difficult to enter into the mystery and majesty of the Mass. We can be simultaneously used to it yet unaware of all that's going on. It's not a lost cause, however. We can pray the Mass better by learning more about it in order to appreciate it better, and, since *Eucharist* means "thanksgiving", by practicing gratitude. The following tips and reflections might also help.

First, Last, Only

Even when we believe in Jesus' Real Presence in the Eucharist, it doesn't necessarily follow that we're always going to *feel* excited at every Communion. I know the teaching; I try to reflect on whom I'm receiving, revere Him and welcome Him, but even so, I don't always manage it. Too often, I still catch myself thinking about what I need to do after Mass.

---

[22] Quoted in Stefano Manelli, F.F.I., *Jesus, Our Eucharistic Love* (New Bedford, Mass.: Academy of the Immaculate, 1996), p. 30.

[23] Second Vatican Council, Constitution on the Sacred Liturgy *Sacrosanctum Concilium* (December 4, 1963), no. 10. And no. 7 reads: "Every liturgical celebration ... is a sacred action surpassing all others; no other action of the Church can equal its efficacy."

[24] Ibid., no. 7.

More than a few sacristies display the exhortation: "Priest of God, celebrate the Mass as if it were your first Mass, your last Mass, your only Mass." How helpful it would be for us all to take that same attitude toward the Eucharist.

What if seasoned communicants could reawaken an appetite for something we now take for granted, for *Someone* we've forgotten to acknowledge, distracted by His disguise? How wonderful to approach the altar with the eagerness of a First Communicant, longing for the Lord, hungry to receive what we until then could not.

And what about receiving as if it were one's *last* Communion? Wouldn't that clear away the mental cobwebs? Wouldn't that help one to enter into prayer more deeply, to strive more ardently to meet Him? If I recognize each Communion as possibly my last, then I will make a good Last Communion ... because one of them *will* be my last; I just don't know which.

We take for granted what we assume will always be there. The secret to appreciating the Eucharist is to recognize how precious and powerful it is. I've heard it said that if we opened ourselves to all the graces available in Communion, receiving Him only once would be enough to perfect us. Believing this and approaching Communion as if it were one's *only* Communion would naturally heighten one's efforts to make the most of it.

We never know when our last day will come. We can prepare by receiving our Lord as if it were our First Communion, our last Communion, our only Communion.

Freshening up for the Deity

There's a reason First Communion outfits are white and dazzling. A white garment is a symbol of a purified soul, hence its use in Baptism too. While it's important to dress well for Mass, we should pay even more attention to our *soul's* "appearance". Just as no parent would bring a daughter to her Baptism or First Communion in a soiled dress, none of us should saunter up to receive Holiness Himself with a soiled soul. We should go as carefully through life keeping our souls pure as a little girl protecting her pretty white dress on her big day. Fortunately, if we do stain our garment, we have in the confessional a terrific dry cleaner, which not only is *free* but can remove absolutely any stain: from little spots to whopping-big splotches.

Jesus was the first to use the image of attire to symbolize our spiritual state when coming to Mass. In the parable of the king's banquet, Jesus speaks of a guest not wearing a "wedding garment". The king asks him the reason; the guest gives none and is thrown out. This might not seem fair, since the king told his servants to invite everyone;[25] we might assume the man was too poor or didn't have time to change. However, Bible scholars have noted that ancient kings would supply wedding garments to those in need, just as certain fine restaurants keep extra neckties on hand. Hence the man's lack of proper attire is due, not to circumstances beyond his control, but to laziness, stubbornness, or indifference. He didn't respect the king enough to dress appropriately.

The point our Lord is making here is that everyone—bad or good, rich or poor—is invited to the feast, but it's important to come with the proper dispositions. All sinners are welcome, but we must also repent. We are, in fact too "poor" in our sinfulness and with our human limitations ever to deserve to come or dress properly. But if we ask, He'll take care of it. A superb way to prepare for Mass then is to utilize the Sacrament of Confession.

To make it a modern parable, imagine a young woman had the chance to meet her favorite celebrity. Wouldn't she try to make the best impression she could? If she were ready to go, and her mother stopped her, asking delicately if she had perchance "run out of deodorant ...?", wouldn't she dash back to her room and do something about it? Or if the young lady knew the celebrity's best friend, wouldn't she listen to his advice? If he said that her hero loathed peach-scented cologne, would she wear it anyway? I don't think so. We need this outlook when approaching the Eucharist. Could there be anyone more admirable or exciting to meet than God Himself? Yet we rarely give any thought to how we appear to Him. Many of us no longer try to please Him but take His unconditional love for granted.

Ironically, we *do* know His best friend on earth, and she happens also to be our own Mother: the Church. We could have the "inside scoop" on what is pleasing to the Number One VIP in the Universe, but we refuse to listen to her. Too often we treat her as a nosy busybody, when actually she is an immortal queen, ancient yet ever-young, full of wisdom. No one on earth knows better than she what pleases Christ, having been His confidante for two thousand years. So if *she* says we

[25] See Mt 22:1–14.

need the cleansing of Confession, let's get it. And if she says the King of the Universe wants us at His banquet every Sunday, let's not miss it for the world.

Enhancing Your Worship

Something else you can do is *act* prayerful, even if you don't feel it. Act as if you believe, and belief will follow. Some might deem this "phony", but it won't be if your intentions are right. If you act contrary to how you feel *in order to* deceive, trick, or impress someone, then it's a sham. But if you want to feel something, then acting accordingly will help the feelings develop. Putting what you want to believe into practice also promotes greater faith. This happens both on a natural level and on a supernatural level, for the Lord rewards a step in faith with more faith. "If you want a quality, act as if you already had it. Try the 'as if' technique", recommends philosopher and psychologist William James.[26] Similarly, going to Mass more often and with a humble, open heart will allow you to receive more and more of the graces the Lord desires to give you. Over time, those graces will build.

Learn about the Mass: what is going on and why. Understanding the structure, history, and significance of the Mass makes a big difference. In addition to what is listed below in "Recommended Works", the "Prologue" and "The Mass" in Matthew Kelly's *Rediscover Catholicism* are great reads.

Preparing for Mass is also invaluable. Looking over or meditating on the Scripture readings ahead of time can help you listen and get more out of them. Get there early. You need time to disengage from the myriad things bouncing around in your brain, all the stimuli you've been taking in and the problems you're trying to solve. You need some silence to enter into this encounter with eternity. Give the Lord your concerns, tell Him what you're sorry for and for what intentions you would like to offer the Mass. Ask Mother Mary to help you pray the Mass well.

---

[26]William James is widely quoted as saying this, though no one bothers to cite *where* he said it. However, he wrote something in the same vein in *Principles of Psychology*, vol. 2 (New York: Henry Holt, 1913), p. 321. C.S. Lewis advised something similar on the topic of loving God or others when we don't *feel* loving: "Act as if you did. Do not sit trying to manufacture feelings.... When you are behaving as if you loved someone, you will presently come to love him." *Mere Christianity* (San Francisco: Harper, 2002), pp. 132, 131.

During Mass, don't just show up like a spectator. The Second Vatican Council's encouragement of "active participation" for the laity doesn't mean becoming an usher or acolyte; it means we should engage, join in, participate. That in turn means listening, praying, singing, etc. When the priest is praying on our behalf, follow along with the missalette or your own missal.

You may have heard that, as members of Christ, we have a share in His being Priest, Prophet, and King. Though not the ministerial priesthood, our priesthood also has a role at Mass: we too can offer sacrifice since we are to offer ourselves with Christ. During the Offertory, imagine yourself lying on the paten with Jesus, offering God your whole life, your whole self. When the priest pours a little water into the chalice with the wine, that represents not only the Incarnation, God becoming man, but also our little sacrifices—a few drops—added to Christ's Blood. This is when we can formally offer Him the sacrifices we've made for love of God since our last Mass.[27]

Imagine

It's extremely easy to find fault with any Mass—whether it is an aspect in which you have some expertise or simply your preference. There's a tremendous value in striving for good liturgy, but bad liturgy should never keep us from coming. Neither the homily nor any other human contribution to the Mass is at all important compared to Christ's. *His* part, while much harder to perceive, is always there, always potent, and always perfect. If we want to appreciate all God is offering us in the Mass and enter into the worship, we must let go of all that bothers us at Mass—whether it's something happening up in the sanctuary or in our pew, we must develop the ability to focus instead on the spiritual realities. This may require closing our eyes at times and concentrating on what's being said or on God during the silence. It may require reading along in the missal. It will require repeated prayers for heavenly assistance. And it requires our imagination.

---

[27] A wonderful way to prepare for Mass is to gather gifts beforehand. In *King of the Golden City*, a sweet allegory written in 1921, a little girl named Dilecta is visited by the King in her hut in the woods. She prepares by gathering flowers and decorating her hut and even the pathway to it. Though Dilecta is poor, she can still please a king. Similarly, countless little sacrifices are within our reach each day; we too can gather loving acts and decorate our souls for His visit to us in Communion.

Imagination is a wonderful gift from God that is misunderstood, forgotten, or improperly utilized in our day. On the one hand, so much is presented to us through visual media that we hardly need to use our imagination anymore. On the other, we're tempted to use it in the wrong way: to imagine confronting an aggravating person or for selfish or illicit fantasies of all kinds. Exercising your imagination in your spiritual life is a *much* better use of it.

When we're at Mass, we are not alone. We are with the angels and saints in heaven as they worship the Lord. They are around us. You can't see them, but you can close your eyes and picture them. That use of the imagination is actually not a fantasy but is helping you grasp a reality. You can imagine your late grandmother sitting next to you at Mass. Our departed loved ones are surely near us, nearer there, in fact, than anywhere else. You can imagine Jesus appearing on the altar at the words of Consecration—again, something you cannot see but is real.

Or imagine you're in Bethlehem on that great night so long ago. Picture the shepherds kneeling in awe, one perhaps kissing the tiny baby's hand reverently, while the tiny fingers curl around his hardened thumb. Or the wise men, splendidly dressed, yet lying prostrate before the manger. Imagine the townspeople unexpectedly having the chance to see Him up close: they wouldn't wait their turn apathetically, looking around at their neighbors or off into space, and then saunter over to the Infant and tap His little hand like workers clocking in a time-card.

Or imagine a time machine took you to the foot of the Cross. Picture yourself beside Mary on her knees there or Mary Magdalen kissing His feet.

We do in fact go to Bethlehem and Golgotha every time we attend Mass. We are actually more privileged than the shepherds or the women who witnessed the events there. We can do more than kiss His little hand or pierced foot—we receive Him into our own bodies. A non-Catholic once said he didn't think Catholics actually believed in the Real Presence. "If I believed what you Catholics say you believe, I wouldn't *walk* up the aisle—I'd crawl on my belly!"[28]

How often have you and I gone sleepwalking up to the altar, received mindlessly, ambled down the aisle, and plopped into a pew? We need

[28] This story is recounted in different ways; see, for instance, "The Presence of the Lord in the Eucharist", by Vic Biorseth, http://www.catholicamericanthinker.com/Eucharist.html (accessed Dec. 1, 2015).

to wake up and realize what we're doing and whom we are receiving. May He open our eyes and help us experience the absolute awe and gratitude we ought. Using our imagination will not only help us concentrate on what we should but also touch our hearts and blow on the coals of our love as well.

Conclusion

When we come to understand the tremendous gift the Mass is, it's easy to see that going once a week really is the minimum. We usually feed our bodies at least twenty times more often. Don't our souls deserve more than the paltry nourishment we typically dole out?

The Mass is God's supreme gift of love and our best chance to please Him with a gift. If we love Him, shouldn't we concern ourselves with what pleases Him most? If Jesus dropped hints of God's love language and the Church has discovered what He likes best, all those who love Him will be glad to learn what is tops with Him. Not only is the Mass His chief gift of love to *us*, it is at the top of His wish list: what He sees as the greatest gift of love to Him.

The value of the Mass can't be overstated. It's much too precious to ration to Sundays only. If you want to make a difference in your life and the world, get to Mass as often as you can.

9

FACE TIME WITH GOD

Spending time in "adoration" (as it's often called) before the Blessed Sacrament is not most people's idea of fun. We feel this way because we don't realize what adoration is.

Rendezvous with a God

One feels silly going out to meet someone who doesn't appear to be there. I know; I once literally did that.

It all started one day in fourth grade. I was gathering my homework only to discover—of all things!—a love note. It was the most thrilling moment of my young life.

A few seconds later, though, I was filled with doubt. Could this be some sort of cruel prank? I had been picked on since second grade by a former friend and her followers. But then I heard that another girl had also received a love note, in a different hand. What was going on?

After we each had received several notes, we came to the conclusion that they were authentic. I began to keep mine in a box marked "Precious".

Then one day our secret admirers invited us to a rendezvous. (The plot thickens!) We were to meet where they could hide behind a fence overgrown with bushes. We were not to try to find out who they were; it was just a chance to talk.

My friend and I duly came, and, after a little while, we began to wonder again if this was a prank, because nothing happened. We felt like fools, standing there talking to the bushes. We began to suspect that no one was really there. At last, when we talked about leaving, we heard some rustling, assuring us that indeed there was someone (or two) unseen listening to us.

For the unbeliever, prayer is as foolish as talking to the air. But even the believer can find going to a church to meet Someone hidden to be like my fourth-grade experience. God invites us to meet Him, then He hides Himself and often doesn't say anything. We can feel as silly talking to Him, who makes no sign of His presence, as I felt that day talking to the shrubbery.

Borrowing an approach from J.R.R. Tolkien and C.S. Lewis, I would say the ancient Greek myth of Psyche and Cupid sheds light on this mystery of God hiding Himself. Psyche (which means "soul", incidentally) was married to someone who claimed he was a god but would never let her see his face. She lived in his palace, surrounded by luxury and servants, but without *him*, at least during the day. He would come to her only in the dead of night and forbade her ever to light a lamp. Her jealous sisters said this was because he was not really a god but a hideous monster. She didn't believe them, but when taunted that she was afraid they were right, she agreed to find out. That night, after her husband was asleep, she lit a candle. What she saw entranced her: the gloriously handsome god of love.

We are like Psyche when we don't comprehend how glorious the Lord is because we can't see Him and find it hard to take Him at His word. But we can learn from Psyche's story. We can choose to believe. We can stir up our love by trying to imagine Him. Theologians say the reason God does not visibly appear to us in all His glory is because He is so wonderful, so perfectly what our hearts desire that we would have no choice but to love Him; our freedom would be lost. So on this side of heaven, we must try to realize how wonderful He is and how marvelous His rendezvous invitation is. We can also learn from the many tales of a ruler who disguises himself to see who his real friends are. Jesus is a King who hides Himself in the Eucharist and waits in the tabernacle to see who loves and believes Him enough to come visit Him.

The One who invites us to meet Him is indeed the God of Love. He is more irresistible than we can imagine, yet He loves and longs for each of us. He too yearns for the day when we'll see Him face to face; in the meantime, He wants us to do the next best thing. Fortunately, He occasionally breaks through our blindness and deafness. If we persevere and prove our faithfulness, we'll catch the rustle of His presence or the whispered sweet somethings we need to hear.

Why Pray in His Presence?

It Delights Him

Why go to church or a chapel with the Blessed Sacrament? Why can't I just pray at home?

The main reason is because it speaks tomes of love to Him. "Of all devotions, that of adoring Jesus in the Blessed Sacrament is the greatest after the sacraments, the one dearest to God and the one most helpful to us."[1] Jesus made it clear in Gethsemane that the presence of His friends brought Him comfort.[2] He is human, remember, and likes to be with those He loves too. Texting, phone calls, and Skype are all nice, but they don't compete with being together.

Jesus manifests an even greater love for us by being there too. He humbles Himself to become our food and in waiting in the tabernacle or monstrance[3] in the hope that we'll come and visit Him. He's called the "Prisoner of Love", for He's chosen to imprison Himself thus for us. This is the one corporal work of mercy we can perform directly for Jesus: visit the imprisoned.[4]

It Helps Us

Angels have no problem adoring God. They love it. It poses no difficulty for them; it is the fulfillment of their being.

We're no angels though. And we never will be. I can say that confidently about us all, even without knowing you personally. That's because this isn't about holiness. Nor is it a lack of hope. It's about species. I can say just as confidently that we are not cats.

Angels are pure spirits. They have a mind and a will, as we do, but no bodies. True, sometimes they appear in human form, but that's a temporary disguise, so to speak, not a permanent incarnation. Human beings, however, are what Pope St. John Paul II called "embodied

---

[1] St. Alphonsus Liguori, *Visite al SS. Sacramento e a Maria Santissima*, introduction: *Opere Ascetiche* (Avellino, 2000), p. 295; quoted in Pope St. John Paul II, Encyclical Letter *Ecclesia de Eucharistia* on the Eucharist in Its Relationship to the Church (April 17, 2003), no. 25.

[2] See Mt 26:38; Mk 14:34.

[3] A *monstrance* (from *monstrare*, "to show") is an ornate receptacle, often made of gold, with a glass center, behind which is a large consecrated Host. It's used in churches, chapels, and processions to allow the faithful to see and adore the Eucharistic Jesus.

[4] See Mt 25:31–46.

spirits". We have a mind, a will, an immortal soul, and a body. That's the way God made us, and it is very good.

Having a body is not without effects. We take in information through our senses, we have physical needs, and it is through the body that we express ourselves. So it naturally affects our prayer. Further, unlike the angels, we do not yet see God; we're fallen, spiritually crippled in a sense, and still on the journey. So when we try to pray, we have to deal with temptations, distractions, emotions, and physical conditions like hunger, sleepiness, pain, or restlessness. This is why, on the one hand, adoration is more difficult for us but, on the other, why it is so good for us.

This is why the Church uses sense-*ible* things like candles, incense, music, stained glass, and beautiful images of God, His saints, and heroic acts in salvation history: to assist our efforts to worship Him. It's a good idea to support our prayer physically as much as we can. In a quiet, dim place, there are fewer sounds and sights to distract us. And we can use that body to express our prayer: kneeling to show humility, sorrow, adoration. Sitting to listen, contemplate, and receive His love. Standing to worship (or to wake yourself up). When alone or with someone who won't be inconvenienced, puzzled, or distracted by it, you can even lie prostrate—sometimes it's simply the best posture for what you're expressing to God. Posture matters.

Place matters too. Gnostic voices in our culture will deny that, but it is obviously true. We don't hold dances in graveyards, but we do erect memorials at battle sites and transform the homes of famous people into museums. Being in the place where something important happened is meaningful to us. Yes, we can pray anywhere, and it won't lessen the prayer's efficacy when we pray wherever we can. But it also helps *us* to pray in a special place. A shrine, place of pilgrimage, or sites in the Holy Land can make spiritual truths come alive in our hearts; it's easier to feel them and realize them on a deeper level when we're there in person.

And so, since we are embodied and affected by physicality, and since Jesus became man and remains an embodied human, and since He keeps His promise to stay with us always,[5] in the Eucharist, then there is no better place for us to pray than in His physical, Eucharistic presence.

[5] See Mt 28:20.

Overcoming Difficulties

An Acquired Taste

I must have been one of the finickiest kids in history; I didn't even like pizza. (I think dinner with me was a big trial for my stepmother, Cheryl, a terrific gourmet cook.) My dad used to say my taste buds would mature someday but that some things, like wine, were an acquired taste. Later my parents and sister jumped on the health-food bandwagon, and my dad eventually gave up all forms of refined sugar. Though as a young adult I ate a wider range of foods and tried to be healthy, I never thought I could go that far. But middle age brings new challenges, and now my diet is healthier than I ever expected. And the interesting thing is that my taste buds *have* adjusted. The girl whose favorite food was Captain Crunch has become a woman who now finds raisins an intensely sweet treat and enjoys vegetables. It's the same with exercise: when you first start, it's dreadful, but if you persevere, you find that you come to need it; you desire it. And so with the spiritual life. Our fallen nature rebels against every new spiritual habit we strive to acquire. It just seems too hard. But if we persist and push past those feelings, we gradually acquire a taste for what we once found repugnant and come to like it, need it.

Adoring our Lord in the Blessed Sacrament is an acquired joy. One usually doesn't feel the benefits right away. At least I began noticing them much more once I was going regularly. Numerous times I've entered the adoration chapel in distress, depression, discouragement, or overwhelming weariness and walked out in peace, with renewed confidence in God and in His working in my life and with new insights and solutions. This is completely different from an "opiate" or any comfort the world has to offer. Drugs—whether recreational or prescription— might improve mood, but they can never give the peace that only the Prince of Peace bestows. Escapes and pleasures are fleeting and superficial. They cannot provide real hope or spiritual strength. But sitting before the throne of God can.

Being There

Some hesitate to come to adoration as they have small children or problems with concentration.

Years ago, a priest friend of ours instituted weekly adoration, and I was trying to attend. I had just two little ones back then, but they were still quite a handful. I remember on one occasion barely having any time to pray: I was just bouncing the baby and fixing things for the preschooler. I wondered if I should bother coming anymore: What was the point?

Then the Lord nudged a thought my way: it was good for us to be there even if I couldn't concentrate. It didn't matter if the girls were clueless about who was there and why we were. They were in His presence, and that had to be good. It had to be good for me too, even if I had little time to pray. In God's presence, we had to be soaking in graces. We were Son-bathing.

Benefits of Adoration

Tremendous benefits come from adoring the Lord in the Blessed Sacrament.

First are the graces. Pope St. John Paul II calls adoration "an inexhaustible source of holiness", through which we "make contact with the very wellspring of grace".[6]

We also gain new insights from the Lord, and our parched souls are refreshed. "Theological insights are gained not only from between two covers of a book, but from two knees before an altar. [Adoration is] like an oxygen tank to revive the breath of the Holy Spirit in the midst of the foul and fetid atmosphere of the world."[7]

Adoring the Lord also benefits the Church, in part due to its connection to vocations. Seminarians are much more likely to come from parishes with perpetual adoration chapels, or at least weekly or occasional adoration. "The *worship of the Eucharist* ... is of inestimable value for the life of the Church."[8] Adoration is also a wonderful opportunity to help someone else and a true act of love. Many chapels supply greeting cards that you can give to the person for whom you prayed. People are often very touched by such a gift.

Best of all is the chance to spend time with our beloved Lord and grow closer to Him. Padre Pio said: "A thousand years of enjoying human glory

---

[6] John Paul II, *Ecclesia de Eucharistia, Eucharist in Relationship to the Church*, nos. 10, 25.

[7] Rev. Fulton J. Sheen, "The Hour That Makes My Day", in *Mornings with Fulton Sheen*, compiled by Beverly Coney Heirich (Ann Arbor, Mich.: Servant Publications, 1997), p. 15.

[8] John Paul II, *Ecclesia de Eucharistia, Eucharist in Relationship to the Church*, no. 25.

is not worth even an hour spent in sweetly communing with Jesus in the Blessed Sacrament."[9] And Pope St. John Paul II noted: "It is pleasant to spend time with him, to lie close to his breast like the Beloved Disciple ... and to feel the infinite love present in his heart.... How often ... have I experienced this, and drawn from it strength, consolation and support!"[10]

Most pertinent to our quest is the chance to show our love to God. If prayer in general is a battle, if it takes extra effort to get to a chapel, if our fallen nature rebels at the idea,... and we go *anyway*, it's a terrific testimony of love for Him and to Him.

> Dear souls, why this coldness and indifference on your part? ... Do I not know that family cares ... and the requirements of your position in life ... make continual calls upon you?... But cannot you spare a few minutes ... to visit and receive this Prisoner of Love! ...
>
> Were you weak or ill in body, surely you would find time to see a doctor who would cure you? Come, then, to One who is able to give both strength and health to your soul, and ... [who] watches for you, calls for you, and longs to see you at His side.
>
> —JESUS (TO SR. JOSEFA MENENDEZ)
>
> BOX 16

Additional Ways to Connect with Jesus in the Eucharist

Besides Mass and adoration, there are other ways to connect with Jesus in the Eucharist.

One is to drop by for a brief visit. Venerable Jean Jacques Olier planned his day thus: "When there are two roads which will bring me to some place, I take the one with more churches, so as to be nearer the Blessed Sacrament."[11] St. Robert Bellarmine dropped by to visit Jesus on his way to and from school. St. Monica, mother of St. Augustine, visited Jesus every morning and evening.[12]

If we can't stop in, we can still show our love and faith in His Real Presence by acknowledging Him when passing a church. Because public

---

[9] Quoted in Stefano Manelli, F.F.I., *Jesus, Our Eucharistic Love* (New Bedford, Mass.: Academy of the Immaculate, 1996), p. 84.

[10] John Paul II, *Ecclesia de Eucharistia, Eucharist in Its Relationship of the Church*, no. 25, citing Jn 13:25.

[11] Manelli, *Jesus, Our Eucharistic Love*, p. 74.

[12] Ibid., pp. 74, 75.

devotions have become uncommon, it can take some courage to adopt them. When I first started, I found myself in an awkward situation. Seated on a bus across from someone I had just met, I saw St. Dominic's Church coming up behind her. I thought it might seem rude if I signed myself while she was speaking. But then she put me to shame by pausing in mid-sentence and solemnly making the sign of the cross. I was impressed with her total unconcern about what others thought. I also realized that my hesitation showed a lack of deep faith. How would I behave if I *fully* believed that He was there?

The other option is to make a spiritual communion. This means inviting Jesus into your heart and communing with Him for a few moments. The beauty of this is that we can do it anywhere, anytime. According to St. Catherine of Siena, the Lord likens sacramental Communion to gold and spiritual communion to silver.[13]

There are a number of prayers of spiritual communion.[14] Or, of course, you can compose something yourself. For example: "Dear Jesus, thank You so much for the precious gift of Yourself in the Eucharist. I long to receive You. Please come to me in a spiritual communion. Thank You, Lord. Help me rest in Your Sacred Heart. Unite Your Heart to mine. Live in me and love through me; enable me to live in You now and forever."

Before returning to heaven, Jesus promised: "I am with you always."[15] He keeps that promise literally and physically in the Eucharist. With all the ways to encounter Him—Mass, adoration, visits, spiritual communions—a simple and superb way to express your love to Him is, in some way, to make every day a Eucharistic day.

2♥ 2♥ 2♥

Spending time with God is to return His love. One who truly seeks to know Him and please Him better must spend time with Him. He "does not give Himself wholly until He *sees that* we are giving ourselves wholly to Him."[16]

---

[13] Ibid., p. 62.

[14] Perhaps the best known is this: "My Jesus, I believe that You are present in the Most Holy Sacrament. I love You above all things, and I desire to receive You into my soul. Since I cannot at this moment receive You sacramentally, come at least spiritually into my heart. I embrace You as if You were already there and unite myself wholly to You. Never permit me to be separated from You. Amen."

[15] Mt 28:20.

[16] St. Teresa of Avila, *The Way of Perfection* (New York: Image Books, 2004), p. 180.

SECTION THREE

LOVING GOD MEANS OBEYING HIM

*"He who has my commandments and keeps them,
he it is who loves me."*

(Jn 14:21)

"If you love me, you will keep my commandments."

(Jn 14:15)

10

THE ODIOUS O-WORD

Of the vows taken by priests and religious, most people would probably consider celibacy the toughest to live out. Influenced by Freud, the secular mind tends to think lifelong celibacy would leave one mentally unhinged. Even for many believers, the idea of giving up a spouse and family for a lifetime seems too hard. Then, our materialistic culture would view the second vow taken by those in religious orders—poverty—as a serious hardship too. The whole vocation idea having already been dismissed, countless people don't ever think about the other vow all priests and religious take, namely, obedience. But according to many living these vows, *obedience* is the real kicker. Upon consideration, it makes sense. Really, the hardest thing to give up is one's will.

Modern culture has little esteem for obedience, admiring instead independence, self-assertiveness, even defiance. Consider how many movies glorify someone who bucks authority (parent, boss, government) and is proven in the end to be right and heroic to have done so.

We don't like people telling us what to do. Not even God.

Freedom

Our age prizes freedom, especially in America, given our country's origins. But we misunderstand the word. We think freedom means doing what we want, as long as we don't hurt anyone else. While the *Catechism of the Catholic Church* describes freedom as the power "to act or not to act", it also points out that exercising freedom "does not imply a right to say or do everything."[1] Flouting laws and rules does not usually result in greater freedom, but it can land you in prison. Real freedom comes from an altogether different quarter. "The more one does what

[1] *CCC* 1731, 1740.

is good, the freer one becomes....The choice to disobey and do evil is
an abuse of freedom and leads to 'the slavery of sin'."[2]

Having free will means God doesn't treat us like marionettes; no
puppet strings make us do His will. He wants us to do it freely. But we
can refuse. We are free to disobey, to go against God's ways. But that
doesn't make it a good choice. The moral law is not like choosing
between strawberry ice cream and coffee ice cream. There is a difference between right and wrong.

To live in the Kingdom of God is to acknowledge God as King. If
we don't want to obey Him, we're free to walk away. No one *has* to
live in the Kingdom of God. If we live outside His realm, we may find
that nothing terrible seems to happen to us—at least at first. We don't
realize we're still enjoying some protection from the nearby castle. But
once that drawbridge goes up and we have no way to cross back over
the moat, we realize the danger of the dark wilderness.

Sadly, it is like the tragic plight of many children running away from
home: instead of finding freedom, they fall into the hands of evil people
who enslave them. The difference is that our heavenly Father is perfect
and His love is infinite, so there's never a good reason to run away.
Moreover, God is the Source of all Goodness. Outside His Kingdom,
there is no chance of finding someone good who will truly help us. In
the afterlife, there is no "neutral" place where we can enjoy good things
without God. Only in this life can we temporarily enjoy His gifts while
shunning Him. He is the source of goodness; if we cut ourselves off from
Him in eternity, we cut ourselves off from every other good as well.

So it is obedience to God that actually leads to greater freedom. It
strengthens us, whereas wrongdoing weakens our will and enslaves us
to pleasure, impulse, or feelings. Olympic athletes reach the pinnacle
of excellence, not by late-night partying, but by listening to the coach
and getting enough rest, good nutrition, and boatloads of practice; those
who obey become free to excel. Similarly, obeying God makes us stronger and able to do greater good. God's ways set us free:

> Your word is a lamp to my feet
>   and a light to my path....
> I shall walk at liberty,
>   for I have sought your precepts....

[2] *CCC* 1733, quoting Rom 6:17.

> Great peace have those who love your law;
>   nothing can make them stumble....
> I will run in the way of your commandments
>   when you enlarge my understanding![3]

Obeying God enables us not only to walk confidently, but even to run; it is the key to freedom.

Obedience to God isn't servile compliance to a tyrant; it is a loving response to a generous Father. Loving parents don't want frightened servants; they hope their children will return their love. God has given us free will so we can freely choose to do what is good and right. Our freedom includes the capacity—not the permission—to choose evil. God hopes we will choose Him. Obeying our Heavenly Father sets us free to be all we're meant to be—*like Him.*

What Does Obedience Have to Do with Love?

When we see warning stickers such as, "Caution! Serious head injury or death may occur. Always use child-restraint strap" or "Do not immerse in water—risk of fatal electrical shock!" we don't think, "Well, who do they think they are? How dare they tell me what to do or impinge on my freedom?" No, we realize the goal of these instructions is protecting our health and lives and those of our loved ones. God's rules are like that. They are for our good; they are like mankind's operating instructions. He made us after all. He knows what is good or bad for us.

We don't always like God's rules, though. A major reason for this is the concupiscence (inclination toward sin) we inherited from Adam and Eve. Another is pride, that tendency underlying so many of our sins. To listen to God, to obey Him, takes humility. It means acknowledging that He knows better than we do and so we should listen to Him.

Obedience requires us to be childlike and trust He's got our best interests at heart. Like any good parent, the Father gives His children rules, not for His sake, but for our sake. A mother who forbids sticking a knife in an outlet or playing in the street made those rules for her kids' own good. She's trying to keep them alive. God's rules are the same: forbidding what could seriously injure or kill us. The Ten

[3] Ps 119:105, 45, 165, 32.

Commandments tell us what we need to do and to avoid in order to stay alive—spiritually alive. His laws are neither arbitrary nor mean; they're necessary for the soul's survival. Jesus' additional commands teach us, not just how to survive, but how to thrive.

Waywardness is dangerous ... like a bog. Bogs can be "green pleasant places to look at, with flowers growing bright and tall", Tolkien said; "but a pony that walked there ... would never ... come out again."[4] In the same way, souls are ensnared by sin. This is why even lesser sins are dangerous. Like Tolkien's pony, if we stray from the Way, even just to nibble a nearby treat, we might take a step farther and then another after tasty flora, until we end up trapped in something pulling us ever downward. Even a little disobedience can lead to a lot of trouble.

How Do We Know God's Laws?

While the Fall and sin have darkened our minds and God doesn't speak audibly to 99.9 percent of us, He hasn't left us rudderless; He has given us means to learn His ways.

Natural Law

First, God has written His law on our hearts.[5] The "natural law" provides essential principles and steers us to the good and away from evil. It is "present in the heart of each man and established by reason, is universal in its precepts and its authority extends to all men".[6] The natural law, then, forms the foundation of individual consciences and good civil law.

Unfortunately, natural law is not sufficient to guide an individual or to establish a just society. "The precepts of natural law are not perceived by everyone clearly and immediately."[7] There's obviously still a lot of disagreement about what is moral and immoral.

Conscience

Another way God enlightens us about what He wants us to do or not to do is something He has planted within each of us: our conscience.

---

[4] J. R. R. Tolkien, *The Hobbit* (New York: Random House, 2013), p. 47.
[5] See Rom 2:15.
[6] *CCC* 1956; cf. also 1955.
[7] *CCC* 1960.

The Fathers of Vatican II described the conscience as man's "most secret core.... There he is alone with God, Whose voice echoes in his depths".[8]

A gift from God, conscience is a power of the soul that judges whether an action is right or wrong. It's a power over which we have only partial control, like our lungs. We can slow our breathing or hold our breath, but only for so long. We can harm our lungs by smoking or breathing polluted air, or we can build our lungs with exercise and healthy living. Similarly, we can harm or help our conscience. We can refuse to educate it, darken it by sin, ignore it, weaken it, and drown it out, but we can't *quite* kill it. The natural law contains the first principles used by conscience, but if we have the opportunity, we must further educate our conscience.

Conscience is a key link to God. It's like a radio tuned to the Heavenly Station. But an element of freedom is the capacity to interfere with the reception. When we first sin, we can usually hear the disapproval of conscience pretty clearly. But we have a choice as to how we'll respond. We can repent, or we can try to stifle the voice of conscience. We can turn down the volume; repeating a sin will naturally do that. We can even try to turn that radio off altogether.

Hearing conscience properly is also dependent on how well we are tuned in. When we don't like what we're hearing, we often try to change the channel. There are a whole host of competing voices out there, trying to influence us. But we can't get too far away from the central, Heavenly Station—we can always kind of hear it, as when a radio is tuned between two stations and both are heard simultaneously.

Conscience is something we're simply given—we didn't ask for it or find it or create it ourselves: it's a part of us like an ear, but its development can be affected. A child raised by thieves, for instance, can be taught that it's wrong only to steal from one's own family. And we ourselves can affect how well conscience works and what shape it takes; thus, we are responsible for forming it properly.[9] Since we're all tempted to "prefer [our] own judgment and to reject authoritative teachings", the *Catechism* says, "the education of conscience is indispensable."[10]

---

[8] Second Vatican Council, Pastoral Constitution on the Church in the Modern World *Gaudium et Spes* (December 7, 1965), no. 16.

[9] "Conscience must be informed and moral judgment enlightened" (*CCC* 1783).

[10] *CCC* 1783.

How does one rightly form one's conscience? The natural law, alone, cannot address every situation.[11] We can look to others for guidance, but we need to be careful here too since social groups or even whole cultures can collectively blind themselves and drown out the voice of Truth. How can we optimize our "radio" reception of the Heavenly Channel?

> The education of the conscience is a lifelong task.
>
> — *CCC* 1784[Box 17]

One reason Jesus came was to solve this dilemma.

Revelation

Thankfully, God did not leave us on our own when mankind's first parents plunged themselves and their descendants into the darkness of original sin. Instead, He reached out to us, sending His Word to reveal His ways. First He taught through the Prophets, but eventually He came in person. Teaching us, living among us, dying for us, rising again, He brought Light, Truth, and the invitation and the means to come home. But then He went back to heaven.

Jesus did not leave us orphans though. He promised to be with His people and guide us. How does He guide us when new theological or moral questions arise? He didn't write a book. (He did later provide one, through the Church under the Holy Spirit's inspiration, but it doesn't answer every new question.) Instead, He gave a Church and the Holy Spirit to guide her.[12]

Heaven's Agents on Earth

The need for such an authority is evident. Circumstances, ideas, and technologies change over time and must be met by a living Church. The principles of the Bible need to be interpreted and applied properly to each age's needs. We cannot rely on individuals' interpretations; that approach ends with as many "popes" as there are people on earth. Witness the fact that scads of new churches are established *each year*. They all differ in their teachings; they can't all be right. Thus each era needs a living, audible interpreter, authorized by God and hence trustworthy.

---

[11] Cf. *CCC* 1787.

[12] See Mt 16:18–19; 18:17–18; Lk 10:16; Jn 14:16–17, 25–26; 16:12–14.

But Jesus didn't leave us thousands of competing churches. He left us *one* Church, with established stewards and the promised guidance of the Holy Spirit, so we could know His will in these matters. When it comes to forming our consciences, we have a reliable guide.

God Wants Me to Obey Them?

After decades of theologians like Charles Curran asserting we could form our own consciences without the Church, many Catholics were already balking at the idea of heeding the guidance of her Magisterium (the official teachings of the pope and bishops united with him). That disinclination to obey the Church rocketed at the turn of the millennium with the scandal of ephebophile[13] priests and the blunders of some bishops in dealing with them. At that point, quite a few Catholics decided not merely to stop listening to the hierarchy but to leave the Church altogether. Then came the scandals of the summer of 2018 (still unfolding as I write).[14] Many people then would ask, *Why should I obey the leaders of the Church?*

As someone who knows too well the horrible and lasting harm molestation can cause, I am the last person to minimize sexual abuse. I also understand the feelings of anger, scandal, betrayal, and utter bewilderment such incidents can cause, for I was devastated when a priest whom I loved and admired was later convicted of abusing a schoolmate of mine during high school.

That certain bishops didn't handle offending priests well is also a serious transgression. Decades ago, it was thought that treatment could cure such a person, so there was some naïveté going on there; still to send him back to a ministry with access to the young was grossly irresponsible. The fact that Theodore McCarrick was promoted at all, let alone to the rank of cardinal, is alarming and likely despicable on the part of some.

To be angry and dismayed over these things is natural and just. Clearly, serious reforms are needed. The best response for Catholics is

---

[13] Sociologist Philip Jenkins points out that the majority of cases of sexual abuse by Catholic priests actually involved teenaged boys (ephebophilia) rather than children (pedophilia); see, e.g., his *Priests and Pedophiles* (Oxford: Oxford University Press, 1996).

[14] In reaction to the Pennsylvania Grand Jury Report, several states have announced they will be opening their own investigations into Catholic dioceses, with more very likely to follow. Links to my Sept., Nov., and Dec. 2018 articles on related topics can be found on my blog at https://where-the-rubber-hits-the-road blogspot.com/.

to channel our anger into helping the Church through this recovery—first by our prayers and sacrifices, as well as by discerning what else God wants us do; many lay Catholics have already stepped up to help in various ways.

However, it's also important to realize a few points.

First, God asks us to obey the pope and bishops only insofar as they are truly His representatives and fulfill their responsibilities to guard and pass on Jesus' teachings as handed on by the apostles, as well as interpreting them as needed *in line with the Magisterial teachings* throughout the Church's history. They're not supposed to change teaching to suit their own whims. If they do, we are not obliged to obey them (more on this below). Nor should the Church be *equated* with the clergy; religious and lay Catholics also *are* the Church and thus also responsible for her. While the majority of bishops fell into error during the Arian crisis, for example, it was the laity who held on to authentic teaching and helped bring the hierarchy back on board.

Secondly, we have to keep in mind that, while truly horrible, the crimes revealed in the Pennsylvania Grand Jury Report peaked in the 1970s and mostly took place before 2002. At this point, at the end of 2018, indications are that, despite McCarrick's promotions and misconduct in the meantime, the measures taken in 2002 to protect minors from predatory clerics, church staff, and volunteers have been successful in preventing most such abuse from happening again. Yes, we still have work to do: our goals must be to bring the number of instances down to zero; we also need to make bishops and cardinals accountable as well and to crack down on serial sexual misconduct in the clergy.

We also must realize that the secular media often do not tell the whole story. Sociologist Philip Jenkins (not a Catholic himself) notes the problem has not only been in the Catholic Church, but also in other faiths and at even higher rates among teachers and coaches.[15] Chris Stefanick put it well: "There were nine credible allegations of child abuse in 2013, out of about 40,000 U.S. priests. That percentage is lower than virtually every other profession that serves children. Of course one case of abuse is too many. Inexcusable. But nine don't sum up the character

---

[15] See Philip Jenkins, *The New Anti-Catholicism: The Last Acceptable Prejudice* (Oxford: Oxford University Press, 2003); see chap. 7, esp. pp. 144 and 148.

of tens of thousands of good men."[16] Nor is it right to misrepresent what happened or to blackball the entire Catholic clergy.

Mary Eberstadt makes another important point: in the 1990s, the "enlightened" were speaking openly and approvingly of "adult-child sex".[17] Eberstadt suggests that when the priest scandal broke, the chance to castigate the Catholic Church was too tempting to pass up, so many of the same people who had treated pedophilia and ephebophilia as "chic" abandoned that stance to excoriate the Church. A surprising and substantial good coming from the priest scandal, then, is that such "enlightened" views are wholly unacceptable in society now.[18]

Other Hurts and Offenses

But these are not the only hurts and offenses people have endured from priests, bishops, and parish or diocesan staff. Fr. Thomas Berg postulates that many Catholics have been hurt in myriad ways, and many who have left the Church have done so as a result.[19]

This is a crying shame. It is tragic that those who have dedicated their lives to following Christ still hurt others, in contradiction to what they believe and the teachings of the Lord. But these unfortunate occurrences are not limited to Church authorities. Every member of the Church is a sinner, and each member should also cry in shame over those we have hurt and the ways we have failed to reflect the face of the Lord and live His teachings.

The fact that there have been in the history of the Church certain shepherds who themselves were seriously sinful is terrible, but not a surprise. Jesus knew it all too well ... in the kiss of Judas. And He warned us too of wolves in sheep's clothing, weeds among the wheat, and hired men who abandon the sheep.[20] But we mustn't let Judas keep us from

---

[16] Christopher Stefanick, "Priesthood" (text below the video; November 24, 2014), https://www.youtube.com/watch?v=xsD_esQoJ6E. See also his "Why Judas Didn't Shake the Faith of Peter", *Real Life Catholic*, http://reallifecatholic.com/portfolio-item/why-judas-didnt-shake-the-faith-of-peter/.

[17] See, e.g., Mary Eberstadt, "Pedophilia Chic", *Weekly Standard*, June 17, 1996, http://www.weeklystandard.com/pedophilia-chic/article/2623.

[18] Mary Eberstadt, *Adam and Eve after the Pill: Paradoxes of the Sexual Revolution* (San Francisco: Ignatius Press, 2012), p. 75.

[19] Fr. Thomas Berg, *Hurting in the Church: A Way Forward for Wounded Catholics* (Huntington, Ind.: Our Sunday Visitor, 2017), introduction.

[20] See Mt 7:15; Mt 13:24–40; Jn 10:12.

Jesus. Jesus is the Head and heart of the Church, which, remember, is His Body. Fr. Berg's book *Hurting in the Church: A Way Forward for Wounded Catholics* offers means to find healing.

Real Authority

Scandal and hurts are not the only obstacles to obeying the Church. After assimilating with an increasingly post-Christian culture influenced by centuries of Protestant and secular opposition to Church authority, many Catholics have only a vague idea that obedience is part of being a Catholic. As for the concept of infallibility, to many it sounds at best doubtful and at worst diabolical. Didn't the pope and bishops come up with this idea just to bolster their own power?

Well, actually, the idea goes back to the time of Jesus; in fact, it was Jesus Himself who came up with it. He made it very clear that authority in the Church is God-given and that He wants us to obey the Church's leaders when He said to His disciples, "He who hears you hears me, and he who rejects you rejects me, and he who rejects me rejects him who sent me."[21]

Consider also the commonly cited moment when Peter declared that Jesus was the Messiah, and Jesus in turn said, "you are Peter [*Kepha*], and on this rock [*kepha*] I will build my Church."[22] When you recall that Jesus also said it's wiser to build on rock than on sand, it becomes pretty significant when He builds something. The only time we hear Jesus speaking of building something Himself is here, and it is His Church. Not surprisingly, he builds her on rock. He picks the rock and points it out to everyone: Peter.[23] Using rock as a foundation secures the building; Peter, therefore, will provide solidity and security for the Church. (And not just Peter, but his successors as well. A foundation that ended in one lifetime wouldn't be terribly stable. Rather, we see in Scripture and accounts of the early Church Fathers that the apostles themselves

---

[21] Lk 10:16.

[22] Mt 16:18. Protestants often stress that the Greek terms used are *Petros* and *petra*, the former meaning "pebble" and the latter "rock" or "boulder". We have to keep in mind, though, that Matthew couldn't use *petra* as a name for Peter because it's feminine, so he used the masculine *Petros*. Moreover, Jesus didn't speak to His disciples in Greek, but in Aramaic. Thus, what Jesus actually said was *kepha*, the Aramaic word for "rock". The New Testament repeatedly calls Peter *Kepha* and *Cephas* (a Latinized version of *Kepha*); see Jn 1:42, Acts, 1 Corinthians, and Galatians.

[23] This would seem to imply that any church not built on *Kepha* is on shaky ground ...

recognized they were to appoint successors to replace themselves, and that need continues.)[24]

That Jesus is giving Peter a very special role in the Church is also clear when He gives Peter the "keys of the kingdom".[25] This signified that Peter held the role of steward or second-in-command in the Kingdom—an office similar to prime minister under a king. Both Isaiah and the Book of Revelation testify to the authority of the one to whom the king entrusts the key: "He shall open, and none shall shut; and he shall shut, and none shall open."[26] Jesus highlights Peter's special role as steward in Luke's Gospel. After Jesus likens being prepared for the Second Coming to servants awaiting their master's return, Peter asks, "Lord, are you telling this parable for us or for all?" Jesus' reply is very personal, as if to say, "You better believe this applies to you, Peter. In fact, your responsibility is even greater." The Lord says, "Who then is the faithful and wise *steward*, whom his master will set over his household, to give them their portion of food at the proper time?" And He goes on to describe what would happen if Peter or his successors, the future stewards, were to abuse the authority of their position.[27]

Further, Christ told Peter alone and later all the Twelve: "whatever you bind on earth shall be bound in heaven, and whatever you loose on earth shall be loosed in heaven."[28] How could He say such a thing if it were possible for the Church to err in religious matters? He would not make binding in heaven any Church law that was contrary to divine law. He could say it because God Himself was going to be the guarantor of their teaching. He had a plan for protecting the Church from error in matters of faith and morals; He revealed it at the Last Supper. "I have yet many things to say to you, but you cannot bear them now", He said, but promised the apostles (the first pope and bishops) that "the Spirit of truth ... will guide you into all the truth."[29]

In addition to this promise of guidance for the Church by the Holy Spirit, Christ also made it clear that Church authority comes from God and is to be respected as such. Even of the Pharisees, He had said, "The

[24] See, for instance, Acts 1:12–26. Consider also that entire epistles in the Bible were addressed to bishops appointed by Paul, giving them instruction: the First and Second Letters to Timothy and the Letter to Titus.

[25] Mt 16:19.

[26] Is 22:22; cf. Rev 3:7.

[27] Lk 12:41–42, 45–46, emphasis added.

[28] Mt 16:19 and 18:18.

[29] Jn 16:12–13.

scribes and the Pharisees sit on Moses' seat; so practice and observe whatever they tell you, but not what they do; for they preach, but do not practice."[30] He was clearly supporting their God-given authority among the Jews as the successors of Moses.

The fact that the Pharisees' own personal lives unfortunately fell far short of God's ways is an example of how infallibility works in the Church. Infallibility isn't the same as sinlessness, nor does it mean that the pope can't make a mistake about anything. Infallibility means that God prevents the Magisterium from teaching error in matters of *faith and morals*. Furthermore, the Church isn't expected to receive every off-handed remark the pope makes or everything he writes as infallible. To be considered infallible, his statement must be declared in a Church document, using certain language common to such instances, clearly showing he means to be teaching *ex cathedra* (from the papal seat, i.e., infallibly). It doesn't happen that often. But the fact that Church leaders are sinners (and they—and we—all are, sometimes serious ones) does not preclude God from teaching accurately through them. He can keep them from teaching error or even prophesy through them without their knowing it. Consider Caiaphas, the high priest who condemned Jesus; it was he who said, "it is expedient for you that one man should die for the people, and that the whole nation should not perish."[31] He had a political meaning in mind, but God used his words to express a spiritual truth. The Scripture even points out: "He did not say this of his own accord, but being high priest that year he prophesied that Jesus should die for the nation, and not for the nation only, but to gather into one the children of God who are scattered abroad."[32] Even though Caiaphas himself was plotting evil, God still chose to use him as His mouthpiece at that moment in virtue of the office he held. How much more will God protect and guide the teaching of those in authority in the Church, which is the Body of Christ?

Thus we have an obligation to obey the teachings of the Church given by her Magisterium, and we can be confident that God is behind those teachings.

Hard Teachings

This obligation includes those Church teachings that are unpopular, hard to understand, or difficult to follow too. This is not easy—I know: I

[30] Mt 23:2–3.
[31] Jn 11:50.
[32] Jn 11:51–52.

struggled with it myself. There was a teaching I didn't like or comprehend at all. When I expressed my hope that said teaching would change in time, a college friend replied, "No, the Church will never change her teaching on that." I found this very annoying. She was very knowledgeable about the Church and obviously holier than I—which my pride also found annoying sometimes, but I respected her. I hoped she was wrong, but she said it so confidently that a small part of me was worried she might be right.

Then the Lord reminded me of a prayer I'd prayed before (He likes to do that kind of thing). You know how Jesus spoke of having a log in your eye? Well, I had noticed *others'* blind spots and how they seemed to be unaware of them. I realized I must have a few too and had asked the Lord to help me recognize and eradicate them. Now it occurred to me that maybe, just maybe, *this* was my blind spot. Maybe, just possibly, *I* was the one who had it wrong.

Now that was not a pleasant thought! I was really attached to my perspective and proud of my forward-thinking position. But then I realized that I was faced with a choice between my opinion and my God. What really mattered, I realized, was what *He* thought about it, not what I thought about it. It cost me a lot, let me tell you, but at last I prayed, "Lord, what you want is most important to me. If I'm wrong about this, please show me. I'll let it go if you help me." What happened next was phenomenal. A great wave of peace washed over me and a sense of God being really pleased with me. At the same time, it suddenly didn't matter anymore. If that *was* how God saw it, I was okay with it. I was even willing to agree.

I looked into it and found that my friend was right. For the first time, I read the reasons behind the Church's teachings. (Before then, I hadn't bothered. I had assumed there weren't any good reasons, viewing it simply as an old custom that needed to be changed.) To my surprise, there were reasons that were quite sound and actually made sense. Having let go of my pride (at least on this issue), I was able to accept it and, over time, even to become an advocate for it. I also learned what the Magisterium was (a term I hadn't heard before) and decided to take Jesus at His word and trust that the Holy Spirit was indeed guiding the Church.

The Church doesn't expect blind or irrational obedience. If we have trouble understanding a teaching, we need to read what she has to say about it. We must educate our consciences. We cannot have an informed conscience if we won't bother to hear the Church out. If we take the trouble to look into it, we will find that Church teachings are never contrary to reason.

So here we have a powerful proof of our love for God: we can accept the way God does things—working through imperfect people—and take Him at His word, trusting that He is guiding the Church through her Magisterium. The one who truly wants to love Jesus will obey His representatives—not for their sake, but for *His* sake.

Earthly Authorities

What about all those—boss, police, government, society—who expect us to obey them? What does God want us to do in relation to them? Are they His representatives as well?

Civil Law

Most people realize it's in their own interest to obey the laws of the land; we recognize that civil society needs laws for our protection. Most of us obey in areas that would otherwise get us into trouble: we wouldn't think of robbery or assault. But many don't think twice about ignoring laws or rules that are socially acceptable to break. There are dozens of examples. Copying copyrighted material; not reporting cash income on one's taxes; breaking traffic laws when the coast is clear; pilfering small items from hotels or supplies from employers; lying about one's age to get a discount, etc., etc. Most people don't give such things a second thought. If you can get away with it, why *wouldn't* you do them? "It doesn't hurt anyone." "This large company can easily absorb it—they're overcharging anyway." "Everyone does it."

But what does God think about it?

How can we know?

Well, He actually addressed this issue in the Bible. While the IRS didn't exist in Jesus' day, the Roman Empire did, and it certainly collected taxes. The Zealots questioned paying the tax—but for religious reasons, not to save a few shekels. What was Jesus' take? "[R]ender to Caesar the things that are Caesar's, and to God the things that are God's."[33] This is about more than tax evasion; Paul instructs us to pay what is due to all authorities: "taxes to whom taxes are due, revenue to

---

[33] Lk 20:25.

whom revenue is due, respect to whom respect is due, honor to whom honor is due."[34]

The principle that earthly authority comes from God runs through Scripture,[35] including direct words from Jesus, such as, "You would have no power over me unless it had been given you from above."[36] Thus St. Paul teaches: "Let every person be subject to the governing authorities. For there is no authority except from God ... Therefore he who resists the authorities resists what God has appointed, and those who resist will incur judgment."[37]

St. Thomas Aquinas, the great theologian, explained that civil government has the right to create laws for the good of society and Christians should obey them as deriving from God's law. This is why governments throughout history across the world have many similarities; they all forbid theft, murder, lying in court, running away in battle, etc.

Of course, there are evil rulers and bad laws. And some laws are disagreeable: they're either a nuisance, or we literally disagree with them. What does God expect of us then? Obviously, when a civil law is contrary to divine law, then "we must obey God rather than men."[38] In such cases, civil disobedience is a good thing. But if a law is merely disagreeable, we ought to obey it anyway (even one we want to change: obey it until we succeed).

When we are obedient to those in rightful authority over us, God takes it as obedience to Himself. Obeying civil authorities then becomes an opportunity to express our love for Him. We can show Him our love by obeying the rule that's a nuisance: by coming to a full stop at that lonely stop sign when there isn't another soul in sight, by buying our own copy of something, or heeding "Please stay off the grass" signs. The quest to love transforms these things utterly; obedience becomes a joy. And the harder it is to obey, the more love we show Him.

Societal Norms

There's another kind of "obedience", unconnected to official law: the unwritten norms of society. Despite our admiration for "rugged

---

[34] Rom 13:7.
[35] See, for instance, Gen 45:8, Ex 22:28; Prov 8:15.
[36] Jn 19:11.
[37] Rom 13:1–2. See also 1 Pet 2:13–17.
[38] Acts 5:29.

individualism", we still engage in a lot of conformity. Many conform to the larger society; others conform to their preferred group of
nonconformists.

Every age and culture has its own way of seeing and doing things; and
each has its blind spots. While people in every time and place have the
same basic sinful tendencies, different societies turn a blind eye to different
sins. The "spirit of the age" in each culture condones or compromises
with those sins it fancies. Our own society, for instance, rightly looks on
slavery with horror but is very comfortable with sins of self-indulgence.

So we must be very careful. If we take an honest look at ourselves,
we realize we're influenced by others. Perhaps we don't agree with the
mainstream on this issue or that trend, but we rarely "go it alone". What
we do or don't do, what we see as being wrong or right, is partly based
on what everyone around us says. If something evil is legal, if everyone
else is doing it, then we have to work hard to see it as wrong. In God's
eyes, goodness is not limited to refraining from what will affront our
neighbors. We need to take on the mind of Christ and see as He sees.
"Do not be conformed to this world but be transformed by the renewal
of your mind, that you may prove what is the will of God, what is good
and acceptable and perfect."[39]

Unfortunately, we can be more obedient to societal norms than we
are to God. But society can be wrong about moral norms. We have to
get beyond the attitude of "Well, there's no law against it" or "Everyone else is doing it, so it must be okay."

Take pornography, for instance. What once was recognized as wrong
has, since its legalization, become in some ways quite socially acceptable
and certainly very widespread. It's far more accessible now, with the
Internet, cable television, and the "adult" shops no longer found only
in the worst parts of town. People even view this stuff on computers at
the public library.

Yet social science now has plenty of data on the results of legalizing
porn.[40] Porn has been shown to be very addictive; it causes a chemical

[39] Rom 12:2.

[40] See, for instance, Matthew Fradd, *The Porn Myth: Exposing the Reality behind the Fantasy of
Pornography* (San Francisco: Ignatius Press, 2017), and Donald L. Hilton, Jr., M.D., "Pornography and the Brain: Public Health Considerations" (July 2015), http://pornharmsresearch.com
/wp-content/uploads/Hilton-Symposium-Speech.pdf. The National Center of Sexual Exploitation and Fight the New Drug provide scores of research at http://pornharmsresearch.com/ and
http://learn.ftnd.org/, respectively.

reaction in the brain that is similar to taking a drug.[41] Not only that, but it is a progressive addiction: over time, one requires more and more of it (in this case, harder and harder versions of it) to get the same effect.[42]

Pornography also impacts those around the addict, because it affects the way he sees other people.[43] Paradoxically, it can lead to rape as well as to impotence as real women don't live up to air-brushed, idealized images. In some cases, when even hard porn no longer satisfies, it can lead to an interest in children, S&M, or other perversions. Serial killer Ted Bundy attributed the foundation for his crimes to an addiction to pornography.[44] Despite all these obvious personal and social harms, pornography is growing more and more socially acceptable.[45]

It is because society and government are not fail-safe moral guides that the Lord came and gave us a trustworthy guide, the Magisterium of His Church, and sent the Holy Spirit to protect her from error when steering us in faith and morals. To obey her is to obey Him.

---

[41] "Pornography 'mimics' sexual intimacy and 'fakes' the body into releasing a tidal wave of endogenous chemicals, which is exactly what pharmaceutical and illicit street drugs do." Dr. Randall F. Hyde and Mark B. Kastleman, "Is Pornography a 'Drug Addiction'?" http://cdn .candeotraining.com/marketing/images/is_pornography_a_drug.pdf. See also, Dr. Judith Reisman, "The Psychopharmacology of Pictorial Pornography" (2003), http://www.drjudithreisman.com/archives/2007/11/the_psychopharm.html.

[42] See, for instance, Donald L. Hilton, Stephanie Carnes, and Todd L. Love, "The Neurobiology of Behavioral Addictions: Sexual Addiction", in *Neurobiology of Addiction* (Oxford: Oxford University Press, 2016), p. 186, also available online: http://www.sash.net/wp-content /uploads/2016/10/Sexual-Addiction-Chapter-from-Neurobiology-of-Addiction.pdf.

[43] The National Center of Sexual Exploitation lists dozens of articles on the criminal behaviors and attitudes linked to pornography at http://pornharmsresearch.com/2013/12 /talking-points-pornography-and-criminal-behavior-and-attitudes-research/.

[44] There are multiple sources on this; see, for instance, "Is There a Connection between Serial Killers/Rapists and Pornography?" September 4, 2016, http://fightthenewdrug.org/is -there-a-connection-between-serial-killersrapists-and-pornography/. Similarly, Russ Warner lists the pornography connection with multiple serial killers in "What Serial Killers and Murderers Think of Pornography", Net Nanny (July 2, 2013), https://www.netnanny.com/blog /what-serial-killers-and-murderers-think-about-pornography/.

[45] "Porn's Harm Is Changing Fast", August 4, 2014, http://fightthenewdrug.org/porns -harm-is-changing-fast/.

OBEDIENCE IN PRACTICE

The Lord didn't just tell us what to do and not to do and leave it at that. Though fully God and existing from all eternity, the Second Person of the Trinity became a human creature subject to obedience and lived it too. Now that took amazing humility, far more than what's required of us. His whole life was one long demonstration of obedience to the Father. "I have come down from heaven, not to do my own will, but the will of him who sent me."[1]

Jesus rarely spoke of His own desires, but when He did, interestingly, it turned out His only desire was to do His Father's will. In other words, Jesus' greatest desire was to obey and please the Father. We see this throughout the Gospels, especially in John. For instance, He says, "I seek not my own will but the will of him who sent me."[2]

Psalm 119 also gives an idea of this passion welling up in the heart of Jesus:

> My soul is consumed with longing
> for your ordinances at all times....
> Your testimonies are my delight,
> they are my counselors....
> The law of your mouth is better to me
> than thousands of gold and silver pieces.[3]

Most revealing are his remarks in Samaria. When Jesus' disciples return with the food He asked them to get, He is no longer interested in it: "I have food to eat of which you do not know." While they

---

[1] Jn 6:38. See also Heb 10:7: "Behold, I have come to do your will, O God."
[2] Jn 5:30.
[3] Ps 119:20, 24, 72. See also vv. 10–11, 16. Similarly, when Jesus came to be baptized, John the Baptist protested. Jesus needed neither repentance nor purification, for He had never sinned, yet He replied, "Let it be so now, for thus it is fitting for us to fulfil all righteousness" (Mt 3:14–15). He expressed His love for the Father in obedience even to laws that did not apply to Him.

were gone, He had saved the woman at the well, but they take Him literally, so He clarifies: "My food is to do the will of him who sent me, and to accomplish his work."[4] For Jesus, doing His Father's will was filling, satisfying, fulfilling. Jesus *wants* to obey the Father because He loves His Father. He wants to please Him. "I always do what is pleasing to him."[5]

If You Love Me ...

In Jesus then, we see a more significant reason to obey than avoiding negative consequences or concern about what other people think. There is a reason to obey in seemingly insignificant matters, even when it's inconvenient or if it's a Church precept we don't understand or don't like. It is the simplest and most beautiful reason in the world: love.

Jesus Himself gave us this reason when He said, "If you love me, you will keep my commandments."[6] Consider human relationships. Anyone with children can appreciate that you feel loved when they obey promptly and cheerfully, and not so loved when they rebel. Those "in love" don't usually issue commands to one another, but they do avoid what offends or hurts their beloved. If their beloved asks them to do or to stop doing something, they comply, out of love. In fact, they look for opportunities to please their beloved.

If we do this for each other, how much more should we do so for God, who as our Creator has the right to our obedience, gratitude, and service? How much more does He deserve after becoming man and dying for us! Is there *anything* we should refuse to do or stop doing for Him?

Jesus not only lived obedience, He also died in obedience. The greatest demonstration of the magnitude of His love for the Father was at the end of His life. In Gethsemane, though desperate to avoid the coming Passion, He still ended every plea to the Father with the caveat, "Yet, not what I want, but what you want."[7] Here we see the depth of Christ's obedience: "he humbled himself and became obedient *unto death*"— and not just any death but "death on a *cross*".[8] His Passion, crucifixion,

---

[4] Jn 4:32, 34. The King James Version uses the word *meat* instead of *food* here.
[5] Jn 8:29.
[6] Jn 14:15.
[7] Mk 14:36, NRSV.
[8] Phil 2:8; emphasis added.

and death were for our salvation but are also a dazzling illustration of loving obedience. His love for the Father outweighed any consideration for Himself, even excruciating pain and death. Obeying the Father's will meant everything to Jesus.

And Jesus explicitly made the connection between love and obedience at the Last Supper: "If you love me, you will keep my commandments."[9] It was so important to Him, He repeated it twice more in the same discourse.[10] This clearly made a deep impression on the beloved disciple, for he not only records these words in his Gospel but also returns to them again in his letters, especially in his first.[11] John even makes it the litmus test of the true disciple: "He who says, 'I know him' but disobeys his commandments is a liar, and the truth is not in him; but whoever keeps his word, in him truly love for God is perfected."[12] Could God have made it any clearer?

Jesus came to do the will of the Father, out of love. And He expects us to imitate Him.[13]

Thy Will Be Done

Many of us pray the Lord's Prayer, the Our Father, but perhaps without much reflection. "Thy will be done on earth as it is in heaven", for instance, are words Christ meant His followers not merely to say but also to live. It is not enough to give intellectual assent or recite the words. After all, He said, "Why do you call me 'Lord, Lord,' and not do what I tell you?" and warned, "Not every one who says to me, 'Lord, Lord,' shall enter the kingdom of heaven."[14] We must live out His teachings. It is by doing the will of the Father that we enter the Kingdom of God.[15]

First we must understand these words. Grammatically speaking, the structure of the sentence "Thy will be done ..." is "passive", and there is a passive meaning to it—as in, accepting God's will. But

[9] Jn 14:15.
[10] See Jn 14:21 and Jn 15:10.
[11] See, for instance, 1 Jn 3:6; 3:24; and 5:3.
[12] 1 Jn 2:3–5.
[13] See Jn 13:15–16.
[14] Lk 6:46; cf. Mt 7:21.
[15] See Mt 7:21.

"passive" in grammar simply means that the doer is not named; hence the doer here must be active. But by whom is His will done? That is the question.

"Thy will be done on earth as it is in heaven" describes the life of Jesus. He is the One who has literally done His Father's will on earth just as willingly, just as lovingly *as* He had done it in heaven. If God the Son, the Second Person of the Blessed Trinity, obeys the Father, who are we not to do likewise? The phrase "Thy will be done" then is a petition that you and I may do God's will—obey Him—the way Jesus obeyed Him and the angels in heaven obey Him.

We are the Body of Christ, but Jesus must find this very frustrating. Imagine if each member of *your* body had free will and a tendency to rebel. Imagine wanting to get a cup of water, but your feet refused to walk to the sink and your hands to get a cup. Your hands and feet might not feel your thirst, but in the long run it would impact them as well. Let's not do this to Jesus, who has indeed said, "I thirst",[16] but lovingly carry out the wishes of our Head. With God's grace, let it be you and I then who actively do His will here on earth the way Jesus and the angels and saints do in heaven: with prompt, cheerful, generous obedience.

It's a Gradual Process

Like so many things in life, it takes time and effort. Really, we should expect obeying God to be arduous: Jesus said as much when He described the path to heaven as narrow and hard, as opposed to the wide and easy road to perdition.[17] That reality should not discourage us: the Lord doesn't expect perfection overnight and stands ready to help us. Instead, we must rely humbly on God and press on with hope and patience. Pope St. John Paul II said one "accomplishes moral good by stages of growth"; it's a gradual process. "What is needed is a continuous, permanent conversion ... in steps which lead us ever forward."[18]

---

[16] Jn 19:28.

[17] See Mt 7:13–14.

[18] Pope St. John Paul II, Apostolic Exhortation *Familiaris Consortio* on the Role of the Christian Family in the Modern World (November 22, 1981), no. 9. He notes, we "cannot however look on the law as merely an ideal to be achieved in the future: [but] must consider it as a command of Christ the Lord to overcome difficulties with constancy" (no. 34).

A law we've previously broken, especially if we broke it habitually, is harder to keep—at least at first. In the physical realm, if I've been spending most of my time lying around eating junk food, it will be hard for me to get up and run a mile. The longer I've been lounging, the harder it will be. But that doesn't mean I can never run a mile. If I persevere in life-style changes, my body will gradually stop screaming in protest, get accustomed to them, and actually become toned and healthy. I'll eventually get stronger and faster and even begin to enjoy running.

It's the same with the spiritual life. Whether God grants us a windfall of grace to overcome something quickly or it takes time, it's always possible. Just keep asking for God's help, and keep trying. It's like riding a bike up a hill. Many quit because they can't go as quickly as on flat ground. But as my cousin Lauren taught me when I moved to San Francisco, you need go only fast enough that you don't fall over. Slow and steady is the secret to riding to the top.

God is patient with us. Just as parents don't expect a baby to learn to walk in a day, He knows it takes time and delights in our efforts as a Father watching His little one toddle about. He cheers us on when we get up (repent) and try again after every fall. And the wonderful thing is that if we persevere, with His grace, eventually we'll *run* in the way of his commandments.[19] So Pope St. John Paul II encourages us "to respond to God's command with serene confidence in God's grace".[20] This confidence comes from a faith-filled and hope-filled certainty that with God, we can do it. *He* is the One who will, with our cooperation, overcome sin within us.

And how do we obtain that grace? As mentioned above, we must ask Him for it. It takes more than an occasional one-liner in the midst of a life otherwise dissociated from Him; we need a regular prayer life and to make use of the means He's set up to replenish our grace. If you own an electric car, you have to recharge regularly, or you'll get stuck somewhere. Prayer and the sacraments are our power stations. All the sacraments give grace, but two are offered without limit: the Eucharist and Confession. We can recharge with these freely and frequently.

Obedience isn't all hard. In fact, the more we obey, the easier it becomes. Here's an example of one of my struggles:

---

[19] See Ps 119:32.
[20] John Paul II, *Familiaris Consortio, Christian Family*, no. 34, quoting his own homily of October 25, 1980.

Growing Up by Slowing Down[21]

I was taught to drive by my teenage brother. And it showed.

I drove fast, boldly, and with a sense of superiority. I managed to believe I also had prudence by comparing myself to reckless drivers. I regarded the speed limit (then 55) as ridiculous and impossible to obey without becoming a road hazard. Since most drivers in Southern California drove well above the speed limit, our family considered driving with the flow of traffic as the responsible way to drive. But I added the stipulation that I could exceed the flow if I was in a hurry, provided I never went faster than I could handle and that someone nearby was going even faster (thus a more likely police target). This philosophy was indispensable to someone chronically running late. Tardiness led to my taking every opportunity to save a few seconds. Between this effort and the anonymity within my car, I lost sight of consideration for my fellow drivers.

The Bumper Sticker

Upon moving to Maryland, I found myself more aggressive than the average Maryland driver. I modified my habits slightly for this new environment but didn't think much about it.

That changed when my husband and I put a pro-life bumper sticker on our car (with a photo of Pope St. John Paul II to boot). I suddenly realized that darting in and out of traffic was not a good witness to the pro-life movement or to the Church. With so much prejudice against both already, any rude moves on my part wouldn't help either. I realized I had been compartmentalizing my driving and my faith. I had to change: I had to be as polite in my car as I was in person.

Sacred Heart Auto League

My efforts had met with only middling success, when a package from the Sacred Heart Auto League arrived. They wrote that Christ cares about every aspect of our lives—driving included—and invited me to pledge to drive in a way pleasing to Him. Thinking, "I need this", I signed the pledge, making a firm commitment in my heart. There was also a prayer to say whenever you got behind the wheel, for God's protection and the grace to drive cautiously, courteously, and obediently. That last one was the sticking point. What did obedience mean here?

---

[21] Originally published as "No Need for Speed", *Faith and Family* (Spring 2009): 33–35.

My husband and I asked a reliable moral theologian we knew, who quoted Aquinas: one is not required to obey a civil law that isn't enforced. A police acquaintance told my husband that the police usually won't pull you over unless you're going at least ten miles over the speed limit. That seemed reasonable. When I tried to implement it, I was surprised at how slow that felt at times. I hadn't really noticed before how fast I was going.

The Influence of Prayer

It wasn't easy, but with the support of my commitment and the grace of prayer, I was able to change. The prayer was essential. I prayed it faithfully. But whenever I got to the word "obediently", I felt a twinge of conscience. Was I really being obedient?

Then my brother did something mind-boggling. Not wanting to get any more tickets, he decided to obey the speed limit at all times. I was stunned. He said it felt so good; he was no longer anxious when he saw police but glad to see them. He even started saying *I* should drive the speed limit. (Big brothers.)

I went on praying the prayer for two years, but it began to get to me. Praying for the grace to drive obediently day after day was like the continual dripping of water on a rock. I thought about how Jesus lived obedience out of love for the Father. Finally, when I realized that I could take it on as a penance and offer it up, I decided to do it. It turned out to be *very* penitential.

The Humiliation

I never realized how much pride I had wrapped up in my driving until it revealed itself at this time, when suddenly I was not cool. I had looked down on those who drove the speed limit. Now I was one of them, and I knew what annoyed thoughts others were thinking about me. (Before, I used to exclaim, "This person is *actually* driving the speed limit!" as if it were deviant. As for people who drove *below* the speed limit, I thought they should be banned from the road.)

I had to change the prayer: I added a heartfelt plea to Mother Mary[22] to obtain heavenly aid, and I offered up the difficulty for a critical intention. Without her intercession, I never could have done it. Doing it as

---

[22] For more on "praying to" saints, see "Models Not Idols" in chap. 24 below.

a penance for my inconsiderate driving in the past helped too. And the cruise control was critical: it would have been impossible without it.

Unexpected Benefits

I can't say that everyone is called to obey the *posted* speed limit. I think a case can be made for driving the *enforced* speed limit. In fact, at times driving the posted speed limit on the highway can even be hazardous. And, of course, some emergencies require speeding.

But I can say that God called me to it and produced some valuable fruits in my life as a result. Over time I saw that this experience could strengthen me in living by my principles even under pressure or despite the disapproval of others. Less stress and more character. Better habits, like leaving earlier and being generous to others. Growth in humility and trust, patience and courtesy. In a word, maturity.

I used to be too worried about being late to be courteous. Now I have time to be magnanimous. Now I see driving as another chance to witness Christ's love. Other drivers are usually pleasantly surprised and grateful when I yield and let them in front of me. I've found that driving "courteously, cautiously, and obediently" means driving *lovingly*.

I'm finally growing up: now I try to drive like my big brother ... Jesus.

Conclusion

There is no better time than now to take out this old-fashioned virtue, dust it off, and give obedience a try. Granted, it's not easy to put into practice. We live in a culture that is different from first-century Palestine, yet we need to apply Jesus' principles to our modern world. That's one of the reasons we need the Church's Magisterium as a living authority to guide us in how to do that. We also need to be open to the Lord's promptings to us personally. "By prayer, we can discern 'what is the will of God' and obtain the endurance to do it."[23]

While obedience may very well prove to be a harder penance than any we've ever undertaken, it is also a surefire expression of love for God. We know we are shouting in His love language when we obey because He said it explicitly so often.

[23] *CCC* 2826, quoting Rom 12:2; cf. Eph 5:17; cf. Heb 10:36.

I love the story about St. Thérèse of Lisieux's obedience. Ardently seeking to please the Lord, she followed St. Benedict's rule of prompt obedience to the monastery bell to the point of laying down one's pen even in mid-sentence. On one occasion when the bell rang, though she had only the final "e" to write in signing her name, she put the pen down and left for her next duty. When she returned, the letter "e" had been appended to her name—in gold. Even if that story is only a legend,[24] there is a spiritual truth in it. That page with the golden "e" *may* not exist on earth, but I'll bet something like it or even better is framed up in heaven.

Obedience for love of God is more than worth it. When we focus on Him and loving Him, it becomes a joy. Jesus implied that it gets easier and benefits us too: "Blessed are those who hunger and thirst for righteousness, for they shall be satisfied."[25] Want peace, joy, love? Obedience is a sure path. Christ has shown us the way:

> Every one then who hears these words of mine and does them will be like a wise man who built his house upon the rock.

> Whoever obeys me dwells in security, in peace, without fear of harm.

> If you keep my commandments, you will abide in my love, just as I have kept my Father's commandments and abide in his love. These things I have spoken to you, that my joy may be in you, and that your joy may be full.[26]

---

[24] Not finding a source for this, I can't offer evidence that that miracle occurred, but she clearly did practice this kind of obedience. See, e.g., Patrick Ahern, *Maurice & Thérèse* (New York: Doubleday, 1998), p. 89.

[25] Mt 5:6.

[26] Mt 7:24; Prov 1:33 (NABRE); Jn 15:10–11.

SECTION FOUR

LOVING GOD MEANS APOLOGIZING FOR TURNING AWAY FROM HIM

Return to the LORD, your God, for he is gracious and merciful, slow to anger, and abounding in steadfast love.

(Joel 2:13, RSVCE)

"Her sins, which are many, are forgiven, for she loved much."

(Lk 7:47)

12

ADMITTING WE WERE WRONG

The more our love for God grows, the more aware we become of how often we fail Him. Learning to *trust* Him more may lead to the realization that *we* have not always been trustworthy. *Spending time* with Him in prayer softens our hearts and opens them to truth. And striving to practice loving *obedience* will naturally open our eyes to our own sinfulness.

When we see our guilt, what are we supposed to do with it?

Guilt: The Big Bogeyman

We're all familiar with the image of a pendulum swinging from one side to the other, illustrating the human and societal tendency to pass from one extreme to its opposite. This is certainly true in the spiritual life too. It's so easy to stray from the straight and narrow, but then often we over-correct and end up going right off the path again, this time on the opposite side.

In the not-so-distant past, there was sometimes an over-emphasis on fearing God and sinfulness that led to anxiety, rigidity, scrupulosity, and judgmentalness. I'm not sure when that began to change, but it has definitely changed. Sin became an old-fashioned notion, passé in enlightened modernity. Even back in 1948, C.S. Lewis noticed "the almost total absence ... of any sense of sin".[1]

> Some are inclined to replace exaggerated attitudes of the past with other exaggerations: From seeing sin everywhere they pass to not recognizing it anywhere; from too much emphasis on the fear of eternal punishment they pass to preaching a love of God that excludes any punishment deserved by sin.
>
> —POPE ST. JOHN PAUL II [Box 18]

---

[1] C.S. Lewis, *God in the Dock: Essays on Theology and Ethics*, ed. Walter Hooper (Grand Rapids, Mich.: Eerdmans, 1970), pp. 243–44. And Ven. Fulton Sheen said: "We are living in the first age in the history of the world that has denied guilt and sin.... There are no sinners. We're just 'patients'." "The Sacrament of Confession", https://www.youtube.com/watch?v=wNZPvk6wB6k.

In the latter part of the twentieth century, you used to hear a lot about "guilt complexes", as though guilt feelings were dangerous and always to be avoided. Our culture encouraged excusing our failings with the reassurance that no one is perfect, or blaming our parents, our kids, our boss, our hormones, our dog—anything but ourselves; or, better yet, not acknowledging that there was anything remiss in our behavior at all. The only thing left to be ashamed of was shame. If you felt guilty, it wasn't because you had actually done anything wrong; it must be that you had "hang-ups" you needed to get over.[2] If truth is relative, then there's not much that's really wrong—except, say, murder, judging other people, or failing to recycle.

Coupled with this crippled sense of sin, we now have an exclusive spotlight on God's mercy. (Don't get me wrong—His merciful love is a critical message! But God's mercy is not *entirely* unconditional; it *does* require one thing: our repentance.) As a result, the common notion of God is now akin to an almighty Santa Claus, who gives only presents and never coal.

I think the ostracization of guilt has worked pretty well; we don't hear much about it anymore. If everything's permissible, what is there to feel guilty about? Our idea of sin is so slim and of God is so nonchalant, it's no wonder hardly anyone bothers to go to Confession anymore.

But why did guilt become such a bogeyman anyway? No one enjoys guilt any more than they do pain, but neither is useless. Pain alerts us that something is amiss in our bodies; guilt does the same with our souls. The function of both is to move us to rectify the cause; the purpose of guilt is to get us to admit our wrongdoing and try to make it right. It's as dangerous to deny or ignore the sense of guilt as it would be to deny or ignore the pain of heart disease.

In the book *Whatever Happened to Sin?* renowned psychiatrist Karl Menninger questioned the wisdom of this cultural whitewashing of sin. "I believe there is 'sin' which is expressed in ways which cannot be subsumed under ... 'crime,' 'disease,' 'delinquency,' 'deviancy.' There *is* immorality; there is unethical behavior; there *is* wrongdoing. And I hope to show that there is usefulness in retaining the concept, and indeed

---

[2] This is not to deny that some people suffer from mental afflictions causing them to fear that their innocuous acts might be sins. But this affects only a small percentage of the population; reassurances to address their irrational fears should not be given to everyone else as well. "It does little good to repent a symptom, but it may do great harm not to repent a sin." Karl Menninger, M.D., *Whatever Became of Sin?* (New York: Hawthorn Books, 1973), p. 48.

the word, SIN." He calls for "reviving the use of the word 'sin'—not for the word's sake, but for the reintroduction of the concepts of guilt and moral responsibility".[3]

Denial

To deny guilt is to deny the truth. Now considering God *is* Truth,[4] this might not be such a bright idea. Archbishop Fulton Sheen said, "There is hope for any civilization which breaks a law but never calls in question the truth of the law; but there is no hope for a civilization that breaks a law and then denies it."[5] And elsewhere: "Sin is *not* the worst thing in the world; the worst thing in the world is the denial of sin.... If I deny that I am a sinner, how can I ever be forgiven?"[6]

Even the world of psychology recognizes the importance of truth and the danger of attempting to live a lie. Serious misconduct that hasn't been adequately "acknowledged" and "atoned for" can lie behind many neuroses.[7] Recognizing the danger of denial, the Twelve-Step movement has made it common knowledge. In fact, eight of the twelve steps deal with sin and denial, including the Fourth: to make "a searching and fearless moral inventory of ourselves".[8]

St. John the Evangelist speaks on this topic several times in his first epistle. "God is light and in him is no darkness at all. If we say we have fellowship with him while we walk in darkness, we lie and do not live according to the truth.... If we say we have no sin, we deceive ourselves, and the truth is not in us.... If we say we have not sinned, we make him a liar."[9]

But while St. John urges us to acknowledge our sinfulness, it's not in order to make us feel bad and stay there. Guilt is meant to move us to

---

[3] Ibid., pp. 46, 48. He also points out that for a psychiatrist to deny sin where it exists would be a failure to provide adequate care. "Would we withhold all censure from a psychiatrist who is giving psychotherapy for 'neurotic' symptoms ... to a man involved in rascality and wickedness of notable degree?... Psychiatrists have finally demonstrated that there is an effective treatment for certain conditions which doctors formerly ignored or mistreated. But do we not repeat the error if we ignore appropriate help available for some individuals whose sins are greater than their symptoms?" Ibid., p. 49.

[4] See Jn 14:6.

[5] Fulton Sheen, *A Fulton Sheen Reader* (St. Paul, Minn.: Carillon Books, 1979), p. 197.

[6] Sheen, "The Sacrament of Confession", https://www.youtube.com/watch?v=wNZPvk6wB6k.

[7] Menninger, *Whatever Became of Sin?* pp. 182, 57.

[8] Twelve Steps of Alcoholic Anonymous, http://12step.org/references/12-step-versions/aa.

[9] 1 Jn 1:5b–6, 8, 10.

act. And, thanks to Jesus, there is something we *can* do. "[I]f we walk in the light," John adds, "... the blood of Jesus his Son cleanses us from all sin."[10] Walking with Jesus means obeying Him; if we wander away, it means coming back, apologizing, and following Him again.

Presumption

The cultural disappearance of guilt arises not only from a denial of sin but also from an indifference to it or an ignorance of its significance. Aside from our fallen inclination to sweep things under the rug, there are several additional sources for this.

Martin Luther may have had an influence in this. He held that justification was a matter of Christ covering up our sins like snow on a dunghill and that our salvation was based on faith alone; it didn't seem to matter if we kept on sinning. He claimed he could commit adultery a hundred times a day and still go to heaven. Obviously, this was hyperbole, and I'm sure he didn't intend to promote infidelity or sin; his focus was on gaining an "assurance of salvation". And no wonder; a look into his personal history shows an obvious proclivity to scrupulosity. Prior to breaking from the Church, he used to go to Confession repeatedly, even within one day, and agonize over every little possible sin, fearing damnation. The remedy he found to assuage his own fears was hardly suitable as a moral theology for everyone else, yet it has grown like a weed.

Another significant influence has been atheistic philosophies over the past few centuries, with the result that some people don't believe in God or sin at all. While self-professed atheists are still a small minority, they make a large impact on others. Catholics and other Christians have swerved sharply away from talking about sin and hell, leading many people to think sin isn't that big a deal. If people are told over and over in various ways that God doesn't really care about these things and not to be so uptight, then they'll believe it. What we watch and read and hear influences our attitudes. The mercy of God doesn't strike even those of us who still think there are plenty of impermissible things as all that exciting. There's been *such* an emphasis on God's love and mercy that we take them for granted.

There's a name for this spiritual nonchalance: *presumption*. St. Paul warned of it: "[D]o you presume upon the riches of his kindness and

[10] 1 Jn 1:7.

forbearance and patience? Do you not know that God's kindness is meant to lead you to repentance?"[11] Presumption is even worse than being taken for granted. To do what you know God won't like and presume that He'll forgive you *without your apologizing* is a little like slapping your mother in the face and then asking her what's for dinner.

Finally, part of our problem is that, being fallen creatures, we begin with only a limited sense of the offensiveness of sin; then our own sins shrink this sense further. On the physical plane, we can become so accustomed to our own odor we no longer smell it; this happens spiritually too: we're unaware of our own soul's "odor". Moreover, we don't realize how putrid sin is to the Lord. Our venial sins are probably more unpleasant to Him than body odor to us—more like a soiled diaper. Mortal sins are like skunk spray. We can't get rid of that stench on our own. For serious sin, we need the special cleansing of Confession.

While guilt feelings should not be disregarded, neither should we swim in them. Thankfully, we're not limited to choosing between denial and despair; there's another choice: repentance. Jesus said, "Blessed are they who mourn"—the right attitude is to mourn our bad actions. "[G]odly grief produces a repentance that leads to salvation and brings no regret", says St. Paul.[12] The healthy way to handle feelings of remorse is to repent with humility and hope.

Sin

What is sin, anyway? There are many ways one could describe or define sin, but essentially it comes down to a failure to love.[13] Sin is the opposite of love.

If love means to seek the good of the beloved, then sin is to seek one's own good at the expense of others. Jesus said that all the Law and the Prophets could be summed up in the two greatest commandments: to love God with all we've got and to love our neighbor as ourselves. But that is precisely what sin refuses to do. Sin puts self before God and before others.

[11] Rom 2:4.
[12] 2 Cor 7:10.
[13] CCC 1849.

Loving anything created more than God is a form of idolatry and a failure to love Him as He deserves. In likening the bond between God and His people to a marriage, and idolatry to adultery, Scripture illuminates how sin wounds our relationship with Him. God is the Bridegroom, so *"sin is not just the breaking of a rule or a law, but the betrayal of a relationship."*[14] We see this in Jesus' exchange with His chief disciple, who had denied even knowing Him.

Do You Love Me More Than ...?

"Simon, son of John, do you love me more than these?"[15] When this verse receives any attention, "these" is often interpreted to mean the other disciples. Some even suggest Jesus singled Peter out because his love was the greatest, but that doesn't make sense to me. After all, "the beloved disciple"—who alone of the Twelve was with Jesus at Golgotha—was right there too. If Jesus did mean "these disciples", He probably meant it ironically. After all, Peter had declared that even if all the others deserted Jesus, *he* wouldn't—essentially a claim to love Him more than they did. That might explain why, given Peter's humble, sorrowful response, Jesus drops the phrase "more than these" when He repeats the question twice more.

Only once did I hear a homily in which "these" was proposed to refer to the fish. I thought, "Uhhh ... love Him more than the *fish*? Come on, Peter wasn't that shallow." But that interpretation, upon further reflection, is worth some consideration. Whether or not that's the primary meaning of the passage, this reading can also bear spiritual fruits.

For most of us, there is no contest between fish and Jesus. But Peter was a fisherman. And he had just made a HUGE catch. This was his career, and those fish represented *Success*. Plenty of people have trouble putting Jesus ahead of their career, success, prosperity, and security. Many don't love Jesus enough to put Him first if it means jeopardizing any of these.

Even those who have put Him first in those areas fall elsewhere sometimes. Any time we put off our prayer to watch a TV show or eat more than we should, any time we choose ease or pleasure instead of

---

[14] Brant Pitre, *Jesus the Bridegroom: The Greatest Love Story Ever Told* (New York: Image, 2014), p. 13; italics in original.
[15] Jn 21:15.

our duty, we are in fact failing to love Jesus more than these. Again, the essence of sin is putting something—anything—before God.

It could be discouraging to reflect on all the stupid things we have, for all practical purposes, loved more than God. But think how gently He treated Peter, who loved his own life more than his Lord. Peter had gone back to fishing, and Jesus repeats the miracle with which He began His relationship with Peter: a tremendous catch of fish. Then He asks him if he loves Him more than these, which could be seen as asking, *Will you make the same choice this time—to drop your nets and follow Me?* It's as if Jesus is giving Peter a chance to start over. Then He asks him the threefold question, Peter's chance to reverse his threefold denial.

Jesus gives us the same chance to start over, reaffirm our love, and follow Him even "where [we] do not wish to go".[16] As a friend pointed out, another possible reading is, "Do you love me more than these fish [love me], who willingly gave up their lives for me?"

When you're reaching for anything you really shouldn't have, even something as innocuous as too many chips, when it seems so hard to resist and so easy to rationalize away, it can be helpful to ask yourself, *Do I love Him more than these?* The little things do matter. Faithfulness in little things is what prepares us to be faithful in the larger. Let's pray and work to make sure we *do* love Him more than these—whatever "these" might be in our individual lives.

Different Levels of Sin

Obviously, eating too many chips is not on the same level as armed robbery. Some sins are worse than others. St. John speaks of different levels of sin: "All wrongdoing is sin, but there is sin which is not deadly."[17] The Church has followed suit, differentiating between *mortal* sin and *venial* sin. The main difference between the two is that mortal (Latin for "deadly") sin kills the life of a soul.

How? All sin hurts our relationship with God, but mortal sin demolishes it. All goodness comes from God, so if we cut ourselves off from Him, we cut ourselves off from the source of the spiritual life for our souls: sanctifying grace. "I am the vine, you are the branches", Jesus said. Apart from Him, we wither up and die, though this isn't immediately

---

[16] Jn 21:18.
[17] 1 Jn 5:17.

apparent on a physical level. We're like candles: in Baptism, one is lit with the Light of Christ. Venial sins make one's flame flicker; mortal sin snuffs it out altogether. The candle is still there, but it is no longer lit.

What makes a sin mortal? The Church lists three elements that make a sin mortal:

1. It must be serious in nature, where grave harm results.
2. The person committing the sin must realize that the matter is gravely sinful.
3. The person must be acting in freedom, with full consent of the will.

If the sin is not of a serious matter, it is venial sin, not mortal. If either knowledge or consent is missing, then the sin is venial, even if it is a grave matter. So what is "grave" matter? "*Grave matter* is specified by the Ten Commandments, corresponding to the answer of Jesus to the rich young man: 'Do not kill, Do not commit adultery, Do not steal, Do not bear false witness, Do not defraud, Honor your father and your mother.' The gravity of sins is more or less great: murder is graver than theft ... violence against parents is ... graver than violence against a stranger."[18]

The *Catechism* also clarifies the other elements: "Mortal sin ... presupposes knowledge of the sinful character of the act, of its opposition to God's law. It also implies a consent sufficiently deliberate to be a personal choice. Feigned ignorance and hardness of heart do not diminish, but rather increase, the voluntary character of a sin."[19]

While mortal sin cuts us off from God, venial sin "allows charity to subsist, even though it offends and wounds it".[20] But this is not to make light of venial sins. Venial sin is nothing to sniff at, because it still wounds the soul. In our physical lives, we don't avoid only those things that will kill us; we also avoid what will injure or maim us.

Fortunately, the Divine Physician is quite capable of spiritual resuscitation and restoring our souls to health. This is wonderful news, but we shouldn't therefore charge into sin, sprightly counting on His healing powers. True, He can heal us, but, like physical healing, it still involves time and recovery. There's residual weakness, the painful tedium of therapeutic exercises, and so forth. It would be as unwise to go back to our mortally sinful ways as to continue unhealthy heart habits after

---

[18] *CCC* 1858, quoting Mk 10:19.
[19] *CCC* 1859, citing Mk 3:5–6; Lk 16:19–31.
[20] *CCC* 1855.

being brought back from cardiac arrest in the ER. You wouldn't cheerfully count on being able to return for another round of electric jolts to your heart, assuming it was immune to wear and tear. (Resuscitation procedures are not fun, sometimes resulting in bruising or even broken ribs.) Nor should we disregard the ravages that sin makes on our souls. Not that God's mercy and healing will run out—no, they are infinite—but sin weakens the will, discourages the heart, darkens the intellect, and builds bad habits. All these lessen the likelihood of repentance, so we can't take sin lightly. "Do not make light even of those sins called lesser", warns St. Augustine. "If you make light of them when you weigh them, be terrified when you count them."[21]

Sin Causes Harm

Sin not only hurts others and damages or breaks relationships, it also hurts the sinner. Sin impacts us physically, emotionally, mentally, and spiritually; it comes with consequences. The repentant drunkard can count on God's forgiveness but not on a brand-new liver. As the saying goes, "God always forgives; men sometimes forgive; nature never forgives."

In the book *On the Banks of Plum Creek*, Laura's mother tells her to stay in the clear parts of the creek. Laura doesn't obey, and when she emerges from the muddy waters, she finds globs of mud stuck to her legs that she can't wash off. Turns out they're not mud globs but *leeches*. When she tries to pull them off, each one stretches and stretches before finally coming off, leaving behind a trickle of blood running down her leg.[22] Sin is like that—it lurks in forbidden places, grabs onto us, holds on tenaciously, and sucks the life out of us.

Early in *A Christmas Carol*, the first ghost, Scrooge's late partner, Jacob Marley, comes clanking up the stairs dragging a heavy chain made of "cash-boxes, keys, padlocks, ledgers,... wrought in steel". He tells Scrooge, "I wear the chain I forged in life.... I made it link by link, and yard by yard; I girded it on of my own free will." A little later, the specter "held up its chain at arm's length, as if that were the cause of all its unavailing grief".[23] Here we have a potent image of a spiritual reality.

[21] St. Augustine of Hippo, *Homilies on the Epistle of John to the Parthians* [1, 6], in *The Faith of the Early Fathers*, vol. 3, ed. William A. Jurgens (Collegeville, Minn.: Liturgical Press, 1979), no. 1846, p. 125.

[22] Laura Ingalls Wilder, *On the Banks of Plum Creek* (New York: HarperCollins, 1971), pp. 130–32.

[23] Charles Dickens, *A Christmas Carol* (New York: Global Classics, 2014), pp. 12, 14, 15.

Sin's consequences are very much like Marley's heavy chains, but we can't see our spiritual shackles. He tells Scrooge, "The strong coil you bear yourself . . . was full as heavy and as long as [mine] . . . seven Christmas Eves ago. You have labored on it, since. It is a ponderous chain!"[24] We too have our sins invisibly bound to us. If we think they are a burden now, just wait until we see them after death. Fortunately, in the Sacrament of Confession we have the chance to be freed of the past dragging after us, freed from the weight of sin.

Getting Free from Sin

In size, venial sins are like leeches: unpleasant as they were, little Laura could deal with them. So too, the Lord gives us the means—through repentance, acts of charity, prayers, etc.—to be cleansed of venial sins.[25] Mortal sin, however, is another matter; it would be more like Laura trying to extricate herself from a giant squid.

When we wander from the Way,[26] our souls are affected. There's tar hidden in the sands on either side of the Lord's path. If you've ever found tar on your feet at the beach, you know you can't get it off with mere water. We are children away from home; we don't have any means—no solvent in our pockets—with which to remove the tar.

But our enemy wants to do more than dirty our feet; he wants to destroy us. Like Br'er Fox trapping Br'er Rabbit with a "tar-baby" in the American folktale,[27] the devil sets even more cunning traps and lies in wait for us.[28] He sets out something big and attractive like a treasure

---

[24] Ibid., p. 14.

[25] These means—which presuppose having remorse for one's sins and not having any unconfessed mortal sins—include saying the Our Father, the use of sacramentals such as holy water, or receiving Communion at Mass. See "Sacramentals", in the *Catholic Encyclopedia*, https://www.catholic.com/encyclopedia/sacramentals, quoting St. Thomas Aquinas, *Summa Theologica* III, q. lxxxvii, a. 3, ad 1um. Cf. Fr. Edward McIlmail, L.C., "Can Sins Be Forgiven in the Absence of Confession?" RC Spirituality, https://rcspirituality.org/ask-a-priest-can-sins-be-forgiven-in-the-absence-of-confession/, and the Rite of Blessing and Sprinkling Holy Water, option B, in *Basic Texts for the Roman Catholic Eucharist*, http://catholic-resources.org/ChurchDocs/Mass.htm.

[26] Jesus called Himself the "Way", and early Christians called themselves "followers of the Way". When we wander from the path to heaven that Jesus became for us, we wander from Him.

[27] See Joel Chandler Harris' *Uncle Remus: His Songs and His Sayings* (1881). The word *Br'er* was short for "brother" in the Southern dialect of that time.

[28] Yes, Satan and the demons are real, and it pleases them no end when people don't believe in them, for such people are easier prey. Scripture refers to them as real, spiritual beings, as does Jesus, e.g., Jn 8:44. Thus the Church has always taught they are a real menace; see, e.g.,

---

Recognizing Your Sins

There are booklets with suggestions for making a good examination of conscience;[a] but here are some tips:

- Consider your actions in the light of the *Ten Commandments* and the impli-
  cations of each one. (The eighth commandment, for instance, prohibits
  not just perjury in court, but gossip and telling lies anywhere.)
- Think of the seven *capital sins*—pride, envy, anger, avarice, gluttony, lust,
  and sloth. Have you fallen into any of these in any way?
- Look at your life-style in the light of the *Beatitudes* and the *works of mercy*.
  How well are you fulfilling these hallmarks of a Christian? We have to
  remember that we offend God not only by what we *do* but also by what
  we *don't* do but should have done.
- The simplest way is to examine your life according to the *two great Commandments*: "Love God with all your heart, all your mind, all your soul,
  and all your strength" and "Love your neighbor as yourself." Reflect on
  your relationships, beginning with God. How have you spurned or disobeyed Him? Have you been striving to please Him?

  Then look at your human relationships. Have you hurt the people in
  your life, especially those with whom you interact most? Have you been a
  channel of God's love to them? Finally, look at your obligations to yourself. Are you taking proper care of yourself? Are you living in a way that
  leads to heaven? Are you striving to grow in virtue? Are you developing
  and using the gifts God has given you?

[a] One such guide can be found at www.theworkofgod.org/Library/examine.htm.

Box 19

---

chest, only, unbeknownst to us, it's covered with tar. If we pick up that
chest, we'll discover we can't put it down or get away from it. It's stuck
to us, and we can't remove it. Sin is as sticky, stinky, and steadfast as tar.

Fortunately, our Savior wants to free us, so He's dispatched His
attendants with the only solvent that can dissolve that tar. All we have

---

CCC 391–92. The experiences of modern-day exorcists and former Satanists melt away skepticism; see, for example, *Former Satanist Becomes Catholic* (CD, Lighthouse Catholic Media), Fr.
Gabriel Amorth's *An Exorcist Tells His Story* (Ignatius Press), or interviews with Fr. Gary Thomas,
whose experiences as an exorcist figure in the movie *The Rite*, in *What You Need to Know about
Exorcism: The Devil, Evil Spirits, and Spiritual Warfare*, CD available at Catholic Answers (https://
shop.catholic.com/).

to do is go back to the Way (repent) and head to a Way-station. God's agent can extricate us from our terrible idol, but only if we come to him and show it to him. If we bring it to him, then he can set us free—not by his own power, but by the solvent given him by our Savior. That's what the Sacrament of Confession is all about.

Repentance

"So long as he is in the flesh, a man is not able to be without sins, at least the lesser ones."[29] We can probably all relate to St. Paul, who says, "I do not do the good I want, but the evil I do not want is what I do."[30] When that happens, what do we do? How do we "get right" with God?

The essential thing is to repent, to be truly sorry. Sometimes that comes easily; sometimes it doesn't. Here are some reflections that might help when it doesn't flow naturally.

Connecting My Sins to His Pains

In a sense, sin hurts God.[31] It certainly hurts our relationship with Him. Everyone who believes that Jesus was God-made-man can agree that *He* was capable of being hurt. If Christ became like mankind in every way then He had to have feelings too.[32] He suffered physically in His Passion and emotionally in Gethsemane.

> Strive to detest [your sins], and to reject them with the greatest abhorrence and contrition of which your heart is capable, bearing in mind that by sin you have renounced God's Eternal Love.
>
> —ST. FRANCIS DE SALES Box 20

---

[29] St. Augustine, *Epistle of John to the Parthians* [1, 6], in *Faith of the Early Fathers*, 3:125, no. 1846.

[30] Rom 7:19.

[31] Those of a more philosophical or a precise theological bent might take issue with that, stating that God is unchangeable, perfectly happy, and thus cannot "be hurt". The problem with emphasizing God's immutability, however, is that, as corporeal beings, we cannot properly picture a God who loves but has no emotions. This does not compute. We associate "no feelings" with being *unfeeling* and end up with an image of a cold, indifferent, and unsympathetic Deity—completely contrary to His revelation of Himself. Instead, in the Scriptures, He uses many anthropomorphisms to describe Himself. So while it isn't precisely accurate to describe God as "jealous" or to refer to His "right hand", He does so because such images express truth in a way comprehensible to us; indeed, such images are truer and more effective than representations that make Him sound distant and uncaring.

[32] See Heb 2:17.

It can be difficult to comprehend, though, how *our* sins, two thousand years later, could affect Him. He already suffered, He already died, He rose and ascended into heaven. Isn't it all over and done with? Yet, the *Catechism* states: "our sins affect Christ himself."[33] After His Ascension, Jesus said to Saul, who was harassing Christians, "[W]hy do you persecute *me*?"[34] Christ is present in the least of His brothers and sisters; thus, whenever we hurt them we hurt Him. But also, in the mysterious workings of time and eternity, our sins hurt Him directly. "It is you who have crucified him and crucify him still, when you delight in your vices and sins."[35]

Perhaps a large part of His suffering in Gethsemane came from foreseeing all the times we would betray Him, all the souls who would reject Him and be lost anyway. When the angel came to Him, perhaps part of the comfort lay in foreseeing the times we would repent, the times we would stand strong, the souls that would be saved. So my actions now add to His suffering or to His comfort.

Another way I can arouse repentance (and gratitude) in my heart for His great mercy is to contemplate my need for it. Relating my sins to His Passion is helpful in this. How often have I, like the disciples in Gethsemane, added to, rather than relieved, His sorrows? They fell asleep when He needed them; they fled when He was taken. Haven't I neglected spending time with Him; haven't I run from the cross, abandoned Him in countless ways?

If every lash of my tongue left a mark, would not my unkind words over a lifetime

> Have mercy on me, O God, according to
>   your merciful love;
>   according to your abundant mercy blot
>   out my transgressions.
> Wash me thoroughly from my iniquity,
>   and cleanse me from my sin!
> For I know my transgressions,
>   and my sin is ever before me.
> Against you, you only, have I sinned,
>   and done that which is evil in your sight.
>
> Create in me a clean heart, O God,
>   and put a new and right spirit within
>   me.
> Cast me not away from your presence,
>   and take not your holy Spirit from me.
> Restore to me the joy of your salvation,
>   and uphold me with a willing spirit.
>   —PSALM 51:1–4, 10–12 Box 21

---

[33] *CCC* 598.

[34] Acts 9:4, emphasis added.

[35] St. Francis of Assisi, *Admonitio* 5, 3, quoted in *CCC* 598.

leave Him as welt-covered and bloody as did the scourging at the pillar? If my every negative, critical, selfish, judgmental, proud thought were a visible barb, would they not amount to a crown of thorns covering His sacred head? If my every sin of omission—every failure to carry my cross—resulted not only in His being burdened with my sins, but also in His falling under their weight, would He not have fallen more than three times?

Then the crucifixion: it's hard to admit one's sins helped fix Him to the Cross, but to accept His gift of forgiveness won on that Cross requires acknowledging it. I recognize those nails as mine. My sins caused Him to suffer because He died in my place. Not only did Christ die for mankind as a whole but also for *each* one of us.[36]

Sorrow, Not Despair

Sorrow for sin is the goal, but not wallowing in it. Yes, we should recognize "he was wounded for our transgressions, he was bruised for our iniquities",[37] but only to help us see straight. Reflecting on what our sins cost Him should not bring us to despair but to repentance, hope, and the road of reconciliation. We must never forget what really held Him on that Cross: love.

> I asked the Lord, "How much do you love me?"
> He said, "This much", and He spread out His arms
> ... and died for me.[38]

Apologizing

"Love means never having to say you're sorry", proclaimed the blockbuster movie *Love Story*. Soon the saying seemed to be plastered everywhere; even today you can get an iPhone cover with that message. Ironically, the line came up later, in *What's Up, Doc?* with the same male lead, Ryan O'Neal. When Barbra Streisand's character spouts that maxim, O'Neal's character replies, "That's the stupidest thing I've ever heard." I think most people would agree the idea is asinine.

---

[36] *CCC* 605.
[37] Is 53:5.
[38] Source unknown.

John Lennon even quipped, "Love means saying sorry every fifteen minutes."

Sure, your beloved may, in love, have already forgiven you beforehand, but *your* love would impel you to apologize anyway. Loving others means caring about their feelings and well-being. If we hurt them in any way, how can we say we love them if we are unwilling to apologize? To love is to care when the beloved is hurt or offended; to care is to seek to reconcile and make amends. This is just as true in a relationship with God as with anyone else.

Sorrow for sins moves us to take that next step of expressing it to Him.

13

THE HARD PART

Confessing

Acknowledging Our Sins

When we truly repent, when we are truly sorry for our sins, love moves us to reconcile with God. The next step, though—to acknowledge we've done something wrong—can be pretty tough. Pride may rise up against it, but any reasonable person will realize that if we've betrayed or hurt someone, the relationship won't be healed if we refuse to admit our guilt.

The Scriptures are very clear on the need to confess:

> When I declared not my sin, my body wasted away ...
> my strength was dried up as by the heat of summer. ...
> I said, "I will confess my transgressions to the LORD";
> then you forgave the guilt of my sin.

> He who conceals his transgressions will not prosper,
> but he who confesses and forsakes them will obtain mercy.

> Return, faithless Israel, says the LORD.
> I will not look on you in anger,
> for I am merciful, says the LORD. ...
> Only acknowledge your guilt,
> that you rebelled against the LORD your God.[1]

St. John also spoke of the need to confess sin,[2] but not merely in private prayer. "In biblical terms 'confession' ... is something you do with your *lips* and not simply in the silence of your heart."[3]

---

[1] Ps 32:3–5; Prov 28:13; Jer 3:12b–13a.

[2] See 1 Jn 1:9.

[3] *Ignatius Catholic Study Bible: The New Testament*, ed. Scott Hahn and Curtis Mitch (San Francisco: Ignatius Press, 2010), p. 469, note on 1 Jn 1:9, citing Mk 1:5; Rom 10:10; Jas 5:16; and *CCC* 2631.

I once heard of a child who hid a splinter in her finger so long she developed gangrene. Just as a doctor cannot heal us if we hide our ailments from him, neither can God cleanse and heal us if we deny and hide our sins. Living in truth is central to following Christ: "[E]very one who does evil hates the light, and does not come to the light, lest his deeds should be exposed."[4] We need to come into the Light: "If we walk in the light, as he is in the light ... the blood of Jesus his Son cleanses us from all sin.... If we confess our sins, he is faithful and just, and will forgive our sins and cleanse us from all unrighteousness."[5]

Psychological Benefits

In order to restore our relationship with God, however, we need to do more than just acknowledge our sins to Him; we also need to confess them—ugh!—to another person.

Even the secular world recognizes how healing it can be to confess one's sins to another person. One "step" of every Twelve-Step program is to make an inventory of all the wrongs one has done. The next step is to tell another person what those wrongs were. The founders understood the importance of St. James' instruction to "confess your sins to one another" and the role that doing so plays in our being forgiven and healed.[6]

There's something about admitting our sins to another human being that requires more of us than acknowledging them to God alone. After all, God already knows about them; it's not like He's going to be surprised or that it will change His opinion of us. But that's not necessarily the case with other humans. Thus, making ourselves vulnerable in this way shows true repentance. It shows that we care more about what God thinks than about what other people think.

And most of the time, if we choose that person well, there is a tremendous psychological relief in exposing our sins to someone else. Though it's something we shrink from, or even fear, if we face it, we find it's not as bad as we thought. Nevertheless, it's still risky, and it probably wouldn't be wise to tell just anyone. That's why the Lord set up a very special procedure—indeed, a sacrament—for the confession of sins, one in which the listener has taken a solemn oath never to reveal what was confessed to anyone.

[4] Jn 3:20.
[5] 1 Jn 1:7–9.
[6] See Jas 5:15–16.

The Sacrament of Confession

Sadly, many don't regard the Sacrament of Confession as good news. Two main hindrances deter people from this sacrament: its reputation and the objection that there's no need for a priest.

Notorious

Regrettably, sacramental Confession has gotten a bad rap. In popular culture, the horrors of the confessional are legendary. I wonder, though, if its infamy really is a *legend*: something of the shadowy past and mixed with fiction and exaggeration. It may be that, years ago, some priests would upbraid a penitent in the confessional. I know people who had unpleasant experiences. This may have been because the priest perceived a lack of contrition or understanding in the penitent or because he had a tinge of Jansenism[7] or rheumatism or was just having a bad day.

At any rate, it's very rare today. Only once did a priest scold me—but that was twenty-five years ago, he tended to be crotchety, and I deserved it. (Sometimes we do.) And I go to Confession fairly often—having made a commitment to confess twice a month twenty years ago—and have gone to a wide array of priests: dozens of parish and diocesan priests in various cities and states as well as retreat masters and those specially trained in counseling or spiritual direction. None has ever yelled at me or called me a miserable sinner. (Though I am one.)

Who Needs a Priest?

The other major objection is this: "Why do I have to go to a priest?" Why not just tell God I'm sorry on my own? Well, you definitely can, and should, tell God you're sorry for your sins.[8] But Confession offers a more thorough cleansing and healing means. If your hands get dirty

---

[7] Though Jansenism, a "particularly dangerous heresy" of the seventeenth century, was condemned by the Church, a "moral Jansenism" lingered for centuries, in which its sentiments survived in a form of "puritanical moral rigorism". *Our Sunday Visitor's Catholic Encyclopedia*, ed. Rev. Peter M.J. Stravinskas, Ph.D., S.T.L. (Huntington, Ind.: Our Sunday Visitor, 1991), p. 529.

[8] "The Church encourages the private confession of sins to God. Ordinarily, however, this should lead us to the Sacrament of Reconciliation." (In *extraordinary* circumstances, when one is truly contrite but it is impossible to get to the sacrament—if you die in an accident, for instance, before you get a chance to confess—God's mercy is still available.) Hahn and Mitch, *Ignatius Catholic Study Bible*, p. 469, note on 1 Jn 1:9.

out in the woods—yes, use a hand wipe. But don't disparage soap and water once they're available.

Still, some might wonder why Catholics are supposed to confess to a priest; why not confess to someone of their own choosing? First of all, you certainly *can* confess to someone else; in fact, we *should* also acknowledge our wrongs to those we have offended and ask their forgiveness too. But really to answer this objection, we've got to review the history of the sacrament.

A Brief History of Confession

Some think Confession is a latecomer in the history of the Church or a "medieval invention". But Scripture and the early Church reveal the truth of the matter to be quite different.

The roots of sacramental Confession stretch back, not to the Middle Ages or the time of Jesus, but to the time of Moses. For instance, Leviticus states: "When a man is guilty ..., he shall *confess the sin he has committed*, and he shall bring his guilt offering to the LORD."[9] And who received those offerings on God's behalf? The priests. "Priestly confession is not a Christian innovation but an extension and sacramental elevation of a practice long observed in Israel."[10]

In Jesus' day, we see an analogous practice: "John the Baptist appeared in the wilderness, preaching a baptism of repentance for the forgiveness of sins." Crowds of people came, and "they were baptized by him in the river Jordan, *confessing their sins*."[11] In the fourth century, St. Basil the Great commented: "Those doing penance of old are found to have done it before the saints. It is written in the Gospel that they confessed their sins to John the Baptist (Mt 3:6); but in Acts they confessed to the Apostles, by whom also all were baptized (Acts 19:18)."[12]

As for the sacrament itself, it was Christ who set it up, realizing our need for it. "The need for repentance, confession, and forgiveness is

---

[9] Lev 5:5, emphasis added. Cf. Num 5:5–7; consider also Sir 4:26: "Do not be ashamed to confess your sins."

[10] Hahn and Mitch, *Ignatius Catholic Study Bible*, p. 469, note on 1 Jn 1:9, with reference to Lev 5:5–6 and Num 5:5–10.

[11] Mk 1:4–5; emphasis added.

[12] St. Basil the Great, *Rules Briefly Treated* [288], in *The Faith of the Early Fathers*, vol. 2, ed. William A. Jurgens (Collegeville, Minn.: Liturgical Press, 1979), p. 26, no. 977.

ongoing throughout the Christian life; otherwise, the Lord would not urge believers to seek forgiveness on a continuing basis [in the Our Father]."[13] The sacrament originated in Jesus' giving His apostles the authority to forgive sins: "If you forgive the sins of any, they are forgiven; if you retain the sins of any, they are retained."[14] So it was the Lord who commissioned His priests to hear our Confessions.

Jesus then raised the practice of confessing sins to a sacrament—that is, a rite not merely symbolic but with real power. Just as Jesus transformed the traditional baptism of Israel used by John the Baptist, a *symbolic* cleansing, into a sacrament that truly and spiritually does what it signifies—a real cleansing of the soul of all sin—so too He made the Confession of sin to priests into a sacrament that truly cleanses souls of sin.

> If we confess our sins, he is faithful and just, and will forgive our sins and cleanse us from all unrighteousness.
>
> — 1 JOHN 1:9 Box 22

In the early centuries of the Church, the need for such a sacrament quickly became clear. Baptism removed all sin, but one can be baptized only once. Those who after Baptism fell grievously and repented were given arduous public penances and were not readmitted to the Eucharist, sometimes for years, until the penance was complete. Many began to postpone Baptism. When the persecutions arose, some Christians apostatized, denying Christ to save their lives. Controversies arose over whether or not to readmit apostates who later repented or Christians who committed another mortal sin after previously performing a public penance. In her early centuries, the Church, through her popes and councils, articulated more clearly the forgiveness offered by Christ in the sacrament and further developed her teachings to meet these challenges. Later, the practice of private Confession became widespread, and public penances became reserved for public figures (such as Henry II, for his part in the murder of St. Thomas à Becket).

The writings of the Church Fathers contain ample evidence that the basic elements of the Sacrament of Confession (or Penance) as we now know it were practiced in the early age of the Church, though there were variations in the details in some places: "The Church has received from Christ the power of remitting or of refusing to remit sins.... This

---

[13] Hahn and Mitch, *Ignatius Catholic Study Bible*, p. 469, note on 1 Jn 1:9, with reference to Mt 6:12 and Lk 11:4.

[14] Jn 20:23.

power extends to all and every sin committed after Baptism.... In the ancient Church public penance was imposed for the more grievous public crimes.... Some kind of confession, not made to God only, but external, is required for the remission of sins.... Confession was made privately to a priest."[15]

In a three-volume collection of the writings of the early Church Fathers, Fr. William A. Jurgens includes quotes on Confession from some very reputable sources; here are just a few. One of the earliest Church documents, the *Didache* (or *Teaching of the Twelve Apostles*, ca. A.D. 140), testifies to the sacrament's use in the infancy of the Church: "Confess your offenses in church ..., and do not go up to your prayer with an evil conscience."[16] Firmilian of Caesarea (d. 268) relates: "The power of forgiving sins was given to the Apostles and to the Churches which these men, sent by Christ, established; and to the bishops who succeeded them by being ordained in their place."[17] On committing "a great sin", Theodore of Mopsuestia (ca. 350–428), writes:

> This is the medicine for sins, established by God and delivered to the priests of the Church.... God, because He greatly cares for us, gave us penitence and showed us the medicine of repentance; and He established some men, those who are priests, as physicians of sins. If in this world we receive through them healing and forgiveness of sins, we shall be delivered from the judgment that is to come. It behooves us, therefore, to draw near to the priests in great confidence and to reveal to them our sins; and those priests, with all diligence, solicitude, and love, and in accord with the regulations mentioned above, will grant healing to sinners. [The priests] will not disclose the things that ought not be disclosed.[18]

And St. John Chrysostom, an influential Eastern Father of the fourth century, brings out the beauty and wonder of this power Christ gave to His priests: "The priests of Judaism had power to cleanse the body

---

[15] Subheadings under the "Sacrament of Penance", in the doctrinal index of *The Faith of the Early Fathers*, vol. 3, ed. William A. Jurgens (Collegeville, Minn.: Liturgical Press, 1979), pp. 382, 383. Jurgens' other headings also paint an instructive picture of the development of the sacrament.

[16] *Didache* [4, 14], in *Faith of the Early Fathers*, vol. 1, ed. William A. Jurgens (Collegeville, Minn.: Liturgical Press, 1970), p. 2, no. 3.

[17] Firmilian of Caesarea, *Letter to Cyprian* [75, 16], in *Faith of the Early Fathers*, 1:245, no. 602.

[18] Theodore of Mopsuestia, *Catechetical Homilies* [16], in *Faith of the Early Fathers*, 2:83–84, no. 1113p.

from leprosy—or rather, not to cleanse it at all, but to *declare* a person as having been cleansed.... *Our* priests have received the power not of treating with the leprosy of the body, but with spiritual uncleanness; not of declaring cleansed, but of *actually* cleansing."[19]

Most famous of all is St. Augustine, a doctor of the Church, who writes: "Let us not listen to those who deny that the Church of God is able to forgive all sins. They are wretched indeed, because they do not recognize in Peter the rock and they refuse to believe that the keys of the kingdom of heaven ... have been given to the Church."[20]

Clearly, the sacrament's format has changed over time. In the seventh century, Irish missionaries spread the practice of private Confession, which led to use of this sacrament more often and the development of its present form.[21] Nevertheless, "Beneath the changes in discipline and celebration that this sacrament has undergone over the centuries, the same *fundamental structure* is to be discerned." This structure has "two equally essential elements": namely, the acts of the penitent: contrition, confession, and satisfaction; and those of God, acting through the Church, who "through the bishop and his priests forgives sins in the name of Jesus Christ and determines the manner of satisfaction".[22]

Reasonable Reasons to Confess to a Priest

Thus to the question, *Why confess to a priest?* the first answer is that this is what Christ Himself set up as the path to reconciliation with God, as both the New Testament and the early Church Fathers testify. And the confession spoken of in the New Testament is "not a general admission of weakness or even sinfulness, but the confession of *specific acts* of wrongdoing (Ps 32:3–5).... Jesus implies as much in John 20:23, where

---

[19] St. John Chrysostom, *The Priesthood* [3, 6, 190], in *Faith of the Early Fathers*, 2:89–90, no. 1120, citing Lev 14:2–3; emphasis added.

[20] St. Augustine, *Christian Combat* [31, 33], in *Faith of the Early Fathers*, 3:51, no. 1579. Additional Fathers quoted by Jurgens on this topic include St. Clement of Rome (the second pope, who died ca. 100); St. Ignatius of Antioch (d. 110, who was himself a disciple of the apostle John); Tertullian (ca. 155–ca. 240); St. Cyprian of Carthage (d. 258); Pope St. Stephen I (d. 257); Origen (ca. 185–253); St. Hilary of Poitiers (ca. 315–367); St. Ambrose of Milan (d. 397); as well as the First Council of Nicaea (325) and the Council of Laodicea (mid-300s).

[21] *CCC* 1447.

[22] *CCC* 1448.

he gives the apostles his own authority to remit or retain sins according to their discretion. *This discretion could not be exercised apart from knowledge of specific sins acquired by the verbal confession of sinners.*"[23]

It Helps Us

Another chief reason we confess to a priest is that it helps *us*. God is invisible, and His voice usually doesn't sound in our ears. The priest is called an *alter Christus*—another Christ; he is Christ's representative as well as a reminder of Christ's presence, and it is to *Christ*, present in the priest, that we confess. Likewise, it is Christ, in the priest, who absolves us from our sin. So it is for our sake that Christ provides someone whom we can see and hear. It is hope-reviving, glorious, and reinvigorating to *hear* those blessed words: "Your sins our forgiven."

Some object that priests are sinful creatures like ourselves. But we go to a doctor, not because he is so healthy, but because he has means to heal us that we lack. It's the same with a priest. St. Basil the Great made this point almost 1700 years ago: "Just as the diseases of the body are not divulged to all, nor haphazardly, but to those who are skilled in curing them, so too our declaration of our sins should be made to those empowered to cure them."[24]

Priests are trained to give spiritual counsel and often have very helpful advice. Moreover, Christ promised to send His Spirit upon them and work through them. Some priests have wandered from the teachings of the Church, but the Holy Spirit can work even in them and offer a beneficial insight to the penitent. Jesus reportedly told St. Faustina: "The person of the priest is, for Me, only a screen. Never analyze what sort of a priest it is that I am making use of; open your soul in confession as you would to Me, and I will fill it with My light."[25]

Church Matters

Whenever we sin, we not only offend God and hurt ourselves, but we also harm the Body of Christ.[26] The Church is that Body; when we sin,

---

[23] Hahn and Mitch, *Ignatius Catholic Study Bible*, p. 469, note on 1 Jn 1:9; citing *CCC* 1461 and 2839. Emphasis added.

[24] St. Basil the Great, *Rules Briefly Treated* [267], in *Faith of the Early Fathers*, 2:25, no. 975.

[25] St. Faustina, *Divine Mercy in My Soul: Diary of Saint Maria Faustina Kowalska* (Stockbridge, Mass.: Marian Press, 2015), p. 610, no. 1725.

[26] Chapter 15 below covers this in greater depth.

we also owe an apology and the making of amends to the Church. Here, then, is another rationale for sacramental Confession, for the priest also forgives us as a representative and on behalf of the Church.

Yet another reason Catholics confess to a priest is obedience. Jesus gave His apostles authority to make "house rules", so to speak (as He had

---

How to Make a Good Confession: A Synopsis

1. Ask the Holy Spirit for the light to recognize your sins and the grace to repent.
2. Examine your conscience. (See tips in chapter 13 above.)
3. Repent of your sins. Ask the Lord to help you resolve not to commit them again.
4. Find out when Confessions are usually scheduled at the location you choose (this may not be your local parish) *or* schedule a private Confession with a priest—this is best if you haven't gone to Confession in years, as it may take some time.
5. Once there, when you walk in, you'll usually have the option to kneel behind a screen or sit face to face with the priest.
6. If you're out of practice, go ahead and tell the priest you may not remember all the steps. He'll walk you through it.
7. Begin with the sign of the cross, saying, "Bless me, Father, for I have sinned."
8. Say how long it's been since your last Confession (or your best estimate).
9. Confess your sins. Usually you don't need to include all the circumstances and provocations; just the sins. (If he needs more information, he'll ask you.) But do include the *number of times* you committed any mortal sins. If you don't know, give him an estimate or a sense of the frequency.
10. Listen to his counsel.
11. Listen to the penance he gives you; ask him to clarify if you don't understand it.
12. Make an act of contrition. This just means you tell the Lord you're sorry for your sins out loud in the presence of the priest. There are formal prayers of contrition, and most confessionals will have at least one available on a prayer card or framed on the wall. You're free to use one of those, compose your own, or simply say, "O God, be merciful to me, a sinner!"
13. The priest will then absolve you from your sins.
14. Make the sign of the cross, thank the priest, and leave.
15. Perform the penance given you right away, if possible; if not, at soon as you can. Write it down or put it on your calendar so you don't forget.
16. Thank the Lord for His mercy, and enjoy having a clean slate!

Box 23

with Moses): "[W]hatever you bind on earth shall be bound in heaven, and whatever you loose on earth shall be loosed in heaven."[27] So if the Church mandates the confessional as the ordinary means of receiving God's forgiveness of mortal sin, then we should obey. Considering that, in the early centuries, Christians had to confess publicly and perform years-long, arduous public penances, we've got it easy now.

Love Does Whatever It Takes

Finally, even if we don't want to or understand the need, going to Confession is an opportunity to prove we are truly sorry. It proves our love of God; it proves our sincerity; it shows we are truly contrite. If an adulterous man wanted to reconcile with his wife, would he be surprised if he needed to approach her through her sister, friend, or lawyer? If I had seriously damaged my relationship with someone I loved, I would do whatever it took to convince that person of my truly being sorry, whether it meant buying flowers, standing on my head, or hopping on one foot. If we're really sorry for having turned our backs on God, then we should be willing to do *whatever* He might want. If God wanted us to apologize by composing an original sonnet of contrition and reciting it in the mall during lunch hour, who are we to argue?

Avoiding Temptation

Real remorse doesn't make accommodation for sin—doesn't tuck it away for later. We can't really be reconciled with God if we're *planning* to sin again. Rather, we need to make what is called a "firm purpose of amendment". This is not unrealistically expecting perfection from now on; it's the resolve to start over, to choose God over sin (especially mortal) from now on, with His help. Sure, we can recognize our weakness, but we can also rely on His grace to enable us to overcome sin. Sincere resolutions require making changes. To avoid falling into old (or new) sins, we must grow in self-knowledge and avoid temptation.

A good place to start is to understand why we sin. Sin is irrational. It hurts our relationships with others, with those we love, and with God, and it hurts us too. So why do we do it?

---

[27] Mt 16:19; 18:18.

What Tempts Us?

St. Thomas Aquinas teaches that the human will moves to what it perceives to be good. Even when we sin, we're not choosing evil for its own sake; rather, we're making that choice because we perceive something good in it. Often what we want is indeed a good thing; the problem is that the circumstances are not good. Food is a good thing; it is not good, though, if we eat too much or deprive others of their share. Sleep is a good thing, but not if one oversleeps and loses his job. Or the good desired is a lesser good. Prosperity is good, but integrity is better; if one can't have both, one is obligated to choose the higher good. Even when someone desires something patently evil, deep down what is really attracting him is a perceived good—it could be independence or self-determination or attention. Whatever tempts us is something that appears good to us.

There are three forces that entice us to choose lesser goods: the world, the flesh, and the devil. All three tempt us to think of short-term gains and disregard consequences and the big picture, to focus on the attractions of the desired good instead of the Greatest Good. The "world" is all we perceive with our senses and the influence of the culture in which we live, what we see our neighbor doing or what we see on TV. We also have an enemy within: "the flesh", which signifies not so much the physical body as a propensity toward sin we inherited from the Fall.

Lastly, there's an enemy deliberately seeking to demolish our relationship with God. Hating God, the fallen angels also hate us and want to destroy us. People often either fear demons excessively or disbelieve in them; both errors are dangerous. We need to recognize diabolical tactics and snares so that with the grace of God we can confidently walk past them.

The devil pretends to be a friend, acting as if all he wants is to grant you something really nice, some treats—which really, after all you've been through, don't you deserve? He preys on your weaknesses and offers rationalizations, presenting the sinful good in the most alluring light possible and insidiously whispering that you can't help yourself anyway. It takes us by surprise, then, to discover his real identity: he is the Accuser (that's what "Satan" means). He's not really on your side; he's not really your co-conspirator in getting enjoyable, if off-limit, delights. It's all a trap. He's like an attorney general who sets up sting

operations, aggressively tempting people to commit crimes and corrupt-
ing them just so he can prosecute them. What our Adversary (another
meaning of *Satan*) really wants is to make sure you spend eternity separated from God.

Temptation then is like chocolate-covered dirt. Satan starts by offering us a tantalizing truffle. We hear a warning that there's something
nasty inside—a trace of dirt or arsenic. "No, no", the devil assures us;
and we want to believe him. So we take it. It's delicious, and we don't
notice anything amiss. When he offers us another, we accept, but maybe
this time we do taste something a little gritty in the middle. But now
we're hooked, and we take more and more, even though each has more
grit and less enjoyment. We can get to the point where we'll swallow a
ball of dirt just because it's got a thin chocolate coating. While Satan's
chief goal is to get us to hell, his next-greatest amusement is to see us
slaves to a sin we no longer even enjoy.

Does God Tempt Us?

The Lord's Prayer says, "Lead us not into temptation." What does that
mean? Why do we ask this? God would never *lead* us into temptation;
Scripture says: "God cannot be tempted with evil and he himself tempts
no one."[28] The *Catechism* explains that the Greek verb used "means
both 'do not allow us to enter into temptation' and 'do not let us yield
to temptation.' "[29]

God does, however, sometimes *allow* us to be tempted. (See chap. 3
above for a discussion on why God allows us to be tested.) It is impossible for us—or even for Jesus—to go through life without experiencing any temptation at all. Such testing helps us recognize our
weaknesses and grow in humility and dependence on Him. Our sins
expose something about us, as C. S. Lewis explains: "If there are rats in
a cellar you are most likely to see them if you go in very suddenly. But
the suddenness does not create the rats: it only prevents them from
hiding. In the same way the suddenness of [a] provocation does not
make me an ill-tempered man: it only shows me what an ill-tempered
man I am."[30]

---

[28] Jas 1:13–14.
[29] *CCC* 2846.
[30] C. S. Lewis, *Mere Christianity* (New York: HarperCollins, 2001), p. 192.

God allows us even to fall in order to teach us humility, because pride is a danger for everyone, and spiritual pride is the worst.[31] Shielding us from all temptation would let us in our blind pride think that we could manage just fine on our own. Better a lesser fall that shakes us up than sailing smoothly to hell. "Lead us not into temptation" then is a prayer of humility, a recognition of weakness and plea for God's help. Humility acknowledges the truth. "I come to the confessional a sinner with sin, but I leave a sinner without sin", Mother Teresa said.[32] "I don't think there is anyone else who needs God's help and grace more than I do."[33]

Know Thyself

The fact is, without God's grace, any of us is ultimately capable of anything. The sooner we realize that, the better. A retreat master recounted that once when St. Teresa of Avila returned from a trip, she found all the sisters whispering. When she learned there was a rumor that she had engaged in some hanky-panky while she was away, she burst out laughing and replied, "Absolutely! that *would* be true—but for the grace of God." Saints always have that attitude. They don't go around thinking how much holier they are than everyone else. With the humility to look at themselves honestly, they know quite well that, left to their own devices, they would be capable of the same. Instead, when they see sin, they say, "There, but for the grace of God, go I."

After humbly admitting our sinful tendencies, we then have to take responsibility for not putting ourselves in the way of temptation. Jesus says, "temptations to sin are sure to come" but also "but woe to him by whom they

> Knowledge of self ... is why the saints could say they were wicked criminals. They saw God and then saw themselves—and they saw the difference.
>
> —St. Teresa of Calcutta [Box 24]

come!"[34] That includes tempting ourselves. We must recognize where we are weak. In order to avoid sin, we must also avoid what the Church

---

[31] Pride is the worst of the capital sins (those which engender other sins). In seeking to put self above others, it is the opposite of love. As C. S. Lewis puts it: "It was through Pride that the devil became the devil: Pride ... is the complete anti-God state of mind." *Mere Christianity* (New York: Macmillan, 1978), p. 109. Lewis' chapter on pride, entitled "The Great Sin", is excellent and was life-changing for me.

[32] Mother Teresa, *Love: A Fruit Always in Season* (San Francisco: Ignatius Press, 1987), p. 76.

[33] Ibid., p. 244.

[34] Lk 17:1.

calls "occasions of sin"—that is, tempting situations.[35] If you're on a diet, you should know better than to wander into an ice cream shop. Gain the self-knowledge to know what is particularly tempting to you, and avoid situations where you're likely to fall. As Mother Angelica put it: "You know, if you are bit by a chained dog, you can't blame the dog. If you put yourself in temptation and you fall you cannot blame anyone but yourself."[36]

Self-knowledge is not meant, however, to serve as an excuse. We're not to say, "I'm so weak; I just couldn't help it", or "I'm such a sinner; there's no hope for me." Yes, realize that "apart from [Christ] you can do nothing",[37] but don't stop there. Live in the miraculous flipside: "I can do all things in [Christ] who strengthens me."[38] We must always remember Paul's words: "God ... will not let you be tempted beyond your strength, but with the temptation will also provide the way of escape, that you may be able to endure it."[39]

If we avoid temptations whenever possible, ask God to help us defeat them, and rely on His grace when they do come, they won't defeat us. Moreover, avoiding and overcoming temptations are more ways to show Him our love and true contrition. Don't doubt that He will notice: "Blessed is the man who endures trial, for when he has stood the test he will receive the crown of life which God has promised to those who love him."[40] When we do fall, He will always take us back. Run to the confessional, where He is eager to embrace and strengthen you.

---

[35] For more, see *Our Sunday Visitor's Catholic Encyclopedia*, ed. Rev. Peter M.J. Stravinskas (Huntington, Ind.: Our Sunday Visitor, 1991), p. 693.

[36] Mother Angelica, *Mother Angelica's Little Book of Life Lessons and Everyday Spirituality*, ed. Raymond Arroyo (New York: Doubleday, 2007), p. 151.

[37] Jn 15:5.

[38] Phil 4:13; see Mt 19:26.

[39] 1 Cor 10:13.

[40] Jas 1:12.

14

THE PAYOFF

Making the Most of Mercy

While it's true that, to appreciate the mercy of God fully, we must realize how much we need it and how little we deserve it; on the other hand, we must be careful not to wallow in guilt. Maybe one reason we avoid considering our guilt is that once we admit it, we're tempted to think we're unforgivable. The point of feeling sorrow for sin is not to be overwhelmed by it but to seek God's mercy and experience His peace. After repenting and receiving the sacrament, we must leave the sin and guilt behind, believing God is our merciful Father, eager to forgive us.

Unchanging Love

No matter what we do, He never stops loving us. We who are changeable and live in a constantly changing world find this hard to comprehend. Here the concept of God as unchanging can help.

God's love is like the sun. When it's warm and bright, we feel comfortable, happy, and energetic. In winter, though, the sun seems cold and distant; in storms or at night, it seems to have gone away. In the desert, it feels unrelenting, merciless, and potentially deadly. But in all these things, the sun hasn't changed at all. What's changed is *our* conditions: in winter our hemisphere receives fewer hours of sunlight, the world has turned, clouds are blocking the sun, or we're far from the water and vegetation we need to survive in the sun. The sun has not changed its position or size or how much heat it gives off. None of its apparent changes are in the sun at all. Rather, the conditions on earth are what is continually changing.

Similarly, when we feel God no longer loves us, the changes are really in *us*, not Him. Straying from Him yields a cold, distant feeling. When we turn our backs on Him, we find ourselves in darkness. When we wander from His fountain of life-giving grace, we're left in a barren desert where His gaze feels unrelenting and merciless, though it's precisely as loving as when it felt balmy and comfortable. When the storms of life roll in, blocking our view of Him, He hasn't gone anywhere: He's still there, above the clouds, loving us just as much.

Infinite Mercy

Sometimes we become so aware of our sinfulness and unworthiness we have a hard time believing God could really forgive us. We focus on the looming size or darkness of our sin until it seems

> God is quicker to forgive than a mother to snatch her child from the fire.
> —ST. JOHN VIANNEY Box 25

too big for even God to forgive. It can also be hard to believe in God's mercy as it is so hard for *us* to practice. But St. Augustine—previously, for decades, himself a serious sinner—said: "Let no one say: 'I did that; perhaps I will not be forgiven.'"[1] God's mercy is bottomless.

Because we have trouble believing God's mercy is infinite, Jesus appeared numerous times to an uneducated Polish nun, Sr. Faustina Kowalska, teaching her about, and asking for a feast commemorating, His Divine Mercy. These private revelations[2] were eventually approved by the Church, and Faustina was declared a saint. In 2000, at her canonization Mass, Pope St. John Paul II added Divine Mercy Sunday to the Church calendar: one week following Easter. It is a day to reflect on and realize in our hearts that God's mercy is *infinite*.

How could any sin be too big or too dark for God to handle? He is infinite Love! St. Thérèse of Lisieux gives a beautiful image of His boundless love: in the blazing furnace of God's love, our sins are like drops of water: they sizzle for a second, then are gone. Similarly, Mother Angelica says that after Confession, one's sins and faults would be as

---

[1] St. Augustine, *Sermon to Catechumens, on the Creed* [7, 15], in *The Faith of the Early Fathers*, vol. 3, ed. William A. Jurgens (Collegeville, Minn.: Liturgical Press, 1979), p. 35, no. 1536.

[2] *Private revelation* is a term used for a claim of supernatural communication from God or His agents to a person on earth; it is distinguished from "public revelation", which ended with the apostles. The Church carefully investigates any such claims by Catholics, considering the soundness of their theological content and any fruits resulting from the alleged apparitions. When the Church determines that a particular claim *does* meet all these criteria (not very often), the private revelation will be "approved", which simply means it was found worthy of belief. Catholics are not bound to believe in any approved revelations, however. Similarly, before canonizing anyone, the Church makes a thorough investigation into the person's life, writings, and miracles attributed to his prayers. Canonization as a saint by the Church, however, does not mean that the saint's writings are considered infallible.

impossible to find as a drop of water tossed into the ocean. "Every day, every minute of the day, throw your drop in the ocean of His mercy", she advises. "Then don't worry, just try harder."[3]

Keep in mind that Jesus died on the Cross *in order that we might be forgiven*. To doubt that He can forgive us could actually be a matter of pride—as if any puny creature could do something so bad that God couldn't forgive it, despite the Son of God's great sacrifice of Himself. It is His Blood—one drop of which is more precious to the Father than the universe—that blots out our sins, provided we seek His forgiveness.

Some worry over the "eternal sin" Jesus speaks of in the Gospels, one that won't be forgiven.[4] The Church has long taught, however, that the only sin that can't be forgiven is the sin of refusing to repent.[5] She assures us: "There are no limits to the mercy of God, but anyone who deliberately refuses to accept his mercy by repenting, rejects the forgiveness of his sins and the salvation offered by the Holy Spirit."[6] This sin has traditionally been called "despair"—but even despair can be forgiven if one repents of it.

The Lord doesn't wish that "any should perish, but that all should reach repentance".[7] Remember the comforting words of Jesus: "The Son of man came to seek and to save the lost", and "There is joy before the angels of God over one sinner who repents."[8] We shouldn't engage,

---

[3] Mother Angelica, *Mother Angelica's Little Book of Life Lessons and Everyday Spirituality*, ed. Raymond Arroyo (New York: Doubleday, 2007), pp. 157–58.

[4] Mark 3:29 reads, "Whoever blasphemes against the Holy Spirit never has forgiveness, but is guilty of an eternal sin."

[5] Aquinas explains that Jesus was speaking of the sin that is "unpardonable by reason of its nature, in so far as it removes those things which are a means towards the pardon of sins. This does not, however, close the way of forgiveness and healing to an all-powerful and merciful God, Who, sometimes, by a miracle, so to speak, restores spiritual health to such men." St. Thomas Aquinas, *Summa Theologica*, vol. 3, pt. II, Second Section, trans. Fathers of the English Dominican Province (New York: Cosimo, 2007), p. 1230. Similarly, Pope St. John Paul II says that " 'blasphemy' does not properly consist in offending ... against the Holy Spirit in *words*; it consists rather in the refusal to accept the salvation which God offers to man through the Holy Spirit, working through the power of the Cross." Pope St. John Paul II, Encyclical *Dominum et Vivificantem* on the Holy Spirit in the Life of the Church and the World, *The Lord and Giver of Life* (May 18, 1986), no. 46; emphasis added. Numbers 46 and 47 of the document provide a lengthy exegesis on this verse.

[6] *CCC* 1864.

[7] 2 Pet 3:9. See also *CCC* 1037: "God predestines no one to go to hell; for this, a willful turning away from God (a mortal sin) is necessary, and persistence in it until the end."

[8] Lk 19:10; Lk 15:10.

then, in "useless looks at our own miseries", Mother Teresa says, but "lift our hearts to God and His light".[9]

Rewards of Reconciliation

Sacramental Confession is a tremendous gift with great benefits. First, we may experience a number of wonderful things: joy, lightness, relief, an increase of love and gratitude, a surge in the desire to obey God better and love Him more, greater compassion for others, humility, and hope. Whether or not we feel any of these, there are certain indisputable, factual gains from braving the confessional: getting plucked from the road to hell (if you confessed mortal sin) and set on the path to heaven; forgiveness; reconciliation with God and with the Church; greater strength for the spiritual journey; a clean soul; and God's grace.[10]

> In Confession you ... receive great strength to help you in avoiding [your sins] henceforth, clearer light to discover your failings, and abundant grace to make up whatever loss you have incurred through those faults. You exercise the graces of humility, obedience, simplicity and love, and by this one act of Confession you practice more virtue than in any other.
>
> —St. Francis de Sales Box 26

Because it's such a wonderful means of growing spiritually, many saints and spiritual writers advise frequent Confession. Though the Church requires Confession only for mortal sins, she still highly recommends availing oneself of its graces for venial sins as well (though one needn't confess *every* venial sin—that could take hours). And while the precept of the Church instructs the faithful to confess at least once a year, she urges going more often; a common recommendation is at least once or twice a month. We don't take a bath only when we're covered with mud or once a year; our souls need "freshening up" more often too. And when you go more frequently, it's easier to remember your sins.

Reportedly, Pope St. John Paul II went to Confession *daily*. Some saints valued the sacrament so highly that they would go even when they had no deliberate sins to confess. They would confess their faults

---

[9] Mother Teresa, *Love: A Fruit Always in Season* (San Francisco: Ignatius Press, 1987), p. 167.
[10] Cf. *CCC* 1468 and 1496.

or even sins confessed previously—not from a fear that they hadn't been forgiven, but out of love, sorrow, and a desire for the graces flowing from the sacrament.

When we love someone, we don't apologize only for major offenses. We're sorry for anything that might hurt or bother our loved ones. Sometimes it might even be something unintentional. If I accidentally break something belonging to my husband or forget to do something he asked me to do, I don't say to him, "Well, I didn't do it on purpose, so get over it." I'm still sorry, and I still apologize. Or when my husband and I speak of old times and recall a time when one hurt the other, we'll apologize again, even though we know the other has forgiven us. It's the same with the Lord. You can bring venial sins and unintentional misdeeds to Confession because you're sorry and want to apologize to the Lord.

At first, it's very difficult to confess one's sins, but just as with eating vegetables or getting exercise, so with the Sacrament of Confession: the more you do it, the easier it gets and the more benefits you enjoy. And just as other good things that require self-discipline lead to being healthy and feeling good, partaking in Reconciliation leads to great joy.

PART TWO

"Love One Another
as I Have Loved You"

LOVING GOD MEANS PICKING UP YOUR CROSS

"If any man would come after me, let him deny himself
and take up his cross and follow me."

(Mt 16:24)

Take your share of suffering as a good soldier of Christ Jesus.

(2 Tim 2:3)

Rejoice in so far as you share Christ's sufferings,
that you may also rejoice and be glad when his glory is revealed.

(1 Pet 4:13)

Parts of this section appeared previously in "Mortification for Moderns", by the author, published in *Voices* 26, no. 4 (Advent–Christmas 2011), pp. 19–21; online edition: http://archive.wf-f.org/11-4-Flood.html.

15

LOVE ENTAILS SACRIFICE

Now we come to a part of the Good News that doesn't strike us as *good*: loving God entails picking up a cross and following Him to Calvary. Yes, this means accepting and enduring the sufferings or crosses He allows in our lives, but He invites us to do more: undertaking something difficult as a sacrifice or penance, as a gift to God. Now the idea of doing penance is often misunderstood (some view it as some sort of masochism) and hardly popular. These then are the two main objections to penances: we think we don't need to do them, and we don't want to.

Who Needs Penance?

A truth our culture abhors is this: not only do we all undergo some suffering, but we actually need to. "It is necessary for us to undergo many hardships to enter the kingdom of God."[1] This includes undertaking voluntary sufferings at times.

Justice

Secular culture isn't alone in objecting to that idea; many of our Protestant brethren do too. They hold that since Christ paid the price for our sins on the Cross, our debt is paid; there's nothing we need to do. This is partially true: *eternal* justice is satisfied for those who repent of their sins to God and call upon the mercy Christ obtained for us on the Cross.[2] But that doesn't mean we're done. Neither Scripture nor the early Church supports that view.

---

[1] Acts 14:22, NABRE. See also 1 Pet 4:12–13; Rom 8:17; 2 Cor 1:5; and 2 Tim 2:11–12.

[2] Ordinarily, this mercy is obtained in the sacraments, but if that is not possible, God has other means for extraordinary cases. See *CCC* 1484.

The New Testament builds on what was practiced in the Old: the Book of Numbers states that after confessing, a penitent should "make full restitution for his wrong, adding a fifth to it, and giving it to him to whom he did the wrong".[3] For instance, the Book of Acts makes clear that we need not only to "repent and turn to God" but also to "perform deeds worthy of ... repentance".[4] In the fourth century, St. Augustine spoke of penitence as a sign of repentance as if it were well known to his contemporaries, stating, "those who do penance ... for the remission of their crimes, however serious" can hope to receive "God's mercy in the Holy Church".[5] And citations from early Church Fathers support the beliefs that "even when guilt is taken away the whole temporal punishment due to sin in not always taken away" and that "there remains after absolution the necessity of making the satisfaction demanded by God's justice."[6]

Wait a second, some might reply, *why does God's justice still demand satisfaction? Didn't Jesus pay the price for us on the Cross?* He most certainly did. He paid the *eternal* penalty for our sins—something we could never have done, no matter how hard we tried.[7]

However, we need to understand that "sin has *a double consequence*":[8] there are not only eternal but also temporal ramifications. Besides the eternal penalty Jesus paid, there is also a temporal penalty, which we are obligated to pay. *Temporal* means "having to do with earthly life". Jesus took care of the debt we owe to God for sin, a debt we could never repay ourselves. Nevertheless, more needs

> Many sins wrong our neighbor. One must do what is possible in order to repair the harm (e.g., return stolen goods ...). Simple justice requires as much.... Absolution takes away sin, but it does not remedy all the disorders sin has caused.... The sinner must still recover his full spiritual health by doing something more to make amends for the sin.
>
> —*CCC* 1459 Box 27

---

[3] Num 5:7.

[4] Acts 26:20, and John the Baptist warned: "Bear fruit that befits repentance" (Mt 3:8).

[5] St. Augustine, *The Enchiridion of Faith, Hope, and Love* [17, 65], in *The Faith of the Early Fathers*, vol. 3, ed. William A. Jurgens (Collegeville, Minn.: Liturgical Press, 1979), p. 149, no. 1919.

[6] William A. Jurgens, "Doctrinal Index", in *Faith of the Early Fathers*, 3:383.

[7] The satisfaction we make "certainly ... is not a price that one pays for the sin absolved and for the forgiveness obtained: No human price can match what is obtained, which is the fruit of Christ's precious blood." Pope St. John Paul II, Post-Synodal Apostolic Exhortation *Reconciliatio et Paenitentia* on Reconciliation and Penance in the Mission of the Church Today, *Reconciliation and Penance* (December 2, 1984), no. 31, III.

[8] *CCC* 1472; see also 1473.

to be done, because all sin injures others and our own souls too. It is only just that we try to repair the damages our sins have wrought on the temporal plane.[9]

Sin isn't committed in a vacuum; it impinges on other people. There is no such thing as a private sin. For one thing, sin weakens our character. This affects how we treat others and makes us more likely to fall again or in other ways, hurting others directly. Furthermore, it's like the natural environment we all share. What we do on our own property affects others. Running a factory that emits billows of black smoke or dumps toxic waste into the waterways is going to impact others beyond our own boundaries. If, on the other hand, we plant trees, which absorb carbon monoxide and emit oxygen, that will freshen the air for everyone, beginning with those closest to us. It's the same in the spiritual realm. Every sin we commit, even in secret, makes the spiritual world a little darker; every Christlike thing we do, even in secret, makes it brighter. Mankind is connected; being one body in Christ means "If one member suffers, all suffer together."[10] Everything we do spiritually helps or spiritually harms everyone else. Thus we need to make reparation to our fellowman as well as to God for our sins.

Look at it this way. If a wayward urchin somehow managed to blow up an abandoned factory building, he would never be able to repay the owner. But if a billionaire stepped in, adopted him, and paid the damages, the boy wouldn't owe the debt anymore. His adopted father would know the boy could never pay him back, but wouldn't it be wrong for the son to do nothing? Shouldn't he rather do whatever he could? Mowing the lawn, shoveling snow, and taking out the trash cheerfully for years would be a pittance in comparison but still be meaningful to his father. Wouldn't it be the just and loving thing to do, a sign of his gratitude and true repentance? Moreover, wouldn't the boy owe something to the community? The state would have every right to require community service of some kind from the boy himself to make some reparation and in the hope of rehabilitating him into a caring, responsible citizen. Similarly, we should show our gratitude to God for His mercy, and acts of penance are one way to do that. Sacramental penance proves the sincerity of our contrition, being "the sign of the

---

[9] See also pp. 192–95, 319, and 324–25.
[10] 1 Cor 12:26.

personal commitment ... to begin a new life."[11] Penance is "community service", not for the state, but for the Kingdom.

Finally, penance helps *us*. It arises from "God's fatherly love ... as a part of a *merciful justice* that re-establishes the violated order for the sake of *man's own good*."[12] Psychology concurs. We saw earlier that most of the Twelve Steps revolve around one's misdeeds. This includes seeking somehow to make amends for those wrongs (Steps 8 and 9). Similarly, Menninger observes that to reduce the stress of an unrelieved conscience, "the logical, reasonable, effective solution ... is to make atonement ... by restitution, acknowledgement, and revised tactics."[13]

Doing Our Part

Another way to understand the need for penance is to remember that when it comes to our purification, as in so many other areas of the spiritual life, there is needed something both from God and from us. Two perennial temptations are to rely too heavily on one or the other. People tend to be either too lazy, expecting God to do everything for them, or too active, relying too much upon themselves instead of God. We have to do both: rely on God and act. In financial matters, we don't just pray and stop there; we still go out and try to find a job. So it is with our sins. He did His part already: paying the eternal debt for them on the Cross. We need to do something too.

St. Paul indicates that Jesus leaves something for us to do: "In my flesh, I complete what is lacking in Christ's afflictions for the sake of his body, that is, the Church."[14] You may wonder, "How could anything be lacking in Christ's sufferings for His Church? He's God! He's perfect, so His sacrifice had to have been perfect and, if perfect, then complete. Right?" His sacrifice is perfect, but He left room for us to be a part of it. After all, we are His Body, and we participate in what the Head does and in what happens to Him—good and bad.[15]

---

[11] John Paul II, *Reconciliatio et Paenitentia, Reconciliation and Penance*, no. 31, III.

[12] Pope St. John Paul II, General Audience (September 29, 1999), no. 3; emphasis added.

[13] Karl Menninger, M.D., *Whatever Became of Sin?* (New York: Hawthorn Books, 1973), p. 182.

[14] Col 1:24.

[15] St. Paul's "words could be misunderstood to mean that the suffering of Christ was not sufficient for redemption and that the suffering of the saints must be added to complete it. This, however, would be heretical. Christ and the Church are one mystical person, and while the

If, after dinner, I do the dishes, while my kids bring them to me, put away leftovers, clear and wash the table and counters, and sweep, it is not because I am incapable of doing those tasks. In fact, I could do them better and faster myself! But I leave them undone so my children can share in the work.

> You have received the spirit of sonship.... [W]e are children of God, and if children, then heirs, heirs of God and fellow heirs with Christ, provided we suffer with him in order that we may also be glorified with him.
>
> —ROMANS 8:14–17 [Box 28]

This is primarily for their sake, so they can learn what it means to be a family, to be responsible and disciplined, and to learn the different tasks involved in keeping a home clean. Similarly, God is perfectly capable of cleaning up the universe all by Himself, but He lets us do some of the work too. He gives us the honor of working with Him, as His children.

Avoiding Sacrifice

We Don't Want To

Another problem is we don't want to do penance. It's hard. Every era, every society, has its weaknesses. Ours is that we've become couch potatoes, satisfied with mediocrity. Compared with our ancestors, "we are less courageous, less honest with ourselves, less self-disciplined, and obviously less chaste than they were. But they were more cruel, intolerant, snobbish, and inhumane than we are. They were better at the hard virtues; we are better at the soft virtues." [16]

Holy Mother Church recognizes how weak we've become and has lowered our penitential obligations to accommodate us. Fasting requirements, for instance, have been greatly relaxed in our time. Until the latter half of the twentieth century, the fast before receiving the Eucharist began the night before, at midnight; now it's just an hour. Catholics' Lenten fasting was once nearly as arduous as Muslims' fasting during Ramadan. A confessor in the Middle Ages might give you a penance of

---

merits of Christ, the head, are infinite, the saints acquire merit in a limited degree. What is 'lacking', then, pertains to the afflictions of the entire Church." Scott Hahn and Curtis Mitch, eds., *Ignatius Catholic Study Bible: The New Testament* (San Francisco: Ignatius Press, 2010), p. 366, note on Col 1:24, citing Thomas Aquinas, *Commentary on Colossians* 1, 6.

[16] Peter Kreeft, *Back to Virtue* (San Francisco: Ignatius Press, 1992), p. 25.

three days' fasting on bread and water, while sitting on the cold floor of a church, without a coat or blanket. Nowadays, we're often told simply to pray three Hail Marys. I don't think this is because we're less sinful than our forebears, just less hardy.

In our day, we can eradicate many discomforts with the flick of a switch, and we're surrounded by messages to take the easy way. But St. Paul warned us not to be conformed to our age.[17] Moreover, as we saw above in the preface, we can get muddled about reality. We can get so caught up in what is right in front of us that we lose track of what's behind it all, as though the things demanding our attention are all there is. Though they're real, they won't last.

Thus the world (with the enthusiastic help of the flesh and the devil) actively distracts us from eternal realities; all three work against the practice of penance. Each encourages us to avoid any and all self-denial and hightail it away from actual suffering. The world is in our face, displaying myriad pleasures and, with the devil, urging us to indulge every fancy and whim, while the flesh is eager to consent. They would have us seek ...

A Life without Sacrifice

There is no such thing as a life with no sacrifice, though we'd prefer to think there is.

Many think it would be wrong for God to ask for sacrifice, so if there is a God, either He is too nice to do so or He is to be avoided. Many shun religion, dedicate their lives to pleasing themselves, and think they're

> Man is made to adore ..., if you give him nothing to worship, he will fashion his own divinities.
>
> —BENJAMIN DISRAELI [Box 29]

thus avoiding sacrifice. But there's no escaping sacrifice, even for those who reject God. Some may think they serve no god, but that's impossible. Whether we admit it or not, the temple of the heart can't be empty. If we refuse to let God in, some other idol(s) will slip in and take His place.[18] And that idol will always demand sacrifice.

If, for instance, I think I'll be happiest with a lot of money and decide to let nothing stop me, I'll put making money above exercise and rest,

---

[17] Rom 12:2.
[18] See also *CCC* 27–28, 44–46, 2113–14, and Rom 1:21–23, 25.

since I've got to put in a lot of hours to advance at work. Since getting that promotion is integral to achieving my goal, I'll put it above being fair to my co-workers and backstab or even lie about them. I'll put gaining wealth above following the law (provided I won't get caught). I may not admit it, but money is my idol, and the sacrifices I make to it are my integrity, my health, and good relationships with my colleagues.

Or let's say what I want most is pleasure. I don't care about the company I work for or pleasing my boss; I only work to pay for my pleasures, so I do just enough to keep my job. I like people with whom I have a good time; if they stop being fun or have problems, I drop them. I spend as much of my life in enjoyable activities as I can, even if they're bad for me. I may not admit I'm worshipping pleasure or sacrificing my conscience, long-term welfare, real friendship, health, and possibly my life to it, but that doesn't change the fact that I am.

If we make sacrifices to the object of our desire, it is an idol. In both those cases, all I've listed are the *temporal* sacrifices. But believers also notice the spiritual price to be paid: the sacrifice of my character, my virtues, and, ultimately, my eternal soul.

Most people aren't as extreme as these examples though. They want money *and* pleasure *and* friends, so they don't sacrifice everything to just one idol. But they still fudge giving much to God. And even those of us who do allow God into the temple of our hearts, being sinners, have at times allowed some minor gods to creep in too. We don't admit that they're idols, so we think God won't mind sharing some space with them. We think we can please Him and them too, and get the benefits of pouring a few surreptitious libations in their direction.

By the word *sacrifice*, most people nowadays mean "the act of giving up something that you want to keep, especially in order to get or do something else or to help someone".[19] We do it all the time. Sacrifice is part of life. Everyone who has ever pursued a goal—from the athlete training for a race to the clerk striving to move up in his company—knows this. Everything comes with a price, and often the price is worth it. Working hard is worth the cost involved to provide for one's family, but not worth the cost of having too little time with them.

If this is how it is in the natural order, why should it be any surprise that it's part of the spiritual order too? Sacrifice is part of following Jesus:

[19] Merriam-Webster online dictionary, http://www.merriam-webster.com/dictionary/sacrifice.

we share in His priesthood,[20] and a priest is one who offers sacrifice. Moreover, growing in virtue and going to heaven have a price too—I have to follow God's commands, even when it means doing something difficult—but that price is well worth it. Any sacrifice I must make—my pride, my grudges, indulging in immoderate pleasure, my pet sins, getting my way—any and every sacrifice is well worth union with God, who alone can satisfy my soul.

If sacrifice is unavoidable, we might as well do it right.

Reasons to Do Penance

The Church has found embracing the cross to be tremendously powerful. Sadly, though, this power for good is greatly overlooked. Once, passing a hospital, Fulton Sheen was seen shaking his head. When his companion inquired, "So much suffering?" Sheen replied, "So much *wasted* suffering." When suffering comes, we can make it a force for good ... or let it go down the drain.

If we're going to suffer anyway—and we all are—we might as well make it useful. All we need to do is hand it over to Jesus; He's the One who can bring good out of it. He was the One who transformed His own murder into the greatest blessing of human history.

Thus Jesus' followers over two thousand years have understood "picking up one's cross" as meaning both accepting bad things that happen as well as the active undertaking of penances: suffering voluntarily. He was the One who turned our perspective upside down, saying, "Blessed are you poor ... blessed are you that hunger ... that weep, ... blessed are you when men hate you ...".[21] From crosses linked to His, God brings good—for others and even for us.

Good for Others

Penance is a potent and multifaceted means of loving others. Chapter 3 above discussed the value and meaning of suffering: participating in Christ's work of redemption and thereby aiding in the salvation of our brothers and sisters. In bearing our crosses, we are "carrying out an irreplaceable service", Pope St. John Paul II says. "It is suffering, more

---

[20] See *CCC* 783.
[21] Lk 6:20–22.

than anything else, which clears the way for the grace which transforms human souls."[22]

We can help people spiritually by undertaking penances and offering them up; penance is a wonderful mode of intercession. This might seem a strange idea if you've never heard it before, but remember Jesus said that sometimes prayer alone is not enough; some situations require fasting too.[23] Adding a sacrifice to our prayer shows God how much we mean it. If a brother puts in a good word with his parents for his sister, who wants to go to camp, that's pretty nice; if the brother also donates his allowance to help her go, that makes an even bigger impression.

The world and our lives are full of people in need. The biggest need, of course, is God. Everyone needs Him, but many don't know it. Those who have rejected Him need the prayers of others to obtain the grace to find or return to Him. They need a miracle. Prayers for that miracle are even more effective when joined to a voluntary penance or the loving endurance of a cross.

Interestingly, God is sending us repeated invitations to help Him save souls. Through His Mother have come recurring calls for fasting and penance not only in the more famous apparitions of Lourdes and Fatima, but also in most of the Church-approved Marian apparitions of the last two centuries, including Our Lady of Akita (Japan, 1973) and Kibeho (Rwanda, 1981).[24]

Pope St. John Paul II saw those who suffer for Christ as mighty: "How often is it precisely ... from them that [the pastors of the Church] seek help and support! ... The springs of divine power gush forth precisely in the midst of human weakness."[25] The elderly who rise at dawn

---

[22] Pope St. John Paul II, Apostolic Letter *Salvifici Doloris* on the Christian Meaning of Human Suffering (February 11, 1984), no. 27. He also explained that it is as members of Him who is "*the irreplaceable mediator and author of the good things*" which are indispensable for the world's salvation" that our sufferings gain their efficacy: "The Church sees in all Christ's suffering brothers and sisters as it were a *multiple subject of his supernatural power*." Ibid.

[23] Mk 9:29.

[24] An *apparition* is an alleged visit of someone from heaven. While claims are many, Church endorsements are few. Hundreds of alleged Marian apparitions have been deemed *not* to be authentic, have not been approved, or have not even been investigated. Thus it is wise not to focus on any apparition that hasn't yet received approval. I know this can be hard; I was once very interested in Medjugorje, benefited from its early messages, and even seemingly witnessed a miracle there. However, while the Church is still investigating, I've backed off. One should never put more trust in a private revelation—even if one is the visionary!—than in the Church; it's too easy to be mistaken. Moreover, we already have everything we need in the Church's teachings. See n. 2 in chap. 14 above for more on how the Church investigates apparitions and private revelations.

[25] John Paul II, *Salvifici Doloris, Human Suffering*, no. 27.

and gingerly hobble into church for daily Mass and the Rosary, the bedridden who offer their pain as prayer, and the cloistered who have given their whole lives as a gift to God, spent in prayer for His people— these are the unacclaimed heroes. These are the prayer giants who keep the world turning.

We can join them; each of us can make a difference. This is what Jesus taught and what His Mother highlights in so many Church-approved apparitions. This is how she's asked us to work on the mess the world is

---

Heavenly Appeal for Penance

One approved Marian apparition very worthy of belief is that of Fatima.

The miracles at Fatima were stupendous and well-documented. An estimated *seventy thousand* people showed up on October 13, 1917, the day Mary had promised a big miracle. Many came unbelieving, including journalists who showed up to scoff and expose the Fatima messages as a hoax. They ended up groveling on the ground when the sun appeared to whirl in the sky and then fall toward the earth. When the sun went back to its place, everyone found their clothes and the ground—previously sopping wet from torrents of rain—to be perfectly dry. The journalists ended up printing articles very different from what they had expected to write, even in the Masonic newspaper. They testified to the miracle they had witnessed.[a]

In addition, there is the witness of the extraordinary lives of the visionaries, especially Francisco and Jacinta, who were recently canonized as saints.

The Fatima story is too big to cover adequately here. There are many resources available.[b] What's critical is Mary's message: essentially a plea to love God and neighbor. She asked us to follow her Son, live in God's grace, do penance, and pray (especially the daily Rosary and the Five First Saturdays),[c] begging God for the salvation of souls.

[a] See for instance, "Circumstances and Dialogue of 1917 Apparitions", *Fatima Network Essentials*, http://www.fatima.org/essentials/facts/1917appar.asp (accessed Nov. 17, 2015). See also http://www.fatimapeaceconferences.com/brazil_2007/transcripts/pc3.asp.

[b] See, e.g., "Fatima: Spectacular Signs for a Skeptical Age", by the author, *Catholic World Report*, Oct. 6, 2017, http://www.catholicworldreport.com/2017/10/06/fatima-spectacular -signs-for-a-skeptical-age/; the book *Fatima for Today*, by Father Andrew Apostoli, and the film of the same name. The latter two are available through Ignatius Press at http://www .fatimafortoday.com/.

[c] For a summary of the latter devotion, see http://www.theworkofgod.org/Aparitns /Fatima/5firstsa.htm.

Box 30

in: one Rosary at a time. Little acts of penance and kindness. Following
the Church's teachings (a penance in itself sometimes). Spending time
with God. If we heed her requests, we will be amazed at the difference
prayer and penance can make.

Gratitude: A Great Motive for Penance

A talented high-school soccer player was once playing in a champion-
ship game. Suddenly, he left the game and sprinted up a nearby hill—
where one could see a house was on fire. He ran into the house and up
the stairs, and he found his four-year-old brother. He rolled him in a
mattress and dropped him out the window into the arms of his neighbors below. He had saved his brother.

On his way out, though, he himself was struck by a falling beam.
Firefighters came and saved his life, but he lost not only his sterling soccer skills but even the ability to walk and talk.

Years later, the younger brother (now seventeen) asked if he could go
to a party one evening. His mother said no; she and his father had to
go out, and so his disabled brother would need him. He exploded,
"What! I have to stay home with that vegetable!" A friend witnessing
this scene could see the older brother in his wheelchair in the next
room: a tear was rolling down his cheek.

When I first heard this (true) story, I was outraged. That ingrate
wouldn't even be alive if it weren't for his brother. The elder one had
risked his life and lost everything else out of love for his little brother.
The latter should have been forever grateful and eager to do *anything*
for him.

Then it hit me like a ton of bricks that I am no better than that
younger brother. While Jesus isn't *visibly* sitting in the next room like
the older brother, haven't I treated Him the same way? I have—every
time I've wimped out on a sacrifice for Him who did even more for me.

An excellent way to express our gratitude to Jesus for suffering and
dying for us is to imitate Him and incorporate self-denial and penance
into our own lives.

Good for Us

Penance is for our own sake. Keep in mind that "even after absolution
there remains in the Christian a dark area due to the wound of sin"
operating as "an infectious source of sin" and resulting in a "weakening

of the spiritual faculties".[26] But there is hope: there is the grace of God, acquired through prayer and the sacraments, and with self-denial, we can fight against the tendency to sin. Just as every sin makes us weaker, so every good action makes us stronger. Penance then makes our wills stronger and helps us not to fall again.

The early Church recognized this and instituted Lent as a period of more intense penitence to train Christians to face persecution. Not all of Christ's followers will end up dying as martyrs, but all must be willing. Jesus said, "Truly, truly, I say to you, unless a grain of wheat falls into the earth and dies, it remains alone; but if it dies, it bears much fruit."[27] Though less likely for us than for the early Christians, still, none of us knows for sure if it will come to that for us, and so we too must be ready. Whether or not we get the gift of laying down our lives for God physically, we can "lose" our lives daily by giving up selfish pursuits: there are a thousand chances every day to die to self. We can pray for God's grace and strengthen our wills to stand fast in the face of death by standing fast and accepting inconveniences, disappointments, and pains when they come our way and by seeking and embracing penitential opportunities too.

Best of all, penance enables us to enjoy union with God sooner—in two ways.

One way that penance expedites our union with the Lord is by lessening our time in Purgatory. Sin can't enter heaven, so, even saved souls can't enter if sin's stain is still upon them; they must first take care of that temporal punishment discussed above. One can do so in this life, through penance and acts of love; whatever one doesn't take care of now will have to be dealt with in Purgatory. The more loving penance we do now the less we'll have there. (Purgatory is covered in much greater depth in chapter 26 below.)

Penance also brings God closer to us *now*. SS. Teresa of Avila and John of the Cross say the experience of contemplation or unitive prayer is possible for each of us, but the clutter of other things in our hearts (sins, worries, attachments) keeps it from happening.

> It is not by sidestepping or fleeing from suffering that we are healed, but rather by our capacity for accepting it, maturing through it and finding meaning through union with Christ.
>
> —POPE BENEDICT XVI [Box 31]

---

[26] John Paul II, *Reconciliatio et Paenitentia*, *Reconciliation and Penance*, no. 31, III.
[27] Jn 12:24. See also Jn 12:25–26.

Spiritual growth can be "choked by the cares and riches and pleasures of life".[28] Teresa and John advise letting go of all that to have God. Penance helps detach us from such things, clear away obstructions, straighten our crooked paths, and smooth out our rough ways, giving Him a direct path to our hearts, so we can enjoy a fuller union with Him even now.[29]

Love: The Best Reason

Love isn't satisfied with doing the minimum. It doesn't hold back but longs to give all. Love wants to pour itself out for the beloved, to spend itself completely. "We love only to the degree we are willing to suffer", according to Fr. John Hardon, S.J. "Love asks no questions; indeed it almost wants to suffer in order to prove its love."[30] Scott Hahn told of a man who fancied a young lady but didn't know how to get to know her. One rainy night, he saw her beside the road with a flat tire. Though he didn't particularly like changing tires in the rain, in this case he jumped at the chance: to be able to help the one he admired was pure joy. Love makes all the difference.

The best reason for doing penance is to express love. Acceptance of suffering is one of the supreme ways to prove our love for God. If the angels and saints now in heaven could envy us anything it would be our chances to suffer for love of God.[31] At the heart of doing penance is the desire to go beyond the minimum: to show God sorrow for our sins, to show Him our love. The cross should not be shunned, but embraced and even rejoiced in—for the love of Christ and the good it yields.

> Love covers a multitude of sins.
> — 1 PETER 4:8 Box 32

When you take up the cross, try to bear it patiently, and offer it to Him as a sacrifice of prayer, it becomes a meaningful emblem—and

---

[28] Lk 8:14.

[29] Is 40:3–4; Lk 3:4–5.

[30] First quotation: Fr. John A. Hardon, S.J., quoted on http://www.religious-vocation.com/redemptive_suffering.html#.VabuOflViko. Second quotation: "The Value of Suffering in the Life of Christian Perfection", conference transcription from a retreat Fr. Hardon gave to the Handmaids of the Precious Blood 1998), www.therealpresence.org/archives/Christian_Spirituality/Christian_Spirituality_011.htm.

[31] This is not masochism, though, not suffering for the sake of suffering. Christians embrace suffering, not because suffering itself is good (it isn't), but because of the good God can bring out of it. "Never the Cross without Jesus. Or Jesus without the Cross." St. Louis Marie Grignon de Montfort. Quoted in *Catechism for Youth: Based on the Catechism of the Catholic Church*, by Carlos Miguel Buela (New York: IVE Press, 2008), p. 99.

powerhouse—of love. This must be why St. Faustina wrote: "Suffering is the greatest treasure on earth."[32]

After Communion, a friend once imagined herself as a child lying prostrate before Jesus. He scooped her up and settled her on His shoulder. Seeing the wound in His hand, she said,

> True love is measured by the thermometer of suffering.
>
> —St. Faustina [Box 33]

"O Lord, I'm so sorry my sins did that to you." He smiled gently and replied, "You're worth it." Can we say that to Him? Whenever a cross comes our way or an opportunity to do penance, can we smile at Him and say, "You're worth it"?

---

[32] St. Faustina, *Divine Mercy in My Soul: Diary of Saint Maria Faustina Kowalska* (Stockbridge, Mass.: Marian Press, 2015), p. 153, no. 342.

16

MODERN MORTIFICATION

Even when we're convinced that we could use more self-denial in our lives, we're not always sure how to go about it. We might be put off by some extreme penances in past ages. Today the Church encourages "patiently bearing sufferings and trials of all kinds" and "works of mercy and charity".[1] She specially recommends three forms of penance: prayer, fasting, and almsgiving, the three about which Jesus gave explicit instructions in the Sermon on the Mount.[2]

Prayer and Almsgiving

If you think of penance as something strictly unpleasant, it may seem strange to include prayer as a form of penance. (If you've experienced how hard prayer can be, it might not seem strange at all.) Prayer, while at times hard, is always a privilege. The purpose of penance is not to suffer per se, but to repair damages; to do good. Prayer is very good and beautiful; thus, offering extra prayers is a great form of reparation. And as sin leaves a wound in the soul, an infection that if neglected can lead to further sin, prayer is essential in healing it.[3]

Almsgiving is a remedy to our attachments. Remember, sin comes from being attached to something more than to God; almsgiving rectifies this in getting our priorities straight. In giving alms, we recognize that everything in this life will pass away. Trying to keep anything is like trying to catch rain in a sieve. It is only what we give away that will give us everlasting joy.

The word *mortification*, which means dying to yourself, or putting to death your sinful inclinations, is essentially a synonym for penance.

[1] *CCC* 1473.

[2] Mt 6:2–18.

[3] See pp. 195–96 above for quote from Pope St. John Paul II, *Reconciliatio et Paenitentia, On Reconciliation and Penance* (December 2, 1984), no. 31, III.

In the light of penance being a medicine to heal the effects of sin, the worth of prayer and almsgiving as forms of penance becomes obvious. (For more on almsgiving and intercession, see chaps. 20 and 27 below, respectively.)

Fasting: The Classic Penance

Fasting seems to be a lost art these days. But Jesus clearly expected His followers to fast; in the Sermon on the Mount, He said, "*when* you fast ...", not "*if* you fast ...".[4]

What many Catholics don't realize is that the Church still regards Fridays throughout the year as days of penance.[5] While abstaining from *meat* on Fridays is no longer required in every diocese, that doesn't mean we're to treat Friday as any other day. Rather, since some folks were missing the point and having lobster on Fridays, the Church has tried to emphasize the *spirit* of the law: it's not the *meat* that matters; it's undertaking a penance in loving remembrance of our Savior, who died on a Friday, that matters. (Similarly, we make every Sunday a little Easter.)

Abstaining from meat is still a normative way to make Friday penitential, but you can undertake a different penance. You could abstain from salt, sweets, social media, TV, or sugar in your coffee. There are countless possibilities. Many Catholics go farther and fast every Friday; some fast on Wednesdays too, as the early Christians did.[6]

> Fast from hurting words and say kind words;
> fast from sadness and be filled with gratitude;
> fast from anger and be filled with patience;
> fast from pessimism and be filled with hope;
> fast from worries and trust in God;
> fast from complaints and contemplate simplicity;
> fast from pressures and be prayerful;
> fast from bitterness and fill your heart with joy;
> fast from selfishness and be compassionate to others;
> fast from grudges and be reconciled;
> fast from words and be silent, so you can listen.
> —ATTRIBUTED TO POPE FRANCIS Box 34

---

[4] Mt 6:16–18; see also Lk 5:33–35.

[5] "Days of Penance", *Code of Canon Law*, nos. 1249–53, www.vatican.va/archive/ENG1104/__P4O.HTM For norms in the U.S., see *Pastoral Statement on Penance and Abstinence* (1966), nos. 18–28, http://www.usccb.org/prayer-and-worship/liturgical-year/lent/us-bishops-pastoral-statement-on-penance-and-abstinence.cfm.

[6] The *Didache* (or *Doctrine of the Twelve Apostles*, ca. A.D. 80–90) exhorted early Christians to fast on Wednesdays and Fridays (8.3). Eastern Orthodox Christians still do today.

Rewards of Renunciation

Fasting delivers quite a few benefits. First, it's good for your health. Next, since there's less meal prep, fasting means more time, which ideally can be spent in extra prayer, reflection, or service. It also reminds us of our dependence on God and makes us more grateful for all we have. When one tries to deal with it merely for a day, one can't help but think of those who face hunger every day; thus fasting gives us more compassion for the poor (plus a little extra money to give them).

Moreover, fasting helps us develop self-discipline. Habitual sins not only make us weaker but also less confident. We don't believe we *can* resist. Starting with small sacrifices, however, means we can go "from victory to victory rather than from defeat to defeat", as another spiritual director, Fr. Louis de Vaugelas, L.C., told me. Our wills become stronger to meet and defeat temptation, and our confidence grows as we realize it can be done. If it seems daunting, keep in mind that with perseverance one can train oneself to do almost anything, and there are lots of ways to fast.

How to Fast

If you want to undertake fasting, how do you go about it? There are many options. Jesus established a high bar, fasting from all food and drink during His forty days in the desert. Human beings usually can't survive more than a few days, *maybe* a week, without water, so that a strict fast is obviously something we're not called to imitate literally—at least not that long. A total fast for a day is not impossible, as many discover when it's required before a medical procedure. But I wouldn't recommend that for most people, especially beginners, because it would be hard to keep up on a regular basis.[7] You would probably try it once and never fast again.

Here's the Church's guide for fast days in the U.S.: one meal, plus two snacks that together do not amount to a full meal. You can fast

---

[7] We must avoid two extremes in self-denial: being too easy on ourselves or taking on too much. Once you're determined to do penance, the devil often tries to discourage you with excessive suggestions. "You could give up that snack, too", "If you *really* loved God, you'd give up dinner altogether", and so on. One needs to distinguish between the voice of heaven and that of hell. The former invites; the latter needles and condemns. The former's suggestions might be challenging, but they yield peace. The latter's hounding leaves one frazzled or negative. It's not so much the idea; the red flag is the nitpicking tone. Keep calm while considering it; ask the Lord to protect and guide you.

more than or less than that, according to what you can manage. If you can handle something stricter, go for it. Those with health problems can make adjustments.[8] I know a hypoglycemic who *has* to eat, so abstains from foods he likes or somehow makes the food he eats less pleasant— for example, eating his spaghetti cold.

A time-honored fast is bread and water. It's basic and cross-cultural, linking us with penitents of the past and the poor today. It's very easy— nothing to prepare. Not terribly interesting, but very doable for most people. If you get light-headed or grumpy, try a high-protein bread, add some butter, or drink a little tea. (Better to lighten it a little than sin against others.)

Another option is a juice fast or a liquid fast. (Adding ice cream, however, or liquefying a candy bar would go against the spirit of the thing.) If all of these seem too hard or you're just getting started, it's a good idea to ease into it. Begin with fasting part of the day or making some sacrifices and building up to a more stringent fast gradually.

Ready-to-Pick Penances

Mother Church encourages prayer, fasting, and almsgiving, but that doesn't mean, of course, that she forbids any other form of mortification. Far from it. Nor, by identifying Fridays, Advent, and Lent as penitential days and seasons, does she mean to limit self-denial to those times. Rather, she reminds us of the need for penance, while leaving a lot of leeway to the individual. The hope is that, in a desire to begin a new life, we will embrace penitence and make it our own. It's not hard to find simple but effective penitential opportunities—they're all around us, every day.

What We Ought to Do Anyway

Self-denial is not just a matter of sacrificing licit goods; God recognizes and accepts the sacrifice involved in renouncing what we should give up anyway or doing what we ought, but don't want, to do. If your doctor says you have to stop drinking, for instance, teetotalism is easier

---

[8] See http://www.usccb.org/prayer-and-worship/liturgical-year/lent/questions-and-answers -about-lent.cfm.

to undertake when embraced as a penance for love of God. Intercession can also enable us to overcome bad habits and even addictions,[9] when knowledge and sheer willpower are not enough. Turning it into a prayer, into a sacrifice for someone you love, makes all the difference. This is especially true if you have people in your life who really need God's help. (And most of us do.)

If we looked at exercise, for instance, as an opportunity to help save a soul, what a difference it could make! We know we should do it but claim we don't have time.[10] But see it as a penance and see penance as a good, and you have a helpful inspiration to fulfill that duty. When you're running and you want to stop, for instance, instead you could pray, "I'll keep going to the next telephone pole, as a sacrifice for so-and-so." You could transform an entire workout into a prayer time, in which every stretch of road or every set of reps was a sacrifice offered for someone you love or someone in need.

Seeking to do penance can give us that boost of motivation we need to live as we ought.

Knights of the Dinner Table

Fasting isn't the only food-related penance. When Jesus sent out His disciples to preach the gospel, He gave them some tough directions—no bag, no money, not even sandals. One is often overlooked: "Eat what is set before you."[11] That would have been *much* harder for me as a kid than going barefoot! But now, I've added it to my arsenal of Helpful Scriptures for Parents. It's a perfect verse to whip out when kids complain about dinner. But adults need to abide by it too, for most of us also have trouble eating as we ought. A diet of only sweets is no better for our souls than for our bodies, so the Lord wants us to eat whatever is set before us at the table of life too: i.e., accept whatever He sends us, trusting it's good for us even if bitter and hard to swallow.

Culinary courage is more than a healthy habit or an apt spiritual analogy, though. It's also a will-builder. I tell my kids to eat their vegetables

---

[9] This is not to say that to overcome an addiction one might not also need outside support or the direction of a physician. Rather, prayer and enduring the difficulties involved as a penance can be critical aids in the process.

[10] Since exercise improves the immune system, gives one more energy, and helps one sleep better, the truth is we don't have time *not* to exercise.

[11] Lk 10:8.

not only for the sake of their health, but also in order to learn to make themselves do the good they find unpalatable. We need that kind of daily discipline or our wills become flabby and weak. At mealtimes, we can start training ourselves and gain the strength to do noble things and conquer greater challenges.

A Life of Adventure

G. K. Chesterton once wrote that "an inconvenience is only an adventure wrongly considered."[12] What is it about an *adventure* that is so much more appealing than a duty or an inconvenience? It must be the idea of being heroic, courageous, overcoming a challenge, for noble reasons, in defense of others. Yet all of that lies potentially in every difficulty we meet.

It doesn't feel like it. No dragons are in sight. But responding to a difficulty with Christlike charity and patience requires heroism and the courage to die to oneself. It can also be done for noble reasons—such as the love of God (nothing nobler) and in the "defense" of others, if we offer it up on their behalf. If no dragons are *visible*, don't doubt that you'll have to fight the world, the flesh, and the devil, at least in your thoughts and inclinations, to rise to the challenge.

This essentially was what St. Thérèse of Lisieux meant by her "Little Way".[13] As a child, she had been trained to look for chances to make sacrifices for Jesus and given a string of ten beads with which to count them each day. As a young woman, daunted by the mortification of earlier saints, she decided to continue her practice, but instead of striving for ten, she would make it her way of life. She would use every opportunity—from a crack in her pitcher to being splashed by a careless nun at laundry time—to turn something unwelcome into a gift to God.

"Make everything you can a penance."[14] When you have a penitential outlook, you find sacrificial opportunities everywhere. Every

---

[12] G. K. Chesterton, *Collected Works*, vol. 27: *The Illustrated London News, 1905–1907* (San Francisco: Ignatius Press, 1986), p. 242.

[13] Many Catholics are familiar with St. Thérèse's Little Way, but she wasn't the first to discover it. Besides Brother Lawrence, whom we met earlier (pp. 77–78), Jean-Pierre de Caussade, an eighteenth-century Jesuit, also wrote about doing one's duty and accepting whatever crosses might come along, out of love for God and as a means of spiritual growth, in *Abandonment to Divine Providence* (also called *The Joy of Full Surrender*).

[14] Before the visits of Our Lady to the three children of Fatima, an angel appeared to them, exhorting them to do penance. When Lucia asked how, this was his answer.

duty, every difficulty, every disappointment, every interruption holds this potential. When you stub your toe, spill your drink, break a dish, lose an unsaved document, you have the chance to "offer it up". Such things might seem useless, but just because spiritual benefits are invisible doesn't mean they're not real. Remember, it's the One to whom we give them who turns them into good. As with the small boy's five loaves and two fish, He can multiply our little gifts into splendid results.[15]

Considering what life is about, one finds that ultimately nothing matters, and everything matters. Nothing matters in that whatever I'm anxious about will be resolved in the best way possible if I entrust it to God. No matter what happens with it, he can bring a greater and longer lasting good out of it. Compared with eternal union with God, nothing else comes close, nothing else matters.

And yet everything matters. Not for its own sake, but because God can use it and because He desires *me* to make use of everything to accomplish His will. In fact, anything I have He gave me for that very reason. Everything I own, everything that happens to me, everything I do can be used for His Kingdom.

> The other things on the face of the earth are created for man to help him in attaining the end for which he is created. Hence, man is to make use of them in as far as they help him in the attainment of his end, and he must rid himself of them in as far as they prove a hindrance to him.
>
> —ST. IGNATIUS OF LOYOLA Box 35

When your goal is God, adventures beckon all around you.

Welcome, Jesus!

It had started out as such a great day for Simon. He was fulfilling the dream of every Jew living outside the Holy Land—to spend Passover in Jerusalem. But just as he reached the gates of the city, a huge crowd surged out. The hated occupiers were leading criminals to execution.

Simon watched with pity and contempt. Then a very bloody one collapsed at his feet. Suddenly Simon's arm was snatched, and he was dragged forward. He opened his mouth to protest, only to find a sword-point just below his chin. "Help him!" the soldier yelled.

[15] Jn 6:1–14.

He complied, but inwardly he rebelled. *Why me? Why must I share in this evildoer's shame? I've done nothing wrong. And why now? Just as I'm reaching Jerusalem! Now I'll be unclean, and there isn't time before Passover to be made clean.* What a grievous disappointment.

At some point, though, Simon must have realized who it was he was helping and must have decided to follow Jesus—beyond Golgotha, to the heavenly city. We know his name; we know the names of his sons; how would Mark know their names unless they had joined the Christian community? We don't know the name of the rich young man, who chose not to follow Him. Simon came to recognize what a tremendous privilege he had been given: to minister to the Christ in His need. No one was closer to Jesus during His Passion than Simon of Cyrene.

Perhaps Simon also realized that Jesus was actually the One who didn't deserve to carry a cross. Jesus was actu-ally helping him to carry what prop-

> Take my yoke upon you, and learn from me.
> —MATTHEW 11:29 Box 36

erly belonged to Simon—and taking the lion's share of the burden. We need to make the same realization in our lives.

I once heard a priest at a conference say it helped to see such trials as chances to meet the Lord, to say, "Welcome, Jesus." When we are pulled out of our way and forced to carry a cross, let's not focus on the cross—but on the One bearing it. See the privilege it is to draw close to Him, the honor to help Him. Realize the cross properly belongs to *us*, not Him; He is actually helping us, not the other way around. Believe that when we are yoked to Him, He carries the heavier portion, and He makes it sweet and light for us. Let's gladly step forward from the crowd and humbly rejoice in every opportunity to be close to the One beneath our cross.

May the Lord give us hearts that appreciate the gift of penance—whether it's one we choose or one that chooses us. Both voluntary and involuntary sufferings have their advantages: accepting without complaint whatever crosses He allows is an excellent way to grow in humility and trust; choosing freely to take on a penance is an excellent expression of love for God.

May He help us recognize in each opportunity the chance to make reparation for our sins, the chance to show Him how sorry we are for having hurt or disappointed or offended Him, the chance to show Him we love Him, and the chance to help build His Kingdom. May He give us hearts that long to spend ourselves as He did, making use of all, knowing that it will help others now, please Him, glorify Him, and redound to our good in heaven. Penance is not something to avoid but a gift to be embraced.

Welcome, Jesus!

SECTION SIX

LOVING GOD MEANS
LOVING THOSE HE LOVES

"Whatever you did for one of these least brothers of mine, you did for me."

(Mt 25:40, NABRE)

"Love one another; even as I have loved you."

(Jn 13:34)

17

THE CHALLENGE OF LOVING OTHERS

Loving our neighbor is an essential part of loving God. Jesus made that clear, dubbing it the second-greatest commandment, right after loving God. Anyone "who does not love his brother whom he has seen, cannot love God whom he has not seen".[1]

It doesn't always come easily. But true love embraces sacrifice: "It hurt Jesus to love us: He died for us. And today it is your turn and my turn to love one another as Jesus loved us."[2]

Love at Home Is Crucial

One day when I was a little girl, I came home from a friend's, telling my mother all I had done to clean there, expecting lots of praise. Instead, she said, "It would be nice if you helped out around here. Love begins at home." I was shocked. I knew Jesus said, "If you love those who love you, what credit is that to you? For even sinners love those who love them."[3] I thought the point was serving people outside your family. I hadn't heard the Scriptures on our duties to our family.[4]

Mother Teresa, besides her work with the poor, was an apostle of family love. When asked what could be done to promote world peace, she replied, "Go home and love your family."[5] Many conflicts in the world begin from heart-wounds that were not resolved in the home,

---

[1] 1 Jn 4:20.

[2] Mother Teresa, *Love: A Fruit Always in Season* (San Francisco: Ignatius Press, 1987), pp. 201, 198.

[3] Lk 6:32.

[4] See, for instance, Sir 7:28, Mk 7:9–12, and 1 Tim 5:8.

[5] "Biography: Mother Teresa", *Biography Online*, www.biographyonline.net/nobelprize /mother_teresa.html.

or even originated there. If you look at the childhood homes of Hitler, Stalin, and Mao, you find some reason for how they turned out.[6] Abusers were almost always themselves abused, and the vast majority of criminals had no father in the home. Study after study shows that the quality of home life—even the frequency of sharing meals—affects academic performance and whether or not youth get involved in drugs or other types of trouble. When the family is what it should be, it is "the environment in which love solves personality problems", says Venerable Fulton Sheen. Not because there are no tensions, but because it is "where the unlovable are loved".[7]

While often our deepest bonds are with family members, putting love for them into action can be challenging for several reasons. First, we tend to take them for granted. We are so used to them, we don't really see them (except when they annoy us). "Do you know the members of your family?" Mother Teresa asked. "Do you care for them; do you try to make them happy?"[8]

Further, in a culture that nurtures self-centeredness, we are caught up in our own pursuits. "I think the world today is upside down", the little Albanian nun said, "and is suffering so much, because there is so very little love in the homes and in family life. We have no time for our children, we have no time for each other; there is no time to enjoy each other."[9] If family members focus on their own wants, there will naturally be clashes and grudges.

Loving family members is also difficult because no one is perfect, and whenever people live together, they're bound to annoy each other at times. We become more careless around family precisely because they already know our faults; we don't bother trying to hide them or overcome them because we expect family members to put up with us anyway. Even when we no longer live together, love can be challenging due to our shared past. We remember their faults and the ways they've hurt us. We've had the same arguments over and over, so when they start to say something, we think we know what's coming next and stop listening.

[6] All three tyrants had violent and tyrannical fathers. Paul Vitz, *Faith of the Fatherless*, 2nd ed. (San Francisco: Ignatius Press, 2013), pp. 134–38.

[7] Fulton J. Sheen, *Children and Parents: Wisdom and Guidance for Parents* (Staten Island: St. Paul's, 2009), pp. 14–15.

[8] Mother Teresa, *Love: A Fruit Always in Season*, p. 31.

[9] Ibid., p. 37.

So the family is fertile ground for either great love or bitter antagonism. But the very things that can tear us apart are also opportunities to deepen and perfect our love. "Love starts at home and lasts at home ...; the home is each one's first field of loving, devotion and service."[10] Family life is like a fitness center, with exercise machines *everywhere*, offering chances to build spiritual muscles and grow in patience, generosity, self-sacrifice, understanding, thoughtfulness.

To get along with anyone, it is vitally important to realize that we can't change others. We desperately want and try to change them, but one can only change oneself. We can influence others, encourage change in others, but only *they* can make changes in themselves. Trying to change others is a waste of time: either they'll resist and resent it, or if they comply just to get us off their backs, then it won't be a lasting change. It can't be until they take ownership of it.

We must always remember that we're not perfect either. We would like to think a difficult person is worse than we are, but we can't know that for sure. We may have been given many more graces; in his shoes, perhaps we would be worse. We don't know his culpability or intentions. But even if he were worse, we are *so* much more like him than like God. Our holiness might exceed his like a poppy compared to a buttercup, but what does that compare to the sequoia-high holiness of a saint or the infinite holiness of God, which dwarfs the universe?

Instead, let's humbly recognize that we have faults, foibles, and weaknesses; it facilitates accepting others' faults, foibles, and weaknesses. When someone annoys us, let's recall that we can be annoying too. Moreover, we can turn irritations into a prayer. If your spouse leaves a damp towel on the bed *again*, choose to hang it up without comment. Instead of a harangue, make it an act of penance for all the times *you*'ve been a wet blanket to others or thrown one on God's plans; then breathe a prayer of repentance and gratitude for your spouse.

Instead of pouring energy into the fruitless attempt to change others, why not work on one's true responsibility: changing oneself? With grace and diligence, we *can* change. Whether it's as small as holding our tongue or as major as overcoming addiction, any victory pleases God. And when we work to change what bothers those close to us, their hearts are softened. To have their wishes heeded is such a pleasant surprise, often they'll respond by making changes too.

[10] Ibid., p. 31.

A Word on Loving Spouses

Marriage is the foundation of a family, and it must be tended carefully, especially in a culture constantly eroding it. One helpful marriage book is *His Needs/Her Needs*, by Willard F. Harley, Jr., which delineates ten desires husbands and wives hold in opposite order. While Christ calls us to rise above earthly desires and seek first His Kingdom, He also wants spouses to communicate His love to each other, and for that each must understand what is important to the other on a natural level. We all tend to assume that others think the way we think or value what we value, but that's simply not the case. What seems insignificant or even silly to you might go a *long* way with your spouse.

Even when it feels like your marriage is a sinking ship, there is still hope and help to save it. Alex Kendrick's *The Love Dare* is a good resource, presenting thirty daily steps to build up or repair one's marriage, and it all focuses on what *you* can do. Dr. Gregory Popcak has a number of great books on marriage and family life, some co-authored with his wife, Lisa; especially noteworthy here is *When Divorce Is Not an Option: How to Heal Your Marriage and Nurture Lasting Love*. Books aren't always enough, but there are powerful outside supports and rescue teams ready to help, such as Retrouvaille, Marriage Encounter, or the Pastoral Solutions Institute.[11]

A Word on Loving Children

The dynamics are naturally different in parenting children as the relationship is not between equals or life partners. With kids, certain annoyances are just part of the package: they're kids, and they don't always know better. So parents *should* help kids overcome bad habits, but with a good measure of acceptance and patience. We all have difficult days and weak points. Perspective is important too. For instance, one must distinguish BIG no-nos from little ones. Drugs deserve a no-tolerance policy; dirty socks in the living room are unpleasant but hardly in the same category. Parents needn't correct every single failure to put something away but can perform hidden acts of charity for their children. One just needs to find that delicate balance.

---

[11] Their websites are as follows: Retrouvaille: https://www.retrouvaille.org/, Worldwide Marriage Encounter: http://www.wwme.org/, and Pastoral Solutions Institute: https://www.catholiccounselors.com/.

Parenting adult offspring is different, naturally. They need continued guidance, and even correction early on, but with more diplomacy. As time goes on, that relationship will continue to evolve; the day may come when the adult child needs to take more of a care-giving role with an elderly parent. What is essential in every stage is love—evident in mutual respect, humble self-knowledge, acceptance, patience, thought-fulness, and generosity. (Humor helps a lot too.)

Reflecting on the thoughtlessness of my own childhood and youth transforms my attitude toward vexations coming from kids. Don't I deserve this? Haven't I ever in my life behaved that way? The present aggravation is a chance for me to make reparation.

It's also important to recall that little acts of service *do* count; they're precious in God's eyes. In a sense, they count more to Him than big notable deeds precisely *because* we don't get any accolades for them—or often even any thanks. And He see that sometimes it takes super-human love to do them, especially with kindness.

Serving a child is our chance to care for the Child Jesus.

❧ ❧ ❧

So loving family members really is a big deal. In her Nobel Peace Prize speech, Mother Teresa said if we could "just get together, love one another, bring that peace, that joy, that strength of presence" to each other in our homes, we could "overcome all the evil that is in the world".[12]

Love of Neighbor

Jesus told us to love our neighbor as ourselves. But just as His audience then wondered, we too often wonder, *Who is my neighbor?* Jesus replied with the parable of the good Samaritan. There He illustrated that my neighbor is not necessarily someone who is in my socio-economic class or with whom I share the same religion or even country. My neighbor may feel like someone foreign to me. My neighbor is anyone I encounter, anyone I can reach.

---

[12] Mother Teresa, Nobel Lecture, (December 11, 1979), www.nobelprize.org/nobel_prizes /peace/laureates/1979/teresa-lecture.html.

When it comes to helping people directly, I can't help everybody. My primary duties are first to my family and then to my neighbor. When someone asks us to help out with a certain effort, we need to discern if God is calling us to serve in that capacity at this time. If you have time and aren't really doing much to help others, go ahead and do it. If you have trouble saying no and keeping up with your present responsibilities, you probably shouldn't. One thing most of us can do is to reach out to our literal neighbors. Nowadays we often have no contact with them. That's what Mother Teresa would say: Start with your family, then move on to the neighbors.[13]

For pointers on serving one's neighbor in daily life, see the charming, humorous page-turner *Small Things with Great Love: Adventures in Loving Your Neighbor*. Author Margot Starbuck provides scores of ideas for people in different circumstances and seasons in their lives. Best of all, she opens readers' eyes to the many opportunities within reach.

What about *Those* People?

We all have them in our lives: people we find difficult. It's tough enough to tolerate them; how are we supposed to love them? Here are three ways:

See Them—Really See Them

Chances are all you see is their disagreeable traits. First, take the time to notice the good in them. If it's hard to find, make it your quest to find something good about that person. Once you do, a great second step is to compliment him on it.

Next, try to understand others, especially those who bother you. "You never really understand a person until you consider things from his point of view ... until you climb into his skin and walk around in it."[14] Believe it or not, that person has a point of view too—and may even have a valid one. "Instead of condemning people, try to understand them.... Try to figure out why people do what they do. That is a lot more profitable than criticism, and it breeds sympathy, tolerance,

[13] "Be that good news to your own people. And find out about your next-door neighbour—do you know who they are?" Ibid.

[14] Harper Lee, *To Kill a Mockingbird* (1960; New York: Grand Central, 1982), p. 39.

and kindness."[15] It's amazing sometimes to discover how differently other people think from the way we do. Once we see things from their point of view, they make a lot more sense.

Now there might be a couple of problems with this. First, the person may not share this inside information with you. In that case, try to imagine what he *might* be thinking. Put the best spin on it you can; give him the benefit of the doubt. This can be hard to do. It might strike us as the height of naïveté. Moreover, we prefer our prejudiced view: our sagacious insight into his nefarious character is much more appealing than trying to see him in a positive light.

The other problem is that he might actually be a nasty person. In that case, consider why he ended up that way: Was someone mean to him? And what a sad and lonely life he'll likely lead if he doesn't change. Such reflections help engender pity and prayer. Seek to find the good that God is bringing out of the situation. You may find it in the mirror.

See Yourself in Them

We feel justified in nurturing animosity toward others when we consider them worse than ourselves. We like to say, "*I* would never do that!" It makes us feel righteous and superior to the disliked person. It also lets us dismiss him as incorrigible and incomprehensible, with no thought that *anything* could excuse or explain his actions or make him anything like ourselves.

I've found that anytime someone has really hurt me and I've taken it to the Lord, He has invariably shown me how I am like that person. When I object, "*I* would never do what she did!" He will help me realize eventually that while that may be true, there are other things I've done. Perhaps I would never make the *particular* scathing remark my neighbor did, but that doesn't mean I've never said anything hurtful. Maybe I wouldn't defame a co-worker in order to promote myself, but I have betrayed my Lord in countless ways. The truth is, I have more in common with this person I dislike—a sinful creature like me—than I do with God, who is all-holy.

See Jesus in Them

Seeing Jesus in difficult people seems impossible. But Dorothy Day, whose cause for canonization is underway, observed one really loves God only as much as the person one likes the least.

Now there's an unsettling thought.

We might wonder how she could say such a thing. She's not trying to discount our love for God but is merely taking Scripture to its natural conclusion. Jesus said whatever we do to the least of His brothers we do to Him, and St. James, if we hate our brother whom we can see, then our love for God whom we can't see is mere fiction. God calls us in no uncertain terms to love everyone, enemies too.[16] If we refuse, then we don't love God enough to obey Him in this. However we treat the least likable of His human creatures, that's how we're treating Him.

This isn't the same as *liking* everyone. *Liking* happens on an emotional level. We find certain people pleasant, and so we like them. *Love*, on the other hand, is an act of the will. To love, remember, is to desire the good of another. We are to desire the good for each person, including our enemy,[17] and the best good is living in union with God forever.

Still, seeing Jesus in someone we dislike can be really difficult. It's an art we need to learn and practice. You can begin by reflecting on how much Jesus loves this person. Jesus knows him inside and out; He knows his faults better than you do, but He also knows all he's been through, all his good qualities, and his potential for holiness. Jesus sees all that and loves him. Next, imagine Jesus behind him, asking you, "See this guy? He's My brother, but he doesn't really know Me. He needs to be loved. Will you be a channel of My love for him? I died for him; I love him; I want him to spend eternity with Me. Will you help?"

It also helps to consider that just as one can serve angels unawares, that's true of the Lord too. There are quite a few stories of saints who reached out to an outcast to find later that it was Jesus in disguise. St. Francis had an intense revulsion for lepers. One day, when he saw one, he fought his inclination to run the other way; instead, he got off his horse, embraced and kissed the leper, and gave him all the money he had. When Francis turned around, the leper was gone; he believed it had really been Jesus. When St. Martin of Tours saw a man in rags

---

[16] Mt 25:40, 1 Jn 4:20, and Mt 5:44.
[17] For more on enemies and forgiveness, see chap. 20 below.

in the cold, he cut his cloak and gave half to the man. That night in a dream he saw Jesus wrapped in it.

Jesus is in that person we find so hard to love—that is what we need to get through our thick skulls. As Mother Teresa put it: "Each one is Jesus, only Jesus in a distressing disguise."[18] If someone seems impossible to love, ask Jesus to love that person for you and in you. He can do it. Consider St. Thérèse of Lisieux's victory:

> There is in the Community a Sister who has the faculty of displeasing me in everything, in her ways, her words, her character, everything seems *very disagreeable* to me. And still, she is a holy religious who must be very pleasing to God. Not wishing to give in to the natural antipathy I was experiencing,... I set myself to doing for this Sister what I would do for the person I loved the most.... I wasn't content simply with praying very much for this Sister who gave me so many struggles, but I took care to render her all the services possible, and when I was tempted to answer her back in a disagreeable manner, I was content with giving her my most friendly smile, and with changing the subject of the conversation....
>
> Frequently when I ... had occasion to work with this Sister, I used to run away like a deserter whenever my struggles became too violent. As she was absolutely unaware of my feelings for her, never did she suspect the motives for my conduct....
>
> One day she [asked]:... "What attracts you so much toward me; every time you look at me, I see you smile?" Ah! what attracted me was Jesus hidden in the depths of her soul; Jesus who makes sweet what is most bitter.[19]

The good news is that, just like the mountain in Dante's *Purgatorio*, which becomes easier to climb the higher you go, so also does it become easier to love those we find disagreeable, once, with prayer and grace, we start trying.

---

[18] Mother Teresa, *Love: A Fruit Always in Season*, p. 179.

[19] St. Thérèse of Lisieux, *Story of a Soul: The Autobiography of St. Thérèse of Lisieux*, trans. John Clarke, O.C.D., 3rd ed. (Washington, D.C.: ICS Publications, 1996), pp. 222–23.

18

LOVE BEGINS IN THE MIND

I remember as a little girl learning that one mustn't say mean things to other people. I pondered a moment and then cheerfully said to my mother, "It's okay to *think* mean things, as long as we don't *say* them, right?" But she said, "Oh, no, honey, we can't even think mean things about people." I was devastated. *How is that even possible?* I wondered.

And why is that? What harm is there in merely *thinking* unkind thoughts?

Well, it's risky: like harboring a violent felon in your home.[1] If we allow ourselves to think unkind thoughts, they begin to take root and grow in our hearts, and eventually they'll spill over; what we think affects what we say and do. Immoral thinking and immoral actions reinforce each other. "Although [the ungodly] knew God they did not honor him as God or give thanks to him, but they became futile in their thinking and their senseless minds were darkened. Claiming to be wise, they became fools.... God gave them up to a base mind and to improper conduct."[2]

What we think is of grave import: it has eternal repercussions. "I the Lord search the mind and test the heart, to give to every man according to his ways, according to the fruit of his doings."[3] And this is why "thoughts, words, and deeds" are so often grouped together: they are all intertwined and begin with the mind. "The good man out of the good treasure of his heart produces good, and the evil man out of his evil treasure produces evil."[4]

---

[1] Jer 4:14.

[2] Rom 1:21–22, 28. "Persistence in sin has damaging effects on the human faculties: the mind gradually darkens to a point of intellectual blindness, and the heart gradually hardens and grows cold to the love and laws of God." Scott Hahn and Curtis Mitch, eds., *Ignatius Catholic Study Bible: The New Testament* (San Francisco: Ignatius Press, 2010), p. 258, note on Rom 1:21.

[3] Jer 17:10.

[4] Lk 6:45; cf. Mt 15:18–19. The ancient Hebrews regarded the heart as the seat of thought as well as emotion. Jeff A. Benner, "Ancient Hebrew Word Meanings: Heart", Ancient Hebrew Research Center, www.ancient-hebrew.org /27_heart.html.

Immoral thinking not only leads to hurtful words or wrongdo-ing; willed thoughts themselves can be sinful. Jesus made that clear: "[E]very one who looks at a woman lustfully has already committed adultery with her in his heart."[5] If we think we're better than another, for instance, inwardly listing the ways we're superior, that's a sin, even if we never share or act on those thoughts. Such reflections feed pride, foster self-centeredness, and damage our future thought patterns. They beget more sinful thoughts; they darken the mind and darken the soul.

Consorting with the Enemy

What about the thoughts that pop into our minds: Are they sinful? First, know that merely having a thought is not itself a sin, precisely because it can occur involuntarily.[6] For something to be a sin, it must be chosen. It's what we do with the thought that matters. Do we dwell on it? Do we welcome it and develop it? In those cases, then, yes, the train of thought becomes sinful.

Secondly, realize that some thoughts do not arise from ourselves. Demons are real, and they do try to tempt and influence us. Sometimes a chemical imbalance, mental malady, or other physiological or psycho-logical factor can produce unwelcome thoughts in our minds. Again, we are not morally responsible, even if we cannot immediately shake off these types of thoughts despite our best efforts; there is no sin, as long as we are not consenting to the thoughts.

What is key in every case is what we *do* with the thought. Thoughts that pop into our minds are like strangers at the front door. We can't always keep them from coming up and knocking, but we don't have to invite them in. When a bad thought stands at the threshold of your mind, the first step is to recognize it as an enemy and shut the door in its face. The thought may not give up right away but try to gain entry any-way. Just because you have to struggle doesn't mean you're responsible for the presence of this intruder. Nor does it mean it's a lost cause. What God cares about is that you're trying to chase it away, not welcoming

---

[5] Mt 5:27–28.

[6] If ideas or images pop into our minds from illicit sources we've willingly consumed, how-ever, we are responsible for having exposed ourselves to them in the first place. If we repent of that, then any subsequent involuntary memories of them are not sinful (unless we choose to dwell on them), but an unfortunate consequence of sin.

it to settle in your heart. Call upon Him and on your guardian angel to help you.

Often the hard part is recognizing evil thoughts as evil; they don't always appear so at first. Thoughts against neighbor include critical, prideful, jealous, envious thoughts—in a word, selfish thoughts, those in which we put down our neighbor or elevate ourselves. Everyone we encounter has faults, so we can't help but notice some of them. Such a realization is not immediately sinful; it depends on what we do with it. Do we add it to a mental list of this person's deficiencies, feeling smug that we don't have that particular fault? Do we lose respect for that person or remember that we too have faults? Do we wonder if we might even have that particular weakness and not realize it? Do we interiorly say, "There but for the grace of God go I"?

Our neighbors also have strengths or gifts that we desire. Do we harbor envious, jealous, or competitive thoughts? Or do we thank God for blessing them in this way and for blessing us in other ways? Can we be happy for our neighbors? Do we remind ourselves that they surely also have crosses and difficulties, many of which are hidden from us? St. James warns, "[W]here jealousy and selfish ambition exist, there will be disorder and every vile practice."[7]

Another way to sin against our neighbor is to entertain judgmental thoughts; however, as there is some confusion about what judgmentalness actually is, it deserves a section of its own.

What, Me Judgmental?

If you saw a young woman laden with a baby and a heavy diaper bag, and holding a toddler by the hand, while she struggled to open massive cathedral doors for her empty-handed husband, what would you think? I doubt you would conclude, "Oh, that poor man! No doubt, though he looks perfectly healthy, there must be something wrong with his arms that prevents him from being the gentleman he would like to be." I know I wouldn't think that. I would probably think something more like, "Why doesn't he help her? What a dysfunctional relationship!"

But, in fact, the first conclusion was the right one. I know, because I was that woman; at one time my husband had a serious nerve condition in both arms. Beyond the pain, difficulty, and worry, one of the hardest parts was knowing that people were often misjudging him.

[7] Jas 3:14–16.

When we hear Jesus' words, "Judge not" (or "Do not judge"), this is not what we think of. *Judging* is greatly misunderstood today. The trend now is to think expressing disagreement with someone is judging them—at least in the area of sexuality. In seeking to love the sinner, according to the adage, "Hate the sin; love the sinner",[8] many deny sin is a sin for fear of making anyone feel bad.

It's not judgmental, however, to point out a danger. Once when I was out walking with my friend, her toddler got hold of a leaf and began sucking on it. Though aghast, I didn't say anything, assuming my friend was okay with it. When she noticed, she gasped and grabbed the leaf out of her child's mouth, fearing it was poisonous. I felt awful; my fear of being seen as judgmental had outweighed my judgment. Sin is just as dangerous, and sometimes our duty is lovingly to warn someone when they're going astray, unwelcome as it may be. That's not judging. (However, if it isn't done gently and lovingly, it probably won't help.)

The judging that Jesus forbids is usurping God's place and gauging someone's heart or eternal destiny. We can often know if an *action* is moral or immoral; what we can't know is the culpability of the person acting. We don't know if this one's conscience was properly formed; we don't know that one's circumstances or intentions. There are a host of physical and psychological conditions that could impact someone's knowledge of God's law and ability to act accordingly. We can't look at people and deem they are going to hell because of this or that. We can't even judge ourselves properly. Only God knows all the factors; only He can judge.

The other thing to consider is that we too are sinners. Perhaps we're not as bad as someone else, but is the credit all ours? If I'm honest with myself, I can see the truth of the phrase, "There, but for the grace of God, go I." If I could do the sin of X, Y, or Z, even with the faith and grace God has bestowed on me, then without His grace, what would I *not* be capable of? Without His grace, any of us is ultimately capable of anything.

Since our society equates calling something a sin with judging and shuns—even judges—such judging, there's hardly any action that society would call sinful anymore. However, we often can definitively say that an action is wrong even when we can't tell if the person doing it is sinning. *Sin* is when we do something we know is objectively wrong

---

[8] This saying of Gandhi, which was actually a paraphrase of St. Augustine, so well encapsulates the teaching of Jesus that it is often mistakenly attributed to Him.

but do it anyway. While it would be judging to conclude that another has sinned without knowing his mind and intentions, it is not judging to acknowledge wrongdoing as objectively wrong.

Ironically, at the same time, it's perfectly fine in society to talk about others' choices. That isn't seen as judgmental; it's just ordinary conversation. And while our culture frowns on judging someone's actions, there's no problem judging someone's heart and intentions. Co-workers, fellow drivers, neighbors, or strangers do something, and we impute to them a motive. *He wants my job. She did that on purpose. He cut me off to spite me*, etc. But how often do we really know why someone did something or if he intended or foresaw its negative impact on us?

We also don't excuse others the way we do ourselves. We like to think God is on our side—He's seen what we've been through; He understands. But when *someone else* is grumpy, we tend to think, "Gee whiz, what a grouch!" or "What does she think, the world revolves around her?" Even when we know someone had a difficult day, we don't make allowances as we would for ourselves, but think, "Yeah, well, we all have tough days sometimes; get over it."

We act this way for a couple of reasons. We jump to conclusions out of a modern-day terror of gullibility. But giving people the benefit of the doubt is not naïve; it's a recognition that we don't know what's going on inside them. Excusing our own behavior but not others' is usually due to plain old selfishness. Loving your neighbor as yourself means developing a greater readiness to excuse others—whose motives we can't know—than ourselves, whose motives we can.

We've got to remember what Jesus said *after* He said, "Do not judge", namely, "so that *you* will not be judged." To make sure we fully understand, He adds: "For in the way you judge, you will be judged; and by your standard of measure, it will be measured to you."[9] In other words, God will be *as* generous, *as* forgiving, and *as* understanding to us as *we* are to others.

Thoughts and Feelings

Our feelings have a huge influence on our thoughts, for the two are intertwined. Frequently, people don't know how to control them or at

---

[9] Mt 7:1–2 (NASB), emphasis added.

what point sin enters into the mix. As with a thought occurring to us, so with the upsurge of a feeling—that moment is premoral (not yet moral nor immoral); once it's there, however, we choose what to do with it. Powerful emotions are burdensome to many Christians because they're even harder to control than thoughts. But not impossible. And, as we'll see below, our thoughts are one of the best ways to control them.

Temptations to give undue sway to our emotions arise from the modern cult of feelings. It shows up in phrases like "Follow your feelings" and "Do what your heart tells you." Our society has gone beyond validly taking emotions into account to giving them supreme rule. It's getting to the point where the feelings of an individual can eclipse truth or the common good.

What are feelings? What is their purpose? They have several functions. One is to serve as indicators: fear warns us of danger and prepares us to deal with it; guilt tells us we've done wrong; anger, that something should be changed; and contentment, that things are safe and as they should be. Feelings were also meant to be our servants: to support us in doing what we ought. Initially, all our faculties were in alignment; the mind, will, and emotions were all directed to pleasing God. But ever since the Fall, they've been out of whack; one's feelings may go completely contrary to one's will or to what one's mind recognizes to be right.

Feelings are like horses: powerful and potentially very helpful. But after the Fall, they became wild horses that could carry us away or cause a lot of damage. Denying them isn't the answer though. If you stuff a colt into a spare room, it'll tear the room apart. Instead, you need to tame it, train it. Like horses, emotions need to be harnessed, directed, their energies channeled.

How do we deal with feelings or get them back "in whack"? One step is to check the source—whether the feeling has a bodily, mental, or spiritual origin.

Sometimes feelings have a bodily origin. St. Francis called his body "Brother Ass", seeing it as his servant—a sometimes stubborn, contrary one, but with legitimate needs. To see your body that way can help you discern when its cries are valid and when they can be ignored. Perhaps a better image for our day is a child. Just as a parent with a child, we have a duty to take care of ourselves. We need to pay attention to nutrition, exercise, sleep, and recreation, or our bodily needs will affect our emotions. If a child moans about getting up, you check to see if she's really sick or simply trying to avoid going to school. Then you treat her accordingly—either keeping her in bed or making her get up and get moving. In the same way, we should heed or ignore our emotions. Treat your feelings like a child—they can be childish!

Sometimes feelings have a physiological and/or mental origin, like depression. Although today there's much more awareness about mental afflictions than in the past, many still think there's a stigma to them. We don't want even to consider that it might happen to us. But why should we be ashamed of a chemical/hormonal imbalance or emotional wound? That attitude and the resulting inaction only hurt us more. Whatever the cause, there's no shame in finding out and obtaining the help we need. I myself experienced postpartum depression after the births of my two youngest. The first time, I didn't know what was happening and felt like a terrible person. Later I learned the symptoms; when it happened again, I recognized it and was able to get help. I couldn't believe the difference it made in my life and ability to handle daily difficulties.

Other times negative feelings arise from sin. If one is ignoring conscience, what would ordinarily be experienced as guilt might manifest itself in other ways, some resembling depression or desolation. So when we're feeling low or far from God, we need to consider if there's some sin behind it. Once we recognize it, we need to repent and rectify it.

In all these cases, there are steps we can take when the cause of difficult emotions is within ourselves and thus lessen their power or ameliorate them.

Ruling Your Thoughts and Feelings

You are like a kingdom and each of your faculties has its role: your will is the monarch, your mind, the court counselor, and your feelings are the people. When feelings form a mob, it's critical not to abdicate. And just as a counselor might take a bribe and misuse his influence, our minds can be swayed by feelings. No matter how rebellious the feelings or rationalizing the mind, however, it is always up to the will, in the end, to decide. Don't let the mob, the mind, or the devil convince you otherwise. The will can always cut through the uprising and say, "Enough! I don't care what you say; we're doing it God's way."

Due to original and personal sin, however, our wills are weak. Like the French monarchy in the fifteenth century, we need a Joan of Arc to regain the kingdom. We mustn't be like Charles VII, though: he didn't always listen to Joan and abandoned her, though she had had him crowned. It's not enough to obtain grace; we have to *use* it, believing it's really there, even when we can't feel it. Joan of Arc didn't look like someone who could win back a kingdom, but as God's chosen instrument, she did. Too often, we don't believe in the efficacy of God's grace. Yet with it, we can establish dominion over even an army of rebellious feelings.

Thought-Power

Much, if not most, of the time, our feelings flow from what's going on in our lives. When things don't go the way we like, negative emotions arise. In order not to sin in difficult moments, the first thing to remember is that interpretation makes a *big* difference. If I'm sitting on a bus and a passerby steps on my foot, my feelings will differ depending on why my toes got squashed. If a girl looking at her iPhone carelessly treads on me, I'll feel annoyed, whereas if someone stomps on my foot on purpose, I'll feel angry or frightened, depending on how big he is. But if someone accidentally steps on my foot as he's running to save a child falling out the window, I won't mind at all. So how we *think* about something plays a critical role in how we feel about it.

Fr. John Hampsch, C.M.F., with a background in psychology, says thinking the same thought over and over actually forms a groove in the brain. When our minds stray anywhere near that idea, our thoughts slip into this same old groove. When they're on the dark side, psychology terms them "automatic negative thoughts". But it works the other way as well. We can choose to reroute our negative notions by recalling positive truths. One can counter, "I can't stand her" with "Jesus loves my co-worker as much as He loves me. She has good qualities too", etc.

The mind, then, like an esteemed counselor to the king, has a huge influence in one's personal kingdom. Its first duty is to be well-informed—and by sound sources. A counselor who simply spouted off the top of his head in proud self-sufficiency would be of no use; one formed by evil influences would be worse. If the mind is going to help us to love God, then it must first "try to learn what is pleasing to the Lord".[10] We don't know this automatically. The Lord's thoughts are as high above ours "as the heavens are higher than the earth".[11] So St.

[10] Eph 5:10.
[11] Is 55:8-9.

Paul advises: "Do not be conformed to this world but be transformed by the renewal of your mind"—and then points out: "This is the only way to discover the will of God and know what is good, what it is that God wants, what is the perfect thing to do."[12] Thanks be to God, He has revealed what is pleasing to Him in the Scriptures and given us the Church to guide us in understanding His word, so we can learn to think like He does.

It is also helpful to take positive action. It is critical to pray through negative thoughts and feelings, and one can also choose certain prayers ahead of time for foreseeable situations. If the feelings continue, try redirecting your thoughts or energies. Go do something else if possible. Pour your energy into something positive and offer up the effort. It's imperative to get out of oneself. Fr. Benedict Groeschel, in *Arise from Darkness*, recommends serving others as a fail-safe method of moving out of any kind of darkness.

Thinking Well of Others

Our thoughts affect other people too. People live up to what you expect of them.

Dr. Grazie Pozo Christie experienced this working as an ER doctor in a high-crime district, where she often treated violent felons. Safety was never an issue, however. "When the felon walks ... into the medical area, he becomes a new person.... He's no longer seen as a dangerous person ... and you know what? He becomes a *not*-dangerous person."[13] She attributes this to his knowing that "his social class, his financial status, even the handcuffs that showed he was violent and dangerous, would mean nothing to me. He would get the best care I could give him, because he was a human being, and my patient."[14] All that would change his demeanor: "In the nine years I spent in that hospital, not once was I treated with anything less than perfect courtesy. I never once felt any fear when left alone with a violent felon,

---

[12] Rom 12:2 (2b is the Jerusalem Bible translation).

[13] Dr. Grazie Pozo Christie, interview with Teresa Tomeo, *Catholic Connection,* June 16, 2015, hour 2, www.avemariaradio.net/audio_archive/catholic-connection-june-16-2015-hour-2/.

[14] Dr. Grazie Pozo Christie, "Assisted Suicide Means the End of Medicine", *The Federalist* (May 20, 2015), http://thefederalist.com/2015/05/20/assisted-suicide-means-the-end-of-medicine/.

many times my size. I could rely on them implicitly for civility and even gallantry."[15]

What we think of others, and what we expect of them, can be a powerful influence. Goethe is widely quoted as saying, "If I treat you as though you are what you are capable of becoming, I help you become that."

Our thoughts also affect how we relate to others. Og Mandino advocates approaching others with conscious love: "In silence and to myself I will address [everyone I meet] and say I Love You. Though spoken in silence these words will shine in my eyes, unwrinkle my brow, bring a smile to my lips, and echo in my voice; and his heart will be opened."[16]

Conclusion

Fr. Lawrence Lovasik wrote a lengthy book on kindness; when I first saw it, I wondered how anyone could say so much on the topic. But as I read it, I felt smaller and smaller. I never realized how many ways I had failed to be kind. Lovasik maintains *thought* as a first step of kindness:

> If you want to be pleasing to God and to grow in holiness, you must strive to develop kind thinking. If you have a correct world of thought, your soul will be healthy and your whole approach to life will be correct. And in no field of spiritual endeavor will your efforts be so necessary and so rewarding as in the love of neighbor.
>
> The opportunities for the practice of kind thoughts are countless. But such a practice takes generous and continuous effort.[17]

If loving one's neighbor is integral to loving God, then if we want to please Him, we'll have to master our thoughts; when they are conformed to His, our feelings and actions will follow suit.

---

[15] Ibid.

[16] Og Mandino, *The Greatest Salesman in the World* (1968; New York: Bantam Books, 1985), p. 61.

[17] Rev. Lawrence G. Lovasik, *The Hidden Power of Kindness* (Manchester, N.H.: Sophia Institute Press, 1999), p. 97.

19

LOVE BRIDLES THE TONGUE

A frequently overlooked part of loving our neighbors is how we speak of them. In a sobering study of how seriously God regards our words, however, Mark Kinzer writes: "I know of few verses in all of Scripture more spine-chilling than [these]: 'On the day of judgment men will render account for every careless word they utter, for by your words you will be justified, and by your words you will be condemned.' "[1]

Why does God care so much about what we say?

Power of Words

God cares about speech due to its potency. Remember how Genesis describes God creating the world? God spoke, and it came to be. In the Book of Isaiah, He says: "For as the rain and snow come down from heaven, ... making it bring forth and sprout, ... so shall my word be ...; it shall not return to me empty, but it shall accomplish that which I intend, and prosper in the thing for which I sent it."[2] Most significantly, John the Evangelist describes the Second Person of the Blessed Trinity as "the Word of God". Obviously, God's words are extremely powerful.

While our words do not have the same miraculous force, they do have power. Words can do great good ... or great harm: "Death and life are in the power of the tongue."[3] The tongue's might is developed in the Letter of James: "If we put bits into the mouths of horses that they may obey us, we guide their whole bodies. Look at the ships also;

[1] Mark Kinzer, *Taming the Tongue: Why Christians Should Care about What They Say* (Ann Arbor, Mich.: Servant, 1982), p. 27, quoting Mt 12:36–37.
[2] Is 55:10–11.
[3] Prov 18:21. This is a recurring theme in the Book of Proverbs; see also, e.g., Prov 12:6, 13–14, 18.

though they are so great and are driven by strong winds, they are guided by a very small rudder.... So the tongue is a little member and boasts of great things. How great a forest is set ablaze by a small fire!"[4]

Those sincerely striving to please the Lord must take seriously the power of their words. "If any one thinks he is religious, and does not bridle his tongue but deceives his heart, this man's religion is vain."[5] Hence, on treating others kindly, Fr. Lovasik devotes twice as many pages to words as he does to actions.

Cutting Words

Whoever coined the saying "Sticks and stones may break my bones, but words will never hurt me" invented a snappy comeback, but unfortunately it's not true for most people. Rather, "The blow of a whip raises a welt, but a blow of the tongue crushes the bones. Many have fallen by the edge of the sword, but not so many as have fallen because of the tongue."[6] Sadly, there are many ways words can be weapons beyond the obvious—slander (lying maliciously about someone) and insults,[7] such as ridicule, sarcasm, caustic criticism, and harsh correction.

Wrathful tongue-lashing is also injurious. "Angry words cause smarting wounds that are hard to heal, and sometimes never heal. They are like knife stabs to the heart. Only too often, in the recklessness of anger,... you may give vent to words you will perhaps someday regret bitterly.... By harsh words, you write on the souls of men that which you cannot rub out."[8]

Fault-finding is something people justify by saying they are only speaking the truth. This dialogue from *Anne of Avonlea* illustrates so well what's wrong with this line of thinking:

> "Mrs. Lynde ...," growled Mr. Harrison, "... is a confirmed busybody and I told her so."

---

[4] Jas 3:3–5. James also says, "If any one makes no mistakes in what he says he is a perfect man, able to bridle the whole body also.... For every kind of beast and bird, of reptile and sea creature, can be tamed and has been tamed by mankind, but no human being can tame the tongue—a restless evil, full of deadly poison" (Jas 3:2b, 7–8).

[5] Jas 1:26.

[6] Sir 28:17–18.

[7] See Ex 20:16 and Mt 5:22.

[8] Rev. Lawrence G. Lovasik, *The Hidden Power of Kindness* (Manchester, N.H.: Sophia Institute Press, 1999), p. 160.

"Oh, that must have hurt her feelings very much," said Anne reproachfully. "How could you say such a thing?..."

"It was the truth and I believe in telling the truth to everybody."

"But you don't tell the whole truth," objected Anne. "You only tell the disagreeable part of the truth...."

..."You must excuse me, Anne. I've got a habit of being outspoken and folks mustn't mind it."

"But they can't help minding it.... What would you think of a person who went about sticking pins and needles into people and saying, 'Excuse me, you mustn't mind it ... it's just a habit I've got.' "[9]

Many people who avoid saying negative things to someone's face have few qualms about saying them behind his back. Yet even if the person never learns of what we said, our words have still hurt him, for we've damaged his reputation. Almost everything we say about someone has the potential to build him up or tear him down. This is why it's so important to avoid gossiping and uttering careless words about others.

St. Philip Neri once told a habitual gossip, for her penance, to take a pillow to the top of a tower on a windy day, cut it open, and shake the feathers out. Then she was to go down and recover every feather. She objected that that would be impossible. He responded that it would be easier than retrieving or repairing the damage of every harmful word she had spoken.

Kind Speech

On the other hand, we must also remember how mighty a power for *good* our words can be. "Pleasant words are like a honeycomb, sweetness to the soul and health to the body."[10] St. Paul advises us to "encourage one another and build one another up." He even asserts that words suitable to the occasion "may impart grace to those who hear".[11]

When we hear someone being denigrated, we can be a power for good in his defense. We can bring up his good qualities or what we like about him. We can point out that no one knows what's going on in another person's life or heart and that we should give people the benefit

---

[9] L. M. Montgomery, *Anne of Avonlea* (1909; New York: Bantam Books, 1978), pp. 67–68.
[10] Prov 16:24. Cf. also Prov 10:20; 15:23; 16:13; and 25:11.
[11] 1 Thess 5:11; Eph 4:29. Cf. Rom 15:2.

of the doubt. If we know something about the matter, we should convey what can help explain the person's behavior. (Only, that is, if such explanation can be given without revealing what should remain private; if not, we can say he had a good reason for what he did or that there's more to it than meets the eye.) Whenever we can, we should serve as peacemakers.[12]

Of course we should also say positive things about others directly to them and in their presence. Everyone needs encouragement sometimes. Most of us are much quicker to point out what's wrong with others or what they've done badly than to mention and commend them for what they've done right. Somehow, so much of that gets passed over without comment; we take those things for granted. We can be so profuse in our criticism and so stingy with our praise.

For this reason, parents and teachers are advised not only to correct children but also to "catch them" doing good. In fact, it's been said that for every criticism, children need to hear five positive things to build them back up. If you want to see children bloom, give them praise.

Remember, loving our neighbors begins in the mind. If we're looking for good in them, then we'll begin to notice the good that they do. The next step is to say something about it. Thank people for what they do, even when they're simply doing their duty. (Duties aren't always easy or pleasant to perform.) Go farther and pay them a compliment. Imparting honest admiration is not flattery, and it just may be what your neighbor needs to hear.

Love as Word Containment

Considering the above and other ways to sin with speech—exaggerating, dominating the conversation, boasting, name-dropping, grumbling, taking God's name in vain, promoting sin, cursing, foul language, and blasphemy—another way to love with one's mouth is to keep it shut.

Listening—A Lost Form of Love

Most people tend to let their tongues wag too much, and *everyone* has said something they've later regretted. "God gave you one mouth and

---

[12] "Blessed are the peacemakers, for they shall be called sons of God" (Mt 5:9).

two ears", says Fr. Lovasik, suggesting we should listen twice as much as we speak.[13] St. James counsels, "Let every man be quick to hear [and] slow to speak."[14] Doing so gives us time to take in what the other is saying and consider how best to respond. My high-school religion teacher Fr. Giampietro Gasparin notes that if people really listened, there would always be a pause before their response; if we're ready with a reply, there's a good chance we've missed something.[15]

Moreover, it's loving to ask people about themselves; if they give short answers, show interest by asking for more details. Love wants to know the loved one better.

Quit That Belly-Aching

One day as a college waitress, I came to work exhausted. Whenever possible, I would lean on the counter in back. I was telling my coworker how awful I felt, when I noticed he wasn't saying anything, just looking at me. Suddenly I realized this was at least the fifth time I had told him this. I said, "I guess you're probably getting sick of hearing about this." He just said, "Uh, yeah."

When something's bothering you, it's easy to complain. But that doesn't help; it just spreads the misery. "After you've said it once, it becomes a complaint. That's a good rule of thumb. Make your announcement and then keep the follow-ups to yourself. Nobody wants to hear that."[16] The ideal would be not to say it even once. One quality saints share is striving to suffer in silence. Sometimes we have a duty to share our trouble, especially if it's something serious, with someone who can help. Or we might need to explain why we're grumpy or unable to help with something. But if it's a minor problem, it can be a holy and beautiful thing to share it only with God, and then, not as a complaint, but as a prayer of sacrifice for someone else.

Instead of complaining, we could look for something positive in the situation. How can we rejoice and give thanks as St. Paul exhorts[17] if there's nothing to rejoice about or to be thankful for? Paul is implying

---

[13] Lovasik, *Hidden Power of Kindness*, p. 175.

[14] Jas 1:19. See also Prov 10:19; 13:3; 15:28; and 17:28.

[15] Prov 18:13 comments: "If one gives answer before he hears, it is his folly and shame"; cf. Sir 11:8.

[16] Mother Angelica, *Little Book of Life Lessons and Everyday Spirituality*, ed. Raymond Arroyo (New York: Doubleday, 2007), pp. 125–26.

[17] Phil 4:4; 1 Thess 5:16.

that in any situation we can find God's hand there, something for which to be grateful.

St. Paul's admonitions hearken back to the paradoxes of the Beatitudes. Jesus described a series of difficulties as—despite appearances—actual blessings. "*Blessed* are the poor,... the meek,... those who mourn,... those who hunger and thirst for righteousness,... those who are persecuted." God is challenging us in every situation to find His love. Sometimes the only thing we can find is the honor and privilege of suffering with Him and for Him and His people. If, instead of grumbling aloud or inwardly, we accept that cross and even thank Him for it, we'll find that He makes it easier, more bearable. When we pick up a cross and carry it, we discover that it comes with grace; it's part of the package. In every difficulty, we have a chance to love God and neighbor—and that's so much better than just sitting there complaining.

Keeping Confidences

We're also prone to sharing what should be kept private. This can range from simply talking about other people's business to telling secrets. Fr. Lovasik advises:

> Should you happen to come to the knowledge of your neighbor's hidden fault, let charity seal the knowledge in your heart as in a deep grave. Never open this grave before the eyes of man without a very serious reason. When you are tempted to speak about another's secret faults, ask yourself, "Why should I do this?"...
>
> ... Never speak of even the lesser sins and faults of others. When circumstances arise where it is permissible to speak of them, make your remarks with moderation, and exclude bitterness and hatred. It is virtuous to respect the absent, for they have no opportunity for explanation or self-defense.[18]

Even worse is to start rumors, for then we're saying what may not even be true. It's bad enough to suspect others or their motives, and it's wrong to gossip, but to combine these in passing on presumptions could be a grievous sin, especially if the matter is serious or gravely damages the person's reputation. Passing on a rumor is also immoral, sometimes mortally so.

---

[18] Lovasik, *Hidden Power of Kindness*, pp. 174, 175. Cf. Prov 17:9 (NABRE): "Whoever overlooks an offense fosters friendship, but whoever gossips about it separates friends."

In fact, even heeding any of these things is wrong.[19] We share in the sin when we stay and listen without murmur to unnecessary toxic remarks about someone. Rather, we have an obligation to defend that person by pointing out the falsity or uncertainty of the remark, countering it with a quality or virtue of that person and/or by redirecting the conversation.

Difficult Situations

Unpleasant Tidings

Negative communication isn't always avoidable. At times we need to correct someone; at times we need to confront someone. Sometimes we're angry, or someone is angry with us.

With respect to correction, you should discern whether it's really necessary and if it's really up to *you* to do it. We can convince ourselves we're justified in correcting someone, when really it's just something that bugs us. If someone simply has a different way of doing something or it's really none of our business, we should just shut up and offer it up. Ditto if you aren't in the right position to correct someone. When it *is* up to us, we must be brave but also gentle.[20]

> Touch the sensitive nature of the reproved with a tenderness like that of Christ. Make commendations of the good qualities in the person freely and generously.... Speak briefly but definitely regarding the objectionable point. [Lengthy] teaching and sermonizing are ineffectual.... Let the reproved realize that you are merely making recommendations for his true welfare.... If the tables were turned ..., you know well enough that you would want to be dealt with considerately.[21]

St. Francis de Sales must have done something like this. When, as bishop of Geneva, he received a request he could not fulfill, he replied with such a gentle, loving, and reasoned no that the petitioner felt as satisfied as if receiving a yes. "The mind of the wise makes his speech judicious, and adds persuasiveness to his lips."[22]

---

[19] "Whoever pays heed to slander will not find rest, nor will he settle down in peace" (Sir 28:16).

[20] "A soft answer turns away wrath, but a harsh word stirs up anger" (Prov 15:1).

[21] Lovasik, *Hidden Power of Kindness*, pp. 183–84. The entire chapter on this topic—chapter 12, "Use Kindness in Correcting Others"—is excellent (as is, actually, the whole book).

[22] Prov 16:23.

There are times when we need to confront someone or give unpleasant news. I faced this when I was in effect a single parent. My husband was working in another state, and I stayed behind with the kids trying to sell the house. During that time, three occasions arose in which I had to tell others things they wouldn't like. I had to confront a contractor about unsatisfactory work; after many months, I had to let our realtor (a close friend) know we needed to try another realtor; and, hardest of all, I had to tell a neighbor with whom we had had a previous misunderstanding that her daughter was vandalizing our house (she

> **Memorare**
>
> O most gracious Virgin Mary,
> recall that never was it known
>   that anyone who fled to
> thy protection, implored thy help,
>   or sought thine intercession
>   was left unaided.
> Inspired by this confidence,
>   I fly unto thee,
> O Virgin of virgins, my Mother.
>   To thee I come,
>   before thee I stand,
>   sinful and sorrowful.
> O Mother of the Word Incarnate,
>   despise not my petitions,
>   but in thy mercy,
> hear and answer me. Amen.
>
> Box 37

didn't want us to move away). I absolutely dreaded all three conversations. But there was no one else to do it. So in desperation, I got on my knees and prayed the best novena I knew. When there isn't time to do a nine-day novena, Mother Teresa advised praying nine Memorares in a row. I beseeched my heavenly Mother[23] for her prayers before each exchange. And each went beautifully. The work was redone at no extra cost. My friend was gracious and understanding about trying another realtor, and my neighbor was very apologetic and helpful. I was amazed. Since then I have always resorted to nine Memorares when facing difficult conversations, and Mary's intercession[24] has never let me down.

---

[23] As adopted siblings of Christ and members of His Body, we not only have the same Father but also the same Mother as He. When Jesus said to the beloved disciple, "Behold, your mother!" (Jn 19:27), He was speaking to you and me too. John always refers to himself as "the beloved disciple", in part to allow us to put ourselves in the story; each of us is the beloved disciple. And, like John, we should welcome Mary into our homes, into our hearts. What a tremendous gift from Christ: His own Mother, a perfect mother, who understands us, loves us, prays for us.

[24] The Catholic Church has long acknowledged Mary as an incomparable intercessor. Twice the Gospels show Mary and Jesus having a difference of opinion; both times, Jesus acceded to her wishes (Lk 2:41–51; Jn 2:1–10). At the same time, the Second Vatican Council explains that Mary's influence originates from, and is completely dependent on, "the superabundance of the merits of Christ", the one Mediator: Second Vatican Council, Dogmatic Constitution on the Church *Lumen Gentium* (November 21, 1964), no. 60. I treat the common misunderstanding of the Catholic practice of "praying to" Mary and the saints at greater length in chap. 24 below.

238

Be Angry, But Do Not Sin

Then there are the times when we're provoked. Scripture calls us to be "slow to anger" and use a "soft" not a "harsh word".[25] While some people heed only a stern voice, generally, raising your voice in anger is not a good idea. Giving in to anger a little easily leads to succumbing to it and, thus, to sin. If we get a grip from the beginning, we're more likely to maintain control. Also, expressing anger loudly gives the impression that we're out of control. The other person will put up a wall against the anger and against the message as well. (Does this sound hard? It is! Do I have this down pat? No way. But as with anything else, this is not impossible—with God's help.)

There are also things we can do. A friend of mine decided to pretend there was something wrong with her voice so that she *couldn't* raise it. If we can foresee an aggravation, we can pray in advance for the grace to handle it as Christ would. If your co-worker keeps making cutting remarks, come up with a charitable reply in advance or plan to say nothing and offer up the annoyance for him. If your child makes you late to work every day, devise an effective consequence, warn her, and calmly carry it out when she does it again. These steps defuse anger because its root is the desire for something to change, and such actions *do* make a change.

For unexpected aggravations, the recommendation is to count to ten to give you a chance to gain control. When my kids were little, I didn't find this sufficient, so I turned it into a counting prayer: "One, two, three, *O Lord help me*; four, five, six, seven, *with help from heaven*; eight, nine, ten, *through Mary,*[26] *amen.*" Usually I would have to pray it several times. But sometimes I would forget, so I would pray in the morning for help to keep my temper. St. Thérèse fled from the room if she felt she couldn't control her tongue.

Another effective method is to write about it. Writing produces thought, so it may help you see things in a new light, especially if you pray while writing or address it to the Lord. Some situations are also

---

[25]Jas 1:19; Prov 15:1.
[26]Short for, "through Mary's intercession—Sweet Mother Mary, please pray for me!—Amen." Jesus is pleased when we love and honor His Mother as He does and ask her to present our needs to God on our behalf. As a child, Jesus turned to her when He needed something; as His Body, shouldn't we do the same? And aren't we to become like little children to enter the Kingdom of heaven?

better handled in writing. We have time to consider and can revise, which we can't do while talking and certainly not when ranting.

When We're in the Wrong

Then there are the cases when someone is angry with *us*.

If we've done wrong, we must admit it and apologize ... humbly. Sometimes we have trouble doing this. When we're upset, simply to say the word "Sorry" or admit we're wrong feels like a *huge* concession, no matter *how* we say it. If we say it loudly and precede it with a "Fine!" it still feels like something pretty humble. But if someone behaved that way to us, would we feel mollified? Peaceful? Hardly. We should apologize to others as we would like them to apologize to us. A shoddy apology is an additional offense. Instead, take some deep breaths, pray a little, calm down, and deliberately modulate your voice, tone, volume, and expression. It doesn't hurt to explain, "I am truly sorry; my feelings are just taking a little while to catch up."

If someone is unjustly angry with us, we should try to listen calmly and then peaceably explain the mistake/misunderstanding. If we've apologized and tried to explain but no efforts at mollification are working, then we can leave it at that and end the conversation charitably. Turning the other cheek doesn't mean being a doormat. Jesus was not a doormat. Even during His Passion, He was usually silent, but He spoke up and defended Himself at times.

The Lord taught me this when my husband and I were newlyweds moving into our first apartment. James dropped me off while he parked. Our apartment number was "302", and so I thought it was on the third floor. But since there were no apartments on the ground floor, ours was actually on the fourth floor. So naturally the key would not work in the lock. While persistently trying to unlock the door, I thought I heard the floor creaking inside, but I dismissed it as my imagination. Then there was an unmistakable sound in there. I looked up and saw "202" on the door, realized my mistake, ... and fled up the stairs in mortification. Immediately someone came barreling out of #202, baseball bat in hand. He was a big guy with a bigger temper. I tried to explain my mistake, but no matter what I said he just kept yelling, "I almost killed you! You better thank God I didn't kill you!" (We later found out that he had been a Green Beret in Vietnam and returned paranoid and abusive.) Finally, as he began coming toward me threateningly, I realized my apologies were only making him angrier. So, by the grace of God, I said slowly, "I made a mistake, and I'm very sorry." Then I went into our new apartment and closed the door.

On the other side, though, I fell on my knees and indeed thanked God that the man hadn't killed me; I prayed for him and for our future as neighbors. The Lord answered that prayer: the man meekly showed up with his girlfriend and started carrying our furniture up the three flights of stairs. I don't think we could have done it without him. Clearly, God's hand was at work.

Speaking the Truth in Love

A sadly common failure to love others is in lying to them. God gave us the power to converse so we could share our thoughts, convey information, etc. It's an abuse of that gift to communicate what is not true with the intention to deceive. Jesus revealed Himself to be *the* Truth and called the devil "the father of lies". Whose side do you want to be on?

What about "white lies"? They seem more loving than the bald truth. It's *not* loving to reveal what should be kept private, gossip, hurl unkind truths, etc. Without love, the truth can be brutal. What harm is there in a little white lie? Well, there are a few problems with it.

First of all, it doesn't help people if we sweep unpleasant facts under the rug. If someone asks for feedback on what they're wearing or their performance, and we say, "Great" when it wasn't great, we could actually do them a disservice. The honest input of others is important in self-evaluation. If my outfit actually looks silly, believing it looks great doesn't help me, especially if it diminishes others' impression of me. If you tell a friend she has a great voice when it's really just adequate, she may waste her time and true talents.[27]

Secondly, white lies erode trust. If we go around saying things we don't mean, people begin to notice and distrust what we say. Our praise becomes meaningless. The weightiest compliments are from those who don't compliment often or don't exaggerate.

This doesn't mean, though, that we are to be blunt and insensitive. We shouldn't volunteer or divulge everything we know. A good rule is to "speak the truth in love." There are ways to say things delicately or avoid saying something hurtful. And the closer we are to someone, the easier it can be to say certain things. So if your friend's outfit looks

[27] Or make a fool of herself, as in the case of *Florence Foster Jenkins* (2016 movie).

ridiculous, you don't have to choose between bluntly announcing that fact or lying to her. You could say how much you prefer another outfit or suggest something that might work better for the occasion; or how much better another color or style suits her. There are lots of ways to present a truth that puts someone in a better direction without hurt or offense. We can find ways to speak truthfully *and* lovingly.

The other debatable kind of lie is one told to protect someone. The typical example is of the Nazis at the door asking if you're hiding any Jews. Obviously, you shouldn't betray those in your care. You are not required to disclose the truth to those who will misuse it. Still, it's better to avoid lying. The best thing to do in such a situation is to use "discreet language".[28]

Those not living in such dire circumstances can still face awkward questions. But there are responses that betray neither truth nor others' rights. We can say we're not at liberty to answer that question or that it's a personal or confidential matter. Or we can keep silence, change the subject, or reply with a question in turn ("Why do you ask?" is a great one). We can also limit our answer to that which wouldn't hurt others. A caller doesn't need to know whether I'm not at home, taking a nap, washing my hair, or just in a bad mood; all my child needs to say is that I'm not available. The essential information has been conveyed; the details are neither important nor any of his business. Just because someone asks a question doesn't mean you have to answer. Jesus never felt obligated to answer his enemies. He was the master of replying with another question or with an unexpected twist that foiled their schemes. But He didn't lie. Nor should we.

Conclusion

What we say or refrain from saying is a key aspect of loving our neighbor. Thus anyone who wants to please God must tame his tongue.

---

[28] *CCC* 2489. In *The Hiding Place*, the Nazis asked the author's niece where her brothers were, intending to force them into military service. She said, "Under the table." They pulled aside the tablecloth, but no one was there. But she hadn't lied. Under the table was a rug, beneath which was a trap-door to the cellar, where her brothers were hiding. It might seem daunting to think of such an answer under that kind of pressure. And if one couldn't, then a white lie would be exponentially better than betraying someone. But we can have faith in God's help. Those living in such a society could pray regularly to the Holy Spirit for help to meet such quandaries.

So let's pray with the Psalmist: "Set a guard over my mouth, O LORD, keep watch over the door of my lips!" and "Let the words of my mouth and the meditation of my heart be acceptable in your sight, O LORD."[29]

---

[29] Ps 141:3; Ps 19:14. See also Sir 28:25–26.

20

LOVE IN DEED

*Love ... is not content with fair words. The effect of love is an eagerness
to be up and doing.... Love seeks to assert itself by deeds.*

—Fr. Lawrence Lovasik

Jesus made it crystal clear that doing the work He did—reaching out
and helping people—is an essential part of following Him. He spoke of
it as a matter of heaven or hell. In the parable of the sheep and the goats,
those who served the needy went with Him to eternal life; those who
passed them by doing nothing went to eternal punishment.[1] Now He
didn't mean that the *only* thing you had to do to go to heaven was serve
the needy. You've also got to repent, believe, obtain and maintain the
life of grace by the sacraments, prayer, and obeying His commands, and
so forth. But He was making it very clear that merely *saying* we believe,
while doing nothing, is not enough. Words are cheap. "If a brother or
sister is poorly clothed and in lack of daily food, and one of you says
to them, 'Go in peace, be warmed and filled,' without giving them the
things needed for the body, what does it profit? So faith by itself, if it
has no works, is dead."[2]

Visible Mercy

Pieces of the Piñata

What is good about Western society today is its compassion. Such an
attitude was not always so prevalent. In fact, it was the Church, imitating

---

[1] Mt 25:31–46.
[2] Jas 2:15–17; see also the whole passage: 2:14–26.

Christ, that inspired and spread compassion for the poor, the sick, the underprivileged. Thus, many people in and out of the Church admire Pope Francis' championing of the poor. Unfortunately, too often we think about how *other* people need to do more, not about how *we* might need to as well. We mustn't think too highly of our own generosity. After all, the average American has luxuries that even the wealthy of past ages could envy (air conditioning and automobiles, for starters). Our homes are cluttered with things we don't need. We may give, but most of us could probably give a good bit more.

Life is like a piñata scramble. The moment the candy bursts from the piñata and cascades to the ground is exciting, but hardly fair. There are always those who get more than others, being closer or faster or more aggressive. Similarly, the world's goods aren't distributed fairly. We need to be as mature as those children who notice the little ones who didn't get much and share with them.

With global media and multiple letters of appeal, we can see the needs of people around the world, and it is a good and holy thing to send alms to the poor in faraway countries. But you can't help *everyone*, so you can feel overwhelmed. One idea is to focus on supporting a few worthwhile charities. It's important to give also to charities serving the needy locally, for we have a special obligation to support those in our own locale.

But how much should one give? How much is enough? That's a question each must answer, after prayer. We should talk with God about it regularly and whenever circumstances change. Mother Teresa gave a good rule of thumb: Give until it hurts. Give so that you must go without something. Laura Ingalls Wilder gives a touching example of this. Her family had started a new farm and had little money to spare. Pa had been saving up to replace his cracked boots; finally he had enough and went to town to buy them. But he came home wearing his old patched pair and without the money. While he was there, he heard that the new church needed $3 more to buy a bell—exactly what he had in his pocket. So he gave it to them—all of it.[3]

Giving like this is hard, but keep in mind that giving helps the giver too. We need to give, and give until it hurts, to rid ourselves of what holds us back. Mother Teresa felt that in making appeals she was doing the *donors* a favor. Fallen beings living in a materialistic culture, we

[3] Laura Ingalls Wilder, *On the Banks of Plum Creek* (New York: HarperCollins, 1971), pp. 188–91.

become attached to things so easily. But life isn't a game in which the winner is the one with the most toys at the end. No, those with the fewest attachments gain the highest rewards.

Greed is a trap. Literally so, in Africa. A secured, narrow-necked jar with a banana inside is set as a trap for a monkey: it can get its hand in the jar, but once it clutches the banana, its hand can no longer fit through the neck. Rather than let go and escape, it hangs onto the banana and is captured. Similarly, though we value freedom so highly, we don't realize we're slaves to our possessions and passions. True freedom is the ability to let go of anything that keeps us from the fulfillment of our being. God is our goal, our fulfillment; He alone is worth clinging to. Indeed, it is He we need, so we should drop anything and everything to cling to Him.

> When we attend to the needs of those in want, we give them what is theirs, not ours. More than performing works of mercy, we are paying a debt of justice.
>
> —St. Gregory the Great [Box 38]

Sins of Omission

Giving money is good, but not enough.

In examining our consciences, we usually focus on what we've *done*, forgetting to consider also what we've "failed to do".[4] But Jesus warned: "As you did it *not* to one of the least of these, you did it *not* to me."[5] He loves all people, including those who are not yet members of His Body; He calls us to show His love by tending their needs. If we neglect them, we neglect Him. Christians must *see* Christ in others and *be* Christ to others. "When Jesus comes amongst His own, His own don't know Him! He comes in the rotten bodies of our poor; He comes even in the rich choked by their own riches. He comes in the loneliness of their hearts.... Jesus comes to you and me, and often, very, very often, we pass Him by."[6]

Christ is our Head. If your toe is stubbed, don't *you* feel it? The downside of having us as His Mystical Body is having disobedient members. How much worse it must be to see someone you love in danger, but your legs are too lazy to run, your voice refuses to yell, and your hands stuff themselves in your pockets instead of reaching out to save. Words attributed to Teresa of Avila make the point so poignantly:

---

[4] Confiteor prayer, from the Mass.

[5] Mt 25:45; emphasis added.

[6] Mother Teresa, *Love: A Fruit Always in Season* (San Francisco: Ignatius Press, 1987), p. 42.

"Christ has no body now but yours. No hands, no feet on earth but yours. Yours are the eyes through which he looks compassion on this world. Yours are the feet with which he walks to do good. Yours are the hands through which he blesses all the world. Yours are the hands, yours are the feet, yours are the eyes, you are his body. Christ has no body now on earth but yours."

From the parable of the sheep and the goats come the "corporal works of mercy"—a list of ways tangibly to serve others: feed the hungry, give drink to the thirsty, clothe the naked, shelter the homeless, visit the imprisoned, tend or visit the sick, and bury the dead. To love God means to get up and do these things. Sure, you can't do every one every day, but pray and consider which you could do and when. Help out at a soup kitchen or parish food bank; have protein bars and water bottles on hand to give to beggars; donate items to the Salvation Army; volunteer at the St. Vincent de Paul Society or Habitat for Humanity; join a prison or hospital ministry; visit a nursing home. Volunteering as a Big Brother, in literacy programs, or for charities offering social services are just a few other ways to help those in need. The possibilities are myriad.

It's the Little Things...

It isn't only the big things that are worthwhile. The little things we do for others are significant in God's eyes. Jesus said, "Whoever gives to one of these little ones even a cup of cold water because he is a disciple ... shall not lose his reward" and "He who is faithful in a very little is faithful also in much; and he who is dishonest in a very little is dishonest also in much"; and of the widow who gave a couple copper coins, He asserted that she had given more than all the rest.[7]

Little things can also be significant to the recipient. One time I greeted a homeless Vietnam vet on the street and apologized that I had nothing to give him. He said, "That's okay. For someone just to *see* me, to acknowledge I'm a human being, means a lot to me."

As mentioned above, St. Thérèse, seeing herself as "a very little soul", who could "offer God only very little things",[8] decided to make use of every opportunity to prove her love for Him: "not allowing one little sacrifice to escape ... [but] profiting by all the smallest things".[9] She

[7] Mt 10:42; Lk 16:10; Mk 12:43.
[8] Thérèse of Lisieux, *Story of a Soul: The Autobiography of St. Thérèse of Lisieux*, trans. John Clarke, O.C.D., 3rd ed. (Washington, D.C.: ICS Publications, 1996), p. 250.
[9] Ibid., p. 196.

strewed them as flowers before the Lord, to "perfume the royal throne with their sweet scents",[10] confident that "the smallest actions done out of love are the ones which charm His Heart."[11] Mother Teresa followed and spread St. Thérèse's "Little Way". "Never think that a small action done to your neighbor is not worth much. It is not how much we do that is pleasing to God, but how much love we put into the doing."[12]

One potent little thing is to show courtesy. Fifty years ago, then-Bishop Fulton Sheen observed that courtesy was disappearing. (What would he think of the state of affairs today?) Opening the door for someone, offering to help, letting another go first, smiling, looking others in the eye, saying, "Thank you" or "Have a nice day", and giving a compliment—are all little things, but they can have a big impact. People are touched when we go beyond what is required or what's asked of us. It gives them hope that there's still some decency in the world and opens them to believing in the goodness and care of God. As Sheen put it: "Courtesy is love in action."[13]

Beyond serving others in ways they can see, one who loves God will also be on the lookout for those opportunities that only He will see. Medieval artists sometimes created beautiful images for Him alone, in the rafters of a cathedral, beyond the view of any human eye. We too can do hidden acts of charity. They offer a chance to express an even purer form of love. An admired act of service brings an earthly reward: the esteem of others. When you do something no one knows about, you give up such esteem, "and your Father who sees in secret will reward you."[14] (But we should never shirk a service out of fear of what others might think.)

Spiritual Mercy

While tending to earthly needs is important, there's more to loving our neighbors than that. They also have spiritual needs, which are even more important.

[10] Ibid.

[11] St. Thérèse of Lisieux, Letter to Léonie (July 12, 1896), in *Letters of St. Thérèse of Lisieux*, vol. 2: 1890–1897, trans. John Clarke, O.C.D. (Washington, D.C.: ICS Publications, 1988), p. 270.

[12] Mother Teresa, *Love: A Fruit Always in Season*, p. 120.

[13] Most Reverend Fulton J. Sheen, *The Power of Love* (New York: Simon and Schuster, 1965), p. 82.

[14] Mt 6:4, 6.

So, in addition to the corporal works of mercy, there's a list of spiritual works of mercy: to instruct the ignorant, counsel the doubtful, admonish sinners, bear wrongs patiently, forgive offenses willingly, comfort the afflicted, and pray for the living and the dead. Most of them make the corporal works of mercy look like a piece of cake. Instructing the spiritually ignorant or counseling the doubtful seems intimidating, admonishing the sinner sounds downright dangerous, and bearing wrongs patiently and forgiving offenses come easily only to a saint.[15] But that's what loving God ultimately means and ultimately requires— that we become saints. (A saint is one who is in heaven. Not all the saints are canonized; there must be millions of unknown saints whom we'll discover only when we join their ranks.) So when God gives us such opportunities, we would do well to do our best to minister to our neighbor in these ways as well. The spiritual works of mercy may be harder, but that just means we need to lean even more heavily on the help of the Lord—and that's always a good thing.

Some people launch, run, or assist big apostolates like Catholic Answers to give spiritual instruction, counsel, and loving admonition. Others, as priests, sisters, and brothers, give their whole lives to such endeavors. But smaller opportunities also come up for the rest of us. A friend might share a problem or ask for advice, and the Lord is there, prompting you to speak up on His behalf. Plenty of chances to comfort, bear wrongs, forgive, and pray for others come our way all our lives. (More on praying for the dead in chapter 26, below.) With His grace and guidance, we can step up and perform spiritual works of mercy. Probably the hardest work of mercy, and the hardest form of loving neighbor, is to forgive those who have hurt us or our loved ones. It's so big an issue it needs its own section.

Forgiving Others

Why Should We Forgive Others?

We must forgive because we can't get to heaven otherwise. Why is that? It has to do with the nature of heaven: If God is our Father, how can we be enemies with any of His children? There can't be any discord

---

[15] Praying for the living and the dead will be treated on pp. 331 and 326–28 below, respectively.

in the heavenly home. Also, it would be hypocritical to ask for forgiveness from God while refusing it to His beloved child, to leave our sin at the gate while trying to bring our brother's sin in and put it back on him or trying to keep him from going in at all.

Conciliatory Correspondence

I'm not claiming that forgiving is easy to do. As a young adult, I had trouble forgiving someone who had really hurt me when I was young. I wanted to forgive and forget, but I couldn't. One Sunday, a sense of hypocrisy dawned on me as I prayed the Our Father. I tried to forgive him and prayed for him, but the feelings would not subside, so I brought it to my spiritual director, and we decided I should tell him how I felt instead of keeping it bottled up. Fr. Luke said I could write him, but I had to do it a certain way: I was to begin and end positively; in the middle, I was to simply list the things that had hurt me, without elaboration, exaggeration, or recrimination. Just the facts. And I was to use "I" language: "When you did this, *I* felt . . ."

It wasn't an easy letter to write. In fact, I wrote a venting letter first, then threw it away.[16] But I followed Fr. Luke's wise advice and received a most healing response. The recipient admitted it was good I had *written* him rather than telling him in person, as he would have just gotten defensive. But a letter gave him time to reflect and realize what I had said was true. He then apologized so sincerely and gallantly that all my bitterness melted away and a wave of such love rose up within me that I almost wished he had done more so I could have the joy of forgiving him more. There was no merit of mine in such a reaction; it was wholly from God. It gave me an intimate understanding of His loving mercy and His joy in forgiving us.[17]

Of course, it doesn't always happen that way. We may have to wait a long time for someone to apologize, or he may never do so. A common stumbling block is misunderstanding what forgiveness is. It's not having warm feelings toward and being close buddies with the one who hurt us. While that's wonderful if it does occur, it's simply not in our power to

---

[16] Don't ever send a venting letter. I had done so once before with someone close to me and have regretted it ever since. I was a little afraid of her and sent it without even rereading it, thinking I would never have the guts to tell her how I felt otherwise. It was thoughtless and cowardly. I'm thankful she was gracious and forgiving.

[17] See all of chap. 15 in Luke's Gospel, especially vv. 6, 9, and 32.

make that happen. For one thing, we can't simply decide to feel something; feelings aren't like that. Secondly, we can't make the other person repent. It's hard to *feel* forgiving toward someone who isn't sorry.

And yet, our heavenly Father calls us to forgive even if that person isn't sorry. One reason is for *our* own sake. My sister first told me this wise insight: holding a grudge is like drinking poison and expecting the *other* person to die. Bitterness often hurts the one nursing it more than the one to whom it is directed. Thankfully, forgiving doesn't require warm feelings for the forgiven. Forgiveness is a choice, an act of the will. Nor does forgiveness require forgetting or making oneself vulnerable to one who's proven himself untrustworthy. To forgive is to let go of vengeance. It means putting the matter of justice in God's hands. It means acknowledging that God's been merciful to us, and hence we must be merciful to others. It means praying for that person. Loving our enemy means wanting the best for him, and the very best thing of all for anyone is to come to know and love God, repent of all sin, and live forever with Him in heaven. We can pray for these things even for an enemy, because in order for him to receive them he has to recognize his sins and repent. We can pray that he is given the grace to do so.

The Unforgivable

The problem comes when someone has done something so monstrous that he is—at least to any ordinary human—simply unforgivable. It seems almost dishonorable to speak of forgiving someone like Hitler or, in our own day, the 9-11 suicide pilots. Surely, the hardest commandment Jesus gave was to love our enemies, to forgive and pray for them.

Mercy seems unthinkable, for instance, for someone like Adam Lanza, who brutally shot down little children. But nothing is impossible with God. And upon reflection, that young man is very pitiable. Something was awry in him. Such heinous deeds deserve the torments of hell, no doubt. And yet, and yet ... can we not pray that somehow, some way, in his very last moments he had the grace of repentance? God is outside time; even now our prayers can touch those final moments. Lanza may not "deserve" prayer, but which of us wants what we really deserve?

It would seem that many in Sandy Hook recognize this. I interviewed Amy Taylor, a Franciscan University graduate who was working in Sandy Hook that horrible day, for an article in the alumni magazine. Divine mercy figured very prominently in her story. She prays for Adam Lanza: "If any soul needs mercy and prayer, it's him. I recall what St. Faustina said: 'The greater the sinner, the greater his right to God's mercy.'" Apparently Amy's attitude was not singular, for she described billboards in the area that read: "We are Sandy Hook. We choose love."[18]

Forgiving One I Loathed

I myself experienced the impossibility of forgiving one who did something detestable. Thoughts of my unknown molester (see chap. 3 above) raised in me violent tendencies of which I had previously thought myself incapable. Forgiving him was hardly my first inclination.

However, forgiving proved to be an integral part of my healing.

In my life-changing meditation chronicled in chapter 3, forgiveness also played a big role. Fr. Blair had told me that victims of sexual assault, having been *treated* as shameful objects, saw themselves that way too. During that fateful prayer time when I realized I hadn't been rendered a shameful object, I saw myself covered with tar that began breaking up and floating off. I wondered where it would go. Naturally, it began to settle on the molester. I saw it land on him and cover him. For the first time, I felt sorry for him. How horrible to have that shame and know it really belonged to you. How much worse to be guilty than to be victimized. Then I wondered what his destiny would be.

There was no doubt I was in the realm of the miraculous now: I went from wanting to rip off the face of my assailant (a face I still could not remember) to worrying about his eternal salvation. Then it occurred to me that I was in a unique position to do something about it. I saw that I could offer up all the pain, all the rage, all the as-yet-fruitless frustration for *him*, for his salvation. God was sharing His power to bring good out of evil ... with me, giving me the chance to bring good out of this evil.

I knew the grace was there. I said yes. Then the healing that had begun with realizing that God had not abandoned me now poured forth as through a crumbling dam. I walked out of that church a different person. I expected the pain to go on but that it would now have a purpose: I would make it useful by offering it up as a sacrifice for my enemy. The funny thing is I experienced such healing I really haven't had much to offer up since then.

[18] Cf. "Mercy in the Midst of Tragedy", by the author, *Franciscan Way* (Autumn 2013): 31.

God Makes Mercy Possible

In *The Hiding Place*, Corrie Ten Boom recounts her time in a concentration camp and her sister Betsie's incredible sanctity, which kept surprising her. For instance, struck in the face by a Gestapo agent, Betsie said, "I feel so sorry for him."[19] Witnessing the beating of a "feeble-minded" girl at the camp, Corrie asked, "What can we do for these people? Afterward I mean. Can't we make a home for them and care for them and love them?" Betsie replied, "I pray every day that we will be allowed to do this! To show them that love is greater!" Later on, Corrie realized: "I had been thinking of the feeble-minded, and Betsie had been thinking of their persecutors."[20]

Again and again, Corrie was shocked by Betsie's ability to forgive and pity their enemies. Sometimes Corrie felt a certain outrage at her sister's mercy. But Corrie learned from her sister's example. After Betsie's death and the end of the war, Corrie did set up a home to help people recover from the horrors of the war. She also traveled around giving talks, telling Betsie's story and encouraging people to forgive.

She found herself unable to do so, though, when face to face with a Nazi guard from her camp. Beaming, he thanked her for her message of God's mercy, hand thrust out to shake hers. But she couldn't lift it, even after asking the Lord to help her to forgive him. It was only when she prayed, "Jesus, I cannot forgive him. Give me Your forgiveness" that she could take his hand. When she did, a profound love sprang up in her heart for him. "And so I discovered that ... when He tells us to love our enemies, He gives, along with the command, the love itself."[21]

Similarly, St. Maria Goretti and her mother are models of forgiveness. In 1902, when Maria was twelve years old, they shared a house with another family of tenant farmers, whose son, Alessandro, was secretly reading violent material and pornography. He became obsessed with Maria; failing to seduce her, he tried to rape her. When she resisted, he stabbed her repeatedly. Even then, Maria's concern was for his soul. She kept saying, "Oh Alessandro, how unhappy you are! You will go to hell!" She was rushed to the hospital, but with fourteen major wounds, little could be done for her. Her pastor gave her last rites, and

---

[19] Corrie Ten Boom, John and Elizabeth Sherrill, *The Hiding Place* (New York: Bantam Books, 1971), p. 130.
[20] Ibid., pp. 209–10.
[21] Ibid., p. 238.

she willingly forgave Alessandro, "for the love of Jesus", saying, "I want him to be with me in Paradise.... May God forgive him."[22] She suffered without murmur and died the next day.

Maria's intense love of God, willingness to suffer, and Christlike mercy were not fruitless. Eight years after the unrepentant Alessandro was sentenced to thirty years of hard labor, he had a vivid dream in which Maria, surrounded by lilies, assured him of her forgiveness. As a result, he repented, became a model prisoner and later a Capuchin brother. After his release, he went to Maria's mother to beg her forgiveness. She said she could not withhold it since her daughter had forgiven him. Alessandro willingly testified in the cause for Maria's beatification and attended her canonization with her mother, Assunta, in 1950.

A similar case of amazing forgiveness occurred more recently: the Clarey family forgave the murderer of their eleven-year-old daughter, who also died defending her purity. Within days of Katie's death, asked by a reporter if she had anything to say to the murderer, her mother said, "Yes ... We would like to tell him we forgive him." Stunned, the reporter asked how that could be possible. Kathie replied: "It is what God asks of us. It might not be our way, but it is His way. We ask in the Our Father every day, 'Forgive us our trespasses as we forgive those who trespass against us.' We do not necessarily understand it, but we must trust in what Jesus tells us to do."[23] After her astounding words were broadcast on television, the Clareys' phone rang off the hook with callers saying she had inspired them to forgive those they found hard to forgive.

Katie's father, Mike, explains, "When we say we forgive the man who killed Katie, it is not a denial of what happened. It is not a denial of justice. Forgiveness is like love. It is an act of the will. Ultimately you surrender to Our Lord, and He applies the grace after that."[24]

While we may not be guilty of anything so evil, none of us is innocent either. A sinner, I hope, not for what I deserve, but for God's mercy, won by the Precious Blood of His Son Jesus. That same sacrifice is not only more than enough to win mercy for all the Alessandros and Adam Lanzas out there, but—much as we might shudder at the thought—was

---

[22] Ann Ball, *Modern Saints* (Rockford, Ill.: TAN Books, 1983), p. 170.
[23] Mike Clarey, "Forgiving the Unforgivable", in *Amazing Grace for Those Who Suffer*, ed. Jeff Cavins and Matthew Pinto (West Chester, Penn.: Ascension Press, 2002), p.118.
[24] Ibid., p. 119.

shed for that very purpose. May God's mercy be showered upon them, their victims, and all who mourn for them. And may all be given the miraculous grace to forgive.

Conclusion

"*If any one says, 'I love God,' and hates his brother, he is a liar; for he who does not love his brother whom he has seen, cannot love God whom he has not seen.*"[25] Christ joined us to His body; how can I say I love Him, while stabbing His shins? If I hurt any part of Him, I hurt Him.[26]

If we truly want to love God, we must love others—our family, our neighbors, our enemies. Jesus said, "You are my friends if you do what I command you."[27] His first command in this regard He gave through Moses: "You shall love your neighbor as yourself." But then He upped the ante: "Love your enemies and pray for those who persecute you", then raised it higher still: "Love one another; even as I have loved you."[28] And how has He loved us? He's loved us to death, and an excruciating one at that.[29] We must love our neighbor and our enemy. True love of God demands it. Hefty dependence on God enables us.

It's not a matter of *liking* everybody or pretending horrible things didn't happen. It's a matter of treating others as we would like to be treated.[30] If we want God's mercy, we must show mercy. Sometimes that means noticing others' needs and ministering to them. Sometimes it means forgiving them: asking God to have mercy on them and to bring about their repentance.

Blessed are the merciful, for they shall obtain mercy.[31]

---

[25] 1 Jn 4:20.

[26] Now don't think, "Ah well, then it's okay for me to hate those who are *not* members of His Body", because that's not true. Everyone who is not currently a member of Christ's Body is a potential member. Everyone is invited. Don't forget St. Paul started out as Saul, an enemy of the Christians, "breathing murderous threats against the disciples" (Acts 9:1, NAB). After meeting Jesus, he became one of His most ardent and active followers.

[27] Jn 15:14.

[28] Lev 19:18; Mt 5:44; Jn 13:34.

[29] "Greater love has no man than this, that a man lay down his life for his friends" (Jn 15:13).

[30] "As you wish that men would do to you, do so to them" (Lk 6:31).

[31] Mt 5:7.

PART THREE

"Be Perfect as Your Heavenly Father Is Perfect"

SECTION SEVEN

LOVING GOD MEANS
FOLLOWING HIM

"I have given you a model to follow, so that as I have done for you, you should also do."

(Jn 13:15, NABRE)

"Do you love me? . . . Follow me."

(Jn 21:17, 19)

21

FOLLOWING JESUS

Jesus told His disciples to follow Him. But what does that mean? It involves more than "following" someone on Twitter—it affects your whole life. It means to learn what He taught and to obey it. It means imitating Him: to live the way He lived, to do what He did. "Our Lord and Savior sometimes gives us instruction by words and sometimes by actions. His very deeds are our commands; and whenever he acts silently he is teaching us what we should do."[1]

For Jesus, imitating His Father was an essential part of loving Him.[2] Little children do this all the time; they *want* to do what they see their parents doing. They consider it an honor and a privilege.

> He who says he abides in him ought to walk in the same way in which he walked.
>
> —1 JOHN 2:6 Box 39

(Another reason we must become like little children to enter the Kingdom of heaven.)

Following the Way

Jesus said the way to heaven was "narrow". That suggests it's easy to stray off. Not only that, but compounding the problem is our tendency to take a pendulum ride from one side to the other. Upon realizing that we've strayed, we over-correct. We may touch the Way briefly as we shoot past it full-speed, but we end up on the other side. The tendency to over-correct may be due to over-enthusiasm. Laziness sneaks in too: we prefer oversimplification to seeking and reflecting on what the Church or Scripture has to say about the subject. Very likely, there's

---

[1] St. Gregory the Great, homily, quoted in *The Liturgy of the Hours*, vol. 4 (New York: Catholic Book Publishing, 1975), p. 1495.
[2] Jn 5:19.

a touch of pride involved: we've found The Answer, and we won't abide any qualifications. I suspect the evil one exploits this human inclination as much as possible. He doesn't care which side we're on so long as we've lost the Way.

Of course, we may drift from the narrow way without correcting at all—because we never realize that we're astray. All we notice is how far off *those* people are, over on the other side. Going off even a little bit on any side is dangerous, particularly if we don't get back on right away. Geometry shows that even a small departure eventually results in a wide separation. Happily, unlike any other way, this One can reach out and help us if we fall, for He *is* the Way.

The key then is to keep our hearts set on Jesus, not on this good or that. After all, He is the Source of all goodness. Any good quality finds its perfection in Him, without being in contradiction with any other. He is Truth; He is Love. In Him they do not conflict. Justice embraces Mercy in His Passion on the Cross. He keeps them all in balance, not in contradiction. Any time we focus on something other than Christ, we'll start following it instead. But if we focus on Him, we'll eventually find all good things. Following Him requires focusing on Him.

Universal Call to Holiness

"Be perfect, as your heavenly Father is perfect."[3] Jesus' call is not to do the minimum to stay out of hell, but to be *like Him*. Holiness isn't just an *option* for the super devout; it's *required* for all who want heaven. "Strive for ... the holiness without which no one will see the Lord."[4]

You might say, *Wait: only saints are holy; not the rest of us.* Nope. Aware that many Catholics saw holiness as just for clergy and religious, the Fathers of Vatican II clarified: "In the Church, *everyone* ... is called to holiness"—all people in their differing circumstances.[5] Mother Teresa

---

[3] Mt 5:48.

[4] Heb 12:14. "Personal sanctification is required for attaining the vision of God in heaven (Mt 5:8; Rev 22:4). This includes being made holy or sanctified by the grace of God, first of all in Baptism (1 Cor 6:11). However, the Lord also wills us to 'strive' for an increase in sanctification by the exertion of our will in living the gospel to the full (Rom 6:19; 1 Thess 3:12–13, 4:3). [This is] ... indispensable for reaching heaven." Scott Hahn and Curtis Mitch, eds., *Ignatius Catholic Study Bible: The New Testament* (San Francisco: Ignatius Press, 2010), p. 434, note on Heb 12:14.

[5] Second Vatican Council, Dogmatic Constitution on the Church *Lumen Gentium* (November 21, 1964), nos. 39 and 40.

echoed them: "It is nothing extraordinary to be holy. Holiness is not a luxury of the few. Holiness is a simple duty for you and me. We have been created for that."[6]

We would like to think following Christ is just a matter of giving up some bad things and doing a few good things. But half-measures aren't what the Lord has in mind.

> The Christian way is different: harder, and easier. Christ says, "Give me All. I don't want so much of your time and so much of your money and so much of your work: I want You. I have not come to torment your natural self, but to kill it.... I don't want to drill the tooth, or crown it, or stop it, but to have it out. Hand over the whole natural self.... I will give you a new self instead. In fact, I will give you Myself: my own will shall become yours."[7]

Don't let the idea of becoming holy intimidate you; let it invigorate you. The grain of wheat has to "die" to what it has been in order to grow, but if it does, it will become something much greater and find its fulfillment.[8] So too with us. The call to holiness is a thrilling prospect because with it comes the promise that, if we respond, we will become like God.[9] We needn't be frightened, because the Lord knows we can't do this on our own. But with our permission and cooperation, He will be the One to do the transforming.

Initial Steps

The key to holiness is Jesus. If we cooperate with Him, He can make us actually holy. He doesn't merely hide our sinfulness; He gets rid of it.[10] Members of His Body truly become part of Him. The more securely

---

[6] Mother Teresa, "Mother Teresa: Something Beautiful for God", *Catholic Planet*, http://www.catholicplanet.com/articles/article115.htm. This doesn't mean *everyone* must go off as missionaries to a distant land; there's plenty to do wherever we are. Part of loving God is to discern how He's calling us to live out holiness. This is particularly true for the young, but discernment is ongoing for everyone, as God can call us to new missions along the way.

[7] C.S. Lewis, *Mere Christianity* (New York: HarperCollins, 2001), pp. 196–97. What Lewis calls "the natural self", St. Paul calls the "old self" or "old man". Cf. Rom 6:6 RSVCE 1st ed.; Eph 4:22–24; and Col 3:9–11.

[8] Jn 12:24.

[9] 1 Jn 3:2.

[10] Is 1:18; Ps 103:12. See also *CCC* 1987.

grafted we are onto that Vine, the more open we are to His filling us, the more we will be transformed into Him. To become one with Christ is to become holy.

Always Seeking

We can't physically see and follow behind Him. To imitate Him, then, we must know Him and what He wants of us. We can't be content with what we know but must keep seeking to know Him better and understand His teachings better, so as to live them out more fully, more perfectly.

Unfortunately too many treat Confirmation as a kind of graduation from religious education. No, no, no. It's not the end; it's the *beginning* of living as an adult in the faith. It's saying, "Yes, I choose Christ and to follow Him. I agree with what I've learned, and now I take it upon myself to live this out." Could an eighth- or ninth-grade education in the faith be sufficient for that? Many wouldn't consider that enough education for living in the world; why would it be sufficient for one's spiritual life? A lifetime is too short to learn everything God has revealed to the Church. Not even eternity will be long enough for us to plumb the depths of knowing God. It's essential to continue learning the faith throughout our lives.

Nowadays there are more resources available to the ordinary believer than at any other time in the history of Christianity. There are many excellent books out there (see the Recommended Works below for starters), as well as CDs, DVDs, conferences, local talks and retreats in many areas, the global Catholic TV network EWTN, and over five hundred Catholic radio stations in the U.S. If you live in an area without EWTN or Catholic radio, both are accessible via the Internet. For most of us, there's no excuse for not being lifelong learners in the faith.

Reading great books and watching or listening to inspiring talks on the faith are essential, but we must also go beyond these to sharing and discussing them with others.

Spiritual Support

Not long after marrying, my husband and I ended up across the country from my family, where I knew no one but him. Though we knew the faith, loved each other and God, and were dedicated to His ways, it was a lot harder than expected. We had trouble finding fellowship; and the few Christian friends we made often moved away. We didn't have much accountability or support. We finally found community seven years later ... and by then I was starving. I no longer thought my faith was all that strong. I knew how weak I was and how much I needed fellow believers.

We can't go it alone; we're not meant to. God didn't create us each with our own little planet and communicate with us directly, and He generally doesn't speak audibly or give us infused knowledge. Instead, He made us social beings who need each other. "The eye cannot say to the hand, 'I have no need of you,' nor again the head to the feet, 'I have no need of you.' "[11]

When Jesus sent out His disciples to evangelize, He didn't send them solo, but in pairs. Later on, after His Ascension, when the Twelve separated and went farther afield, they still had helpers with them. Peter had Mark, and Paul had Barnabas and later Luke, and others as well. And throughout the history of the Church, we can see that the lives of the saints are intertwined.[12] Keep in mind too that God enjoys giving to us through others (and to others through us). "Now there are varieties of gifts, but the same Spirit; and there are varieties of service, but the same Lord.... To each is given the manifestation of the Spirit for the common good."[13]

As the Body of Christ, we need each other. It's hard enough to walk the walk without wandering away, but it's just about impossible to grow spiritually without the support of our siblings in faith. We *need* each other. We need encouragement and the examples, prayers, and wisdom of others. Fellow followers are indispensable if we are to grow and to stay faithful.

We can learn a lot from other people when, for instance, they share what they've read and experienced and especially their perspectives. Each of us has a unique vantage point and relationship with God. We can help each other understand Him a little better (provided we don't start spouting things contrary to His teachings). When I first started attending

---

[11] 1 Cor 12:21; cf. all of chap. 12 in 1 Corinthians.

[12] Think of the apostles, along with St. Paul, Mother Mary, Mary Magdalen, Martha and Mary; think also of Cosmas and Damian; Ambrose, Augustine, and Monica; Cyril and Methodius; Francis de Sales and Jeanne de Chantal; John of the Cross and Teresa of Avila; John Bosco and Dominic Savio; Thérèse of Lisieux and her recently beatified parents, Louis and Zélie Martin; and the newly canonized siblings Francisco and Jacinta.

[13] 1 Cor 12:4–5, 7. See also Vatican II, *Lumen Gentium*, The Church, no. 12.

Gospel reflections where each was to share what the passage said to her, I thought, "Ho-hum. I guess I'll just say the obvious; what else is there?" I was so wrong! I would share what seemed blatantly obvious to me, and someone would say, "I never thought of that before!" But I couldn't be proud of my insight, because every single time someone else in turn would say something *I* had never thought of before.

We also need accountability: fellow followers who know us and will notice if we fall off the wagon, whatever particular wagon we need to ride. Their presence keeps us from crumbling in the face of a world ready to ridicule us for our faith; they help us live with integrity.

Unfortunately, while some parishes present many ways to connect parishioners, others don't offer much beyond the sacraments. And for some sad, strange reason, many Catholics are not very good at reaching out to each other and super shy when it comes to our faith. (We don't have any problem complaining about the Church—local or universal—but we don't often share what's going on inside ourselves.) Many show up for Sunday Mass and that's it.

But that's not enough. Like the early Christians, we need to form communities in which we support each other. If your parish has small groups, great; join one. Go to the Bible study or whatever activity suits you. If there isn't a parish group for you, seek out others who follow what He taught and who will help you grow more like Jesus. Check out what's available in the diocese: there may be a third-order Franciscan, Dominican, or Carmelite group in your area, or an ecclesial movement such as Opus Dei or Regnum Christi, a Rosary cenacle or charismatic prayer group. Or get involved in something faith-based: volunteer at a soup kitchen, home for pregnant girls, nursing home, or apostolate. If you can't find anything, consider starting something. You could host a book club to discuss a book[14] or Bible study in your living room.

We're not meant to live the faith alone.

Feedback, Correction, and Guidance

Thanks to the Fall, each of us is quite capable of fooling ourselves. In ordinary life, at some point, most of us need some frank but necessary feedback: as when we're about to go out with a zipper down or determined to say something really stupid to the boss. We also need feedback

---

[14] A few suggestions: *Rediscover Jesus, Seven Big Myths, Rediscover Catholicism, Courageous Virtue.*

in the spiritual life. "I really don't think that idea could be from the Holy Spirit because that's not what Jesus taught." Or "No, honey, don't fast today; you're still getting over that cold." Or "You know, St. So-and-So went through the same thing, and this is what she did ..."

Knocking Off the Barnacles

Sometimes our friends and family are too nice or too biased to give us frank and objective feedback, however. That's why we also need those who aren't as concerned or who just don't like us. Many saints humbly accepted criticism—and even were grateful to those who disliked them—because they wanted to know their faults.[15] God allows difficult people in our lives to help knock off some of the barnacles of sin from our souls. Like anything medicinal, it doesn't feel good at the time, but if we take it well, it will be for our greater good in the long run.

I once collaborated with another Christian whose personality was very different from mine. We had opposite strengths and weaknesses and quite different ways of thinking and doing things. In one way, that made us a perfect fit for the work at hand. But it also meant we frequently irked or hurt each other—unintentionally. At the time, it was a very painful cross for me. Not only when she accidentally hurt me, but also when I had to face the fact that *I* could be a difficult person in someone else's book. It was humbling to discover that others found me annoying and to get a close-up look at my faults. Fortunately, both of us were dedicated to Christ and obeying His command to love one another. Over time, we came to appreciate each other's gifts, to understand each other, and even to try to please the other, yielding in what was important to her. We became much deeper friends—and better people—precisely by passing through that difficult valley. Vexing as it was, we're both grateful for how God used us to our mutual benefit, and our love for each other is tender and true.

Spiritual Direction

Often the best guidance in following Jesus comes from a good spiritual director. This should be someone who knows and upholds the

---

[15] Even when a particular accusation is false, saints are conscious of other sins for which they deserve rebuke and so humbly accept this as just. Getting to that point must be difficult (I wouldn't know—I'm still working to get there), but we can all make steps toward that place, which must be one of peace.

teachings of the Church, is living a holy life, and preferably is trained in spiritual direction or at least has a lot of wisdom and experience. Such a director is invaluable in helping one discern God's will in large and small decisions and gently challenges you to grow in areas where you need to grow but perhaps would rather ignore.

Good spiritual directors are not easy to find; try calling the diocese for a recommendation. Those in religious houses (for example, Dominican) usually have a little more time than the average parish priest. If you can't find one, try spiritualdirector.com and/or try to find a good confessor. Just as it's good to have a regular doctor who knows your history, it's best to have a regular confessor, if possible. Of course, in emergencies you don't bother about *which* doctor, you just go to the ER; similarly, if you have a mortal sin on your soul and your regular confessor is not readily available, it would be better just to get to any confessional. (You can always fill your confessor in later, if need be.)

Therapy Hurts before It Helps

One day I bent over to pick something up from the floor . . . and threw my back out. So I went to a physical therapist. Her solution was to find tender tense spots on my back, neck, and legs; dig her thumb or elbow deep into the heart of said spots; and ever-so-slowly drag it through my muscle. "Pain" does not adequately describe the feeling produced. I would say, "I can't believe I'm paying you to do this to me", and "You know, if I had an enemy who really wanted to get to me, this would be the perfect way to do it." But you know what? It worked. That was fifteen years ago, and thus far, praise God, I haven't had any recurrence of that back problem.

Feedback that's hard to take is like that. While others can help us recognize those problem areas that we can't see or reach, we don't want to let anyone touch those tender spots. But if we do, we will find it well worth the temporary pain to gain priceless benefits to our souls and our relationships. Whether it comes from a spiritual director, trusted friend, mentor, or even a stranger, it is to our advantage to listen to wise correction or advice when it comes to us.

〰 〰 〰

So don't try to be an island; don't try to live the faith alone. We need each other. We need those farther along in holiness to urge us on;

challenging people to make us grow; comforting people to restore and renew us. And others need us.

A good friend is a channel of God's love. Christlike friends give comfort in our sorrows, a listening ear and extended hand in our diffi-

> Faith is a treasure of life which is enriched by being shared.
>
> — *CCC* 949 ^{Box 40}

culties, a smile in our joys, a cheer in our victories, wisdom in our folly, warning when we're headed toward harm, salutary rebuke when we're wrong, and forgiveness when we're sorry. We would do well to seek good friends and to *be* a good friend.

Always and Everywhere

Learning about God and His ways, praying for holiness, and hanging out with holy people are all good, but not enough. We also need to *do* something, live it out. We must be His followers every day and everywhere. Many of the recommended practices of previous chapters herein can be done privately. Now let's examine how to take it to the streets.

22

WHERE YOU LOOK AND HOW YOU LOOK

Before taking Jesus to the streets, we should give a little thought to our appearance first. God called me out on this some years ago, letting me know that being His follower had to affect the way I dress too. What does it mean to follow Jesus in the area of clothing? While it won't be literal for most people—in a first-century-style tunic and cloak—we can glean certain principles from what Jesus said and the reflection of the Church.

The Gospels don't say much about what Jesus wore, but given His instructions when He sent His disciples out to preach, we can assume it was nothing fancy; nor was it likely that the One who had "nowhere to lay his head" would wear the "soft robes" of the rich.[1] On the other hand, He did speak of a man not suitably attired for a wedding, and on Golgotha, He was wearing a seamless tunic: the garb of the high priest, who made the sacrifice of atonement on behalf of the people.[2] Plainly, Jesus saw some value in being dressed appropriately for the occasion. In our day of extreme informality—where people wear pajamas to the grocery store—this principle might give us pause. Especially when it comes to church.

This was a perspective I had to learn. Having grown up in Southern California, then among the most casual areas in the country, I was a little scandalized at college in Ohio when I saw all the fuss some girls put into getting ready for Sunday Mass. I thought the focus was too much on themselves, and God couldn't care less how they looked. My friend Annamary enlightened me, though, on how the motive could be a holy one: you would naturally dress up to meet a VIP at a formal affair; could there be anyone more important to meet than Jesus? While God does care much more about what's in our hearts than on our backs, He's still pleased when we wear our best at Mass as a sign of respect to Him.

[1] See Mt 10:9–10; 8:20; 11:8.
[2] Mt 22:11–12; Jn 19:23.

It's also an act of charity to our neighbor to dress in a way that isn't distracting or inappropriate—by being flashy, slovenly, or immodest, for example.

Good Christians can disagree about precisely what it means to dress appropriately, so how can we know? I can't think of a better source than St. Peter's Basilica in Rome. While there is no Church document outlining inches or fabrics or those kinds of details, the basilica itself does have a dress code, which can be a good guide for worship at our own parish as well. Admission is free, but tourists not properly dressed are turned away at the doors. If the Vatican deems it inappropriate simply to enter and view the basilica with bare shoulders or knees (on men or women), then we probably shouldn't show up that way to worship at any church.[3]

Another principle we can glean from the Gospel is to take care where we look and how we look. Jesus revealed lust to be a serious sin when He said, "Every one who looks at a woman lustfully has already committed adultery with her in his heart."[4] But dressing immodestly can tempt others (especially men) into this serious sin; thus the wearers (especially women) must also recall Jesus' warning, "Woe to the man by whom temptation comes."[5]

The problem is that often we don't realize when we're doing that.

What Many Women Don't Know about Men

I was in my thirties before I learned that in thinking of myself as a decent dresser (i.e., modest) I was naïvely mistaken. I hadn't understood why even ordinary attire could evoke lecherous looks or darting glances. It's not as simplistic as I had thought: namely, that certain men were lustful creeps, while others were normal and mature. Rather, the vast majority of men—whether they show it or not—are affected by the same phenomenon. The sight of a female form has a much greater effect on a man than most women and girls would guess.

[3] At St. Peter's Basilica and the Sistine Chapel, the dress code for both men and women requires that knees and shoulders must be covered. Wearing shorts, short skirts, tank tops, or even sleeveless tees will get you turned away. See http://www.papalaudience.org/dress-code (accessed Aug. 18, 2016).

[4] Mt 5:28.

[5] Mt 18:6–7.

While human beings do not operate by instinct as animals do, we're still affected by our body's promptings. You could say we all have "buttons", in a sense. Certain buttons are standard (just about everyone has them), though some are more sensitive or powerful on some individuals than on others. But what many don't realize is that men and women have some buttons that differ. At least, some buttons on one gender seem to be protected by a glass cover and thus are usually much less accessible than on the other gender.

That certainly is the case here: seeing someone of the opposite sex dressed immodestly has a much bigger impact on most men than on most women. Popular culture has long recognized this. For instance, whenever the voluptuous girl-rabbit comes along in the old cartoons, Bugs Bunny's eyes bulge out and he stumbles around as though drunk. The girl-bunny never does that. It seems to be the way we're wired. For instance, a neuroscience study tracking brain activity while the subject was viewing sexually arousing stimuli showed significantly more activity in the amygdala (an area associated with emotion and sexual arousal) of men than women. The highest amygdala activity in women was in response to photos of *nonsexual* couple interaction.[6]

It seems to me that God gave husbands a very sensitive visual-stimulus button as a means of continuing our species. Before the Fall, I imagine, only the sight of his wife would set it off, but since original sin threw our body-mind-soul equilibrium out of whack, just about any woman can activate it. That's why humans started wearing clothes in the first place.[7]

Or you can think of it as a trigger. Humans have certain physiological triggers: "mouth-watering" foods really do trigger the production of saliva, the mere smell of bacon triggers a release of digestive enzymes, and the power of chocolate over most women is proverbial. Likewise, seeing the female form triggers a chemical reaction in a man's brain.[8] Moreover, this particular trigger is usually pretty powerful. It's like a

---

[6] Stephan Hamann, Ph.D., et al., "A sex difference in amygdala response to visual sexual stimuli", *Nature Neuroscience* 7 (Apr. 1, 2004): 411–16.

[7] See Gen 3:7. See also Pope St. John Paul's *Theology of the Body* (1979–1984), passim, but esp. audiences "12. Fullness of Interpersonal Communication", "14. Revelation and Discovery of the Nuptial Meaning of the Body", and "29. Relationship of Lust to Communion of Persons". Available online at EWTN: https://www.ewtn.com/library/PAPALDOC/JP2TBIND.HTM.

[8] Dr. Judith Reisman, cf. "The Psychopharmacology of Pictorial Pornography Restructuring Brain, Mind, and Memory", http://www.drjudithreisman.com/archives/2004/12/pre-2005_entrie.html (accessed Feb. 17, 2016). In a private email to me, she wrote: "Anything that applies to images on a page applies to images walking down the street" (Mar. 14, 2005).

high-energy young dog: even when he's asleep, if you rattle his leash, he'll leap up and race to the door, ready to go.

The sight of an immodestly dressed woman is such a strong stimulant that it can involuntarily conjure up in a man's mind an image of how she looks unclothed. If he's seen pornography (and most men have),[9] that will only intensify the reaction. In fact, often he can avoid this only by immediately looking away and thinking hard about something else ... like kitty litter. This takes a great deal of self-control and, really, grace. Without grace, why would he want to do that? Only with a well-formed conscience would he even bother. In a culture full of arousing images, he needs a lot of prayer and grace to do so. (How difficult daily life must be for such men, when sometimes every fifth or sixth person they see obliges them to exercise this self-control. For a woman, it would be like being on a diet with every sixth person she passes wafting a tray of chocolate truffles under her nose.)

Mutually Clueless

All this will come as an eye-opener to many females. Most are unaware of how potent this trigger is, largely because our experience is so different. Sure, women can be tempted by immodestly dressed men, but (a) men don't dress immodestly nearly as often, and (b) the effect is usually drastically less powerful. Think of a man wearing a Speedo: the effect on many women is to make them look away and laugh, thinking what an absurd exhibitionist he is.

Moreover, it isn't considered polite for a man to show his reaction if a woman is dressed immodestly, so it's often not apparent what's going on in his mind. Thus, many females are fairly clueless about the effect they're having. Many who consider themselves "good girls"—my younger self included—are actually tempting men to sin while being quite unaware of it.

Meanwhile, some men think women have the same trigger or at least know what they're doing. They conclude that an immodestly dressed

[9] Family Safe Media reports that nine in ten *children* have been exposed to porn by age sixteen (http://familysafemedia.com/pornography-statistics/#anchor4). And sadly, with the prevalence of Internet porn today, it's a problem even among Christians: in 1996, 53 percent of survey respondents at an event for Promise-Keepers (Christian men dedicated to marital fidelity) admitted looking at Internet porn in *the previous week* (http://www.safefamilies.org/sfStats.php). That was over twenty years ago; since then, with the advent of smartphones, it has only become worse.

woman *wants* to be ogled at. After all, there are some women who purposely dress immodestly to attract attention, fully aware of the effect.

Many men, however, do know that females can be naïve about this, though they may not realize how naïve. So why don't they say something? Three probable reasons: it doesn't occur to them; the likely backlash deters them; and some enjoy the show too much to try to quell it.

So when choosing an outfit, females have to be extra careful not to choose the leash-rattling variety. The trouble is discerning what clothes fit that description.

Practical Principles

Our culture has some double-think going on here. We have an incredible increase in raciness (many of the fashions of today were the hallmark of a prostitute less than a generation ago) with a simultaneous denial that it's of any significance. Anyone who questions it is labeled a prude. But if it's really so insignificant, why do so many ads take full advantage of it?

Though we may recognize that our culture's morals are shrinking steadily, we're not always aware how much our culture influences us. Surrounded by immodesty, we may recognize it only when it's extreme. If we merely avoid what society considers to be immodest, we will not be modest enough. We must not conform ourselves to the world's view but to God's.

Moreover, since the male mind works differently in this area, many females need some enlightening. For instance, when a woman sees another woman wearing a strapless dress, she'll just see a woman in a strapless dress. But a man's mind might automatically leap from the bare shoulders and neckline to what the rest of the bare torso probably looks like.

So between our cultural astigmatism and this imagination dissimilarity, many women and girls need a little help in recognizing immodesty. I know I sure did. Here are some factors to keep in mind (which apply to males as well, by the way).

Factors of Immodesty

THE SKIN FACTOR is what we usually think of when it comes to "immodesty". But it's made light of now because standards have changed so much in the past century; the sight of a mere ankle is no longer titillating. But then, a lot more than the ankle is being shown today, and a great deal of visible skin is still risqué. Too much information yields too much imagination.

But immodesty isn't merely a matter of showing too much skin. In fact, other factors can be more alluring. Some people look more immodest in a pair of snug pants than in a swimsuit. Why? Well, pants can accentuate the shape while hiding imperfections. Which brings us to ...

THE SHAPE FACTOR is the kind of immodesty most commonly overlooked by Christian women today. Low-cut tops and mini-skirts aren't the only triggers: for countless men, form-fitting pants and tops are too. And "form-fitting" doesn't just mean "tight". We need to expand our notion of what is "revealing" to include what clearly reveals one's shape. Any clothing that accentuates the contours of a curve is probably too shape-revealing. Unfortunately, nowadays, this includes a lot of trendy pants and tops.

THE ACCESSIBILITY FACTOR is also frequently overlooked. It's what makes a mini-skirt more immodest than shorts of the same length. Hence loose skirts above the knee, being dicey in the wind, are risqué, but even tailored skirts can be too accessible if they're significantly above the knee. We can't be naïve about how music videos, racy movies, and pornography have exacerbated the unfavorable tendencies of the post-Eden male imagination. They play on that theme all the time. Even items that only appear to be accessible, such as scooter skirts and skorts, are problematic. Many a man won't realize they include shorts. He sees what appears to be a mini-skirt, and the accessibility factor kicks in.

The fashion for young men of pants half-off in the back is another example of the accessibility factor. Thankfully, it is finally waning.

Finally, there's THE PROVOCATIVE FACTOR. Clingy, silky materials are also suggestive even without being close-fitting (hence their use in lingerie). Colors and styles with steamy cultural associations—like red lace or fishnet stockings—are psychologically provocative too.

Two Tips

A young man came up with a wonderful principle summing it all up so well: he advised a female friend to dress in a way that drew attention to her

> ### The *Catechism* on Modesty
>
> "The forms taken by modesty vary from one culture to another. Everywhere, however, modesty exists as an intuition of the spiritual dignity proper to man."
>
> — *CCC* 2524
>
> "Modesty inspires a way of life which ... resist[s] the allurements of fashion and the pressures of prevailing ideologies."
>
> — *CCC* 2523
>
> "Modesty protects the mystery of persons and their love."
>
> — *CCC* 2522 ^{Box 41}

face, not her form. Clothing that's skimpy, accessible, or provocative, or that reveals too much shape will do the opposite. Drawing attention to your face reminds others of your personhood.

Secondly, turn to Mother Mary. She's essential for women, since we can't ask *What would Jesus do?* in this situation, but we can ponder what Mary would wear in our day. If she would deem an outfit immodest, we should too. Both sexes can benefit from her potent prayers and her brown scapular, which has a practical use here.[10] A private devotion, it's not worn like a necklace but under your clothing. If your top can't cover the scapular, even with the help of safety pins, that's an indicator it's probably immodest.

Challenges to Changing

Now it's not an easy thing to change how we dress.

First, we might worry that dressing modestly means having to look totally out of it. This is especially true for females; our attire plays a large role in our self-expression and, often too large a role in our lives. And then, it's a hundred times easier for males to find modest clothes. Thus females may be feeling some dismay about the possibility of finding any clothes without one of these factors, especially the younger generation. I know! I have five daughters—and the only who's easy to buy clothes for is the kindergartner.

But don't give up. God always provides a way to obey Him.[11] There are companies that sell modest clothes; some online companies sell *only* modest clothing. If you can't find any modest choices, ask; if they don't

---

[10] The brown scapular's spiritual power is discussed below, pp. 299–300.
[11] I Cor 10:13.

have any, your asking will raise awareness. Second-hand or consignment shops often have more modest options and are cheaper to boot.

One can also work with or supplement one's wardrobe to make it more modest. Pants that are too form-fitting can be paired with a tunic or top long enough to cover the seat. If the top is too revealing, you can add a shrug, tee, or camisole. If you're handy with a needle, you can alter or add as needed—like a piece of lace across a low neckline. Originality and nonconformity have been very fashionable for decades now. Here's a great opportunity to think outside the box.

Modesty Motivators

Most of these options involve a lot of hassle, I admit. It may not seem worth it. It's easy to get discouraged and throw in the towel (or scarf, in this case). But we need to remember the bigger picture, to think of more than our vanity and convenience. There are three good reasons to take the trouble to dress modestly: for our own good, for others, and for the Lord.

For Our Own Sake

Jesus told us not to throw our pearls before swine.[12] No one but a spouse has a right to know just how sexy you can look. Everyone else needs only to know you as a person. Dressing modestly emphasizes your personhood and upholds your dignity.

For the gals, once we realize what effect dressing immodestly may have, don't we *want* to watch what we wear? It's one thing to be attractive; it's another to conjure up intimate details about oneself in the mind of potentially *any* man one meets. Granted, a man who wants to lust can do so even if you're dressed modestly, but why make it effortless for him? Why *encourage* men to view you as an object? Immodesty draws attention away from your richness as a person.

Moreover, immodest clothing puts us in some danger with aggressive males. No, it isn't fair, but it is an unpleasant fact. This is due in part to pornography, which has grown more perverse and sometimes violent. It's commonplace in pornography to portray women as either

---

[12] Mt 7:6. Yes, in context He meant theological pearls, but we can apply the same principle here.

(1) wanting to be assaulted or (2) enjoying it when it happens. These gross falsehoods feed the heinous idea that a woman who gets raped was "asking for it" if she was dressed immodestly. On the contrary, even if she was stark naked, that would not give anyone the right to touch her. But that doesn't mean that dressing modestly is to subscribe to these blame-projecting attitudes of predators. Modest attire is no more an endorsement of such abominable notions than avoiding dark alleys at night is an approval of mugging.

Dressing modestly is in our own interest. Not only for safety's sake, but also because it is a way showing respect for ourselves and communicating that we expect respect from others.

For the Sake of Others

Jesus said we are to be in the world, but not of the world. Our moral standards must differ from those of the world. What that means in daily life requires prayerful reflection and constant vigilance to make sure we're not adopting the wrong cultural norms. Though some are called to be radically countercultural, like St. Francis, most of us are called to dress "normally". (Generally we'll have more opportunities to witness effectively to others if they don't label us on sight as "weird".) But we're never called to compromise Christ's standards. To be "salt for the earth" means standing out in some ways. Salt adds flavor and helps preserve against decay. Modest and attractive attire helps people realize there's more to being human than sex appeal. When we dress that way, we remind others of our dignity, reveal inner beauty, and are examples to others.

For the Sake of the Lord

We should be concerned most of all with what our Lord thinks. Loving Him means trying to please Him—in everything. Even in the smallest details, we should consider what He wants us to do.

Custody of the Eyes

Much of this chapter thus far applies more to women than to men—at least on a practical level. But men have responsibilities here too. They too need to watch what they wear—that it's modest and appropriate to the situation. And they in turn have a responsibility that applies more to them than to women, though it does apply to women as well. Since men have this sensitive trigger, they have a grave responsibility to guard it. The traditional term for this is "custody of the eyes".

Sam Guzman, who writes a blog called *The Catholic Gentleman*, has four great tips on how to practice custody of the eyes in our day of ever-available sexual stimuli. First, be careful about what you allow yourself to be exposed to; Guzman mentions TV, movies, etc., but it's also a must to install filters on all devices. You also need to be careful where you go; some men might find simply sitting on a beach to be an occasion of sin and thus to be avoided.

When encountering temptations in person, Guzman recommends looking a woman in the face, because "it is essentially impossible to lust after someone's face. The face is the icon of each person's humanity."[13] He acknowledges, however, there are some situations where the best thing to do is just to look down at the floor. Finally, fasting and prayer are indispensable. Guzman ends with advising hope in God's help. "Yes, temptation is everywhere, but we are not helpless victims.... Through prayer, fasting, and practice, we can learn to take control of our eyes and avoid temptation. This isn't quaint and archaic—it's basic to spiritual survival."[14]

I would add: turn to Mary. A devotion to Our Lady is weighty in overcoming lust and an addiction to pornography. The Immaculate Mother of Jesus is the perfect image of pure womanhood; think of her when you're tempted to objectify women. And her prayers are formidable; turn to her and use her aids, the scapular and Rosary (see chapters 25 and 27 below).

Conclusion

The Lord is calling males to guard their eyes and speak up. Challenge your peers to esteem and practice purity in look, word, and action. Prayerfully and carefully say something to the women and girls in your

---

[13] Sam Guzman, "Custody of the Eyes: What It Is and How to Practice It", *The Catholic Gentleman* (June 12, 2014), https://www.catholicgentleman.net/2014/06/custody-of-the-eyes-what-it-is-and-how-to-practice-it/.

[14] Ibid.

lives too: husbands, ask your wives to save certain outfits for your eyes only; fathers, affirm your daughters' inner beauty, teach them to expect respect and how to keep it, and hold them to a family dress code; young men, encourage sisters and friends to wear modest attire, especially by complimenting them on it when they do.

And the Lord wants Christian women to set an example for the world. There is a fledgling modesty movement in our country. Imagine the impact we can have if we each dress modestly and band together to demand more modest fashions from the clothing industry.

The world applauds being "dressed to kill". The thing is, the way we dress really could kill ... someone's soul. Maybe our own. A better phrase would be "dressed to keep"—dressed to keep your dignity, to keep others from seeing you as an object, to keep close to God. And if ever we "dress to impress", let's dress to impress and please the Lord.

23

FOLLOWING HIM AT WORK

Living a holy life must encompass all parts of your life. We can't compartmentalize our faith; we can't just be Sunday Christians or private Christians. We are called to bring Christ with us into the workplace, school, playing fields, market, and public square.

God in the Workplace

Perhaps one of the scariest places to identify as a Christian is at work. Pushing God out of public life has become more and more common over the past fifty years. The idea of wearing one's faith on one's sleeve can provoke some anxiety.

Risk Analysis

A key way to overcome fear is to face it. Often our fears are undefined. Ask yourself: What exactly am I afraid of? Ridicule, ostracization, being passed over, losing my job? How likely is it? What's more likely? How would it play out if this actually came to pass? How bad would it be? Could I trust God to help me? How bad is it in the light of eternity? Usually you find the likely outcome isn't as catastrophic as vague anxiety would lead you to believe.

I can't promise that those who live their faith at work will never suffer for it. It's possible a co-worker or boss might try to bring you down. Some people are definitely persecuted, but that should be no surprise to us. Christians have suffered and been martyred for their faith since the beginning of the Church; why should we expect to get through this "vale of tears" unscathed? " 'A servant is not greater than his master'. If they persecuted me, they will persecute you."[1] Christians have lost their

---

[1] Jn 15:20.

jobs because of their faith in recent years—even in America, the "Land of the Free"—and the trend might get worse before it gets better.[2] But God is worth every sacrifice. "The sufferings of this present time are not worth comparing with the glory that is to be revealed to us."[3] In fact, our sufferings contribute to our future and unending joy: "For this slight momentary affliction is preparing for us an eternal weight of glory beyond all comparison."[4]

Keep in mind, though, that the Lord also takes care of us, even in this life.[5] Most will not lose their jobs because of their faith. The greater risk, really, is to lose one's faith because of one's job. Of the two, the latter is much more dangerous in the long run.

I can understand the apprehension, however. When my husband was in graduate school and I was the main breadwinner, I found myself having to risk a job for the sake of conscience. A large portion of my freelance work at that time was copy-editing medical research articles. One day I noticed a drastic change: aborted fetuses and fetal parts started appearing in the lists of materials used in the experiments. I was appalled. Was that even legal? (It had just become so, under President Bill Clinton, though most people were unaware of it.) I didn't know what to do; I worried that if I told my client I didn't want to work on them I would lose that source of income.

If there's anything I dread as a knee-jerk people-pleaser, it's confrontation. So I prayed, took a deep breath, and told the editor I didn't feel comfortable working on that kind of article. She blinked once or twice and then said, "Okay, next time just look through the stack first and don't take any articles you don't want, and I'll give them to someone else." I was lucky.

Of course, it wasn't luck, but God's Providence, which is there no matter what we go through. Lawyer Carl Cleveland recounts how, because he refused to go along with corruption and commit perjury, he was falsely accused and imprisoned for over two years. And yet, God

---

[2] See *The Criminalization of Christianity: Read This before It Becomes Illegal*, by Janet L. Folger (Sisters, Ore.: Multnomah Publishers, 2005), for numerous examples of ways that Christians are being silenced at work and elsewhere. Keep in mind that her book was published in 2005, and things have only worsened since then.

[3] Rom 8:18.

[4] 2 Cor 4:17.

[5] Lk 12:22–34; Mk 10:29–30.

brought many blessings out of his suffering, and in the end he was vindicated and set free.[6]

It's not just in the secular sphere that we might suffer for putting God first. Numerous Protestant ministers have had to find new professions because of their religious beliefs. Jeff Cavins, Marcus Grodi, Scott Hahn, Alex Jones, Al Kresta, Dwight Longenecker, Steve Ray, and Paul Thigpen are among the famous ones. Each in following Jesus found to his dismay that He was leading him to the Catholic Church. Each faced the daunting prospect of resigning, after preparing and dedicating his life to ministry. Each knew that family, friends, and congregants wouldn't understand, that some would feel hurt and might even end the relationship. Each came to the edge of a precipice, beyond which was a thick fog, and took a leap of great faith ...

And all were caught in the loving hands of our Father. All are now esteemed authors and speakers many of whom began new apostolates. God was faithful to them, providing not only new jobs for them, but employment in which they could work for His Kingdom directly and make use of their education, background, and considerable gifts.[7] They have brought much wisdom, enthusiasm, and fire with them, benefitting many Catholics, myself included.

It comes back to trust. Can we trust that He'll take care of us? It may seem more practical to put our trust in worldly wisdom than in a God who may not see things the way we do. But in reality, that is to build on sand. Conforming to the world's rules is no guarantee that we'll keep our jobs. Recessions hit; market forces and new technologies force out established industries; downsizing occurs; companies go out of business or out of the country; personal injuries happen.

My own husband went through this. Right after getting his master's degree in classical guitar, with a year's worth of performances scheduled,

---

[6] Read Carl's full story, "My Thorn in the Flesh", in *Amazing Grace for Those Who Suffer*, ed. Jeff Cavins and Matthew Pinto (West Chester, Penn.: Ascension Press, 2002), pp. 31–59.

[7] Jeff Cavins is the founder of the Great Adventure Bible study program; Marcus Grodi, founder of Coming Home Network and host of the television/radio show *The Journey Home*; Scott Hahn, professor at Franciscan University and founder of the St. Paul Center for Biblical Theology; Alex Jones (deceased), a deacon and evangelization coordinator for the Archdiocese of Detroit; Al Kresta, president and CEO of Ave Maria Radio and host of "Kresta in the Afternoon"; Fr. Longenecker, a Catholic parish priest and blogger; Steve Ray, an avid Holy Land and pilgrimage guide and filmmaker; and Dr. Thigpen, a journalist and the editor at TAN Books.

he suffered a nerve injury that snuffed out our dreams of a concert career for him. And yet, while we've never enjoyed American-style abundance, the Lord has always provided for us. Moreover, James is actually thankful. He's found great fulfillment in other musical ventures and apostolates, which he believes have brought forth more glory to God and fruit for the Kingdom than his concert career was likely to bring.

Clinging to God is truly the most sound advice of all.

How Do You Bring God into the Workplace Anyway?

The best way to begin, naturally, is to consider how Jesus must have worked. While his years working as a carpenter are not described in Scripture, we know enough of His life and His principles to ascertain what qualities and attitudes He must have brought to His work.

Obviously, He was a man of integrity, honesty, and justice. He would never have cooperated with corruption. Nor would the Messiah who later evaded being crowned king and who washed His disciples' feet have been looking out for "number one". We can't imagine Him being a slacker: He was eager to begin His mission when He was only twelve;[8] He began His ministry healing late into the night, rising early to pray, and moving on to the next town.[9] Mark reveals Christ's zealous pace by using the word "immediately" at every turn.[10] Finally, Jesus brought love (caritas) to the workplace. No gossiping or back-biting for Jesus. Nor would He have ever put profit or success above any person. People were always primary to Him, second only to His Father. I would bet a fortune that during the hidden years of His life He prayed for His clients and offered up His work for others.

We too can work the same way ourselves, imitating Christ's integrity, humility, honesty, work ethic, and charity. We can also offer our work as a gift to the Lord, completing it as well and as cheerfully as we can and as a prayer for God's people.

Be Who You Are Wherever You Are

I found being openly Christian fairly intimidating at my first job out of college, as a secretary in the corporate world. I used to relieve the

---

[8] See Lk 2:41–51.

[9] Mk 1:32–38.

[10] Mark writes "immediately" nine times within thirty-some verses in his first chapter.

receptionist during her lunch hour and was allowed to read when it was quiet. I wanted to bring a spiritual book but was too chicken at first. Then I did bring it, but quickly put it face down when anyone came in. But recalling Christ's warning that if I was ashamed of Him, He would be ashamed of me before the Father,[11] I stopped hiding it.

That little act—reading a spiritual book in public—was all God needed. I didn't have to brandish it around or preach to anyone; I just had to sit there and read. Several co-workers asked me what I was reading; then three of them, separately, started sitting down and talking about spiritual things with me. Two were searching and asked a lot of questions. Once, to my amusement, while one was talking with me, the other happened to walk through, and the first quickly went silent, not knowing that the other had been talking God with me minutes before.

My friend Mark Erickson is a great example of bringing Christ with him wherever he goes, including the workplace. He owns his business, so he has no fear of being fired, but he still has clients. He confidently and cheerfully brings God and his faith into conversations regularly; it comes naturally to him. He has absolute trust in God and doesn't worry what anyone thinks.

One time, for example, a piece of machinery kept malfunctioning overnight. When an employee brought this to Mark's attention, he replied, "I could try to figure it out, but I don't have time right now. So I'm just going to pray over the machine and ask God to watch over it while we're not here tonight." The employee was incredulous as Mark put his hand on the machine and asked the Lord to bless it and keep it running.

His employee looked at him and said, "You really think that's going to fix it?"

Mark responded, "Not only do I think it, I guarantee it."

Sure enough, the machine was still running in the morning, and they haven't had a problem with it since. The employee wondered how Mark could have known. He explained, "When we turn to God, He's going to do something. He may not do it the way we think He should do it, but He's going to come through. He is faithful when we come to Him in prayer."

Mark's prayer not only fixed a machine; more importantly, it made a powerful impression on his employee. You never know what God will bring out of our faithful witness to Him.

---

[11] Lk 9:26.

A much more dramatic instance happened in New York. Everyone at his office knew Al Braca was a Christian, and some gave him grief about it. "According to [his wife] Jeannie, Al hated his job; he couldn't stand the environment.... But he wouldn't quit. He was convinced that God wanted him to stay there, to be a light in the darkness."[12] His colleagues' attitude changed the day a jet crashed into their building and exploded several floors below them. There was no escape, only certain death. On that terrible day in September 2001, many turned to the Christian who had been brave enough to be himself despite their ridicule. Al shared the gospel with about fifty of them and led them in prayer, preparing them to meet their Maker. Be who you are—His faithful follower—wherever you are, and *He* will do amazing things!

Work as Prayer Revisited

Another way to bring God into the workplace is to invite Him.

First, pray *at* work, if possible. I know someone who used to take her break in the supply room, praying the Divine Mercy chaplet for her colleagues during the Hour of Mercy.[13] You might find like-minded co-workers with whom to pray before/after work or during breaks.

Next, make your work a prayer. Yes, chapter 6 above discourages making work one's *only* form of prayer, but that's not to rule out prayer while working *altogether*. How else could we fulfill St. Paul's advice to "pray always"? Work becomes prayer first when we present it to God as a gift in a morning offering; this gives all our works "a supernatural character".[14] We can also designate each task for a certain intention. A friend prayed for each family member as she folded their laundry items. Another made a chart to keep track of her intentions.

Those in religious orders transform work into "a sacrifice, an oblation for love of God", first by accepting whatever work is assigned to them.

---

[12] See Christin Ditchfield, "A Light in the Darkness", *Focus on the Family*, 2002, available online at http://worklife2.org/worklife_articles/lightindarkness.html.

[13] St. Faustina reported the Lord asking her to pray at the hour of His death each day, remembering His Passion; He described the three o'clock hour as a time of special mercy. *Divine Mercy in My Soul: Diary of Saint Maria Faustina Kowalska* (Stockbridge, Mass.: Marian Press, 2015), nos. 1320, 1572.

[14] "Work, Prayer Flow Together in Lives of Religious Men and Women", by the author, *OSV Newsweekly* (Sept. 25, 2013), https://www.osv.com/TheChurch/SacredScripture/Old Testament/Article/TabId/2413/ArtMID/19690/ArticleID/11231/Work-prayer-flow-together -in-lives-of-religious-men-and-women.aspx.

"We try to cultivate a holy indifference regarding the concrete details of the work we do", said Fr. Johannes Smith, F.F.I. "Fulfillment is not in the details of the work ... [but] in doing them with a generous heart ... with love."[15] This leaves no room for shoddy work. You can turn any job, even if you hate it, into something meaningful and beneficial by doing it for love of God. This approach fulfills what St. Paul wrote: "Whatever your task, work heartily, as serving the Lord and not men."[16]

Prayer is very feasible while performing manual tasks. Brother Isidore Mary says that while working, he "adores God, and keeps company with Mary". This may sound lofty, but he says, "Eventually, you can get to the stage where throughout your whole work you keep up the conversation with God, just offering the little things, the things that are hard, for the salvation of souls."[17]

Naturally, work that requires more thought or conversation is a different matter. Though it's hard, that kind can still be transformed into prayer. We can call upon the Holy Spirit for help and inspiration, pray aspirations (brief, simple prayers), and use sacred images as visual reminders. A time-honored method is to pen an acronym at the top of a page and to pray it at the beginning of the work at hand. One can dedicate a work to "Jesus, Mary, and Joseph" under "JMJ", or pray "AMDG" (Ad Majorem Dei Gloriam) and do it for the greater glory of God. While most of us can't write such things at the top of our work projects, we could at the top of our to-do lists or calendars, or even on post-it notes. And even when we can't actually type something at the top, we can still pray brief prayers before starting a letter, proposal, etc. My friend Leigh's kitchen inspired me so much—with quotes from Scripture and the saints posted on all her cupboards; I played copy-cat and came up with my own batch. I taped "All for Jesus" at the top of my computer in the hope that I would remember for whom I was working and why.

Life-Work Balance

But there's more to life than work. We workaholics have to remember that. Healthy life-work balance is a hot topic, but achieving it is another thing. Sometimes it can still seem impossible.

[15] Ibid.
[16] Col 3:23.
[17] "Work, Prayer Flow Together".

I get this. When people learn I have six children, they often say, "I don't know how you do it all!" And I respond, "I don't." Take a look at my house; you'll see what I mean. (Actually, come to think of it—please don't look at my house.) There's never enough time to take care of everything. I keep trying to put God first, then my family, then my work, but it's like trying to balance an egg on end, it keeps tipping over. Keeping those priorities in right order means entrusting one's time and tasks to the Lord, trusting that if we don't get to everything, it will be okay. A few years ago, I had to do this—under doctor's orders. That meant I had to trust that God would take care of it. Not long after, there was a lull in my freelance work: while it gave me more time, the next month's bills were looming. But just in time, our family won third-prize in the annual parish raffle—won, in fact, the exact amount to make up the difference. He is trustworthy.

Here again, we can learn from the life of Jesus. We can be sure Jesus didn't neglect His family. He wouldn't violate His own teachings by failing to provide for His Mother[18] (Joseph evidently having died). He worked at His trade until He was thirty years old before launching His work of saving mankind. He was very likely saving up for that ministry, especially funds for Mary's sustenance in His absence.[19] He certainly had His responsibility toward her in mind when dying on the Cross, for He entrusted her to the care of the beloved disciple.[20]

On the other hand, Jesus didn't exceed the limits of His mission. People stopped Him constantly, and He welcomed these interruptions as opportunities to love. He knew He could trust His Father's will. However, He didn't come close to healing everyone, even just in the Holy Land. There were many good things He didn't get to. From this balance in Jesus, we can learn to say no to those things that we're not called to do. We can't say yes to everything; we have limits, and thus we must say no sometimes, even to good things. It comes down to sharing His priorities. We must simply seek God's will and trust in Him.

Still, God does not send us a morning memo (oh, how I wish He would!). I personally find it very challenging to discern which of the myriad duties looming over me I should do first. And so I added this to

[18] See Mk 7:9–12, where he reproaches adult children who neglect to care for their parents. Cf. also 1 Tim 5:8.

[19] I like to think He was also offering up His daily work as a prayer for those whom He would later encounter.

[20] Jn 19:26–27.

my morning prayer: "Blessed Holy Spirit, guide me each moment of the day. Enable me to know Your will and en-grace me to do it. Let me get done today what You want me to do, and only that; help me to let go of everything else. I entrust it all—what I get done and what I don't—into Your hands. Your will be done, O Lord. The whole purpose of my life is to please You." I've also recently adapted the Serenity Prayer: "Lord, grant me the serenity to let go of the things You're not calling me to do, the courage to do the things You are, and the wisdom to know the difference." Finally, when we're unsure, we can pray: "Lord, I think I should do X, so if You don't want me to, please make that clear ... or stop me."

I take great comfort in these words of St. Teresa Benedicta of the Cross (*aka* Edith Stein): "When night comes, and you look back over the day and see how ... much you planned that has gone undone, and all the reasons you have to be embarrassed and ashamed: just take everything exactly as it is, put it in God's hands and leave it with him. Then you will be able to rest in him—really rest—and start the next day as a new life."[21] At the end of the day, if we're seeking His will, we can trust that the Lord is guiding us, and not worry too much about it.

---

[21] Edith Stein, *Wege zur inneren Stille*, collected articles, ed. W. Herbstrith (Frankfurt: Kaffke Verlag, 1978), p. 48, quoted in Walstraud Herbstrith, *Edith Stein: A Biography*, trans. Fr. Bernard Bonowitz, O.C.S.O., 2nd Eng. ed. (San Francisco: Ignatius Press, 1992), p. 101.

24

HANG OUT WITH THE PROS

In our efforts to follow Christ, we can rely on our friends in high places. Each of us has a formidable ally always at our side, devoted to our eternal well-being, a true friend in a world of temptation and disappointment. We would be wise to call upon our guardian angels frequently.

The angels are not our only heavenly friends. The Church has long turned also to the saints, but before discussing that, we must clear up some common misconceptions first.

Myths about the Saints

Erroneous rumors that Catholics "pray to the dead" and "worship" saints—though the Bible clearly forbids both—are widespread, confusing even some Catholics. Now I can see how such misconceptions could arise; some individual Catholics have evidently taken this too far. The Second Vatican Council warned the faithful against "abuses" and "excesses" in the "vital fellowship with our brethren who are in heavenly glory".[1] Let's look at each myth.

No Dialogue with the Dead

As for the charge that Catholics communicate with "the dead", Jesus pointed out that those who die in friendship with God are not dead.[2] When Jesus used the word *dead*, He was usually referring to the spiritually dead, not the physically dead. There's no doubt we shouldn't have any contact with those in hell. Further, what the Bible forbids is conjuring up the dead, i.e., an occult attempt to speak with them.

---

[1] Second Vatican Council, Dogmatic Constitution on the Church *Lumen Gentium* (November 21, 1964), no. 51.

[2] "Have you not read what was said to you by God, 'I am the God of Abraham, and the God of Isaac, and the God of Jacob'? He is not God of the dead, but of the living" (Mt 22:31–32).

The Church concurs: supernatural communication can rightly take place only through God; trying to go around Him is not only disobedient, disrespectful, and superstitious, but also very dangerous.[3] The only other means are evil spirits. At best, a séance or "channeling" will be a fraud; at worst, it will be demonic. Don't forget that the devil can pose as an angel of light[4] ... or as a late relative. The Lord was not forbidding *all* interaction, however. Consider the Book of Hebrews: after recalling the prophets and heroes of salvation history, the inspired author likens this life to running a race, as in an arena, in which "we are surrounded by so great a cloud of witnesses".[5] This doesn't sound as though those in heaven are oblivious to those on earth, but as though they are involved and cheering us on.

Consider also our interdependence with *all* members of His Body, in heaven and on earth: "For just as ... all the members of the body, though many, are one body, so it is with Christ.... God arranged the organs in the body, each one of them, as he chose.... The eye cannot say to the hand, 'I have no need of you,' nor again the head to the feet, 'I have no need of you.'... But God has so composed the body ... that the members may have the same care for one another."[6]

When communicating with the saints, what Catholics do is ask for their intercession. Our "prayers" to them are requests for their prayers *for* us. That's what *to pray* means: "to ask". This meaning was once commonly used with other humans: the archaic term *prithee* is a contraction for "I pray thee". When we "pray" to the saints, we're not conjuring or worshipping them.

Even so, some Protestants think it's an insult to God to go to the saints with a request. But no one thinks that when it comes to a VIP in this life. You wouldn't walk right up to a world leader and ask a favor, would you? Approaching through an intermediary isn't an insult but a sign of respect. Now, what's different with the Lord is that He *wants* to have an intimate relationship with us and for us come to Him with our requests. But even a prince must show deference to his father, the king. Similarly, we still owe Him reverence as the Lord of the Universe. So going to the saints can actually be an act of humility and sign of respect to God.

[3] See *CCC* 2115–17, especially 2116.
[4] 2 Cor 11:14.
[5] Heb 12:1.
[6] 1 Cor 12:12, 18, 21, 24–25.

And asking their intercession isn't an avoidance of God, nor does it take away from our relationship with Him any more than when we turn to friends or fellow believers and ask for *their* prayers. When we're in particularly desperate straits, we tend to turn to someone who's really holy and ask for his prayers because Scripture tells us, "The prayer of a righteous man has great power in its effects."[7] It also helps to turn to someone whose faith is strong, especially if we feel ours is weak.[8] Similarly, Catholics (and Orthodox and some Anglicans) turn to the saints, who are obviously holy people with great faith. Their prayers are very powerful. Nor does that minimize the role and power of the mediation of Christ, the "one mediator between God and men".[9]

God himself accomplishes and provides everything that mankind needs, but in the richness of his plan he also chooses to entrust his creatures with a share in his work. Jesus is the one great high priest..., and yet he calls Christians a "priestly people" and invites them to share in his priesthood.... In the same way, Jesus, the "one mediator," entrusts a share in his work of mediation to his creatures by allowing and enabling us to pray to God for each other.... The passage that calls Jesus the "one mediator ...", also urges *all* Christians to bring "requests, prayers, intercession and thanksgiving" to God. Most of us have experienced how we can be channels of God's grace to others and how others can bring grace to us.[10]

No Idolatry

The second source of confusion is our statues. I could see why this might raise an eyebrow; the Lord did say, "You shall not make for yourself a graven image, or any likeness."[11] But He could not have meant us to take this too strictly, for not long after, He *commanded* the Jews to make images. For the mercy seat of the ark, He bade them to "make two cherubim of gold".[12] And when the people were beset by serpents,

[7] Jas 5:16. This idea is all over the Bible; see Ps 34:14; Sir 35:16–17; Jn 9:31; Heb 5:7, for starters.

[8] Mt 21:22; 13:58.

[9] 1 Tim 2:5.

[10] Alan Schreck, *Catholic and Christian: An Explanation of Commonly Misunderstood Catholic Beliefs* (Ann Arbor, Mich.: Servant Books, 1984), pp. 171–72, citing Heb 8:1, 1 Pet 2:91, Tim 2:1–6.

[11] Ex 20:4.

[12] Ex 25:18.

the Lord told Moses, "Make a fiery serpent, and set it up as a sign; and every one who is bitten, when he sees it, shall live."[13]

No, the problem wasn't graven images per se; it was what the ancient peoples did with them. Immediately after the forbidding of images comes the command, "you shall not bow down to them or serve them."[14] The issue is idolatry. This is even clearer in the wording of the commandment in Leviticus: "You shall make for yourselves no *idols* and erect no graven image or pillar, and you shall not set up a figured stone in your land, to *bow down* to them."[15] Images, including "graven" ones like statues, are fine, so long as you're not worshipping them and offering them sacrifice. Most modern people feel no temptation to do that. But that doesn't mean we're off the hook. Our idols are more likely to be money, pornography, food, alcohol, or other pleasures, or intangible things like power or prestige.[16]

Catholics generally find the idea that we worship statues to be rather funny. No one considers the visitors to the Lincoln Memorial in D.C. to be worshippers, even though the statue there is imposing and housed in what looks like a temple. I no more worship the statue of St. Joseph in my living room than I do the photo of my dad on the mantelpiece. A photo is an image too, and Catholics use statues (and paintings) the same way we all use photos: to display those we love or admire and to feel closer to those who are far from us. Even kissing a statue is not some weird form of worship any more than kissing the photo of a faraway sweetheart would be. The Church has long allowed the fashioning of images[17] and already hashed out this whole iconoclast controversy back in the 700s and 800s. The last of the Church Fathers, St. John Damascene, was particularly eloquent and persuasive on this topic.[18]

It is true that we venerate the saints, but keep in mind that *to venerate* means "to honor", not "to worship".[19] The Church has always

---

[13] Num 21:8.

[14] Ex 20:5.

[15] Lev 26:1; emphasis added.

[16] See chap. 15 above, especially the section on "A Life without Sacrifice".

[17] See *CCC* 2132, 2141.

[18] See St. John Damascene, *On Holy Images* or *Apologia against Those Who Decry Holy Images*.

[19] The meaning of *worship* in English has evolved over time. The word can crop up in connection to saints in other times and places where it includes the meaning "honor", e.g., the use of "Your Worship" even now in Britain in addressing a magistrate. People no more "worship" saints than they "worship" a judge. Due to this difference from modern American usage, the terms *adore* and *adoration* better describe "the total, consuming reverence" that the Church teaches we are to give to God alone. "Saint Worship?" Catholic Answers tract, http://www.catholic .com/tracts/saint-worship. Cf. *CCC* 2114.

distinguished between what she gives to the saints (*dulia*, or "honor") and what she gives to God (*latria*, or "supreme worship"). As one of the Apostolic Fathers put it in the second century: "We worship Christ as God's Son; we love the martyrs as the Lord's disciples and imitators, and rightly so because of their matchless devotion towards their king and master. May we also be their companions and fellow disciples!"[20] The Fathers of the Second Vatican Council echoed this: "We seek from the saints 'example in their way of life, fellowship in their communion, and aid by their intercession.'... Our communion with those in heaven ... in no way weakens, but conversely, more thoroughly enriches the latreutic worship we give to God the Father, through Christ, in the Spirit."[21]

Neither does venerating the saints detract from God. In fact, rightly ordered relationships with the saints give glory to God and please Him. The Lord delights in faithfulness and holiness; He enjoys celebrating it.[22] Jesus even promised, "If any one serves me, the Father will honor him."[23] And since any human person who made it to heaven got there by being a member of the Mystical Body of Christ, then whenever we honor one of them, we honor Him.[24]

> Love one another with brotherly affection; outdo one another in showing honor.
>
> —ROMANS 12:10 [Box 42]

Further, when we love people, we're delighted when they love each other too. Patrick Madrid makes a great analogy of this, depicting a young man saying to his beloved:

> "I love you with all of my being.... *But* ... I don't want to know anything or anyone that has to do with your past or your family. All I want to do is focus on you." Isn't that absurd? Yet how many people are walking around with exactly that attitude toward Christ? This whole idea of "me-and-Jesus and that's it" is completely unbiblical. The biblical attitude is: "Lord, I love you and anything that pertains to you: your friends, your family, where you lived, what you said."[25]

---

[20] *Martyrium Polycarpi*, 17: *Apostolic Fathers* II/3, 396; quoted in *CCC* 957.

[21] Vatican II, *Lumen Gentium*, *The Church*, no. 51. *Latreutic* is the adjectival form of *latria*, the supreme adoration reserved for God alone.

[22] He bragged about Job to Satan, for instance; see Job 1:8.

[23] Jn 12:26.

[24] 1 Cor 12:26.

[25] Marcus Grodi and Patrick Madrid, "The Truth about Mary" (talk), *The Rosary and Divine Mercy Chaplet* CD (Fairview Park, Ohio: Mary Foundation, 2008), track 16.

God is Love; He wants us to love Him first but also to love each other. He is our *Father*—which makes us siblings. He wants us to be a family, a loving family that helps and honors one another.

Moreover, the saints have no interest in gaining personal glory. They're saints—that means they're really holy, not really vain. They love us as their little brothers and sisters and want to help us reach our heavenly Father.

Models Not Idols

The life of Jesus is our primary example of how to love God, but the lives of the saints also display how it's done concretely. Most of us do not live in Palestine; about half of us are not male; and none of us lives in the first century; thus our circumstances in life differ from Christ's. Plus we all have differing personalities, talents, callings, experiences, and crosses. Yet we can all find someone with whom to relate, whose circumstances are similar in some way to ours or whose life inspires and instructs us in how to imitate Christ in our own. There's nothing wrong with imitating someone who's imitating Christ; Paul repeatedly instructed people to do just that.[26] Seeing how other friends of Jesus followed Him and put His teachings into practice is extremely helpful. We need these examples, the more the better. God wants us to be inspired by them.

Finding such a model is particularly beneficial when we're going through trials; it helps us psychologically and spiritually. Serious trials or calamities often make it difficult to trust in God and His plan or to wait patiently. Sometimes it *feels* easier to entrust to another human person our desperate pleas to God, especially one who's gone through something similar.

Back when I was homeschooling our (then) five children, with some part-time work mixed in, I used to turn to St. Elizabeth Anne Seton on my difficult days. She had had five children and taught them in her home (and she taught other children too). When my husband went to find work in another state, I had another connection to her, for she had had to raise her children without her husband too. Knowing she understood what I was going through was a comfort. Then I

[26]See 1 Cor 4:16; 11:1; Phil 3:17; 1 Thess 1:5–6; 2 Thess 3:7; Heb 6:12; 13:7.

would think about how much worse she had it than I. Her husband had died, whereas mine called me every night and came home once a month. As a widow, she had gone from wealth to poverty, because she converted to Catholicism and all their relatives disowned her. Born two centuries before I was, she didn't have all the conveniences I take for granted—running water, a car, washing machine, dryer, phone, computer, heater, air conditioning. And finally, she had to let go of her children and trust in God in a way that I have yet to face: two daughters died young, and one son went off to be a sailor (pretty risky). Recalling her faith, steadfast trust in God, and surrender to Him in all circumstances—similar to, yet harder than my own—helped keep me from wading too far into self-pity and strive instead to imitate her as she imitated Christ.

Our patron saints are the holy ones whose lives or trials bear some connection or similarity to ours.[27] St. Anne, the mother of Mary, who had trouble conceiving a child, is a patron saint of the childless; St. Dymphna, who was killed by her insane father, is patron saint of the mentally ill; and St. Patrick, who brought the gospel to Ireland, naturally became its patron saint.[28]

Accounts of how the saints lived out their love for God can inspire us to do the same. Two great examples are the recently canonized saints Francisco and Jacinta Marto.[29] Their spirit of generous penitence is very inspiring: though they were mere children, they embraced penances and sacrifices to offer up for endangered souls. Their example is a little intimidating, but we can ask their intercession for us to be granted the grace and strength to imitate them.

Another huge gift many saints offer is their wisdom. Here we have the advice and experience of people with the same goal as ourselves: to live their lives out of love for God. And not just any people: they have actually achieved that goal—so successfully as to be deemed "heroic".

[27] Some Protestants object to the idea of patron saints, yet they accept angels being assigned to us. If God charges His angels to help certain individuals and groups, why not His saints as well? Similarly, friends often say to someone grieving, "Now you have an angel in heaven looking after you." I'm not sure how this theologically incorrect (humans can't become angels) but comforting thought is different from having a saint looking after you.

[28] Many saints have more than one area of patronage or overlapping areas. St. Anne is also the patron of grandmothers, expectant mothers, and Canada; and Ireland also claims St. Bridget and St. Columba as patron saints.

[29] With their cousin Lucia, they were the Fatima visionaries. See pp. 194 above and 330–31 below.

Their writings have so much to offer us: a gold mine of knowledge and expert counsel from those who have "been there, done that" ... superlatively.

A Little Help from Our Friends

In the saints we have thousands of examples of what it means to love God, how to live a life dedicated to pleasing Him. We honor them as members of His Body, our older brothers and sisters in faith and those who have fought the good fight and kept the faith, who have run the race and wear a crown. Now they cheer us on and help us follow Him too.

Give the saints a chance. Take a look at their lives—varied in circumstances but united in utter devotion to Him—and learn what loving God with all one's strength looks like.

25

LIVING IN JESUS

Becoming holy is not ethereal or merely wishful thinking; we have to work at it. We can start with the opportunities the Lord provides us every day. When my father was in college, he and his roommate used to toss items at each other—when the other's back was turned. If Dad heard "Joe-o" in a certain tone, he knew something was *already* in the air and would turn in a flash, ready to catch anything. What a great way to approach daily life that would be—trying to catch everything God might toss our way.

In addition, there are methods to grow in holiness. You can even set goals and plan out steps to reach them. A tried-and-true approach is to work on gaining one virtue at a time. Start by taking some time in prayer (preferably a

> It is part of the love of God to acquire and to nurture all the virtues which make a man perfect.
> —St. Alphonsus Liguori Box 43

guided retreat) to figure out your weaknesses: where you tend to fall repeatedly and why. Based on that, discern what virtue the Lord wants you to pursue, which best counters that fault or weakness. Then, with the help of a spiritual director, think of concrete ways you can grow in that virtue.

For instance, if pride is your root sin (the one that gets you into the most trouble), you might work on humility—or generosity, thoughtfulness, or trust in God, depending on how your pride has been manifesting itself. You could resolve to form new habits to help you develop that virtue. For examples: to pray first thing in the morning so as to rely on God instead of self, compliment a co-worker each day, pray the Litany of Humility a few times a week, add a daily Mass to your weekly routine, do a hidden act of charity each day, keep a gratitude journal thanking God for all He's done for you.

It's a Journey

We must always remember that sanctification (becoming holy) is a process, a journey. We will stumble and fall, and the evil one will pounce and try to discourage us: *Why do you even try? This will never work.* But God doesn't see it that way. He's not surprised we don't get there in a day, nor should we be. He delights in holding your hand and helping you along, even more than the most doting father delights in helping his toddler learn to walk. The humble aren't surprised by their own falls into sin, but say to God, "And so I will always do—unless You help me!"

It's also important to know that God offers us all the graces we need for our state in life[1] and every situation. But we need to ask for and cooperate with God's grace. Again, we must find a balance between relying on God and expecting Him to do everything. Life is like a vacuum cleaner. If you don't turn it on, I don't care how much you move it around, it's not going to accomplish anything. But if you turn it on and just leave it there, only one narrow rectangle will get clean. You've got to turn it on *and* move it around. God supplies the power; you have to apply it.

It might seem a contradiction to say both that we shouldn't be surprised when we fall *and* that God gives us all the graces we need. But it's true. Only rarely does He give us such a superabundance of grace that we just float along. More often, the grace is there, just not all that apparent. I think *The Return of the King* movie provides an excellent illustration. When Mount Doom begins to collapse, Frodo and Sam flee, while the ground falls away beneath each foot just after it leaves the ground. Cynics might view that as the height of poor authorship[2] and reliance on coincidence, saying, "Well, isn't that convenient? The ground remains just long enough for them to run away, step by step." It reminds me, though, of the ways of Providence. He provides the ground for us to walk on every day, and we don't notice. But even when everything is falling apart, He makes sure it's there for us—though we still have to sprint. God gives us graces, but we must still do our utmost.

---

[1] Single adults have the graces of Baptism, Confirmation, the Eucharist, and Confession available to help them. The married have those plus the graces flowing from the Sacrament of Marriage to deal with the aggravations they sometimes give each other and receive from their children. Clergy and religious have extra graces on hand from their ordinations and consecrations.

[2] I don't agree with that opinion, but I should point out that this particular incident is not in the book.

Boosts and Shortcuts

The Lord is compassionate and merciful. He knows becoming holy isn't easy for us, so He generously proffers assistance in many ways. Unfortunately we too often disdain, disbelieve, or dismiss them. Here are two fail-safe shortcuts: Mary and the Eucharist.

Mama Gives Us a Boost

Some people are leery of Mary, due to the many myths about the Church's Marian teachings. First let's clarify that Catholics do *not* worship Mary. We don't regard her as a goddess or the fourth person of the Trinity. Rather, imitating Jesus, we honor her, and we appeal to her as did the faithful in the early Church and the Fathers, who recognized Mary as the "New Eve".[3]

All Mary wants is to glorify God and please Him.[4] Of all the saints, she is the disciple par excellence, giving the best example of someone who fluently spoke and lived out all the love languages of God. Moreover, if He uses *us* as instruments, how much more fitting that He do so with Mary: her pure docility and perfect obedience[5] to Him make her

---

[3] St. Irenaeus, *Against Heresies* (3, 21, 4), and St. Justin Martyr, *Second Apology*, 100, in *The Faith of the Early Fathers*, vol. 1, ed. William A. Jurgens (Collegeville, Minn.: Liturgical Press, 1970), p. 62, no. 141, and p. 93, no. 224. Henri de Villiers, "The Sub Tuum Praesidium", Feb. 3, 2011, www.newliturgicalmovement.org/2011/02/sub-tuum-praesidium.html#.WSojjoWcHIU. If it seems we give more honor to Mary than to other saints, well, that's true: while to the saints we give *dulia* (honor), to Mary, we give *hyperdulia* (greater honor), because of the singular role she played in salvation history. Still, *hyperdulia* is not *latria*—the adoration and worship due to God alone. "No creature could ever be counted as equal with the Incarnate Word and Redeemer." Second Vatican Council, Dogmatic Constitution on the Church *Lumen Gentium* (November 21, 1964), no. 62.

[4] "I am the handmaid of the Lord; let it be to me according to your word"; "My soul magnifies the Lord, and my spirit rejoices in God my Savior" (Lk 1:38, 46–47).

[5] The angel Gabriel's greeting to Mary, "Hail, full of grace", points to her sinlessness. The word he used, *kecharitomene*, means "completely, perfectly, enduringly endowed with grace". Fr. Mateo, *Refuting the Attack on Mary: A Defense of Marian Doctrines* (San Diego: Catholic Answers, 1999), p. 21. Tim Staples explains how "remarkably precise" the Greek past participle is. "If Mary had been anything less than perfectly filled with grace, there would have been multiple ways for Luke to have expressed it." Tim Staples, *Behold Your Mother: A Biblical and Historical Defense of the Marian Doctrines* (San Diego: Catholic Answers Press, 2014), pp. 62, 63. Foreseeing what Jesus would do, God gave Mary in advance the sanctifying grace Adam and Eve had lost and could not pass on to us and Jesus would win back for us on the Cross. He was still her Savior, a fact she herself acknowledged (Lk 1:47). Mary was the vessel through which God became man; it is understandable that He would want her to be pure of all sin. "As the Only-Begotten has a Father in heaven, whom the Seraphim extol as thrice holy, so he should have a Mother on earth

an incomparable instrument. That's why He gives her the ability to lend us a hand in getting closer to Him. Devoted to helping us love Him better, her perennial message is "Do whatever He tells you."[6]

Among the myriad Marian devotions and sacramentals[7] by which God assists those who seek Mary's aid, perhaps the most pertinent to following Jesus is made of two small squares of brown wool, attached by strings.[8] The brown scapular is a sacramental worn against one's heart. Like a friendship bracelet, it's a sign of one's relationship with Mary; like a wedding ring, it's a reminder of promises. The promises are made both *to* our Blessed Mother and *by* her.

To those who faithfully wear the brown scapular, Mary makes wonderful promises. First and foremost: to keep them from going to hell. *How can she make such a promise?* some might ask. Others see it as a superstitious, Get-Out-of-Hell-Free license to sin. But a closer look reveals this is not the case. What Mary is promising here is to aid us in our journey to heaven, *but* we have to do our part. We must faithfully walk the walk; we must in turn promise (1) to follow the teachings of the Church, (2) to live chastely according to our state in life (married, single, religious/clergy), and (3) to pray certain prayers or follow certain practices (most commonly, praying daily a five-decade Rosary).[9]

For centuries, the brown scapular and the Rosary have been associated, as Mary's two chief gifts to her children, with a shield and a sword.[10] Popes couldn't comment on all the possible devotions out there, but

---

who would never be without the splendor of holiness." Pope Pius IX, *Ineffabilis Deus* (December 8, 1854), www.newadvent.org/library/docs-pio9id.htm. Cf. Stefano Manelli, F.F.I., *All Generations Shall Call Me Blessed: Biblical Mariology* (New Bedford, Mass: Academy of the Immaculate, 1995), pp. 130–33, and Mateo, *Refuting the Attack on Mary*, pp. 19–23.

[6] Jn 2:5.

[7] Religious objects blessed by a priest are called *sacramentals*. They have no power on their own; the Lord grants graces through them according to the disposition of the recipient. See "Sacramentals", in *Our Sunday Visitor's Catholic Encyclopedia*, ed. Rev. Peter M.J. Stravinskas (Huntington, Ind.: Our Sunday Visitor, 1991), p. 848.

[8] In 1910, Pope Pius X instituted a scapular *medal*, which could be worn instead for those already invested in the cloth scapular. See http://www.ewtn.com/library/CURIA/CDFMEDL .HTM.

[9] Of course, if one falls, that doesn't mean it's all over; one just repents, confesses if necessary, and goes on.

[10] The Rosary is treated at length in chapter 27 below. Many brown scapulars have an attached miraculous medal, which is a third very popular Marian devotion, so named for the many miracles associated with its use. For more information, see Stephen Breen, "St. Catherine Labouré and the Miraculous Medal", available at EWTN's online library, http://www.ewtn.com/library /mary/medal.htm.

more than a few have recommended these. I can testify to their efficacy in my own life. The years when I succumbed most to sin, doubts, or anger at God were precisely the years when I was not wearing the scapular or praying the Rosary. Once I returned to them, I could better receive God's grace; I was set free and have never committed a serious sin since. Mary's intercession has been huge in my spiritual life, in more ways, I'm sure, than I even realize.

To anyone who feels that overcoming sin is impossible—especially sins of the flesh or addiction—the brown scapular and Rosary are powerful boosts. For all who turn to Mary as Mother, she's a shortcut to God: she lifts them up and gives them to Him.

Living in Jesus

To follow Jesus, we must learn to think as He thinks. We can grow in this by prayer and studying Scripture, the lives of the saints, and His updates, that is, the Church's Spirit-led teachings on how to live out His word in our changing world. But we mustn't neglect perhaps the best chance to know Him and follow Him better: the Eucharist.

We examined this incredible gift earlier, in chapters 8 and 9, but a discussion of following Christ would be incomplete without connecting it with the Mass, "the source and summit of the Christian life", and Christ Himself, the source of all holiness.[11] Fusing with Christ requires physically receiving Him often. The gift of Himself comes with the grace and strength to think and act as He would, as we never could on our own. Receiving Jesus into our very selves helps us walk with Him—even, in a sense, to walk *in* Him. The tricky part is we so easily dawdle, stop, or walk away. It's tough to stay with Jesus; we must tread carefully. It takes a lifetime of practice, growth in virtue, and purity of heart. But the lives of the saints prove it can be done. Indeed, the aura around saints in old paintings seems to show this: saints bring Jesus wherever they go, and His presence within them shines through.

> I keep up the Holy Hour ... to grow more and more into His likeness.... We become like that which we gaze upon. Looking into a sunset, the face takes on a golden glow. Looking at the Eucharistic Lord for an hour transforms the heart in a mysterious way.
>
> —ARCHBISHOP FULTON SHEEN Box 44

---

[11] Vatican II, *Lumen Gentium, The Church*, nos. 11, 47.

The Eucharist offers us the best chance to become more deeply rooted in Him and better able to follow Him. I'm not talking only of weekly Mass but of daily Mass whenever possible. And not only visits to the Blessed Sacrament but a regular *holy hour* because becoming like Christ also requires time with Him in person.

Many are thinking, *I don't have time for that.* I know: I'm time-management-challenged, and it already seems impossible to get everything done as it is! But every time I make the time for God, He

> The Eucharist is the secret of my day. It gives strength and meaning to all my activities.
>
> —POPE ST. JOHN PAUL II Box 45

takes care of it. Moreover, prayer changes *us*. It makes us more loving and peaceful, which is much more valuable than checking off every item in one's planner. Stepping into the presence of God is not exactly stepping *out* of time, but it is stepping *into* eternity, into the intersection of time and eternity, where they overlap. Prayer is the only occasion where we can both spend something and save it too. Time spent in prayer is never lost or wasted; indeed, it is saved in eternity. Remember, when we invest our time with God, there are great returns.

Spending time in an adoration chapel can also be a little intimidating. We can sense it's something sacred and special and intellectually recognize its value, while at the same time wondering what on earth to do and fearing that we'll just be bored. Not a very appealing package.

Holy Hour?

Why an HOUR*?!*

The tradition of spending an hour with Jesus arose from His request in Gethsemane: "Could you not watch with me one hour?" Those who love Him have for centuries replied, "Yes!" and done so in His physical presence in the Eucharist. Of course, we can adore the Lord in the Blessed Sacrament for less than an hour (or more than an hour, for that matter). For many years, I could only manage a holy half-hour. A visit of any length is pleasing to Him.

What to Do

The idea of making a holy hour is rather daunting; it seems an awfully long time to fill up. Thankfully, the Church has produced an ample array of prayers and

(continued)

> ### Holy Hour? (*continued*)
>
> devotions. Many chapels stock prayer books, such as *An Hour with Jesus* or *Visits to the Most Blessed Sacrament*.
>
> I always begin by thanking God for being there and also for getting *me* there. (I consider the latter perhaps to be the bigger miracle.) I try to stop and appreciate what a tremendous gift this personal time with the Lord of the Universe is.
>
> Worshipping God is a great thing to do. Hymns or spiritual songs can be a real aid; you can recite them silently, or if you're alone with God, you could even sing aloud. If you sing from the heart, He'll be delighted no matter how bad your pitch might be.
>
> Ideally, conversing with God should form a good portion of our time there. He wants us to treat Him as a Friend as well as Father and Lord. So make a spiritual communion too.
>
> Box 46

Back in the late '90s, I joined an ecclesial movement (similar to a lay religious order). Of our prayer commitments, trying to make a weekly holy hour was the one I struggled with most. It was so hard to fit into my schedule, and when I did go, I often spaced out, then felt guilty. Several years ago, I decided to make it a regular part of my life, rather than just hit or miss. (Okay, I'll go ahead and do the math: it took me thirteen years to get to that point!) Our parish has an adoration chapel open twice a week, and one of those days I'm there anyway, shuttling kids to choir rehearsals, so I decided to go then but wasn't ready to *commit* to that hour. I didn't need to: someone was already signed up for that slot. After a while, however, she asked me if I could replace her as the adorer for that hour as another time would work better for her. I was really hesitant, but finally I took the plunge. And I'm *so* glad I did. I don't see it as a duty anymore; now I see it as a privilege. Now I long for it. I wish I could spend more time there. Sometimes I wish I could live there.

> Do you want many graces? Go and visit the Blessed Sacrament often.
> —St. John Bosco Box 47

Conclusion

Following Jesus, then, is integral to expressing love for God. It means striving to grow in holiness, because He is holy. It takes prayer, obedience, and dying to our own will. It means keeping Jesus company all the time, wherever we are: at work, at home, at play. Following Him affects everything from the way we drive to the way we dress; it affects our whole life.

I like to imagine the refrain of John Denver's song "Follow Me" as a personal invitation from Jesus: to follow Him wherever He goes, His example in what He does, and in loving those He loves (everyone), to become a part of Him, to hold His hand and follow Him anywhere and everywhere.

SECTION EIGHT

LOVING GOD MEANS
EAGERLY AWAITING HIM

O God, you are my God, I seek you, my soul thirsts for you. . . .
When shall I . . . behold the face of God?

(Ps 63:1; 42:2)

"When I go and prepare a place for you, I will come again and
will take you to myself, that where I am you may be also."

(Jn 14:3)

[B]ecause of the surpassing worth of knowing Christ Jesus my Lord
[and for] his sake I have suffered the loss of all things, and count
them as refuse. . . .
[O]ur commonwealth is in heaven, and from it we await a Savior,
the Lord Jesus Christ."

(Phil 3:8, 20)

Hark! my beloved is knocking. . . .
My beloved put his hand to the latch, and my heart was thrilled within me.

(Song 5:2, 4)

Come, Lord Jesus!

(Rev 22:20)

26

DETERMINING OUR DESTINATION

This world is like Grand Central Station, and we're waiting. Sure, we can buy some lunch and look around, but we must be careful not to get so absorbed in shopping that we forget to buy a ticket, lose it, or miss our train. A consideration of the traditional "Last Things" helps us understand what we're supposed to be doing here.

You're a Mist, Soon to Vanish[1]

It's so easy to forget one's own mortality. We generally shy away from thinking about it and even have a hard time really believing it. Yes, yes, we know intellectually that we'll die someday, but it's so hard to believe on an emotional level and to act accordingly.

The fact is, we could die any day. I've personally known quite a few people who died unexpectedly, starting with schoolmates killed in car accidents. There was a neighbor, a runner who appeared in great shape—only one day he didn't come back from his run. He had died from a massive heart attack. I knew two people—a new friend in her twenties and a family friend in her seventies—who died in very similar circumstances: each was happily engaged in conversation when she suddenly collapsed, succumbing to a brain aneurysm. And only an hour after seeing her doctor, an in-law with the flu lay down for a nap and never woke up again. Yet even when we know people who've died suddenly, the possibility of it happening to *ourselves* just doesn't seem real. The solid fact of one's own eventual death is so hard to grasp.

We need to increase our awareness, however, or we become overly invested in this world. When death seems interminably remote, how

[1] Jas 4:13–15.

hard it is to focus on eternity rather than what's right in front of us; few are willing to delay gratification *that* long. But as St. Augustine says, it's absurd to lose eternal goods in the pursuit of temporal ones.[2]

What makes the saints extraordinary is their ability to perceive, believe, and live out this spiritual truth; they're not taken in by the illusion of permanence. A quote attributed to St. Clare of Assisi reminds us: "Our labor here is brief, but the reward is eternal.... Do not let the false delights of a deceptive world deceive you."[3] St. Paul frequently urges us not to let our minds get fogged up by the day-to-day trivialities always clamoring for our attention. "Set your minds on things that are above, not on things that are on earth."[4] Instead, we should prepare ourselves: "Every athlete exercises self-control in all things. They do it to receive a perishable wreath, but we an imperishable."[5]

> **What Will Last**
>
> Nothing's so solid
> it can't crack or crumble.
> Nothing outlasts time.
> "All things pass; all things pass."
> All joys, all sorrows
> —today's, tomorrow's—
> all pleasures, all pains,
> all shall fall away.
> Things may evolve;
> they may even revolve
> for eons on end.
> But all will devolve
> in the End.
> No thing outlasts time.
>
> All persons do.
>
> Box 48

My life, your life, everyone's lives will come to an end. Are we living with our ultimate destiny in mind? How does one prepare for it? Fr. Martin Connor, L.C., a wonderful speaker and retreat master, sets himself a "death-day" each year. He picks a day some six to nine months off and regards it as if the doctor told him that's how long he has to live. It helps him keep his priorities straight. If you knew you had only a week, what would you make sure to do? What temporal, relational, and especially spiritual matters need to be addressed?

And what happens if we're not prepared to meet our Maker?

---

[2] Augustine, *Sermon on the Mount*, 5, 16, https://www.ccel.org/ccel/schaff/npnf106.v.ii.vi .html.

[3] St. Clare of Assisi, Letter to Sr. Ermentrude of Bruges, nos. 5–6, in *Francis and Clare: The Complete Works*, trans. Regis J. Armstrong, O.F.M. Cap., and Ignatius C. Brady, O.F.M. (Mahwah, N.J.: Paulist Press, 1982), p. 207.

[4] Col 3:2.

[5] 1 Cor 9:25. In those times, winners were given a laurel or olive wreath.

Making the Most of the World-Womb

We shouldn't procrastinate considering what will happen after death. It's challenging, though; it's hard to remember that this life—enchanting as it can be—doesn't merely exist for its own sake; rather it is more about getting ready for the next. It's hard to believe in a Father we can't see.

But really, refusing to believe in Him is as ironic as a fetus refusing to believe in his mother. The fetus can't see his mother, though surrounded by her and receiving everything he needs from her. We are even more dependent on our heavenly Father, who is even closer to us. Just as we once grew and developed in our mothers' wombs in preparation for our entry into the world, so is this world a place of preparation. In the womb, we develop physically; in the world, we develop spiritually; this is the place to prepare for the next and final life—*real life.*

The difference between time in the womb and time in the world is *choice.* In the womb, we didn't choose to develop; our cells just followed the DNA program with no input from us. We couldn't be too busy to grow a foot; we couldn't decide against developing a nose. But in our current state, we do have a choice. Some people *are* too busy to grow in virtue; some people do decide against developing their spiritual gifts or choose to dispense with a conscience.

Growth in the "world-womb" is as critical as growth in the maternal womb. A baby can get by without lungs in the womb, but he can't stay there forever. We can scrape by in this world without grace, but we can't stay here forever. We can no more survive in the next life without sanctifying grace than a baby who had refused to grow lungs could survive outside the womb.

Being sinners, most of us are not working on our development the way we should. We're too busy kicking and twirling. Fortunately, God has a terrific neonatal unit. The less prepared we are, the more time we'll need to spend in the NICU; but no matter how purgatorial it may be, we'll be thankful for it. And the Divine Physician in charge there can save even those who repudiated all development—provided they give Him permission and call upon His mercy before being born into eternity. However, in Purgatory, unlike in NICU, we will not be able to develop any further. It is a time of purification, not of growth.

Death is a kiln that sets us for eternity; even the Potter can't mold us after we've passed through the kiln. And if we, the clay, have always hardened ourselves against the Potter, rejecting the softening of His grace, then the kiln will make us crumble. But those who have submitted to His (admittedly painful) kneading, stretching, molding work will be transformed from lumps of clay to beautiful, elegant vessels of great depth. The joy of heaven is God's love, and everyone there will be filled with His love—though how much each of us can hold depends on how we have responded to the Potter. The more we have let Him stretch us and hollow us—the more emptied of self we are—the more love we can contain. To receive His love, we have to let Him make at least a dent in our self-absorption; He can fill even a thumbprint.

But why be satisfied with that? Better make use of this special, limited period in our existence. As babes, we had nothing to do with our development; what a gift (yet terrifying responsibility too) that it's up to us what shape we'll be in when we finally meet our Father face to face.

Divine Proposal

At death, we will reach the destination we ourselves have determined by our life's choices. As author and speaker Fr. Larry Richards puts it in many of his talks, when we meet the Lord, He will give us what we want the most. If during life, we didn't want God the most, He won't force us to spend eternity with Him. If we loved ourselves and our sins the most, we will get ourselves and the harvest (i.e., consequences) of our sins for all eternity.

At the moment of death, it doesn't matter as much *where* we are on the road that leads to heaven at one end and hell at the other; what matters most is which way we're headed—if we've turned our back on God or turned back *to* Him. Yes, if we've traveled long on the road toward Him, our bliss in heaven will be greater, but if we went the wrong way and then turn back—even just before the very gates of hell—we will still have bliss in heaven. The danger is this: the further you travel away from God, the harder it is to turn back.

Perhaps the most prevailing image in Scripture of the relationship of God to His people is that of the Bridegroom to His bride. The Lord God, Creator and King of the Universe, has made a proposal to each of us, to *you*: come and live with Me in love forever. Our time on earth is the time to consider that proposal and prepare for the day of being united with God—or not.

Anyone baptized has at least technically accepted God's proposal. If you were baptized as a baby, your parents betrothed you to Him on your behalf, but you have the chance—a lifetime of chances—to confirm or break that betrothal, as do those who were baptized later in life. Those who have not yet heard the gospel are awaiting an emissary to make the proposal on Christ's behalf. If no one ever does, they still have the signs of the Creator in nature and their conscience, which whispers a hint of the proposal to them in urging them to do good and avoid evil.[6] The hundreds of choices all of us make each day are in one direction or the other. Choices to go against His will in grave matters are inherently choices against Him and thus choices that sever the betrothal.

Breaking the Betrothal

Just as a young lady who breaks her engagement has to give back the engagement ring, if we don't choose Christ, we don't get to keep His gifts—and everything good is a gift from God.

A Helluva Concept

Many people today laugh at the idea of hell. They think, if it exists, only people like Hitler are there. If that were true, why did Jesus speak more often of hell than of heaven? And why do some who have been resuscitated say they went to hell—even though previously they didn't believe in it?

Based on the Word of God, the Church teaches that hell does exist, but she doesn't presume to say who's there. We also know that it's eternal and indescribably horrific. Revelation calls it "a lake of fire".[7] The worst part, though, is the "eternal separation from God, in whom alone man can possess the life and happiness for which he was created and for which he longs."[8]

---

[6] "Those also can attain to salvation who through no fault of their own do not know the Gospel of Christ or His Church, yet sincerely seek God and moved by grace strive by their deeds to do His will as it is known to them through the dictates of conscience (Mk 4:14). Nor does Divine Providence deny the helps necessary for salvation to those who, without blame on their part, have not yet arrived at an explicit knowledge of God and with His grace strive to live a good life (Lk 12:32)". Second Vatican Council, *Lumen Gentium* (1964), no. 16.

[7] Rev 20:14–15.

[8] *CCC* 1035.

St. Teresa of Avila is one of several saints who visited hell in spirit during their lifetime. In Teresa's account, she actually experienced a tortured night in a red-hot, cramped space with her name on it. (Jesus is not the only one preparing a place for each of us in the afterlife.)

I admit hell is a hard teaching. It's hard to comprehend how our good, loving, and merciful God could send almost anyone to such horror for eternity. I have a very tough time getting my mind around the awful fact that hell lasts forever. I don't understand it, but I accept it as true, based on Scripture and the Church's teaching.

The key thing to know is that anyone in hell has freely chosen to go there. When the Light came into the world, some "loved darkness rather than light.... For every one who does evil hates the light, and does not come to the light, lest his deeds should be exposed."[9] Some people, when they come face to face with God, flee to hell because they can't stand the sight of themselves in the light of God's goodness. C. S. Lewis put it: "There are only two kinds of people in the end: those who say to God, 'Thy will be done,' and those to whom God says, in the end, '*Thy* will be done.' All that are in hell, choose it.... No soul that seriously and constantly desires joy will ever miss it. Those who seek find. To those who knock it is opened."[10]

Catholic apologist Mark Shea says it's all about relationship with God:

> Hell is not some arbitrary punishment that God sticks on us.... It is ... looking squarely at the offer of relationship with God and man, systematically destroying that relationship, and blaming everybody else.... It is the human heart walling itself off finally and utterly from relationship with God and man in idiotic pride. It is any of us, making the final choice to be bricked round in the furnace of ourselves.... Heaven is simply the fruit of a life that pursues relationship with God on His terms, and Hell is simply the fruit of a life that pursues its own course on its own terms.[11]

Sin Goes to Gehenna

Another enlightening consideration is that no sin can enter heaven. Perhaps this is why Jesus described the gate leading to life as "narrow": we can't take any baggage with us but have to leave everything behind.

[9] Jn 3:19–20.

[10] C. S. Lewis, *The Great Divorce* (New York: HarperOne, 2001), p. 75.

[11] Mark Shea, "We Are Saved by Christ, Not by Rules", *National Catholic Register*, Aug. 8, 2015, https://www.ncregister.com/blog/mark-shea/saved-by-christ-not-by-rules.

Meanwhile, the gate to perdition is wide; you can bring whatever you want—all your pet sins—but if you do, you'll perish with them.

All sin is destined for Gehenna.[12] Since sin is a turning away from God and hell is the farthest place from Him, hell is sin's natural home; sin is drawn inexorably to hell like iron to a magnet. No matter how it may glitter, sin is no treasure but a lead deadweight. When our lives run out, when we reach the precipice of death, if we cling to mortal sin, we'll plummet down with it. But if we're clinging to our Savior, we'll rise with Him to His heavenly Kingdom. We can't embrace the Savior and mortal sin at the same time. We've got to choose.

Catching on Fire

The sun is an image I've found helpful in comprehending the conundrum of hell.

The sun, over one hundred times bigger than the earth, is 93 million miles from the earth: the perfect distance. Any closer would be too hot; any farther too frigid. This is a pretty good deal for us since, being the ultimate energy source for every living thing on earth, it happens to be essential to our existence. It gives light and warmth; its power and beauty have fascinated mankind across time. Moreover, God is the supreme Artist, and that incredible ball of fire is one of His most poetic creations, rich in symbolism. In so many ways, He is like the sun in our lives.

As intriguing as our human race has always found the sun, we've never been, and never will be, able to visit it. There is no substance known to man that could protect us from the intensity of its rays if we tried, like Icarus, to get close to it. Just as we could never survive a flight to the sun, neither could we survive coming in our natural state into the direct presence of God, hence the Old Testament belief that seeing the face of God meant death. Not to say there was anything wrong with God; rather, His holiness and power, His divinity, were too much for a puny creature to bear. It would be like coming face to face with the sun.

The only way something could come close to the sun and survive would be if it were ablaze too.

---

[12] A ravine near Jerusalem, Gehenna had been a place of child-sacrifice. In Christ's day, it was an ever-burning trash heap, where criminal corpses were flung, hence His very apt image for hell (e.g., Mt 5:22, NABRE).

Scripture likens the love of God to fire, and Jesus said He had come to set the world on fire and wished it were already blazing.[13] This sheds light on the mystery of hell when it seems incompatible with a loving, merciful God. This life is our time to be lit with the fire of Christ. St. Paul says it is in

> We cannot be united with God unless we freely choose to love him. But we cannot love God if we sin gravely against him, against our neighbor or against ourselves.... To die in mortal sin without repenting and accepting God's merciful love means remaining separated from him for ever by our own free choice. This state of definitive self-exclusion ... is called "hell."
>
> — *CCC* 1033 Box 49

dying to ourselves and letting Christ live in us, in being members of His Body—becoming the same substance as the Son—that we gain eternal life.[14] It is only in having His life within us that we can live eternally. God is love. We must become like Him; we must love. The more we love and the more united we are to Him, then the more prepared we are to meet Him. If we catch fire with His love, then as little flames we can dance in close proximity to the fiery Son.

The thing is, it is only in this life that we can become fire ourselves. In the next life, we can only burn. If we are flames of the Divine Fire, then, like the burning bush, we will burn without being consumed. If we refuse to undertake this transformation, then when we encounter God, we'll burn up. Hell is painful to those who go there because, having refused the transformation, they can't enjoy God's burning love. If we have made only a partial transformation (the case for most of us) then that which is not of God in us, what is not already aflame, will be burned away, though we ourselves, St. Paul assures us, will be saved.[15]

The Bridegroom's Palace

The chief purpose of life then is to prepare for heaven, but sadly, some people don't find the idea of heaven particularly appealing. They hear about harps, robes, and clouds, and they're just not all that interested. But again, heaven means eternal union with Infinite Love, the fulfillment of

---

[13] "Our God is a consuming fire" (Heb 12:29; Lk 12:49). See also Ex 3:1ff., Deut 4:11–12, and Lk 3:17.

[14] Rom 6:3–11; Gal 2:20; 2 Tim 2:11.

[15] 1 Cor 3:15.

our being. Heaven will definitely *not* be boring! Harps and clouds are meant to help us imagine the unimaginable. If they don't help you want to get to heaven, forget them. There are better images.

Aligning with the figure of the Bridegroom, the image for heaven the Lord used most often was that of a wedding banquet—often a king's. Most people aren't personally familiar with royal banquets, but we can imagine the elegance, beauty, intricate finery, the best of everything. And most have been to wedding receptions and know the best are occasions of joy, celebration, dancing, laughter, delicious food and wine, and the enjoyment of being with friends and family. *God's* wedding banquet has got to be even better.

One of my daughters used to worry that she wouldn't be happy in heaven. She asked if there would be this or that in heaven. I would ask her to imagine a poor child who had never had any sweets or desserts except those chalky little candy hearts that are strangely ubiquitous around Valentine's Day. Imagine him being invited to a party at a palace and feeling anxious about whether or not there would be any candy hearts there. If he was told no, but there would be lots of other delightful things, like *chocolate truffles* and *ice cream sundaes*, he would have to trust that such treats were actually better, even though he had no concept of what they were like. In the same way, heaven holds joys we can't even imagine here. If there are no candy hearts there, it's because there's something even better. We won't miss them. I can't say in detail what will or won't be there, but I can confidently assert that we'll be perfectly happy there.

C. S. Lewis tried his hand at depicting heaven more than once. In *The Great Divorce*, the borderland of heaven is more real, more vivid, and more solid than life on earth. In his *Last Battle*, many of the heroes and heroines from the entire Chronicles of Narnia series are gathered together in the outskirts of heaven. They're all youthful, enthusiastic, full of life and joy, laughter and energy. They discover one delight after another as they come "further up and further in", including all the good things of their former lives—only bigger, "more real" and "more beautiful".[16]

All of these are only images, and all fall short. Human language and experience are insufficient to express what heaven will be like. "No eye has seen, nor ear heard, nor the heart of man conceived, what God has prepared for those who love him."[17] These are the words of St. Paul,

---

[16] C. S. Lewis, *The Last Battle* (New York: HarperCollins, 1994), p. 224.
[17] I Cor 2:9.

who also reports of a man who in Christ was caught up to the third heaven, and many theologians hold that he's speaking of himself; he didn't try to describe Paradise, though, saying only that he had "heard things that cannot be told, which man may not utter".[18] The point is that heaven is better than we could possibly imagine. The Lord Himself revealed that in heaven we'll enjoy endless peace, joy, love: "I came that they may have life, and have it abundantly."[19]

"Eternal life consists of the joyous community of all the blessed, a community of supreme delight" and "in the complete satisfaction of desire, for there the blessed will be given more than they wanted or hoped for.... Whatever is delightful is there in superabundance. If delights are sought, there is supreme and most perfect delight."[20]

The greatest joy of heaven will be union with God, our Father who created us, our Savior, and our Sanctifier. On earth we often hope and expect our loved ones to love us perfectly, but they never do; they can't because they are imperfect and finite; just as we are and thus we can't love them as perfectly and infinitely as they want. But God is the satisfaction of that deep, aching, never-quite-fulfilled desire in our hearts to be loved, loved perfectly and infinitely. He is also the Source of everything we desire and love: He is Goodness, He is Beauty, He is Truth, He is Love. Being with Him will be our fulfillment, and we will be perfectly happy forever.

Before departing, Jesus said, "I go to prepare a place for you."[21] These are the words of a bridegroom. In ancient Israel, though betrothal carried all the legal obligations of marriage, the bride would live with her parents while the bridegroom would build or prepare a home for her. The marriage would be finalized when he came to bring her to their new home; at that point, the week-long wedding banquet was celebrated. The Lord has proposed the same to us; He's the Divine Bridegroom, preparing a heavenly home—a new heavens and a new earth[22]—for us.

---

[18] 2 Cor 12:2, 3.

[19] Jn 10:10.

[20] Thomas Aquinas, Coll. super Credo in Deum: Opuscula theologica 2, Taurini 1954, pp. 216–17; quoted in Liturgy of the Hours, vol. IV, Second Reading for Saturday, 33rd Week of Ordinary Time (New York: Catholic Book, 1975), p. 564.

[21] Jn 14:2.

[22] Is 65:17; Rev 21:1–2.

DETERMINING OUR DESTINATION

And what are we doing as we wait? Brides everywhere search for the perfect dress; many take extra steps to get in shape. Traditionally brides also prepared a trousseau of beautiful, useful items for the new home. For such a perfect Groom, should we not spiritually do at least as much?

Restoring Our Wedding Garment, Option One: Pitstop in Purgatory

We saw in chapter 8 above that Jesus likens the soul to a wedding garment. If every sin stains and tears the wedding gown, then it needs cleansing and repairs. One could say that the Sacrament of Confession removes the stains, and penance repairs the tears. But what happens if our efforts are too little or too late? If we're heading the right way on the path of life—toward God—but our souls aren't ready for the wedding feast when we die (our gowns have spots or rips), then He has provided a solution.

Purgatory is God's gracious gift to the not-quite-prepared for the wedding; it is the anteroom of heaven, where we can get cleaned up and the holes in the delicate lace of our souls reworked and repaired.

Many don't believe in Purgatory, so let's begin with the reasons behind the Church's teachings for it.

Support for the Reality of Purgatory

I won't attempt to *prove* the existence of Purgatory, which most Protestants dispute and even many Catholics question or misunderstand; to do the topic justice would take a book. But I will touch on the basics and some points that help me to understand it—which may help others too.

Purgatory and the Bible

It is true that one can't find the word "Purgatory" in the Bible. But neither can you find the words "Trinity" and "Incarnation" there. But you can find the roots of these doctrines in the Bible. One important passage supporting the doctrine of Purgatory is not found in many Protestant Bibles or is relegated to an appendix called "Apocrypha". Disliking the passage, Luther removed the entire book in which it is found (the

Second Book of Maccabees).[23] It regards some fallen Jewish soldiers, found to have been wearing amulets (a sin) when they died:

[Judas Maccabeus] also took up a collection,... to the amount of two thousand drachmas of silver, and sent it to Jerusalem to provide for a sin offering. In doing this he acted very well and honorably, taking account of the resurrection. For if he were not expecting that those who had fallen would rise again, it would have been superfluous and foolish to pray for the dead. But if he was looking to the splendid reward that is laid up for those who fall asleep in godliness, it was a holy and pious thought. Therefore he made atonement for the dead, that they might be delivered from their sin.[24]

Even to one who wouldn't accept this passage as scriptural, it is historical evidence that Jews living about a century before Christ believed their prayers and sacrificial offerings could aid the dead. This wouldn't make sense if the departed were in hell, because hell is final. And if they were in heaven, they wouldn't need the help. It indicates a third possibility. Jesus implies the same in speaking of forgiveness "in this age or *in the age to come*".[25] Apart from Purgatory, how could that be possible? "The Bible clearly implies a place for an intermediate state of purification after we die."[26]

---

[23] Luther removed the Deuterocanonical books from his Bible, since they weren't in the Jewish Bible of his day. But that canon was established nearly a hundred years after Christ's birth, by a Jewish council rejecting the Deuterocanonicals because they appeared first in the Septuagint (the Greek translation of the Old Testament). It is suspected, though, that the real reason was their desire to reject the Christian interpretation of the Old Testament. Jesus and the apostles clearly accepted the Septuagint because they quote it (over three hundred times) as did the early Church Fathers. When the early Church held councils in the fourth century, to decide which books belonged in the Bible, they included all the Deuterocanonicals. Indeed, all Christians accepted them, and they were included in all Christian Bibles, until Luther came along. He also rejected a few New Testament books, especially the Book of James, which explicitly countered his "faith-*alone*" theory. Other Protestant denominations followed suit and cut the Deuterocanonicals, though they restored the New Testament books. Ironically, they accepted the decisions of the Catholic Councils of Hippo and Carthage in determining the New Testament canon, but, when it came to the Old Testament, they decided to rely on a council that rejected Christ. See James Akin, "Defending the Deuterocanonicals", EWTN Library, www.ewtn.com/library /ANSWERS/DEUTEROS.HTM.

[24] 2 Mac 12:43–45 (or 46 in some translations).

[25] Mt 12:32, emphasis added. See also *CCC* 1031.

[26] Andres Ortiz, "Where Is Purgatory in the Bible?" *Catholic Answers*, www.aboutcatholics .com/beliefs/where-is-purgatory-in-the-bible/.

Where Is *That* in the Bible?

The implication of this common question is that all matters of faith must be stated explicitly in the Bible. But where is that premise found in the Bible? You can look, but you won't find it.[a] Nor will you find explicit teachings on the Trinity or the hypostatic union (that is, Jesus was one Person with two natures, divine and human). These doctrines are present in the Scriptures but not named or explicated. They came to be understood and defined over time by the Church in a process called the development of doctrine.

What you *will* find in the Bible is St. John plainly stating that the Gospels don't contain everything Jesus said or did ("were every one of them to be written, I suppose that the world itself could not contain the books that would be written") and St. Paul exhorting, "stand firm and hold to the traditions which you were taught by us, either by *word of mouth* or by letter."[b] Indeed, oral teachings were all the earliest Christians had. Then for a few centuries they had Gospels and epistles, but it wasn't always clear which were authentically apostolic and truly inspired by God. It wasn't until the fourth century that the Bible finally came together as we know it, when the Catholic Church officially designated which books belong in the canon of Scripture, especially in the New Testament.[c]

It was under the guidance of the Holy Spirit and by the authority granted by Jesus Christ that the same Catholic Church that gave us the Bible also gave us teachings such as Purgatory.

[a] Some cite 2 Tim 3:15–16, which affirms that Scripture is "inspired by God and profitable for teaching". This is very true ... but not the same thing. Moreover, Paul was speaking solely of the Old Testament, since the New did not yet exist.

[b] Jn 21:25 and 2 Thess 2:15; emphasis added.

[c] *Canon* means essentially the "official list". For more information, see the fascinating book *Where We Got the Bible: Our Debt to the Catholic Church*, by Henry G. Graham (1911).

Box 50

We saw earlier, in chapter 15 above, that sin results not only in an eternal penalty (which Christ paid on the Cross for all who will accept the gift) but in a temporal or earthly one as well. If we don't make reparation for our sins now, then we will still owe the temporal part of the debt the Lord left for us to pay ourselves. Jesus Himself warns of such a debt when He says: "Make friends quickly with your accuser, while you are going with him to court, lest ... you be put in prison; truly, I say to you, you will never get out till you have paid the last penny."[27]

[27] Mt 5:25–26.

This sounds like hell, for how can you pay a debt if you're in prison? But in the debtor's prison of Jesus' day, a debtor did stay until his family or friends could pay the debt for him.[28] This is precisely what the Catholic Church teaches: the souls in Purgatory owe a debt and can do nothing for themselves but need the prayers and sacrifices of their family on earth, the Church.

Most people, Pope Benedict XVI surmises, have an "openness to truth, to love, to God", but it gets covered by what is base in their concrete choices. What

> Sin has *a double consequence*. Grave sin deprives us of communion with God and therefore makes us incapable of eternal life, the privation of which is called the "eternal punishment" of sin. On the other hand every sin, even venial, entails an unhealthy attachment to [created things over the Creator], which must be purified either here on earth, or after death in the state called Purgatory. This purification frees one from what is called the "temporal punishment" of sin. These two punishments ... [follow] from the very nature of sin.
>
> —CCC 1472 [Box 51]

then "happens to such individuals when they appear before the Judge? Will all the impurity they have amassed through life suddenly cease to matter?"[29] There are many biblical passages on the need for cleansing, such as the Book of Revelation, which declares, "nothing unclean shall enter [heaven], nor any one who practices abomination or falsehood".[30]

Another Bible passage pertinent to the doctrine of Purgatory reads as follows:

> Now if any one builds on the foundation [Jesus Christ] with gold, silver, precious stones, wood, hay, straw—each man's work will become manifest; for the Day will disclose it, because it will be revealed with fire, and the fire will test what sort of work each one has done. If the work which any man has built on the foundation survives, he will receive a reward. If any man's work is burned up, he will suffer loss, though he himself will be saved, but only as through fire.[31]

---

[28] See *Catholic for a Reason: Scripture and the Mystery of the Family of God*, ed. Scott Hahn and Leon J. Supernant, Jr. (Steubenville, Oh.: Emmaus Road, 1998), p. 220. An in-depth portrayal of a debtors' prison appears in *Little Dorrit*. Charles Dickens was quite familiar with the prison as his own father was imprisoned there when Charles was twelve.

[29] Pope Benedict XVI, Encyclical Letter *Spe Salvi* on Christian Hope, *Saved in Hope* (November 30, 2007), no. 46.

[30] Rev 21:27. See also Ortiz, "Where Is Purgatory in the Bible?"

[31] 1 Cor 3:12–15; see also v. 11. Regarding the phrase "suffer loss", "The Greek OT uses this verb to denote personal suffering ... as well as financial penalties.... The Gospels use it for the

Bible scholars Scott Hahn and Mitch Curtis comment:

> Some ..., whose efforts are shabby and imperfect, will pass through God's fiery judgment like a man who barely escapes a burning building with his life. This prelude to salvation will involve painful spiritual consequences, which, though severe, will spare them eternal damnation.... Purgatory is a final stage of purification for those who are destined for heaven but depart from this life still burdened with venial sins or with an unpaid debt of temporal punishment.... Passing through fire is thus a spiritual process where souls are purged of residual selfishness and refined in God's love.[32]

The Need for Purgatory

C. S. Lewis (not a Catholic) believed in Purgatory, saying it is *we* who desire purgation:

> Our souls *demand* Purgatory, don't they? Would it not break the heart if God said to us, "It is true, my son, that your breath smells and your rags drip with mud and slime, but we are charitable here and no one will upbraid you with these things, nor draw away from you. Enter into the joy."?
>
> Should we not reply, "With submission, sir, and if there is no objection, I'd *rather* be cleaned first."
>
> "It may hurt, you know."
>
> "Even so, sir."[33]

Similarly, St. Catherine of Genoa, a mystic and doctor of the Church, says: "To see God when full satisfaction had not yet been given to Him ... would be unbearable to the soul. It would sooner go to a thousand Hells to rid itself of the little rust still clinging to it, than stand in the divine presence when it was not yet wholly cleansed."[34] The first time I read that, I found it to be rather too much of a hyperbole ... until I remembered a memorable day at a country club.

---

frightful prospective of losing eternal life.... In 1 Cor 3:15, it refers to spiritual damage." Hahn and Mitch, *Ignatius Catholic Study Bible: The New Testament*, "Word Study: *Suffer loss* (1 Cor 3:15)" (San Francisco: Ignatius Press, 2010), p. 288.

[32] Ibid., pp. 288n–289n, citing *CCC* 1030–32.

[33] C. S. Lewis, *Letters to Malcolm: Chiefly on Prayer* (1963; repr., Orlando: Harcourt, 1992), pp. 108–9; emphasis in original.

[34] Catherine of Genoa, *Fire of Love: Understanding Purgatory* (Manchester, N.H.: Sophia Institute Press), p. 75.

One summer, a friend invited me to go horseback riding. We had a great time, riding along trails in the California desert. Afterward we were chatting happily driving home—I thought—when her mom parked in the lot of a ritzy country club. Apparently I didn't get the memo about this part of the day. The club was equipped with fancy private showers, but unlike my friend, who had brought along a fresh outfit, all I had were my dirt-caked, horsy clothes. You see, riding on a warm day means you and the horse sweat, especially where you come in contact— and, if I remember correctly, I had ridden bareback. And though horses are brushed daily, they aren't bathed all that often. So I had large swaths of brown along my pants, bearing the distinct odor of horse.

While I don't remember anyone looking at me strangely or turning up their noses, I still *felt* like a skunk. I couldn't get comfortable anywhere we went in the club, and I certainly didn't want to sit down on the fine furniture. While those there were well-to-do, fashionable, and *clean*, they were still strangers whom I would never see again. If I nevertheless felt so mortified, contemptible, and out of place among other humans, how would I feel appearing grimy with my own sin in the presence of *God*, who is perfectly holy, whose beauty, glory, and power are beyond imagination, and who is the deepest desire and only satisfaction of my heart?

What Will Purgatory Be Like?

Nowadays, many of those Catholics aware of the existence of Purgatory think it will be over soon and won't be too bad. St. Francis of Assisi, however, reportedly chose three days of suffering on earth over one day in Purgatory when a heavenly vision offered him this choice on his deathbed. This story raises two important points to consider.

First, it testifies that St. Francis viewed the pains of Purgatory as worse than any suffering on earth. Such is the long tradition in the Church. St. Augustine, for instance, wrote: "This fire of Purgatory will be more severe than any pain that can be felt, seen or conceived in this world."[35] The *Catechism* does not attempt to describe Purgatory but avers it is "entirely different from the punishment of the damned".[36]

---

[35] Augustine, xli *De Sanctis*, quoted in Thomas Aquinas, *Summa Theologica*, vol. 5, pt. III, Second Section and Supplement, trans. Fathers of the English Dominican Province (New York: Cosimo, 2007), q. 2, a. 1, p. 3006. See also Catherine of Genoa, *Fire of Love*, p. 24.

[36] *CCC* 1031.

Pope Benedict XVI suggests that "the fire which both burns and saves is Christ himself, the Judge and Savior." He remarks: "In the pain of this encounter, when the impurity and sickness of our lives become evident to us, there lies salvation. His gaze, the touch of his heart heals us through an undeniably painful transformation 'as through fire'. But it is a blessed pain, in which the holy power of his love sears through us like a flame, enabling us to become totally ourselves and thus totally of God."[37]

Thus, despite the pain, the souls in Purgatory rejoice to be where they are and in knowing they will never sin again. St. Catherine of Genoa, who was given an extensive vision of Purgatory, reported, "The soul that has the least stain of imperfection accept[s] Purgatory as though it were a mercy."[38] The souls there also rejoice that they are being prepared for what they most desire: to be with God. (The greatest suffering of Purgatory is the longing to be with Him, whom they saw at their personal judgment.)[39] So, despite the pain, "no happiness can be found worthy to be compared with that of a soul in Purgatory except that of the saints in Paradise."[40]

So ... Who Goes to Purgatory?

The short answer on who goes to Purgatory is this: everyone going to heaven must pass first through purification, either in this life or in Purgatory.[41] The Catholic Church teaches: "All who die in God's grace and friendship, but still imperfectly purified, ... undergo purification, so as to achieve the holiness necessary to enter the joy of heaven."[42]

The second point to consider from St. Francis' story is this: If someone as holy and ascetic as he still required even a "day"[43] in Purgatory,

---

[37] Benedict XVI, *Spe Salvi, Saved in Hope*, no. 47.

[38] Catherine of Genoa, *Fire of Love*, p. 49.

[39] Aquinas, *Summa Theologica*, q. 2, a. 1.

[40] Catherine of Genoa, *Fire of Love*, p. 23.

[41] Exceptions to this include young children who in Baptism were purified of original sin and died before committing any personal sin.

[42] *CCC* 1030. The *Catechism* also notes another possibility: "A conversion which proceeds from a fervent charity can attain the complete purification of the sinner in such a way that no punishment would remain" (*CCC* 1472). For most, however, there is suffering in this life if not in Purgatory.

[43] How time works in Purgatory is a mystery. While the souls there are no longer subject to the turning of the earth or the beating of their hearts to mark the passage of time, they are, in being purified, still subject to change, another aspect of time.

what will the rest of us need? Reflecting on these things can really spur you to see penance in a whole new light.

Restoring the Wedding Garment, Option Two: What We Can Do Now

One who has begun practicing the "love languages" covered herein is already preparing to meet the Bridegroom. We can make all our ordinary duties, all our actions, indeed our every breath into a prayer, a gift of love to God and reparation for our sins. Still, our penances alone can go only so far in expunging the stains from our souls, so the Lord has given us additional ways to prepare for the wedding banquet and fill our flasks with oil.[44]

God Is Merciful—Even Indulgent

Through the Church, the Lord gives powerful means to make reparation for sin: indulgences.

Now, before anyone freaks out, let's establish that indulgences are not what most people think.[45] An indulgence "is not a permission to commit sin, nor a pardon of future sin; neither could be granted by any power.... It does not confer immunity from temptation or remove the possibility of subsequent lapses into sin. Least of all is an indulgence the *purchase* of a pardon."[46]

Indulgentia, the Latin origin, means "remission" as well as "leniency" and "kindness". With the powers to "forgive sin or to retain sin" and to "loose and bind" given her by Jesus Himself, the Church offers many "indulgences" by which we can remit some or all of the temporal

---

[44] See Mt 25:1–13.

[45] A catalyst behind Martin Luther's revolt against the Catholic Church was the misleading preaching about indulgences by a Dominican friar (Johann Tetzel) in Luther's region of Germany. The Church condemned Tetzel's exaggeration, which implied that passage to heaven could be bought, and he repented. The Church formally clarified her teaching on indulgences in the Council of Trent (1545–1563) and sought to "correct the abuses that have crept in" as well as any "other disorders arising from superstition, ignorance, irreverence, or any cause whatsoever ... so that the benefit of indulgences may be bestowed on all the faithful by means at once pious, holy, and free from corruption." Quoted in "Indulgences", in the *Catholic Encyclopedia*, http://www.newadvent.org/cathen/07783a.htm.

[46] Ibid., emphasis added. The passage also notes: "It is not the forgiveness of the guilt of sin; it supposes that the sin has already been forgiven [in the Sacrament of Confession]."

punishment connected with our sins.[47] Its worth is based on the infinite value of Christ's merits, not on any action of ours; it's not something we "earn".

The Lord's indulgence is so great it can even be total: a "plenary indulgence" removes all temporal punishment incurred up to that point in one's life. The four requirements to gaining a plenary indulgence testify to the Church's sound teaching. Besides performing an indulgenced act (more on this below), these requirements are ...

1. sacramental Confession;
2. Eucharistic Communion;
3. prayer for the pope's intentions;
4. no attachment to sin, even venial.[48]

(That last one is the kicker.) Ideally, the three actions are to be done on the same day as the indulgenced act, but may be done within twenty days (before or after).[49] If any of these requirements are not met or incomplete but you are contrite, you can still gain a partial indulgence.[50]

These requirements demonstrate that indulgences are based on the saving power of Christ's Cross, true repentance, and the mercy of God. Clearly the point of the requirements is to show God how sorry you are for your sin and that you intend to straighten up your act from now on. The disposition of detachment from sin also prevents one from just going through the motions, and the requirement to receive the Eucharist demonstrates that Christ is the power source of the indulgence. The

---

[47] See *CCC* 1471.

[48] The fourth is the needed "disposition" or attitude of heart. In addition, "in order to be capable of gaining indulgences one must be baptized, not excommunicated, and in the state of grace at least at the completion of the prescribed works" and "have at least the general intention" of gaining an indulgence. Apostolic Penitentiary, *Manual of Indulgences*, trans. from 4th ed., of 1999 (Washington, D.C.: United States Conference of Catholic Bishops, 2006), p. 17, no. 17. (The Apostolic Penitentiary, in case you're wondering, as I did, is the Roman dicastery in charge of indulgences. The name comes from the Latin word for "penitence", and the *Catholic Encyclopedia* calls it "chiefly a tribunal of mercy" [New York: Robert Appleton, 1912, p. 148].)

[49] The norm used to be eight days but was changed in the Jubilee Year of 2000. See Apostolic Penitentiary, "The Gift of the Indulgence", www.vatican.va/roman_curia/tribunals/apost _penit/documents/rc_trib_appen_pro_20000129_indulgence_en.html, and "Norm of Confession for Gaining a Plenary Indulgence" http://www.ewtn.com/library/curia/apconfes.htm.

[50] While one must meet the other requirements for each plenary indulgence, a single sacramental Confession can serve for several plenary indulgences. Multiple partial indulgences can be gained per day but only one plenary indulgence.

immense, blessed result of a plenary indulgence—the satisfaction of all temporal punishment for sin—is purely the indulgent mercy of our loving God, who, like the father in the parable of the prodigal son, is eager to welcome us home.[51]

Some examples of indulgenced acts include the following:

- thirty minutes of Scripture reading;
- praying the Rosary with others or before the Blessed Sacrament;
- adoring the Lord in the Blessed Sacrament for at least thirty minutes;
- making a pilgrimage to a holy site;
- praying the Stations of the Cross;
- making a retreat of at least three full days.[52]

These are just a few examples. There are many others tied to saying certain prayers at certain places or on particular feasts, for example, renewing your baptismal promises at the Easter Vigil Mass or devoutly participating in a Divine Mercy service on Divine Mercy Sunday.[53]

Many of the things Jesus calls us to do—our duties for love of God, giving to or serving others, making sacrifices, and giving witness to the faith—have a partial indulgence attached to them.[54] You could even obtain a plenary indulgence every day simply by praying a daily Rosary at church or with others and fulfilling the other indulgence requirements listed above.

An awareness of Purgatory helps us keep on track, with our hearts and minds set on the things above, not on things that are on earth.[55]

Praying for the Dead

One of the spiritual works of mercy is to pray for the dead. Understanding Purgatory should inspire compassion in us for the poor souls there

---

[51] Mother Church also mercifully provides additional options for gaining a plenary indulgence to those who cannot fulfill all the requirements: e.g., granting mental recitation of public prayers to the deaf and mute, granting exceptions on Confession and Communion to those residing where sacraments are infrequent "provided they have contrition for their sins and have the intention of receiving these sacraments as soon as possible" and to those duly disposed and at the point of death without recourse to the sacraments. Apostolic Penitentiary, *Manual of Indulgences*, p. 19, no. 25, and p. 54, no. 12.

[52] "The Enchiridion of Indulgences", a digest of works and prayers listed in the *Enchiridion of Indulgences* (1968), Catholic Online, www.catholic.org/prayers/indulgw.php.

[53] The Sunday after Easter. For more information, see "The Divine Mercy Sunday Indulgence", https://www.ewtn.com/devotionals/mercy/indulgence.htm.

[54] "The Four General Concessions", *Manual of Indulgences*, pp. 21–36.

[55] Col 3:2.

now—not only a concern for our loved ones, but for all the suffering souls, especially those with no one praying for them specifically. The good news is there is much we can do for them.[56] The following prayer of St. Gertrude is held to be very efficacious, as it's tied to the Mass—the most powerful prayer of all:

> Eternal Father, I offer Thee
> the most precious Blood of Thy divine Son, Jesus,
> in union with all the Masses said throughout the world today,
> for all the holy souls in purgatory,
> for sinners everywhere, sinners in the Universal Church,
> those in my own home and within my family. Amen.[57]

Moreover, we can say other prayers or make little sacrifices throughout the day for the souls in Purgatory. In fact, we can even make partial or plenary indulgences for them.[58]

Another loving thing to do is to have Masses said for those who have died. You can arrange this at your local parish, a seminary, or with a religious order, making a donation of whatever size you see fit—not as a commercial transaction, but as a sacrifice on behalf of the departed soul and in grateful support of the priest offering the Mass.

Unfortunately, "we are apt to leave off too soon praying for [our departed loved ones], imagining with a foolish and unenlightened esteem ... that they are freed from purgatory much sooner than they really are."[59] We needn't fear our prayers will insult them. If they're in Purgatory, they'll be grateful, not insulted. If they're heaven, they'll be too holy to be insulted by your kindness, and no prayer is ever wasted: God will apply our prayers to another soul in need.

---

[56] See *CCC* 1032.

[57] Prayer of St. Gertrude the Great, in *Prayers, Promises, and Devotions for the Holy Souls in Purgatory*, ed. Susan Tassone (Huntington, Ind.: Our Sunday Visitor, 2012), p. 72.

[58] Realizing that we really need only *one* plenary indulgence, one could even entrust them all to Mother Mary, asking her to reserve the last one for oneself and apply the rest to poor souls in Purgatory. Indulgences can't be applied to other living persons, however. That might seem unfair at first, but it makes sense. Mercy requires repentance, and while we can strive to be truly repentant ourselves and we know those in Purgatory must have repented or they wouldn't be there, we can't make another person repentant. Of course we still can (and should) pray and make sacrifices for the living.

[59] Fr. Frederick Faber, *Purgatory*, quoted in Susan Tassone, *Thirty-Day Devotions for the Holy Souls* (Huntington, Ind.: Our Sunday Visitor, 2004), p. 76. Fr. Faber's book is available at TAN Books.

Because of the blessed mercy of our lavish Lord, we can make a difference for the holy souls in Purgatory. In the fourth century, St. John Chrysostom urged: "If Job's sons were purified by their father's sacrifice, why would we doubt that our offerings for the dead bring them some consolation? Let us not hesitate to help those who have died to offer our prayers for them."[60]

Perfect Love Casts Out Fear

Sometimes my little one doesn't want to listen to me; she wants her own way even when it isn't good for her. If, when I speak sternly and remind her of unpleasant consequences, she finally obeys, I'm glad. But I would be happier if she obeyed out of love. It's the same with the Lord. While fear is good if it moves us to repentance and obedience, love is better. "For fear has to do with punishment, and he who fears is not perfected in love",[61] says the apostle John, through whose writings the theme of love runs like a stream of gold. Love is better because it's more pleasing to Him and because love is what fulfills us, our *raison d'être*.

"There is no fear in love, but perfect love casts out fear", assures John.[62] Let's make reparation for sin, but out of love, not fear. Let's ask the Lord to enlarge our love and work with Him in removing every blot from our souls before the Wedding, for love of the Bridegroom.

Ready and Waiting

These reflections show why we can't be presumptuous or complacent. Those doing more than the minimum must still keep striving to go higher. The spiritual life is like climbing up a down-escalator: to descend, you don't have to turn around and start walking; all you have to do is stand still. It's so easy to sink into complacency, especially if we compare ourselves to our self-centered culture rather than to Jesus and His saints.

Those in love ache when apart from the beloved. Those in love with God long to see Him face to face. They think about it and prepare

---

[60] Hom. in I Cor. 41, 5; PG 61, 361; cf. Job 1:5; quoted in *CCC* 1032.
[61] I Jn 4:18.
[62] Ibid.

for it. St. Dominic Savio had already figured this out as a youth. St. John Bosco asked some boys playing soccer what they would do if they learned they would die the next day. One boy said he would run to Confession, another would pray before the Blessed Sacrament. Dominic replied that he would keep on playing soccer. He wasn't callous—he was prepared. He had already attended to his spiritual and earthly duties, so he was free to enjoy a little recreation (also a duty, though a lesser one).[63] Dominic didn't see any need to stop playing, as he believed it was God's will for him to play soccer right then—and he had dedicated himself to doing God's will at all times.

Perhaps that is the secret to being ready.

---

[63] Recreation is a human need, physically, mentally, and emotionally. Playing soccer was also an important way that Dominic could connect with the other boys and thereby more effectively be a good influence on them.

27

THE ONLY THING WE CAN BRING
WITH US: OTHER PEOPLE

One who loves God cannot but assist in what He most desires—the salvation of souls. The purpose of this life, then, is to grow continually in love for Him and get ready for heaven, but also to bring as many souls with you as possible. Loving others is more than being kind to them. Real love is concerned with the others' welfare, particularly their eternal welfare. So loving others has to include praying for them and sharing the gospel with them.

Prayer: Foundation of a Fruitful Apostle

Helping Those Headed toward Hell

We saw above that people go to hell; does God care? Oh yes. "God predestines no one to go to hell", states the *Catechism*; He doesn't want "any to perish, but all to come to repentance".[1] He desires the salvation of all.[2] If you want proof that God cares, look at the Cross. *That's* how much He cared; that's how much He wanted to save people from hell. He cares *Passion*-ately.

As members of His Body, we should participate in His saving work. If He cares so much, so must we. And thinking of those who might suffer without end can really motivate us to do whatever we can to prevent that. After the visionaries of Fatima were given a vision of hell, they took on many challenging penances and became powerhouses of prayer for souls at risk of going to hell—although they were mere children.

---

[1] *CCC* 1037, quoting 2 Pet 3:9.
[2] "God our Savior ... desires all men to be saved and to come to the knowledge of the truth" (1 Tim 2:3–4).

Jacinta, at age nine, even underwent surgery without anesthesia, offering it up for the conversion of sinners ... until she passed out.

Christ underwent His Passion to save not just us but everyone from sin and eternal punishment. To show Him gratitude and to love those He loves, we can join in His loving crusade for souls, in which He gave His life and shed His Precious Blood: we too can pray, fast, and make whatever sacrifices He may ask of us to help souls be saved.

Necessity of Prayer

Efforts to share the Good News must be based in prayer, or they cannot succeed. Prayer is indispensable—apostles need it, hearers need it, and the Holy Spirit must be invoked.

First, "Apostolic activity must spring from intimate union with Him."[3] Dom Jean-Baptiste Chautard found this vital fact to be so overlooked that he devoted an entire book to it: *Soul of the Apostolate* helps readers root their apostolates in a rich interior life with Christ. And the way to develop this union is regular prayer and use of the sacraments.

To be an apostle, you must develop the heart of Jesus in your own ribcage. Spend time with Him, do whatever He tells you, and decrease, so that He may increase in you. Meditate on death and eternity, and nurture a holy concern in your heart for souls headed away from God. Ask Him to fill your heart with a desire to be part of His rescue team.

Secondly, those who don't know God can't come to know Him without help: human help, yes (more on that below), but even more, divine help—in theological terms, "actual graces". The graces to be open, to listen, to recognize and accept truth, to believe, to act.

Finally, the Holy Spirit is the One who converts hearts; if we don't invite Him into our efforts, they will ultimately be fruitless. On our own, we can do nothing.[4] He's also the One who equips us with the gifts, graces, and inspiration to carry out this work—which is, after all, His.

Intercession is crucial.

---

[3] Second Vatican Council, Decree on the Adaptation and Renewal of Religious Life *Perfectae Caritatis* (October 28, 1965), no. 8. The Second Vatican Council also wrote on the apostolate of the laity: see *Apostolicam Actuositatem, Apostolate of Lay People* (November 18, 1965), no. 4.

[4] Jn 15:5. Yes, we can act without requesting God's help, but only because He's given us life, freedom, and the faculties to do so. Anything we do "on our own" will disappear on Judgment Day like straw in a fire (1 Cor 3:12).

Rosary: Power Prayer

An extremely potent form of intercessory prayer is the Rosary. Sadly, it is often misunderstood or regarded negatively; we'll begin then by answering doubts and correcting myths.

Protestant Objections to the Rosary

Scott Hahn tells how, as a Protestant, he tore apart his late grandmother's rosary, triumphant in setting her free from a chain of Catholic superstition. Since other religions also use prayer beads, some Protestants view the Rosary as pagan. But Eastern Orthodox Christians also use prayer beads. Moreover, just because other religions do something doesn't mean Christians need to reject it. In almost every religion, people kneel in prayer—should we eschew that too?

Another major objection stems from there being fifty Hail Marys in the Rosary. Some think this is what Jesus was talking about when He warned against using "vain repetitions" in prayer "as the heathen do".[5] But who knows what vain repetitions Gentiles

---

Definition and Development of the Rosary

The Rosary arose from a desire for the illiterate (most people, centuries ago) to pray like the religious, who prayed all 150 Psalms daily or weekly. It gradually took the form of 150 Hail Marys, each compared to a rose, hence the name, meaning "garland or wreath of roses".

Later, these prayers were divided into fifteen *decades* (groups of ten), each focusing on a *mystery* in the lives of Jesus and Mary. For centuries, there were three groups of five decades: the Joyful, Sorrowful, and Glorious Mysteries. In 2002, St. John Paul II added the Luminous Mysteries, on the public life of Jesus.

The *Rosary* (capped) then is this form of prayer, usually meaning five decades; a *rosary* (lower-case) is a string of beads on which to keep track of the prayers: one small bead for each Hail Mary and one larger bead between each decade for an Our Father and Glory Be.

For a brief history of the Rosary, see D.D. Emmons, "Where Did the Rosary Originate?", *Our Sunday Visitor Newsweekly*, September 1, 2015, www.osv.com/TheChurch /LiturgyandPrayer/Article/TabId/666 /ArtMID/13698/ArticleID/17911/Where- did-the-rosary-originate.aspx. For an in-depth history, see "The Rosary", *Catholic Encyclopedia*, www.newadvent.org/cathen/13184b .htm.

Box 52

---

[5] Mt 6:7, NKJV.

said two thousand years ago? Jesus couldn't have been criticizing any and all repetition. (If He was, then we who use spontaneous prayer are in trouble too, for we often use pet phrases.) He Himself prayed in the same words repeatedly in Gethsemane; the Lord ordered repetition of the First Commandment; and in Revelation, the four living creatures "*never cease* to sing, 'Holy, holy, holy, is the Lord God Almighty, who was and is and is to come!' "[6] Moreover, repetition aids one in entering into meditation. The Orthodox repeat the Jesus Prayer ("Lord Jesus Christ, Son of God, have mercy on me, a sinner") throughout the day as a way to obey St. Paul's injunction to "pray without ceasing" but also as "a prayer that leads to the deepest mysteries of the contemplative life".[7]

Still, some view the prayer as "*vain*". Chapters 24 and 25 above have already addressed doubts about prayers to Mary and other saints, so here let's examine the "Hail Mary" prayer. It's largely scriptural: the first two-thirds come straight from the Gospel of Luke, only the names of Mary and Jesus are added;[8] the final third, though not scriptural, is historical and humble. It consists of a title, "Holy Mary, Mother of God", that the Council of Ephesus affirmed early in the fifth century, based on what Scripture says of her, and a request: that she "pray for us sinners" at the only two times in life we are certain to have: "now and at the hour of our death".

Finally, there's more to the Rosary than reciting prayers: there are "mysteries" on which to meditate at the same time. The mysteries are largely from the life of Christ—from His Incarnation and birth, through His ministry, Passion, and death, and on to His Resurrection and Ascension. Thus the Rosary helps one to remember the significant moments in Christ's life. Meditating on them keeps Him, His teachings, and how He suffered for us from fading from our minds.

Moreover, we "ponder" them with Mary, His tiptop disciple. St. Luke says Mary kept in her heart the things she witnessed in Jesus' life

---

[6] Deut 6:7; Rev 4:8; emphasis added.

[7] 1 Thess 5:17 (Douay-Rheims); Bishop Kallistos Ware, quoted in Benedict Groeschel, C.F.R., *Praying Constantly* (Huntington, Ind.: Our Sunday Visitor, 2010), p. 83.

[8] "Hail [Mary], full of grace, the Lord is with you!" is exactly the heavenly accolade with which Gabriel the archangel addressed her (Lk 1:28), and "Blessed are you among women, and blessed is the fruit of your womb [, Jesus]!" is precisely how Elizabeth, inspired by the Holy Spirit, greeted her (Lk 1:42).

and *pondered* them.[9] They were mysterious things, words and occurrences she didn't always comprehend at the time.[10] Contemplating the "mysteries" of the Rosary helps us know Christ and His ways better and to understand and handle better His mysterious working in our own lives. And doing so *with Mary*, who actually witnessed them and first pondered them, is to meditate under the guidance of the best spiritual director and the holiest saint. Anyone who perseveres in praying the Rosary and striving to meditate with Mary is sure to grow closer to Christ as well as in wisdom, understanding, and virtue.[11]

The Rosary is saturated with Scripture and focused on Christ.

Catholic Reluctance

Catholics have their own problems with the Rosary. Many don't know much about it and find the idea of praying it highly unattractive—too boring or too daunting. It's true that the Rosary is surprisingly hard to pray. It's a simple prayer, but it's difficult to make oneself do it. It only takes fifteen to twenty minutes, but often there's a huge reluctance—even aversion—to overcome. It's as appealing as rolling a boulder uphill. To me, that's a sign that the evil one is pulling out all the stops to prevent us from praying it, which is a testimony of its effectiveness.

But we can overcome such obstacles. Using Rosary meditation booklets makes it much easier to concentrate and more fruitful.[12] And perseverance is key. Like brushing your teeth, once you gain the habit, it becomes a normal part of your day. And it's *well* worth it.

Super-Power for Earthlings

The Rosary is a beefy form of intercession. In our family, we've seen its efficacy in solving problems and answering heartfelt prayers of all kinds. What motivated us to commit to a daily five-decade Rosary was the simultaneous health crises besetting my mother and my husband's

---

[9] Lk 2:19 and 51.

[10] Lk 2:50.

[11] "The Rosary ... is at heart a Christocentric prayer ... [containing] all the *depth of the Gospel message in its entirety*.... It is an echo of the prayer of Mary, her perennial *Magnificat*.... Through the Rosary the faithful receive abundant grace, as though from the very hands of the Mother of the Redeemer." Pope St. John Paul II, Apostolic Letter *Rosarium Virginis Mariae* on the Most Holy Rosary (October 16, 2002), no. 1.

[12] There are many. My favorite is *The Scriptural Rosary* from Christianica (http://thescriptural rosary.com), which gives a Scripture verse for each bead.

mother. One was in the hospital with mysterious blood-pressure and heart problems plus a new Alzheimer's diagnosis; the other had serious heart problems, a spot on her brain, and lung cancer. We feared we would lose both, but my mother-in-law recovered and lived another eleven years, and my mom, against all odds, is still with us now, thirteen years later.[13]

It can be hard to believe that something as simple as a Rosary can make much of a difference in our lives, let alone history. But it has. In fact, the Feast of Our Lady of the Rosary was established in honor of the Rosary's spectacular effects on October 7, 1571. When a huge Turkish naval force was threatening Europe, Pope Pius V called on the faithful to pray the Rosary, and miraculously, a much-smaller Christian alliance defeated it. And the Rosary continues to affect history. Day after day, its sixty-some little prayers have the effect of drops of water. Even stone gives way to water droplets—if there are enough of them. The Iron Curtain rusted from the sprinklings of countless Rosaries and crumbled soon after Pope St. John Paul II consecrated the world to Mary in 1984. Also in the 1980s, the dictatorship of Ferdinand Marcos in the Philippines was washed away in a bloodless revolution riding on a tidal wave of Rosaries.

The Rosary is mighty. No wonder Padre (now St.) Pio—that holy, twentieth-century, demon-wrangling, miracle-working monk—had such confidence in its power; no wonder he called it "my weapon". May we remember and utilize this vital force at our disposal.[14]

Evangelization

Prayer is essential, but we must also evangelize.

Most people don't associate evangelizing with Catholics. Of course, that shows how history books and mass media in our time have short-changed the Catholic Church. But even acknowledging her evangelical record over the past two thousand years, when we think of evangelization, modern-day American Catholics are not typically what come to

---

[13] Of course, not all our prayers have been answered yet or in the way we had hoped, but many have, and the Rosary has helped sustain our faith in adverse circumstances or when God saw fit to answer in another way.

[14] To learn how to pray the Rosary or obtain a free Rosary CD, visit CatholiCity at www.catholic.org/prayers/rosary.php.

mind. Nor do we usually think of ourselves that way either. But that too is not how it should be.

"Evangelizing is in fact ... the Church['s] ... deepest identity", Pope St. Paul VI declares, in an apostolic exhortation most Catholics have never heard of, *Evangelization in the Modern World*. (It's a good read: not too difficult or lengthy, and very inspiring.) In it, he also points out, "The presentation of the Gospel message is not an optional contribution for the Church"; indeed, he asserts, "She *exists* in order to evangelize."[15]

Even upon learning this, most Catholics would still see evangelization as a calling given only to a few special people who are super-holy and endowed with extraordinary talents to carry out an extraordinary task. An ordinary Catholic would hardly expect to *meet* such a person, let alone *be* one. The next shocker, however, is that *each* Christian, each *Catholic*, is called to evangelize. Not just clergy and missionaries. Everyone—lay people too. Whether we're ordained, religious, married, or single—we all share the same fundamental *vocation*, the vocation of the baptized: to follow Jesus to heaven and bring as many people with us as possible.

This doesn't mean evangelizing as a group: "*Each* one of them [is] to cooperate in the external spread and the dynamic growth of the Kingdom of Christ in the world."[16] Paul VI explains why: Lay people are placed "in the midst of the world and in charge of the most varied temporal tasks.... Their own field of evangelizing activity is the vast and complicated world of politics, society and economics,... of culture, of the sciences and the arts,... of the mass media."[17] The laity have access to people the clergy don't.

This means you. Each of us has been given certain talents, and God has put us in a certain place and time, with our personality, background, experiences, and even weaknesses, all

> The person who has been evangelized goes on to evangelize others.... It is unthinkable that a person should accept the Word and give himself to the kingdom without becoming a person who bears witness to it and proclaims it in his turn.
>
> —POPE ST. PAUL VI[Box 53]

---

[15] Pope St. Paul VI, Apostolic Exhortation *Evangelii Nuntiandi* on Evangelization in the Modern World (December 8, 1975), nos. 14, 5; emphasis added.

[16] Second Vatican Council, Dogmatic Constitution on the Church *Lumen Gentium* (November 21, 1964), no. 35; emphasis added. See also *CCC* 904.

[17] Paul VI, *Evangelii Nuntiandi, Evangelization in the Modern World*, no. 70.

just right to touch certain people at certain times. Each has a mission, with certain souls to reach.

Are You Prophetable?

Prophesizing is not primarily predicting the future, but speaking God's truth. It's not just the heroic and legendary who are called. Each member of Christ's Body is to share in His role as prophet.

I'm not brave enough, you say. *It's counter-productive to get on a soapbox*, etc., etc. You don't have to get on a soapbox. You don't have to eat locusts and shout that the Kingdom is coming. Those were the callings, respectively, of Frank Sheed and John the Baptist. Your calling is different. Each person has an individual calling. Each of us is called to give witness—but how and to whom will naturally differ not only from person to person but even from day to day.

My uncle is a perfect example of this.

One day at the airport, after being paged, my brother was approached by an older gentleman asking if he was related to a frat brother with the same last name. The man (Bill)—forty years later—still remembered Uncle Domingo, though the latter had had to drop out of his first semester of college due to what turned out to be the beginnings of schizophrenia. But it wasn't the symptoms of mental illness—if he had even seen them—that Bill remembered. Nor was it so much my uncle's intelligence, impressive athletic and artistic talents, striking good looks, or natural confidence that he recalled. It was Uncle Domingo's character that stuck with him. On "hell night", they were required to perform a silly, crude, humiliating rite. My uncle refused. He didn't care what the others thought of him; he didn't care if they wouldn't let him in the fraternity as a result. He just calmly said he wouldn't do it. (And he got in anyway.)

Domingo's convictions made a huge impression on Bill, and he became curious about the Catholic faith. A couple of years later, Bill became Catholic and considered Domingo his godfather (though since he wasn't available, he asked Domingo's kid brother, my dad, instead). It would have amazed my uncle if he had known. Most of the rest of his life was spent in an institution or halfway house. He never would have guessed the impact he had had on Bill's life.

Nor would he have guessed that he could continue to witness to Christ. Once a star athlete and sharp dresser, in later life, he became haggard, resembling an aged van Gogh, shuffling in baggy, tobacco-scented clothes. If he had known about Bill, he would have thought, "Well, he knew me before all this. No one would want me to be his godfather now."

But he was a good godfather. I know, because he was *my* godfather. He may not have been able to buy me gifts or take me places, write me letters, or whatever godfathers typically might do. But I'm sure he prayed for me. And I know he still does, for when I ask for his intercession, the results are often quick and impressive. Most of all, he gave me the gift of example. He was the most humble person I have ever met.

His humility also affected other family members and friends. I know my father and one of their childhood friends were both moved by it over the years. Who knows who else was touched? Only the Lord, who called him to witness to Christ in a halfway house.

No one feels adequate to God's call. But that doesn't matter, for it is He who works; we're only his instruments.

Going from Disciples to Apostles

If you feel unqualified—good, because you are. Humility is the ideal beginning; it means God can work with you. And if you let Him, He will work not only with you and in you but also on you—indeed, He will transform you. Just look what He did with St. Peter.

Peter was my grandmother's favorite saint. She found his foibles endearing and encouraging: even the first pope had his shortcomings, yet God chose him and used him. Being less wise and less humble, I thought as a kid that the disciples were rather dense, particularly Peter, who was brash too. It's also easy to scoff at the disciples for sitting around in the Upper Room for nine days after the Ascension, though Jesus had commissioned them to make disciples of all nations. What a way to start. That isn't fair though. After all, He did tell them to go back to Jerusalem and wait for the Holy Spirit. If the Spirit decided to wait nine days, what could they do about it? Finding fault with the disciples is like critiquing professional athletes—as if I could do so much better in their place. And once you put yourself in the disciples' sandals and imagine how daunting their mission was, disparagement melts away. How *do* you go about evangelizing the world? Suddenly praying a lot and waiting on the Holy Spirit sound like excellent ideas.

The second chapter of Acts, moreover, shows how right Grandma was and how wrong I was. After the Holy Spirit came and set them on fire, the transformed apostles went out into the streets of Jerusalem, praising God in multiple languages. Then Peter—who, from fear, had denied Jesus and hidden from the authorities—went out into the street, gave an impromptu speech, and converted three thousand people on the spot. This demonstrates that the foundation of evangelization is prayer, and its power is the Holy Spirit.

But this story is about more than admiring the apostles as they deserve; it's clear that we must imitate them. The same commission has been handed on like a baton to each of us, and we're called to get out there and do the best we can. By God's generosity, we've received the Good News—but not just for our own sake.[18] Jesus said, "Every one to whom much is given, of him will much be required."[19] Most of us, though, settle down for years in the Upper Room: hardly praying; just hiding. But if we've been baptized into Christ and confirmed, the Spirit is already living within us. He's already given each of us the gifts we need to fulfill our particular mission, and He wants to transform us into apostles too.

A *disciple* is a pupil or learner; an *apostle* is one who is sent. Christians are to be lifelong disciples—always learning from the Master; but we must also go out and share what we've learned.

Those hiding out in the Upper Room are surrounded by unopened gifts, while outside there's a massive wildfire of sin and disbelief ravaging the land and leaving devastation in its wake. God has an infinite ocean of mercy and grace within reach to pour down and save everyone. But He needs *you* to grab a hose and get to work.

Be Prepared

To be His ambassadors, we need to be prepared. You can't give what you don't have.

Begin with knowing and living the faith. We need to educate ourselves constantly. While a lifetime is too short to learn all there is to know about the Lord and His teachings, we still need to learn as much as we can. Not only for our own fulfillment, but also because we can't

---

[18] "You received without pay, give without pay" (Mt 10:8).
[19] Lk 12:48.

explain what we don't understand. The transformed Peter counseled, "Always be ready to give an explanation to anyone who asks you for a reason for your hope."[20]

And it's crucial that we put what we learn into practice, that we *live* the faith. If you're reading this, good chance you're already living it, but we can always live it better. If we think we've arrived, we'll become pompous and superior, and no one will find that appealing; no one will see Christ in us. And the essence of evangelization is revealing Christ. Humble recognition that we're still on the journey with a long way yet to go is essential. (On the other hand, we shouldn't feel that we need to be highly advanced in holiness before we can witness to the gospel. God uses anyone who lets Him, no matter where they are on this pilgrimage to heaven.) We need "constant conversion and renewal, in order to evangelize the world with credibility."[21]

For that, again, we must fill up with Him, avail ourselves of God's grace, especially by Confession and the Eucharist. Without a steady influx of grace, we can't live out the faith well, to our own detriment as well as to that of those who are watching us. (And don't doubt that people *are* watching.) Striving to live out our faith, to be faithful followers and imitators of Christ, is a witness in itself. A powerful one. "The first means of evangelization is the witness of an authentically Christian life.... 'Modern man listens more willingly to witnesses than to teachers, and if he does listen to teachers, it is because they are witnesses.' "[22]

So if you've begun adopting any of the practices suggested in this book, you're already evangelizing. When you pray, trust in God, obey His commands, acknowledge your faults, and try to make amends for them (parts 1–4 above), you automatically become someone who is noticeably different from the average person. If you let the Lord live in your heart, if you are seeking to please Him, it will show. You will begin to exhibit a peace, joy, and wisdom that stands out and causes people to wonder what makes you tick.

Likewise, when you deny yourself, love and serve others, act mercifully, and imitate Jesus (parts 5–7 above), people will notice that too. Kindness, patience, courtesy, thoughtfulness, magnanimity, and

[20] 1 Pet 3:15, NABRE.

[21] Paul VI, *Evangelii Nuntiandi, Evangelization in the Modern World*, no. 15.

[22] Ibid., no. 41, quoting Pope St. Paul VI, *Address to the Members of the Consilium de Laicis* (October 2, 1974): *AAS* 66 (1974): p. 568. Cf. Second Vatican Council, *Apostolicam Actuositatem, Apostolate of Lay People* (1965), no. 6.

disinterested service are less common these days. When we start living out these principles, we are already evangelizing because we are demonstrating the Good News. Through this wordless witness, such Christians stir up irresistible questions in the hearts of those who see how they live: Why are they like this? Why do they live that way? What inspires them?[23]

We do need to go on, though, and do more: we must also evangelize consciously. "Even the finest witness will prove ineffective in the long run if it is not explained, justified ... and made explicit.... There is no true evangelization if the name, the teaching, the life, the promises, the kingdom and the mystery of Jesus of Nazareth, the Son of God are not proclaimed."[24]

And "[h]ow are men to call upon ... and believe in him of whom they have never heard?... Faith comes ... by the preaching of Christ."[25] The Second Vatican Council Fathers remind us that "a true apostle looks for opportunities to announce Christ by words, addressed either to non-believers with a view leading them to faith, or to the faithful with a view to instructing, strengthening, and encouraging them to a more fervent life."[26] And those who look will find.

But don't bluster. Or rant or lecture. Immediately after Peter says to be always ready, he cautions, "yet do it with gentleness and reverence."[27] Don't turn your Bible or *Catechism* into a cudgel. Bludgeoning people with the truth is not evangelizing. You won't convert or aid anyone without love and respect. We must always beware too of pride, which has a nasty tendency to sneak into our conversations and twist them into contests. Discussions can quickly derail into quarrels, in which the point becomes winning a fight, not winning over a soul.

On the other hand, this is exactly why many Catholics don't speak up in the first place: they're afraid of saying the wrong thing.

But What Do I Say??

Often the biggest hurdle we face in trying to evangelize is figuring out what to say.

---

[23] Paul VI, *Evangelii Nuntiandi, Evangelization in the Modern World*, no. 21.
[24] Ibid., no. 22
[25] Rom 10:14, 17. See also 2 Cor 5:14 and 1 Cor 9:16.
[26] Vatican II, *Apostolicam Actuositatem, Apostolate of Lay People*, no. 6.
[27] 1 Pet 3:15, RSVCE.

The easiest and most natural thing to do is to let down the God-speak guard. Even in countries that ostensibly have religious freedom, there's still a cultural damper on speaking about one's faith outside one's own circles. Many of us habitually clam up about that part of our lives. So the first thing to do is to stop hiding our faith.

Be true to who you are, be yourself. If you're living your faith, then references to it can drop naturally into your conversation. If you took your kid to a music or soccer camp, you would probably say that without thinking twice. Do the same if it's a vacation Bible camp; don't edit it to just "camp". When you return from a retreat and are asked what you did last weekend, own up to it. Or if someone asks what you did on Sunday, don't skip the hour you spent at Mass. You don't have to force religion into a discussion; just let God's part in your life flow in naturally.

But that's just the first step. We must also bring the Lord into the conversation. There's no need to do this artificially. "There are innumerable events in life and human situations which offer the opportunity for a discreet but incisive statement of what the Lord has to say in this or that particular circumstance."[28] We can always share how the Lord is working in our own lives. Someone may not be open to hearing what the Church teaches about this or that, but it's hard to object to your sharing your own experience. "In the long run, is there any other way of handing on the Gospel than by transmitting to another person one's personal experience of faith?"[29]

Chance meetings offer a great opportunity to evangelize, especially on airplanes. People who aren't open to religious conversations with family or friends are surprisingly open to them with a stranger. There's no past baggage, no hyper-vigilant need to save face, no pride to get in the way. And since one is so much less likely to get huffy with someone one just met, must sit next to for hours, and will probably never see again, it's so much easier simply to explore some ideas together. I've had some *very* interesting exchanges on flights. I have no idea of the long-term results, but that's okay. That part is up to the Holy Spirit.

What's most important is to rely on the Holy Spirit. And He does use us, often when we're not aware of it. A college friend made a big impact on my spiritual life by an offhand remark that I actually found quite annoying at the time. But it made me think and gradually changed my

[28] Paul VI, *Evangelii Nuntiandi, Evangelization in the Modern World*, no. 43.
[29] Ibid., no. 46.

outlook completely. And she had no idea until I told her twenty years later. A priest once shared that after giving a talk at a retreat, four men came up to him separately to thank him for something he had said. In each case, he hadn't actually said what the man found so inspiring. Evidently, for each of them, something he did say started a train of thought in which the Spirit was able to work. The priest was both humbled and encouraged that the Lord was working through him—for it was clearly the Lord, not he, who was having an effect.

Christ promised we need not worry about what to say but should trust the Spirit to give us the words. Sometimes we need to follow Peter's example in Joppa, where he "opened his mouth" and began to preach and the whole household was baptized.[30] Philip also "opened his mouth" when the Holy Spirit sent him to preach to the Ethiopian eunuch.[31] We too can take a deep breath of faith, just open our mouths, and see what happens, see what the Holy Spirit leads us to say. You might be surprised to hear what comes out of your own mouth.

Simple Ways to Evangelize

There are easy ways to start evangelizing.

You can share wholesome, positive messages on social media. Some of these could be explicitly Catholic or Christian, or just hopeful and true. You can order well-written and persuasive leaflets and leave them in public places like bus stops, restrooms, or waiting rooms. Get a bumper sticker; wear a cross or crucifix; display Christian art or Scripture verses in your home, office, cubicle, or locker. Give away excellent, persuasive books, CDs, and DVDs on the faith. Start a Bible study or a book club discussing a work from one of the great Catholic publishers, like Ignatius Press, Catholic Answers, Sophia, Emmaus Road, Pauline, or Our Sunday Visitor. Join the evangelization committee at your parish and explore events your parish could host— lectures, movies, coffeehouses, concerts, half-day retreats. You can book a nationally known speaker or use local talent. Invite friends, neighbors, and co-workers to such events, and lapsed Catholics to special liturgies as well. Support or help out at a local Catholic radio station—it's one of the most powerful and approachable media for

---

[30] Acts 10:34, 44–48.
[31] Acts 8:35.

transmitting the faith around. If you don't have one near you, pray for one and consider working with others to get one.

Your Apostolate

Besides such day-to-day, Kingdom-building methods, we each need to discern what apostolate God is calling us to do. Even if you're bedridden, you're not off the hook. Your apostolate is to pray and/or offer up your sufferings for family, friends, neighbors, and other apostolates.

If you want really to dive into evangelization, there's a new apostolate you can join: St. Paul Street Evangelization. The members simply set up a table in a place with ample pedestrian traffic. They offer free rosaries to those who pass by, speak lovingly with those who stop, give away pamphlets, rosaries, and medals, and answer any questions people may have. In a few short years, this new apostolate has blossomed, with hundreds of teams in seven countries.[32]

Maybe He wants you to join an existing apostolate; there are dozens, and all use some volunteer help. Or maybe God is calling you to start an apostolate. It may be something small; it may be something impossible. (He likes to do the latter: then you and everyone else are absolutely positive it's from Him.)

I know several people who have started apostolates, small and large. My friend Rachel Watkins, a writer, homeschooler, and mother of eleven, developed the Little Flowers and Blue Knights clubs for girls and boys, respectively. These programs teach the children about virtues, saints who exemplified them, and fun ways to imitate them. A friend of ours was part of a team who launched a Catholic radio station in our

> ### What Is an "Apostolate"?
>
> The work of an apostle, ... of all the faithful who carry on the original mission entrusted by the Savior to the twelve to "make disciples of all the nations" (Mt 28:19). The ... purpose is not temporal welfare, however noble, but to bring people to the knowledge and love of Christ and, through obedience to his teaching, help them attain life everlasting.
>
> —*Modern Catholic Dictionary* Box 54

area. (It's wonderful—I listen to it for hours each week.) My own husband was inspired to start two apostolates: the Catholic Corner Books and Gifts and the Foundation for Sacred Arts. (He had a lot of help with

[32] To learn more, visit their website: http://streetevangelization.com/. You can also read *Catholic Street Evangelization: Stories of Conversion and Witness*, edited by founder Steve Dawson (Ignatius Press, 2016).

both.)[33] The former provided Catholic items for the northern Baltimore area; the latter supports sacred artists and promotes beautiful and inspiring works.[34] And then of course there's Joseph Fessio, S.J. While getting his doctorate in Europe, Fr. Fessio discovered some great Catholic theologians and came back to the U.S. wanting to share their work with the English-speaking world. He contacted one publisher after another, but only one was mildly interested. So he started his own publishing company to translate these theological gems. Thus was born Ignatius Press, now regarded as one of the finest Catholic publishers in the world.

Meeting Persecution

You may think, "Yeah, well, evangelizing has consequences." For most of us, the consequences are merely on a social plane. Some might look at you funny, avoid you, or outright ridicule you. That's about the extent of persecution in the West, but in other parts of the world, Christians are losing everything, being driven from their homes, tortured, and even killed. By comparison, what we're likely to face—even job loss—is mild. We must pray for our suffering brethren and should imitate them, even if on a smaller scale. And who knows what may come our way in the days to come? Suffering for Jesus in smaller ways now will prepare us for possible tougher times later.

People admire those who put their money where their mouth is; persecution has a way of producing fruit for the Kingdom. Nothing witnesses better to the truth of the gospel than remaining peaceful, loving, and faithful regardless of persecution. People notice. Confidently and charitably standing firm for Jesus in the face of opposition could lead even to the persecutor's conversion. "The blood of the martyrs is the seed of the Church" has proved true from her beginning to our own day. Even now, certain Muslims are noting the courage and staunch faith of the Christians who prefer being beheaded to denying Christ. Some are not only noticing, but converting.[35]

---

[33] The Catholic Corner's success was due in large part to our partners Joan and Tim Linz, who ran it for nearly twenty years. The Foundation has gone through periods of high productivity and dormancy, benefitting over the years from the support of quite a few, most notably: Reed Armstrong, James Depew, Rachel Ross, Ann Marra, and Mark Nowakowski.

[34] See thesacredarts.org.

[35] See e.g., "Isis Seen Undermining Islamic Faith as More Muslims Convert to Christianity", *Christianity Today*, June 8, 2017, https://www.christiantoday.com/article/isis.seen.undermining .islamic.faith.as.more.muslims.convert.to.christianity/55622.htm. There are additional reasons, but these conversions number in the millions.

Don't be afraid: Jesus turns evil to good. "Blessed are you when men revile you and persecute you and utter all kinds of evil against you falsely on my account. Rejoice and be glad, for your reward is great in heaven, for so men persecuted the prophets who were before you."[36]

Building the Kingdom

Jesus launched His public ministry proclaiming, "The Kingdom of God is at hand." But what does that mean? Where is the Kingdom of God? While ultimately the Kingdom of God is heaven, it begins now. The Kingdom of God is not a place, but a state of being. The Kingdom exists wherever Christ reigns and in the heart of everyone who accepts Him as King.

The essence of evangelization is to extend that Kingdom. Christ's subjects are to bring Him wherever they go and build outposts of His Kingdom wherever they can. Our biggest opportunity lies where we already reign. For most of us, this is our own homes; whether you also run a corporation or merely share a room with a sibling, just about everyone has some say over some space. As ambassadors of Christ,[37] we must establish embassies of the Kingdom, our home country, in foreign lands. It's up to you to transform your domain into a microcosm of the Kingdom.

"We're on a Mission from God"

Like many in our day, when I was young I began to wonder who I was and to be concerned about how to express it: what music, what style of clothes, how I should decorate my room. But life isn't about self-expression; it's about expressing love to God and expressing His love to others. "We're on a mission from God", Mary Beth Bonacci says.[38] Some readers may recall TV shows in which certain angels were sent "on a mission" into people's lives to help them in various difficulties.[39] The angels never got caught up in the trappings of one assignment and begrudged moving on to the next. They never neglected their charges in favor of shopping or work. They saw their clothes as costumes and knew their "jobs" were highly temporary. Everything they had was given them by God solely to help them fulfill their mission.

[36] Mt 5:11–12.
[37] 2 Cor 5:20.
[38] See her excellent book *We're on a Mission from God* (San Francisco: Ignatius Press, 1996).
[39] *Highway to Heaven* and *Touched by an Angel*.

It's really no different for us. The word *angel* means "messenger", and the word *apostle* means "sent". All the baptized are called to be apostles. Our missions don't require us to move about as often as the TV angels, so God doesn't *miraculously* supply us with the clothes, homes, and skills we need to fulfill them—but He still gives them to us. We usually have to do something too, but our share in obtaining them is part of the assignment. Likewise, anyone we meet is potentially part of our assignment. It's just as incongruous for us to forget our mission—getting caught up instead in our jobs, possessions, or activities—as it would be for Raphael[40] to do so. Like the angels, we're here on assignment, not here to stay.

Our situation reminds me of a passage in a wonderful children's book, *The Phantom Tollbooth*, describing a "magnificent metropolis" called "Illusions", in which "the rooftops shone like mirrors, the walls glistened with thousands of precious stones, and the broad avenues were paved in silver", but it is merely a mirage. Next to it is a "wonderful city called Reality", which is indeed real, but invisible. The inhabitants of Reality all rush along "with their heads down", looking at nothing but their shoes.[41]

I don't know if the author Norton Juster intended it as such, but it's a perfect analogy of the temporal and eternal elements of our lives. What we *can* see in our daily lives is like a mirage in that all of it will eventually fade away. None of these things will last forever, no matter how substantial they appear. All we see is like the city of Illusions that way. The real things, those that *will* last, on the other hand, are nearly all[42] invisible, and we're all too busy to notice them.

So the question is, what are you going to do? How will you live your life? Are you going to devote yourself to things that won't last? Are you going to rush around, staring at your scurrying shoes, and take no notice of the people around you? Or are you going to unite yourself to the Savior and help Him rescue as many others as possible?

ɜ๑ ɜ๑ ɜ๑

Loving the Lord involves an eagerness to see Him face to face. Love eagerly awaits His coming and prepares for that day—whether it is the

---

[40] See Tobit, a lesser known book of the Old Testament.

[41] Norton Juster, *The Phantom Tollbooth* (1961; New York: Yearling, 1996), pp. 115–18.

[42] People will last for eternity, but their earthly bodies will pass away. We can't yet see people as they really are or as they will appear in their glorified state in eternity.

Last Day of the world or simply the last day of one's own life. We prepare in two ways: by working on holiness and sharing Jesus with others.

Divine grace in our souls can be likened to the flame of a candle. It's more than a matter of being lit or unlit. I was given a candle with a wider wick—as wide as five standard wicks in a row, and guess what? The flame is larger. By expressing our love for God and striving for holiness, we widen our wicks, and the divine flame shines more brightly in us. A larger flame uses up more fuel—and this is just what we want. Love longs to spend itself for the sake of the Beloved; those who love the Lord long to decrease so that He may increase. May our love burn away all our wax so all that is left is sparkling glass filled with the fire and light of God.

Loving the Lord inherently involves evangelization. When you love someone, you can't help talking about him and how wonderful he is. It's no different when that Person is God. And if the merciful, loving salvation He offers is real, then it's the best news possible; shouldn't we share it with others? How can we keep Him to ourselves? Moreover, the One we love asked us to help Him build His Kingdom, and being the true force behind all evangelization, the Lord can use any of us if we just let Him. How can we say "No"?

He called me to write this book. What is He calling you to do?

CONCLUSION

So there you have eight ways of expressing love to God that we know are very meaningful to Him. You can see how they are interrelated and how one can grow—indeed, must strive to grow—in living them out better all one's life long.

It's also interesting how well they dovetail with the eight Beatitudes Jesus gave us.

Beatitudes and Loving God

In the Beatitudes, Christ promises blessings and rewards for those He describes; they are eight *attitudes* or conditions that lead to blessings. The eight ways of loving God examined in this volume are the *actions* that go along with the Beatitude attitudes.

It's natural for those described by the first Beatitude to *spend time* with God; the "poor in spirit" have the needed attitude for prayer. They know that apart from God they have nothing, that He is the source of all, including themselves. They come to Him to thank Him, to request His help, and to grow closer to such a good and loving God. He rewards them with a Kingdom.[1]

The second Beatitude, "Blessed are those who mourn", takes a little more unpacking. Mourning a lost loved one can indirectly bring us to *repent* if it makes us focus more on eternity and less on the joys of this life. And to mourn is also to grieve over being separated from one we love and to feel sorrow for our sins against and omissions toward them; thus, those who love God mourn the ways they have offended Him and seek His forgiveness. And the promise for such is perfect: "they shall be comforted."

The "meekness" of the third Beatitude is precisely the attitude one needs to put one's *trust* in God. It takes humility to trust Him rather than our own opinions; it takes meekness to accept His will. Doing

[1] Mt 5:3.

349

so goes against worldly wisdom, yet Jesus promises, "they shall inherit the earth."

The natural action for those described in the fourth Beatitude, who "hunger and thirst for righteousness", is to *obey* Him. And the more we love and obey Him, the more we see other areas of unrighteousness in ourselves. Thankfully, the Lord gives us hope: "they shall be satisfied."

The "merciful" of the fifth Beatitude actively *love* others. Love of neighbor often requires mercy: noticing others' needs, responding with works of mercy, and forgiving others. For those who express love of God in mercy, Jesus' reward is sweet: "they shall obtain mercy."

Those who *follow* Jesus, who hear and keep the Word of God, are well described as "the pure in heart" of the sixth Beatitude, for they are wholly dedicated to God. Living only for Him, they are blessed, Jesus tells us, for they will receive what they long for: "they shall see God."

"Blessed are the peacemakers"—this seventh Beatitude in action is to *carry one's cross* for love of God. The Son of God came to make peace between God and man, and those who join their sufferings to Christ's participate in His work of redemption and reconciliation are like Him; they share in his Sonship. And of them, Jesus says, "they shall be called sons of God."

Finally, those who are "persecuted for righteousness' sake" and "because of [Jesus]" find the strength to persevere because in their love for God they *eagerly await* His return. No matter what the cost, they do everything in their power to prepare themselves and others for His return. Not only will their reward be "the kingdom of heaven", but they will have pleased their Beloved in a love language He treasures.[2]

Loving the Lord as He longs to be loved is its own reward, but He still rewards each expression of love with the perfect blessing, as manifested in the Beatitudes.

Unprofitable Servants?

"We are unworthy servants; we have only done what was our duty."[3] This verse can be discouraging if we think it means merely that we can't take credit for anything we do for God, even the most heroic, because

---

[2] The Beatitudes are found in Mt 5:3–12.
[3] Lk 17:10. Some translations use "unprofitable" rather than "unworthy".

He gave us the power and inspiration to do it. This is true, and a much-needed reminder, given our tendency to pride. One could never repay God: the gift of existence alone is too much to repay, never mind the gift of redemption, bought by the Blood of Christ.

However, I would like to think this was not Christ's sole point in this parable. I see another, more subtle meaning in it—an invitation. You see, in the same Gospel (Luke), Jesus also says, "Blessed are those servants whom the master finds awake when he comes; truly, I say to you, he will put on his apron and have them sit at table, and he will come and serve them."[4] Nor was He content merely to *say* this; at the Last Supper, He tied a towel around His waist, got down on the floor, and washed His disciples' dirty feet.[5] A little later, he said, "No longer do I call you servants, for the servant does not know what his master is doing; but I have called you *friends*, for all that I have heard from my Father I have made known to you."[6]

When I add to all this His call to go the extra mile,[7] I see an invitation. He wants us to obey Him, yes, but not with a minimalist attitude. Love doesn't ask, *What's the bare minimum I have to do to keep from getting in trouble with you?* That's not love or friendship; it's begrudging servitude. Often we begin obeying Him out of fear, but He invites us into so much more: a relationship of love. And His example of over-the-top love is an invitation: Why can't we do the same, do more for Him even than He asks?

When we grasp this, we thump our foreheads and cry out, "We are unworthy *servants* [rather than *friends*], for we have done only what we were obliged to do!"

Let's do much more. Let's try to think of something extra we can do for God. Let's give Him more than obligation or begrudging obedience. Let's show some love. Let's get creative and try to surprise Him with gifts of love. (Okay, He knows everything, but maybe He would be willing to shut His eyes, so to speak.) Yes, God is the source of all good, and we owe Him everything, so I guess we can't really do anything "extra" for Him, but He does give us freedom, creativity, and lots of opportunities, so we can give it our best shot.

[4] Lk 12:37.
[5] See Jn 13:3–5.
[6] Jn 15:15; emphasis added.
[7] Mt 5:41.

Realizing like the Prodigal Son that we're not worthy to be called His sons, when He runs and welcomes us back anyway, let's accept His incredible mercy. Let's act like sons, like *the* Son, who showed us how to love God and please Him. Jesus' life and teachings express at least eight divine love languages; let's master them all.

—*October 13, 2018*

PRAYER OF LOVE

Lord of love, You have done so much for me. You have created me and a beautiful, wondrous universe and world for me and all Your children to inhabit, share, and explore. You have taught me love through the good people You have placed in my life. You have revealed Yourself to me through Your creation, Your prophets, Your Word and Son, and His Church, and in touching my life. You've reached out to me countless times, in countless ways, and through many caring people. You've put up with me and forgiven me over and over again. You've showered me with love and grace. How can I make a return to You, O Lord, who are holy, perfect, and almighty, when I am so small, weak, and sinful? I can do so only with Your help.

With Your grace and the intercession of Blessed Mother Mary, I pledge to make my life a gift of love to You. Help me remember each day and each hour to embrace the chances You give me to return Your love. I will endeavor to please You with my life, especially by

- spending time with You;
- trusting You in everything;
- obeying Your commands;
- when I fall, apologizing in the way You want;
- carrying my crosses with You;
- loving and serving others;
- following and imitating You; and
- preparing for heaven and encouraging others to accept Your invitation too.

I can never do this on my own, Lord. Please come and live in my heart and do all this in me. You are Love. Help me to live in You and love You as You want me to love You. I beg this in Jesus' name. Amen.

ACKNOWLEDGMENTS

Writing a book is not easy, especially when raising children and dealing with personality handicaps like time-blindness. In this case, it definitely took a small village to help me pull it off. And many deserve to be gratefully acknowledged.

First of all, I must thank my parents, Jo An Simmons and Joe Amestoy, for teaching me the faith and to love God in the first place. Next, without the encouragement of Fr. Martin Connor, L.C., this book would not exist. If he hadn't believed in me, I would never have begun. And I would never have finished without the ongoing encouragement and support of my beloved husband, James. I also want to thank Jody and Chris Erickson, whose reaching out to me moved the book past the beginning stages.

The *hospitality* of a number of generous souls was also highly valuable. Deborah Bowe, Ann and Tim Combs, and Sandra and Tim Weaver graciously opened their homes to me for mini–writing retreats. Fr. Joseph Workman, my pastor, kindly let me write before the Blessed Sacrament in both the church and the chapel, while parish staff members Susan Simmons and Colleen Houk helped make that feasible.

I'm also very grateful to my *readers*, who gave feedback along the way: Michele Amestoy, Fr. Martin Connor, Jennifer Schmidt, Anne Waters, and especially Tom Amestoy, Paula Wilson and my husband, who both read the entire manuscript, and to my *helpers*, who supported me in a variety of ways, especially Laura Carbone-Rodriguez, Maggie Clark, Ann McCarron, Donna Shumay, Jean Smith, Susan Urban, Anne and Bill Waters—and especially my precious Elizabeth, Emily, Alicia, Alex, Isabelle, and Angelie.

I am humbly and greatly thankful also for every one of the many friends who gave financial gifts. While I can't name them all here, I do need particularly to thank Mark and Loretta Erickson, the Weaver family, Virginia Cramer, Margo Smith, Laura Rodriquez-Carbone, Annamary Boler, Malcolm and Mora Meluch, Karen and Fred Schmeider, Karen McKeogh and the First Catholic Slovak Ladies Association, Paula and Ray Wilson, Anne and Bill Waters, Donna and Don Shumay, Jenny and

Rich Amiot, Jean and John Henderson, Thomas and Molly Sammon, Jerry and Coleen Monroe, Patricia and John Scott, Sally and Teddy Smith, Liz Urban, Cheryl and Richard Cherney, Dan and Kathy Shields, Susan and Mike Urban, Beth and David Van Natta, Karen and Alfred D'Agostino, Cheryl and Mike Cadigan, Julie and Dave McLaughlin, Jill and Dave Thein, Dawn and Tom Beltavski, and Cristina and Jim Kaiser. Without your help, this book would have taken five years longer to write or may never have come to fruition at all.

I cannot forget my heavenly helpers. Thank you, sweet Mother Mary, for your many prayers; my thanks also go to the saints and beloved deceased whose intercession I entreated, especially G.K. Chesterton, St. Thomas Aquinas, St. Teresa of Avila, and my patrons St. Jeanne d'Arc, St. John, and especially my newest, St. John Damascene, and to my guardian angel.

I am deeply grateful to all these supporters. Thank you so very much, and may God bless you all!

Most of all, I must thank our good and gracious God, without whom nothing is possible. Thank You, Lord, for loving me, for Your mercy and patience with me, for putting up with me, for calling me to write, for teaching me so many things in the writing of this book, and giving me what gifts I have while supplementing them with more than a little help from my friends and a whole lot of grace from You. May You be praised and loved as You desire and deserve.

RECOMMENDED WORKS

Why Believe in and Love God?

Fulwiler, Jennifer. *Something Other Than God*. San Francisco: Ignatius Press, 2014.

Hahn, Scott, and Benjamin Wiker. *Answering the New Atheism: Dismantling Dawkins' Case against God*. Steubenville, Ohio: Emmaus Road, 2008.

Horn, Trent. *Answering Atheism: How to Make the Case for God with Logic and Clarity*. San Diego: Catholic Answers Press, 2013.

Spitzer, Fr. Robert J. *New Proofs for the Existence of God: Contributions of Contemporary Physics and Philosophy*. Grand Rapids, Mich.: Eerdmans, 2010.

Why Believe in Christ?

Horn, Trent. *Why Believe in Jesus? A Case for the Existence, Divinity, and Resurrection of Christ*. San Diego: Catholic Answers Press, 2014.

Lewis, C. S. *Mere Christianity*. 1952; London: William Collins, 2017.

Spitzer, Fr. Robert J. *God So Loved the World*. San Francisco: Ignatius Press, 2016.

To Know and Love Jesus Better

D'Elbée, Fr. Jean Coeur de Jésus. *I Believe in Love: A Personal Retreat Based on the Teaching of St. Thérèse of Lisieux*. Manchester, N.H.: Sophia Institute Press, 2001.

Kelly, Matthew. *Rediscover Jesus: An Invitation*. Palm Beach, Fla.: Beacon, 2015.

Pitre, Brant. *Jesus the Bridegroom: The Greatest Love Story Ever Told*. New York: Image, 2017.

Sayers, Dorothy. *The Man Born to Be King*. 1943; Camp Hill, Penn.: Classical Academic Press, 2014.

Sheed, Frank. *To Know Christ Jesus*. 1962; Tacoma, Wash.: Angelico Press, 2013.

Sheen, Bishop Fulton J., ed. *That Tremendous Love: An Anthology of Inspirational Quotations, Poems, Prayers, and Philosophical Comments*. New York: Harper & Row, 1967.

Trust in God and Suffering

Angelica, Mother M. *Mother Angelica on Suffering and Burnout.* Irondale, Ala.: EWTN, 2017.

Cavins, Jeff, and Matthew Pinto, eds. *Amazing Grace for Those Who Suffer: 10 Life-Changing Stories of Hope and Healing.* West Chester, Penn.: Ascension Press, 2002.

Egan, Eileen, and Kathleen Egan. *Suffering into Joy: What Mother Teresa Teaches about True Joy.* Ann Arbor, Mich.: Servant, 1994.

D'Elbée, Fr. Jean Coeur de Jésus. *I Believe in Love: Retreat Conferences on the Interior Life.* Still River, Mass.: St. Bede's, 1982.

Groeschel, Fr. Benedict. *Tears of God: Persevering in the Face of Great Sorrow or Catastrophe.* San Francisco: Ignatius Press, 2009.

Lewis, C. S. *The Problem of Pain.* 1940; New York: HarperCollins, 2015.

Spitzer, Fr. Robert J. *The Light Shines On in the Darkness: Transforming Suffering through Faith.* San Francisco: Ignatius Press, 2017.

Prayer

Alphonsus Liguori, St. *Prayer: The Great Means of Salvation and Perfection.* Veritatis Splendor, 2012.

Angelica, Mother M. *Mother Angelica's Little Book of Life Lessons and Everyday Spirituality.* New York: Doubleday, 2007.

Benedict XVI, Pope: *A School of Prayer: The Saints Show Us How to Pray.* San Francisco: Ignatius Press, 2013.

Burke, Dan. *Into the Deep: Finding Peace through Prayer.* North Palm Beach, Fla.: Beacon, 2016.

———, and Connie Rossini. *The Contemplative Rosary with St. John Paul II and St. Teresa of Avila.* Irondale, Ala.: EWTN, 2017.

Dubay, Fr. Thomas. *Fire Within: St. Teresa of Avila, St. John of the Cross, and the Gospel on Prayer.* San Francisco: Ignatius Press, 1989.

The Scriptural Rosary. Glenview, Ill.: Christianica Center, 2005.

Meditation Books

Alphonsus Liguori, St. *How to Converse with God.* Charlotte, N.C.: Tan Books, 2009.

Bartunek, Fr. John, L.C. *The Better Part: A Christ-Centered Resource for Personal Prayer.* Hamden, Conn.: Circle Press, 2007.

Gabriel of St. Mary Magdalen, O.C.D., Fr. *Divine Intimacy.* 4 vols. San Francisco: Ignatius Press, 1987.

Peter of Alcantara, St. *Finding God through Meditation,* ed. Daniel Burke. Steubenville, Ohio: Emmaus Road, 2015.

Sheen, Rev. Fulton J. *Mornings with Fulton Sheen,* ed. Beverly Coney Heirich. Ann Arbor, Mich.: Servant Books, 2007.

Teresa, Mother. *Love: A Fruit Always in Season*. San Francisco: Ignatius Press, 1987.

Thérèse of Lisieux, St. *Mornings with Saint Thérèse*, ed. Patricia Treece. 1997; Manchester, N.H.: Sophia Institute Press, 2015.

Mass

Guardini, Romano. *Meditations before Mass*. London: Aeterna Press, 2015.

Hahn, Scott. *Lamb's Supper: The Mass as Heaven on Earth*. 1999; London: Darton, Longman & Todd, 2007.

————. *Scripture and the Mystery of the Mass*. Catholic for a Reason III. Steubenville, Ohio: Emmaus Road, 2004.

Howard, Thomas. *If Your Mind Wanders at Mass*. San Francisco: Ignatius Press, 2001.

O'Sullivan, Fr. Paul, O.P. *The Wonders of the Mass*. 1963; Charlotte, N.C.: Tan Books, 1993.

Adoration

Alphonsus Liguori, St. *Visits to the Blessed Sacrament and the Blessed Virgin Mary*. Charlotte, N.C.: TAN Books, 2001.

Manelli, Stefano, F.F.I. *Jesus: Our Eucharistic Love: Eucharistic Life Exemplified by the Saints*. 1996; New Bedford, Mass.: Franciscan Friars of the Immaculate, 2008.

Sheen, Rev. Fulton J. *The Holy Hour*. London: Forgotten Books, 2018.

Obedience

The Catechism of the Catholic Church, 2nd ed. Washington, D.C.: United States Catholic Conference, 1997.

Caussade, Jean-Pierre de. *Abandonment to Divine Providence* (aka *The Joy of Full Surrender*). Atlanta, Ga.: Trinity Press, 2017.

Faustina, St. *Diary: Divine Mercy in My Soul*. 3rd ed. 1987; Stockbridge, Mass.: Marian Press, 2016.

Lawrence, Brother. *The Practice of the Presence of God*. New Kensington, Pa.: Whitaker House, 182.

Ray, Stephen. *Footprints of God: Abraham, Father of Faith and Works*. San Francisco: Ignatius Press, 2015. (DVD)

Can We Trust the Church?

Berg, Fr. Thomas. *Hurting in the Church: A Way Forward for Wounded Catholics*. Huntington, Ind.: Our Sunday Visitor, 2017.

Graham, Henry G. *Where We Got the Bible: Our Debt to the Catholic Church*. London: Aeterna Press, 2015.

Horn, Trent. *Why We're Catholic: Our Reasons for Faith, Hope, and Love*. El Cajon, Calif.: Catholic Answers Press, 2017.

Kaczor, Christopher. *The Seven Big Myths about the Catholic Church: Distinguishing Fact from Fiction about Catholicism*. San Francisco: Ignatius Press, 2012.

Kelly, Matthew. *Rediscover Catholicism: A Spiritual Guide to Living with Passion and Purpose*. Palm Beach, Fla.: Beacon, 2011.

Ray, Stephen. *Upon This Rock: St. Peter and the Primacy of Rome in Scripture and the Early Church*. San Francisco: Ignatius Press, 1999.

Confession

Gray, Tim. *Sacraments in Scripture: Salvation History Made Present*. Steubenville, Ohio: Emmaus Road, 2001.

Hahn, Scott. *Lord, Have Mercy: The Healing Power of Confession*. London: Darton, Longman & Todd, 2003.

Rego, Fr. Richard J. *A Contemporary Adult Guide to Conscience for the Sacrament of Confession*. St. Paul, Minn.: Leaflet Missal, 1990.

Love Those I Love

Kinzer, Mark. *Taming the Tongue*. Marshfield, Mo.: Fruits of Zion, 2015.

Lovasik, Rev. Lawrence G. *The Hidden Power of Kindness: A Practical Handbook for Souls Who Dare to Transform the World, One Deed at a Time*. Manchester, N.H.: Sophia Institute Press, 1999.

Sheen, Rev. Fulton J. *Children and Parents*. New York: IVE Press, 2009.

———. *The Power of Love*. Garden City, N.Y.: Doubleday, 1968.

———. *Three to Get Married*. New York: Appleton-Century-Crofts, 1951.

Starbuck, Margot. *Small Things with Great Love: Adventures in Loving Your Neighbor*. Downer's Grove, Ill.: IVP Books, 2011.

Teresa, Mother. *One Heart Full of Love*. Ann Arbor, Mich.: Servant Books, 1988.

Penance and Purgatory

Apostoli, Fr. Andrew. *Fatima for Today: The Urgent Marian Message of Hope*. San Francisco: Ignatius Press, 2010.

Catherine of Genoa, St. *Fire of Love! Understanding Purgatory*. Manchester, N.H.: Sophia Institute Press, 1996.

Dubay, Fr. Thomas. *Fire Within: St. Teresa of Avila, St. John of the Cross, and the Gospel, on Prayer*. San Francisco: Ignatius Press, 1989.

———. *Happy Are You Poor: The Simple Life and Spiritual Freedom*. 2nd ed. San Francisco: Ignatius Press, 2003.

Salza, John. *The Biblical Basis for Purgatory*. Charlotte, N.C.: Saint Benedict Press, 2009.

Follow Me

Fradd, Matt. *Delivered: True Stories of Men and Women Who Turned from Porn to Purity*. San Diego: Catholic Answers Press, 2013.

Francis de Sales, St. *Introduction to the Devout Life*. San Francisco: Ignatius Press, 2015.

Ghezzi, Bert. *Getting Free*. Manchester, N.H.: Sophia Institute Press, 2001.

Grodi, Marcus. *Life from Our Land*. San Francisco: Ignatius Press, 2015.

Kreeft, Peter. *Back to Virtue: Traditional Moral Wisdom for Modern Moral Confusion*. San Francisco: Ignatius Press, 1992.

Mitch, Stacy. *Courageous Love: A Bible Study on Holiness for Women*. Steubenville, Ohio: Emmaus Road, 1999.

―――. *Courageous Virtue: A Bible Study on Moral Excellence for Woman*. Steubenville, Ohio: Emmaus Road, 2000.

Riccardo, Fr. John. *Heaven Starts Now: Becoming a Saint Day by Day*. Frederick, Md.: Word Among Us Press, 2016.

Richards, Fr. Larry. *Be a Man! Becoming the Man God Created You to Be*. San Francisco: Ignatius Press, 2009.

Sheen, Bishop Fulton J. *Go to Heaven: Spiritual Road Map to Eternity*. San Francisco: Ignatius Press, 2017.

Mary and the Saints

Hahn, Scott. *Angels and Saints: A Biblical Guide to Friendship with God's Holy Ones*. New York: Image, 2014.

Madrid, Patrick. *Any Friend of God's Is a Friend of Mine: A Biblical and Historical Explanation of the Catholic Doctrine of the Communion of Saints*. San Diego: Basilica Press, 1996.

Manelli, Stefano M., F.F.I. *All Generations Shall Call Me Blessed: Biblical Mariology*. Bedford Mass.: Academy of the Immaculate, 2005.

Mateo, Fr. *Refuting the Attack on Mary: A Defense of Marian Doctrines*. San Diego, Calif.: Catholic Answers, 1999.

Staples, Tim. *Behold Your Mother: A Biblical and Historical Defense of the Marian Doctrines*. El Cajon, Calif.: Catholic Answers Press, 2014.

―――. *Friends in High Places*. El Cajon, Calif.: Catholic Answers Press, 2008.

Evangelization

Barber, Terry. *How to Share Your Faith with Anyone: A Practical Manual of Catholic Evangelization*. San Francisco: Ignatius Press, 2013.

Chautard, Dom Jean-Baptiste. *The Soul of the Apostolate.* 1946; London: Catholic Way Publishing, 2014.

Dawson Steve. *Catholic Street Evangelization: Stories of Conversion and Witness.* San Francisco: Ignatius Press, 2016.

Paul VI, Pope. Apostolic Exhortation *Evangelii Nuntiandi* on Evangelization in the Modern World (December 8, 1975).

SOURCES FOR QUOTATIONS IN TEXT BOXES

Box 1: Pope Francis, Apostolic Exhortation *Evangelii Gaudium* (*Joy of the Gospel*) on the Proclamation of the Gospel in Today's World (November 24, 2013), no. 1.

Box 2: From a sermon by St. Alphonsus Liguori, quoted in the *Liturgy of the Hours*, Office of Readings for August 1 (New York: Catholic Book Publishing, 1975), 4:1264–65.

Box 3: St. Thomas Aquinas, *Summa Theologica*, I–II, 26, 4, *corp. art.*; quoted in *CCC* 1766.

Box 4: St. Augustine, Sermon 11 (on Mt 7:7), no 6. Quoted in Francis Fernandez, *In Conversation with God*, vol. 5 (London: Scepter, 2005), 464 (incorrectly cited as Sermon 61). For Sermon 11 in full (an older translation), see http://www.newadvent.org/fathers/160311.htm.

Box 7: St. Faustina, *Divine Mercy in My Soul: Diary of Saint Maria Faustina Kowalska* (Stockbridge, Mass.: Marian Press, 2015), p. 381, no. 995.

Box 11: St. John Chrysostom, *De Orando Deum*, lib. 1, 1. Quoted in *Prayer, the Key of Salvation* by Michael Müller (Baltimore: Kelly and Piet, 1868), p. 57.

Box 13: St. John Vianney, Excerpt from "On Morning Prayers", in *Thoughts of the Curé of Ars*, ed. W. M. B. (Charlotte, N.C.: TAN Books, 1984), 17.

Box 16: See Servant of God Josefa Menendez, *The Way of Divine Love* (Charlotte, N.C.: TAN Books, 1972), pp. 246–47.

Box 18: Pope St. John Paul II, Post-Synodal Apostolic Exhortation *Reconciliation and Penance* (December 2, 1984), no. 18.

Box 20: St. Francis de Sales, *Introduction to the Devout Life* (New York: Vintage Books, 2002), p. 13.

Box 24: St. Teresa of Calcutta, *No Greater Love*, Commemorative Edition (Novato, Calif.: New World Library, 2016), pp. 113–14.

Box 25: Quoted in Pope John XXIII, *Sacerdotii Nostri Primordia*: Encyclical on St. John Vianney, Aug. 1, 1959, no. 93.

Box 26: St. Francis de Sales, *Introduction to the Devout Life* (New York: Vintage Books, 2002), p. 76.

Box 29: Benjamin Disraeli, *Wit and Wisdom of Benjamin Disraeli* (London: Longmans, Green, 1886), p. 207.

Box 31: Pope Benedict XVI, Encyclical *Spe Salvi* on Christian Hope (November 30, 2007), no. 37.

Box 33: St. Faustina, *Divine Mercy in My Soul: Diary of Saint Maria Faustina Kowalska* (Stockbridge, Mass.: Marian Press, 2015), p. 153, no. 343.

Box 35: St. Ignatius of Loyola, *The Spiritual Exercises of St. Ignatius of Loyola* (New York: Cosimo, 2007), p. 19.

Box 38: St. Gregory the Great, *Regula Pastoralis*, 3, 21; quoted in *CCC* 2446.

Box 43: *Liturgy of the Hours* (New York: Catholic Book, 1975), 4:1264.

Box 44: Archbishop Fulton Sheen, *Treasures in Clay: The Autobiography of Fulton J. Sheen* (New York: Image, 2008), p. 198.

Box 45: Pope St. John Paul II, Address to Young People of Bologna (September 27, 1997), no. 3.

Box 47: St. John Bosco, Quoted in Stefano Manelli, F.F.I., *Jesus, Our Eucharistic Love* (New Bedford, Mass.: Academy of the Immaculate, 1996), p. 78.

Box 53: Pope St. Paul VI, Apostolic Exhortation *Evangelii Nuntiandi* (December 8, 1975), no. 24.

Box 54: John A. Hardon, S.J., *An Abridged and Updated Edition of Modern Catholic Dictionary* (New York: Image, 2018), p. 29.

GENERAL INDEX

SCRIPTURE INDEX

Items marked with an asterisk are in the boxed text on the pages.